# THE DELECTABLE NEGRO

SEXUAL CULTURES

General Editors: José Esteban Muñoz and Ann Pellegrini

TITLES IN THE SERIES INCLUDE:

*Times Square Red, Times Square Blue*
Samuel R. Delany

*Queer Globalizations: Citizenship
and the Afterlife of Colonialism*
Edited by Arnaldo Cruz Malavé
and Martin F. Manalansan IV

*Queer Latinidad: Identity
Practices, Discursive Spaces*
Juana María Rodríguez

*Love the Sin: Sexual Regulation and
the Limits of Religious Tolerance*
Janet R. Jakobsen and Ann Pellegrini

*Boricua Pop: Puerto Ricans and the
Latinization of American Culture*
Frances Négron-Muntaner

*Manning the Race: Reforming Black
Men in the Jim Crow Era*
Marlon Ross

*In a Queer Time and Place: Transgender
Bodies, Subcultural Lives*
Judith Halberstam

*Why I Hate Abercrombie and Fitch: Essays
on Race and Sexuality in the U.S.*
Dwight A. McBride

*God Hates Fags: The Rhetorics of Religious Violence*
Michael Cobb

*Once You Go Black: Choice, Desire, and
the Black American Intellectual*
Robert Reid-Pharr

*The Latino Body: Crisis Identities in
American Literary and Cultural Memory*
Lázaro Lima

*Arranging Grief: Sacred Time and the
Body in Nineteenth-Century America*
Dana Luciano

*Cruising Utopia: The Then and
There of Queer Futurity*
José Esteban Muñoz

*Another Country: Queer Anti-Urbanism*
Scott Herring

*Extravagant Abjection: Blackness,
Power, and Sexuality in the African
American Literary Imagination*
Darieck Scott

*Relocations: Queer Suburban Imaginaries*
Karen Tongson

*Beyond the Nation: Diasporic Filipino
Literature and Queer Reading*
Martin Joseph Ponce

*Single: Arguments for the Uncoupled*
Michael Cobb

*Brown Boys and Rice Queens: Spellbinding
Performance in the Asias*
Eng-Beng Lim

*Transforming Citizenships: Transgender
Articulations of the Law*
Isaac West

*The Delectable Negro: Human Consumption
and Homoeroticism within U.S. Slave Culture*
Vincent Woodard, Edited by Justin A.
Joyce and Dwight A. McBride

For a complete list of titles in the series, see nyupress.org.

# The Delectable Negro

*Human Consumption and Homoeroticism within U.S. Slave Culture*

Vincent Woodard

*Edited by Justin A. Joyce and Dwight A. McBride*

*Foreword by E. Patrick Johnson*

NEW YORK UNIVERSITY PRESS
New York and London

NEW YORK UNIVERSITY PRESS
New York and London
www.nyupress.org

References to Internet websites (URLs) were accurate at the time of writing.
Neither the author nor New York University Press is responsible for URLs that
may have expired or changed since the manuscript was prepared.

For Library of Congress Cataloging-in-Publication data, please contact the Library of
Congress

ISBN: 978-0-8147-9461-6 (hardback)
ISBN: 978-0-8147-9462-3 (paperback)

Manufactured in the United States of America
10 9 8 7 6 5 4 3 2 1

Also available as an ebook

# CONTENTS

*Editor's Note*                                                       vii
  *Justin A. Joyce*

*Foreword*                                                             xi
  *E. Patrick Johnson*

Introduction: "Master . . . eated me when I was meat"                   1

1. Cannibalism in Transatlantic Context                                29

2. Sex, Honor, and Human Consumption                                   59

3. A Tale of Hunger Retold: Ravishment and Hunger                      95
   in F. Douglass's Life and Writing

4. Domestic Rituals of Consumption                                    127

5. Eating Nat Turner                                                  171

6. The Hungry Nigger                                                  209

*Notes*                                                               241

*Bibliography*                                                        289

*Index*                                                               303

*About the Author*                                                    309

*About the Editors*                                                   311

JUSTIN A. JOYCE

I never had the chance to meet Vincent Woodard personally. Working through someone's scholarship backward and forward for nearly five years, however, gives you a type of intimate knowledge of the working of his or her mind. From both his work and the reminiscences of his friends, I feel I've come to know something of him and feel I can confidently join his friends, family, and colleagues in their mourning. To have lost such a stunning intellect and cogent writer is truly a tragedy. The exhaustive research that went into this book, along with the cunning analytical mind that guides its prose, bears witness to a scholar driven by a search for new truths and a passion to share his insights.

It is this drive and passion that pushed Vincent, quite literally till the very end of his life. For despite, or perhaps because of, the illness that claimed his life Vincent worked tirelessly, almost obsessively, to complete this book. A simultaneously ebullient and private man, Vincent kept his illness to himself until he could no longer hide it, working all the time at his scholarship. Through his sickness and treatments, he kept working. Through many a disorienting medication, he kept working. Through the fog of severe sufferings, Vincent kept working. Up till his very last moments his scholarship was on his mind, for his final wishes included a plea that his colleagues see this project to completion. The book you have before you, then, is a testament to the care with which these friends dedicated themselves to helping Vincent's hard work come to fruition.

The manuscript for *The Delectable Negro* arrived on my desk, as it were, in 2008. My task then was a seemingly simple one: compile a bibliography for the notes and copyedit the text for submission. As I worked through the text, however, the state of Vincent's notes and missing references within the manuscript, no doubt due to his illness and the earnest pace that drove him to try to complete this manuscript when most people would be more worried over their terminal illness, presented additional challenges for publishing his work. These challenges included incomplete or missing citations, notes and citations that contained factual errors, and specific references within his notes that were either ambiguous or pointed to particular versions of popular texts that could not be identified fully. As I worked to compile the bibliography, it became increasingly evident that there were enough errors in the manuscript that we would be remiss to print it as it stood. To do so would be more than poor scholarship; it would be a dishonor to Vincent Woodard's legacy.

In order to be completely confident of the accuracy of his notes and references, the only proper course was to check *each and every* reference for accuracy. As anyone would imagine, this entailed considerable effort and research time. To work backward through a scholar's research trajectory, tracking down each citation, reference, and mention through archival materials is a colossal undertaking. This herculean task was not completed alone. It is only fitting to acknowledge here the hard work of two student assistants, Matthew Alan Lang at the University of Illinois at Chicago and Andrew Brown at Northwestern University. Without their diligent attention and assistance, Vincent's work might never have seen the light of day. It is fitting here to acknowledge also the incredible tolerance of NYU Press and Vincent's family. Without their enduring patience, *The Delectable Negro* would have been a much poorer tribute to Vincent's hard work.

It is truly unfortunate that Vincent Woodard could not see his own work to press. It is also unfortunate that his manuscript lacked a proper conclusion. In the introduction to the extant manuscript that was passed on to Dwight A. McBride and E. Patrick Johnson, Vincent makes reference to a coda, wherein he planned to extend his discussion beyond the confines of slavery and a strictly white/black dynamic of hunger and homoeroticism:

> For the Coda of the book, "Cannibal Nation," I return more broadly and meditatively to the nineteenth-century concern that the US had become a cannibal nation. I look at instances of US frontiersmen and soldiers consuming or harvesting the flesh of Native Americans. While my focus

has been African American experience, I branch out in the conclusion to suggest how the consumption of black persons coincided with the literal and cultural consumption of other groups seen as expendable or marginal to the US nation-making endeavor. Going deeper into black experience, I tease out, within African American Reconstruction culture, how black people maintained an implicit critique of institutionalized US cannibalism at the same time that they denigrated Africa and saw Africans and African cultural practices as heathen and cannibal. Given that Africans and African Americans had strong, vibrant indigenous traditions that accounted for and even posed remedies for human consumption, I speculate about why such traditions were not more widely acknowledged nor integrated into the public sphere.

Though the material that Vincent planned for the book's coda is lost, his groundbreaking combination of challenging ideas yet goes forth. Countless corrections to references and citations have been made in order to present his work in the best possible light; any errors or omissions that remain are entirely mine. The innovative ideas and approachable prose style in this manuscript, however, are all Vincent.

E. PATRICK JOHNSON

*The Delectable Negro* is a provocative reading of race relations vis-à-vis an almost indiscernible homoeroticism in the nineteenth century. According to Woodard, such homoeroticism was always already there, but "our contemporary framing of homosexuality has obscured our vision." Moreover, he suggests that "the absence of an appropriate linguistic apparatus, the dearth of historical documentation, and the lack of theoretical models with which to excavate homoeroticism from extant historical documents" have all colluded to conceal the presence of this racialized libidinal dynamic. Shaman-like, Woodard sharpens our vision by immersing himself in the archive while relying on what Philip Brian Harper calls the "evidence of felt intuition"[1] to reveal the unsaid and the taboo hidden in plain sight. What is perhaps more enlightening—and frightening—however, is his framing of homoerotic desire in slavery through cannibalism. Woodard deploys cannibalism as more than just a metaphor, as he documents actual instances—in slave and ex-slave narratives, autobiographies, and WPA interviews—of whites' literal consumption of black flesh. Thus, instead of the question Du Bois frames as the most compelling problem facing the Negro in the twentieth century, Woodard argues that another question was already on the forefront of the Negro's mind in the nineteenth century: "How does it feel to be an edible, consumed object?" The erotic charge catalyzed in the process of consumption, according to Woodard, was not unidirectional but also emanated from black men toward white men and toward each other. Indeed, Woodard dares to speak of black men's sexual agency around their own libidinal desires and how those desires and acts were mobilized in the service of their own self-preservation from literal and spiritual consumption. In *The Delectable Negro*, Woodard convincingly analyzes the psychosexual details of consumption as it flowed both ways. The result is a fierce rethinking of the ways in which capitalism, racism, and sexuality functioned within a slave economy that framed the libidinal formation of race relations for generations.

Vincent Woodard's thinking on this topic evolved over a ten-year period, beginning in graduate school. I met him and heard him talk about this research for the first time in 1999 at the University of Texas at Austin, where I had been invited to perform and where he was a graduate student in English and American Studies. Like many self-actualized black gay academics, he understood the precariousness of the profession he had chosen and proceeded accordingly. That is to say, he understood the old adage, "you have to be twice as good," a mantra most black folks were taught growing up, as well as the fact that his gayness would be both a hindrance and an asset within the academy depending on the context and how that identity marker would be *consumed* by his students, colleagues, and critical interlocutors. Working his way through graduate school at the height of queer theory and during the nascent stages of black queer studies meant that Woodard had to negotiate mastering the "established" field of queer studies while also following in the footsteps of his peers and mentors who were waging a critique against queer theory's blind spots to race. In some ways, it was the best time to be in graduate school, to take advantage of the explosion of new work and to be a part of the theoretical and political conversations generated by scholars and activists committed to legitimizing sexuality studies in the academy. But in other ways, the late 1990s and the early 2000s were a challenging time for graduate students who sometimes were overwhelmed by the sheer volume and multiple twists and turns of this emerging scholarship and who sometimes felt trapped—professionally and politically—in a world where just the mere topic of their dissertation or who their advisor was could determine whether or not they were taken seriously as scholars or if they would be viable on the job market.

Vincent and I discussed all of this and more over e-mails and visits during the early years of our friendship. Although he thought of me as a mentor as much as he did as a friend, it was always I who was impressed with the way his mind worked. I'll never forget, for example, the first time he discussed with me his ideas about writing about cannibalism and homoeroticism. At the time, there was nothing I could offer by way of feedback or encouragement—mainly because I thought it would be too intellectually ambitious to imbricate these two topics in the context of slavery. I became a believer, however, when Vincent sent me the first draft of this manuscript in 2005, then titled, "Recovering the Black Male Womb: Slavery, Homoeroticism and Nineteenth-Century Racial Uplift." I wrote notes and questions on just about every page because the ideas were so provocative. I was still unsure, however, if he would be able to successfully pull together everything that he wanted to say and justify all of the claims that he was making.

The turning point came in 2006, at the American Studies Association conference in Oakland, California, where Vincent delivered a paper entitled, "Blood Magic and Sorcery in the State Formation Archive" in which he laid out what would become the key terms of *Delectable Negro* as unearthed in the archive: consumption, hunger, homoeroticism, and slavery. It seemed the entire conference was abuzz with talk about Woodard's paper, and it would be the turning point for Woodard as he began to hone in on two topics that were too taboo for even the most courageous of academics: cannibalism and same-sex desire under slavery.

For those who knew Vincent Woodard and understood his genius, the theorizing and analysis contained in the pages of this book will come as no surprise. And for those who experience it for the first time they will be in for a treat. Vincent knew how to tell a good story, and this one is his finest. And he knew it. That is why in the final days of his life he told his colleague, John-Michael Rivera at the University of Colorado, Boulder, to make sure that this manuscript got to Dwight A. McBride and to me so that we could see that it got published. And that is what Dwight and I have worked toward for the past five years, with the assistance of Justin A. Joyce and a host of undergraduate and graduate research assistants. And quietly but persistently urging us on have been his parents, Vera and Cedric Woodard, who have waited patiently to see the fruits of their son's labor.

I am still in denial about Vincent's passing because I feel his presence so viscerally. He was immediately recognizable as a gender-queer. That day in 1999 in Austin when we first met in a coffee shop, he strolled in wearing a sarong and flowing locks and exhibiting a bohemian confidence. We spent hours talking about poetry, politics, and black people.

Many often mistook his soft-spoken demeanor as a sign of timidity, but soon discovered, as I did, that this could not have been further from the truth. On many occasions I witnessed the lioness in Vincent emerge: Whether dealing with a waiter at a restaurant whose service was insulting or flinging a zinger at a scholar who was being obtuse or apolitical in their presentation, Vincent was deft and deliberate in delivering his thoughts about someone being "triflin." What was so funny about these instances is that as soon as he had his say, the sweet, gentle, nonchalant Vincent would turn back to you and pick up where he left off in the conversation before the object of his wrath had so rudely interrupted him. Plainly, Vincent was a fierce diva, but only when it was necessary. He was centered both in who he was as a person and as an activist. This is probably because Vincent was such a spiritual person and praised the ancestors in every aspect of his life. Now that he has crossed over, his own spirit is traveling the universe, radiating the poetic goodness of his soul. Now, he has left *The Delectable Negro* as his legacy for us to consume. As we partake of it, may we think of Vincent, sashaying through our digestive tract, providing us with nutrients for the soul, but also giving us a little heartburn along the way. Nothing this good ever goes down easy. And Vincent wouldn't have it any other way.

Introduction

*"Master . . . eated me when I was meat"*

In the summer of 2007, I visited Somerset Place in Creswell, North Carolina.[1] At one point, Somerset Place, a historically restored plantation, was the most successful plantation in North Carolina and its owner, Josiah Collins III, one of the largest slaveholders in the state. It is now a state historic site sitting on over 100 acres of lush forest and wetland. My party and I arrived early one Saturday morning, parked near the overseer's quarters, and walked the red cobblestone road down the center of the plantation—past the stocks, past the smokehouse, past the outside cooking facilities—to the gift shop where the tour begins. My travel companions browsed the bookstore while I sat in the adjoined seating area taking in the genealogy of enslaved persons who had formerly lived on the plantation. Someone had conveniently mounted photographs and biographies of these persons on the walls. There was Darius Bennett, a Somerset field hand who had heard the cannons signaling the Civil War. There was Besty Spruil Riddick seated with hands folded before a wooden shack. There was even a makeshift family tree dating back to the first enslaved Africans to arrive on Somerset Plantation.

After a while, all of us there for the morning tour made our way into the seating area where our tour guide finally came in and stood before us. He wore khaki pants, a maroon polo shirt, and glasses; he was blonde-haired, blue-eyed, and stood about 6'3" tall. For the sake of discussion, I will refer to him as Mr. Swellfellow, because he had that

look of a good hometown guy. He probably lived in the same neighborhood as his mother (if not *with* his mother), volunteered with the local
fire department, had a high school sweetheart he was engaged to, went
to church every Sunday, and, as far as I could see, wore honesty about
his face like a child wears a milky mustache. He was totally disarming
and chubby and southern and immediately attentive, standing before
us, leaning on the mantle of the fireplace.

After warming to us, he began by talking about the pictures on the
wall and quickly segued into minor details about the plantation. Not all
of the original buildings had been restored to the plantation. This was
a walking tour that would begin at the overseer's quarters and end at
the big house. A woman who had once tried to escape was put into the
stocks in the wintertime. Her legs froze and they had to be amputated.
Each month, enslaved adults received a ration of a peck of corn and
three pounds of dried meat. "The slaves on this plantation were well
fed," Mr. Swellfellow emphasized, before rattling off more details about
the tour. I tried to stay focused, but my mind returned to the rationed
meat and cornmeal, the fact that hard field labor would have depleted
such rations in a week, and the image of happy, well-fed darkies ever so
casually introduced into Mr. Swellfellow's presentation.

I raised my hand and waited for Mr. Swellfellow to call on me. True
to his namesake, Mr. Swellfellow noticed my hand and welcomed my
question. "Mr. Swellfellow," I began, "I want to go back to an earlier
point you made for clarification. You said that the enslaved were given
a peck of corn and three pounds of meat and then you said they that
they were well fed. But to my thinking, the enslaved must have gone
hungry, especially those working in the fields who would have needed
more substance than this to sustain them in backbreaking, day-long
labor." The smile on Mr. Swellfellow's face dimmed a little even as he
formulated an entirely hopeful response. "The slaves were well fed," he
insisted. "It was not in the economic interest of the master to starve
them and besides, the Collinses were kind and had benevolent relations
with their slaves. They weren't the type to make their slaves go hungry."

"Actually," Mr. Swellfellow," I interrupted, "it *was* in the economic interest of slave masters to starve their slaves; this fact is well
documented in literature written by fugitive slaves. And on the subject of kindness, the so-called kindness of masters hardly ever, to my

knowledge, interfered with their profit motive. What better way to profit than by giving your slaves minimal nourishment while you expect, in return for investment, maximum labor output?" Only after I stopped speaking did I realize I was shaking internally and had taken an edge to my voice. I became aware of my African American travel companions sitting across the room and the few other white tourists who were part of our morning party. Mr. Swellfellow had flushed and begun to sweat. He had become anxious and nervous. Clearly, his National Parks Service tour guide training had not prepared him to deal in a knowledgeable manner with questions of hunger and starvation on the plantation. Perhaps, too, he felt embarrassed, embarrassed at his immediately defensive posture, embarrassed at his rushing to defend the master, and, finally, embarrassed and angry at my daring to challenge what was clearly a sacred memory: contented, well-fed blacks roaming about the plantation.

Needless to say, this initial interaction with Mr. Swellfellow set the tone for the remainder of the tour. When, during the walking tour, he brought up the subject of enslaved persons stealing meat from the smokehouse, I responded by asking why such *well-fed* persons would have provocation to steal meat in the first place? At one point, thoroughly frustrated with the constant reinforcement of the pastoral and goodly nature of life on Somerset plantation, I said to our tour guide so that everyone could hear, "Mr. Swellfellow, it seems to me that you and the state of North Carolina are invested in an image of the masters as goodly and that you are not willing to entertain perspectives of plantation life that go against this reality." Swellfellow, sweating even more profusely, denied my accusations and did his best to avoid me the remainder of the tour.

"The history of slavery continues to have meaning in the twentieth century—it burdens all of American history and is incorporated into public interpretations of the past," write James Oliver Horton and Lois E. Horton.[2] We need look only as far as Somerset Place for an example of a historically laden and contested site of slave memory. There, we see the circumstances of slave existence and the meaning of the master's authority and "good will" as fluid, contested categories of experience regulated by the state and a larger master narrative of slave history. Similar issues regarding the meaning and import of slavery have affected contemporary battlefields and Civil War sites operated by the National Parks Service. As a result of pressure from Civil War heritage interest groups, those who give tours at these sites do not speak of slavery as the major social phenomenon that catalyzed the Civil War.[3] In higher education, another state-regulated realm, the history of slavery continues to shape our lives. A good example of this is Brown University. Brown, like a number of universities on the East Coast, has ties to slavery that trace back to its founder, John Brown. Members of Brown's educational community who have attempted to reconcile the university's historic and economic ties with the institution of slavery have, in the process, encountered staunch resistance from the regents and alumni, among other constituencies.[4] From contemporary debates over national identity to concerns about modern civil rights, the legacy of slavery continues to inform and impact our sense of civic belonging and investment in this experiment called the United States.

Living, as we do, in a society in which many still deny the fundamental tie between the Civil War and slavery helps me better understand, on a systemic level, Mr. Swellfellow's resistance to my insinuations of institutionalized hunger on the Somerset plantation. An admission of institutionalized hunger on the plantation would have required Mr. Swellfellow to alter his notions of the goodly, altruistic master. As well, such an allowance would have required that Mr. Swellfellow consider how sentimental conventions, Christian morals and values, southern state formation and statecraft all informed our discussion of slaves made to hunger on the plantation.

While Mr. Swellfellow had his own geographically bounded (he was from the surrounding area) and personal reasons for denying the existence of slave hunger, my insistence upon the topic arose mostly from the researching for and writing of this book. I had come to know, through my research, that instances of hunger—within such a pristine, well-kept context—were often only indicators of a much larger culture of institutionalized hunger. I had encountered numerous masters like Somerset's Josiah Collins III, who one biographer described as "an autocrat with a will as imperious and a sway as absolute as the Czar himself."[5] Josiah III, I would find out months after my plantation tour, fit the profile of the cultivated, overlording type of master who used hunger and all manner of social conditioning to wring from enslaved people maximum labor and to instill in these persons fear and self-denial. Hunger, with persons such as Collins, was often only the tip of the iceberg. So much more than hunger was at stake in my interactions with Mr. Swellfellow: If he and I could not talk about hunger on the plantation, then we would never (as individuals or a nation) be able to talk about other intersecting issues, such as "social consumption," "ritualized hunger," or "cannibalistic masters" populating southern plantations such as Somerset Place.[6]

For my part, my encounters at Somerset Place disturbed me and catalyzed in me a state of personal and intellectual reflection. Was the nation, not to mention the state of North Carolina, ready for an open and inquiring discussion into the topics of hunger and human consumption on the plantation? Was I ready to and capable of serving as mediator of this discussion, which clearly had a life beyond the book pages I had labored to fill over the years? In the nineteenth century, none but the most radical abolitionists believed the enslaved person's claims about consuming masters and their descriptions of a culture of human consumption pervading plantation life. Over a century later, not much had changed. Not only had we collectively forgotten many of the significant details of slavery that continue to impact the present, but we had also willed ourselves to forget the horrific forms that human hunger and the pursuit of power could take.

Despite our will to forget and desire to reconfigure the past, the reality is that institutionalized hunger and practices of human consumption characterized life on many southern plantations. No topic disturbed and mystified nineteenth-century America like the subject of human consumption under slavery. For the most part, whites during the time responded to this topic, as did Mr. Swellfellow, with an air of secrecy and shame. For example, one of the most notorious incidents of literal black consumption from the nineteenth century involved members of the whaling ship *Essex*, which sailed from Nantucket, Massachusetts, in 1838. White Nantucketers still today have little to say about the incident, especially the fact that the first four crew members to be murdered and eaten by whites were black. Nantucket was known in the nineteenth century as a Quaker and abolitionist stronghold, and its residents then and still today find it hard to explain ship captains operating as "slave drivers," African persons treated in a brutish manner aboard whaling ships, and, more pointedly, the master/slave ideology informing the consumption of the four black men.[7]

Colonial-era Nantucketers were not alone in their self-preserving silence. Slave-owning whites, for different reasons, covered up the reality of black consumption. Take, for example, the circumstances surrounding the consumption of Nat Turner, the black insurrectionist. Black members of the Southampton, Virginia, community left oral records of whites who tried to coerce them into consuming Nat Turner's boiled-down flesh and entrails. Black persons also implied that nineteenth-century whites might have consumed the revolutionary as a medicinal substance. Whites from the time period dismissed such ideas as "folk belief" arising from the backward and infantile culture of "older darkies."[8] To add to this, scholars of Turner's experience have, on the whole, denied, infantilized, or dismissed the observations of black persons.[9]

These scholars, it seems, are not aware of those aspects of U.S. plantation culture that were based in parasitism and a dynamic of human consumption. In *Slavery and Social Death: A Comparative Study*, Orlando Patterson describes slavery as a parasitic institution that white masters strove to conceal in ideology and act. According to Patterson, "the slaveholder," in order to maintain an image of himself as civilized and free of parasitic appetites, "camouflaged his dependence, his parasitism, by various ideological strategies. Paradoxically, he defined the slave as dependent. This is consistent with the human technique of camouflaging a relation by defining it as the opposite of what it really is."[10] *Parasite* is the perfect concept for my purposes, as it implies a range of consumptive acts, some resulting in immediate death but most involving the passage of time and the incremental feeding upon the human host. Most of my examples of consumption, on and off the plantation, range from the literal murder and eating of black persons to what we might think of as metaphoric acts. I refer to these metaphoric acts—which encompass starving, flesh-seasoning rituals, and sexual modes of consumption—variously as consumption, human consumption, metaphoric consumption, instances of social consumption, and even cannibalism. I will explain the historical and contemporary significance of such terms as "cannibal" later in the introduction, but I wanted to acknowledge here that I do use a range of terms to describe instances of consumption.

My cluster of terms challenges the layers of stereotype and imprecise language that have historically characterized the topic of the consumption of slaves. As a common strategy, masters often hid their appetites and hungers in stereotypes and ideologies that attributed these characteristics to the slaves. Patterson describes a reality wherein the master deflected his appetites and hungers onto myths of the chattel slave as dependent, childlike, and somehow ennobled by the master's consumptive needs. In dismissing the bonded person's accusations of consumption as infantile rants, which I point out using Turner's example, scholars have reinforced this slave-owning, ruling-class mentality and have helped to maintain a general code of silence regarding the master's appetites and sycophantic needs.

This pattern of silencing has resulted in the dismissal of the reality of those enslaved persons who frequently described slavery as an outgrowth of the master's homoerotic and consumptive appetites. Within U.S. slavery, black men and women consistently described incidents of human consumption that occurred on literal, metaphoric, and institutional levels of social interaction. These incidents often had a homoerotic or sexual charge to them. John S. Jacobs, for example, referred to his former masters as "human fleshmongers" possessed of an unnatural hunger for human flesh and soul. Naked bodies depicted on the auction block, instances of rape, and sexualized torture coincide with the hunger and satiation described by Jacobs.[11] For Solomon Northup, the "gastronomical enjoyments" and excesses of whites included the sexualized treatment of men such as himself at the hands of slave catchers, overseers, and masters.[12] Harriet Jacobs recorded in *Incidents in the Life a Slave Girl, Written by Herself* how white mistresses acted out hungers for and erotic desires for black women in intimate spaces on the plantation.[13] Issues of sexual dominance and white male fixations on black male virility informed the consumption of Nat Turner.

Acknowledging how scholars of U.S. and transatlantic slavery have largely ignored and dismissed accusations of the cannibalizing of black Americans, I take the enslaved person's claims of human consumption seriously, and I attempt throughout this project to draw attention to how blacks experienced their consumption as a fundamentally erotic, and more specifically homoerotic, occurrence. Given the taboo nature of homoeroticism in the nineteenth century, black people rarely wrote about same-sex experiences or encounters with whites. In the context of consumption, though, this topic was unavoidable. For blacks could not identify, name in language and concept, negotiate, or resist the culture of human consumption they saw pervading plantation life without unearthing the erotic implications of their consumption and, even more, constructing a sexual politics that included homoeroticism. Amazingly, nineteenth-century black Americans, without conscious forethought, created an entirely new language and symbolic system to describe not just their consumption but also the deeper homoerotic nuances of black life under slavery. Linking this personal reality to the larger national, political terrain, they developed strategies of resistance, a politics of moral accountability, and a social vision of human consumption that implicated the most cherished values and tenets of the republic.

When black Americans described instances of the eating, cooking, and consumption of flesh in slave narratives, newspaper articles, speeches, testimonials, sermons, and autobiographies, they not only questioned the national body politic but also tried to understand why and how they had become so delectable, so erotically appetizing, to a nation and white populace that, at least rhetorically, denied and despised their humanity. A New Orleans physician, Samuel A. Cartwright, perfectly captured this denial of and despising of the Negro in his medical writings. Cartwright's popular views depicted the Negro as childlike, lacking civilization, and therefore a completely undesirable species. On the topic of Negro infantile behavior, he writes: "Negroes, moreover, resemble children in the activity of the liver and in their strong assimilating powers, and in the predominance of the other systems over the sanguineous."[14] Comparing the Negro's skin to that of an animal hide, he describes how his "skin is very thick" and how he has a membrane called "plica lunaris, like that which is observed in apes." He reserves his most sweeping comments for so-called African biological and racial inferiority, which in his opinion "has rendered the people of Africa unable to take care of themselves."[15] In reality, of course, enslaved black persons took care of whites, who often acted as sycophantic children in their demands, hungers, and insatiable needs. Under this cloud of delusion, wherein whites depicted the Negro as the helpless adult-infant that they themselves embodied, white hungers for and desires for the Negro could flourish. On the level of acquired taste for the Negro, Cartwright's pseudo-medical science portrays how myths of the Negro child, of the exoticized and animal-like African, stoked white appetites and made the Negro into a delectable, desirous object.

Such references to black people as animal-like, infantile, and disfigured proliferate in pro-slavery rhetoric. They are so common that we do not naturally think of them as indexes of desire—of white people's fixations upon and obsessions with black bodies and sex. Even more, we are not in the habit of reading homoeroticism into comments made by persons such as Cartwright. Within the culture of consumption, there existed numerous examples of homoerotic affection between black and white men, sexualized violence, and incest bonds, among other phenomena. Yet such affections were often veiled or hidden within rhetorics of objectification and abjection. For white men, sex with and sexual attraction to black men was a natural by-product of their physical, emotional, and spiritual hunger for the same.

For black men, on the other hand, homoeroticism was a means of resisting, accommodating, and transforming the discourse of black consumption. For example, in the process of speaking about their sexual consumption, black men crossed gender boundaries, adopted the genders and identities of black and white women, and imagined themselves "giving birth" to new archetypes of the nation. Within black nationalist movements, dating from slavery to the 1960s, black men linked effeminacy and homosexuality with the white desire to culturally and spiritually consume black men. Even black women, in the late twentieth century, linked their discussions of mother hunger and self-consumption during slavery with violent acts of homoeroticism—references to male rape and oral violation. While the culture of U.S. consumption frames my narrative, this is a book as much about homoeroticism as it is about flesh consumption. Through multiple desires, African American men and women successfully resisted their consumption and constructed a racial politics based in the hunger and desire to recover self and collective.

## Transatlantic Origins of Black Consumption

The origins of this U.S. culture of consumption trace back to the first contact between European colonizers and coastal Africans. By the early twentieth century, even Europeans admitted to and documented a connection between European global expansion and a sexual/libidinal appetite for African flesh. A cartoon published in the French journal *Le Rire* in 1911 demonstrates how European hungers for conquest sometimes coincided with a homosexual hunger for African flesh. In the foreground of the cartoon, a porter, soldier, and general gather around a Bakongo man stabbed into a skewer. The Bakongo man spins around and awaits the slice of the butcher knife resting at his knees. A 1937 cartoon published in the Belgium magazine *Hooger Leven* that also depicted Europeans' cannibalism had a caption that perfectly captured the irony of an African turning on a skewer: "Any takers for Negro Soup?" Such cartoons depict a different species of cannibal and an altogether different master narrative of cannibalism informing European expansion into Africa.[16] The word "Congo" is tattooed on the African man's loincloth, establishing a connection between the carving up of Africa by numerous European nations and the carving up of the African male body.

The homoerotic bonds shared among the white men gathered around the African man highlight the promise of "Negro Soup," with the Bakongo (Congo) man serving as a symbol of their common purpose and desire. The African body is spread-eagled before this tableau of male bonding. The general and his captain of arms (who turns the skewer) look across the black man's body into one another's eyes. The other men, bent over the half-naked body, appear to be captivated by their vulnerable prey turning delectably on the skewer. One soldier has his hand on his hips; the other has his palms pressed together and tucked tightly into his groin. The knife in the general's hand resembles a phallus—thick on the bottom and narrower at the tip. With this "phallus" in one hand, the general squats between the African man's legs, holding his calves apart. The Bakongo man is positioned in a manner that provides for easy anal access—the missionary position. In the Belgian cartoon, sexual/erotic tastes are indistinguishable from the palate—the knife and the phallus are interchangeable signifiers.

This cartoon depicts a widespread belief in in Western and Central Africa that Europeans were cannibals. Groups such as the Igbo, Bakongo, Fanti, and Guinea all thought of European interlopers as cannibals.[17] A century earlier, for example, Ali Eisami, of the Bornu people

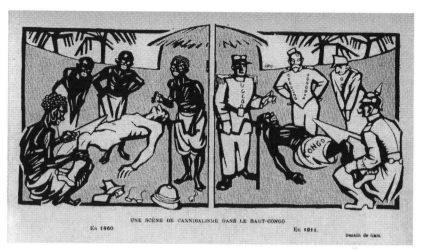

A cartoon published in the French journal, *Le Rire*, in 1911.

Marcel Eemans, "Zum er hog liefhebbers voor negersoep?" © 2012 Artists Rights Society (ARS), New York / SABAM, Belgium.

in Nigeria, described his encounter with a "European cannibal" in a manner laden with terror and homoeroticism. Eisami is transported as a slave throughout many western African regions; slave traders finally bring him and a group of kinsmen to the home of a white minister in Bathurst in 1818. The minister comes out of his home and surveys all of the slaves. He takes a marked interest in Eisami, who recalls that the man "took hold of my hand, and drew me into his house."[18] According-ing to Eisami and the other Africans assembled, the white man strongly desires him, takes a delectable interest in this Bornu man. The terrors and observations of the other enslaved African persons erupt into whispered rumor: "The White man has taken Ali, and put him into the house, in order to slaughter him." Inside the house, Ali imagines his seducer wielding a phallic object, a long knife: "If this white man takes a knife," he thinks to himself, "and I see it in his hand, I will hold it."[19] The threat of sexual domination and dismemberment hovers at the edges of Eisami's imagination. The Africans translate white male phallic power over the effeminized African subject into an erotics of appetite and eating.

The slave trade ferried this culture of homoeroticism and consump-tion aboard slave ships across the Atlantic, where it took root and assumed a number of new forms in the context of chattel slavery. For example, within plantation culture, this culture of consumption took the form of whites literally flaying and smoking African American flesh and overt references in slave narratives to masters literally and meta-phorically consuming their slaves. For the slave, this culture of con-sumption was a fact of daily life, as was amply documented in slave nar-ratives, Works Progress Administration (WPA) interviews of ex-slaves, letters, political treatises, and autobiographies from the antebellum period.

The Belgian cartoon, Ali Eisami, and the literal and metaphori-cal consumption documented in slave narratives, letters, WPA inter-views, and autobiographies are each examples of a horrific dimension of African American experience that is difficult, if not almost impos-sible, to put into language. Toni Morrison referred to this region of African American experience as the unspeakable. In her writing about nineteenth-century literature and slave culture, she makes subtle refer-ences to a white culture of consumption. In an example from *Playing in the Dark: Whiteness and the Literary Imagination*, Morrison describes whites and, in particular, a white slave mistress as "gathering identity unto herself from the wholly available and serviceable lives of Africanist others."[20] Morrison describes a social and emotional form of cannibalism or parasitism taking place in the context of plantation culture. This subject of cannibalism so disturbed the white, educated female audience of Harriet Jacobs's slave narrative that she moved all references to flesh-cooking, flesh-carving, and eating in her slave narrative to one chapter that readers could conveniently skip.[21] Many morally conscious whites registered the disturbing implications of cannibalism and sought to address its national implications. For example, in Herman Melville's *Moby Dick*, or *the Whale* (1851), which the author based upon incidents of consumption of black males at sea, Ishmael draws a parallel between his cannibal shipmate and George Washington, the first president of the United States: "Queequeg," says Ishmael about his companion, "was George Washington cannibalistically developed."[22] Is it possible that our beloved, slave-owning first president and founding father, George Washington, embodied cannibalistic hungers? This question, posed through a fictional character, struck at the heart of American founding mythologies, national issues of hunger and taste, genteel posturing, and ideas of a pure, white paternity.

For African Americans, this question was much more personal and poignant. Most slave narratives contained overt or covert references to flesh-eating. In his *Narrative of the Life of Frederick Douglass, An American Slave* (1845), Frederick Douglass described the entire institution of slavery as a towering, cannibal being: "There stood slavery . . . glaring frightfully upon us—its robes already crimsoned with the blood of millions, and even now feasting itself greedily upon our own flesh."[23] Most of what Douglass knew and felt, though, about this institutionalized cannibalism remains unspeakable and undocumented: "I wish," he says, "I wish I could commit to paper the feelings with which I beheld it."[24]

In part the subject of cannibalism has been unspeakable for black men because of the homoerotic implications of such experiences. Kara Walker, commenting upon European and white cannibalism, has observed that "there is a little bit of masochism . . . so much love and hate involved in eating something; to kill something and eat it. It's very sexual, very sensual."[25] The consumption of black flesh often took place in the context of incestuous plantation dynamics. A master would often choose "a favorite" male slave as the object of his cultivated delight. Black men in such contexts had to negotiate feelings of affection, hatred, shame, sexual degradation, and arousal toward white men. Cannibalism was unspeakable, but cannibalism coupled with the subject of homoeroticism went against conventional ideas of black men as stoic, as embodiments of the valiant struggle of will and mind over body, as agents of reason and political strategy. To speak about "the feelings" associated with his own flesh consumption would have aligned Douglass too deeply with the unspeakable knowledge of the body as sexual and sensual object, potentially undermining the literary and literate authority we have come to associate with his masculinity.

Long before the poignant questions of the color line and the Negro problem registered in the black imagination, it seems that a more pressing problematic confronted the black citizen. In the form of a question, it might have registered as: "How does it feel to be an edible, consumed object?" In other words, how does it feel to be an energy source and foodstuff, to be consumed on the levels of body, sex, psyche, and soul? Answers to such questions had personal and national implications, as the personal plight of the Negro formed part of a larger homoerotic master narrative of colonial conquest and male desire. For the Negro as well as the white person, such questions necessitated a reconsideration of basic American values, such as gentility and social etiquette, colonial drive and hunger, and cherished racial categorizations.

## Linking Homoeroticism to Cannibalism

My study emphasizes homoeroticism over homosexuality. By definition, homoeroticism implies same-sex arousal and draws attention to those political, social, and libidinal forces that shape desire and, ultimately, the homosexual act.[26] The homosexual components of the feasting—partaking of the boiling pot of Negro soup—are less important to me than the racial assumptions, political aspirations, gender codes, philosophical frameworks, and cosmologies that dictated the feelings of arousal on the part of European and white Americans toward black males and hunger for black male flesh. For example, the larger discussion of Negro effeminacy, or the idea of the Negro as the "lady of the races,"[27] shapes European male desire in the Belgian cartoon; it sets the stage for homosexual consumption and makes possible what Eve Sedgwick refers to as homosocial bonding. Segdwick has written about Victorian-era homosocial desire as operating through triangulation, operating through "its relation to women and the gender system as a whole."[28] Her referent for gender is the female body. However, in the cartoons discussed above, the African man functions as the feminized figure; through him, the general, the soldiers, the porters, and the field attendants bond and share in homoerotic desire. The final outcome of the Negro Soup scene is a type of homosexual consumption. However, long before we get to the homosexual act, the machinery of homoeroticism clicks into play, shaping and dictating the meaning and significance of the homosexual act.

David Halperin has cautioned against easy conflations of modern conceptions of sexual subjectivity with those that figured in the emotional lives of premodern subjects.[29] His concerns reflect the general understanding within queer theory of homosexuality as a constructed, historical phenomenon. Medical and psychological discourses at the turn of the twentieth century normalized and pathologized the homosexual personality type. The word "homosexual" was, in turn, reclaimed by same-sex-identified activists, intellectuals, and cultural workers in the 1950s and 1960s. However, the word "homosexual" had no currency in the eighteenth and nineteenth centuries; neither, for that matter, did the word "homoeroticism." Taking to heart the importance and necessity of historical specificity, I do not attempt to homoeroticize black experience in the nineteenth century. That is, I do not attempt to graft an arbitrary language and sexual modality onto the time period. The word "homoeroticism" in my study serves as a referent for a large set of same-sex desires and intimacies that include romantic friendship between men, same-sex incest in the context of plantation patriarchy, the romanticization of and exoticization of whiteness, and literal and metaphoric cannibalism, among other things. All of these terms I identify and extrapolate from their appropriate historical and cultural contexts. Often, though, when a blanket term is called for, I use the word "homoeroticism" to refer to any combination of these subcategories of experience.

By coupling homoeroticism with cannibalism, I have sought to ground the meaning of the word "cannibalism" in the African/

European encounter and in the Middle Passage (the originary site of black erotic/sexual encounter). Paul Gilroy's *The Black Atlantic: Modernity and Double Consciousness* resuscitates the Atlantic as a living symbolic and cultural entity for black people of the African diaspora. Gilroy effectively recasts the Atlantic as a twentieth-century migratory structure (through the image of ships) composed of triangular routes along which black people in South Africa, England, and the Americas have ferried philosophical, political, and musical materials. Like Gilroy, I also appeal to the African diaspora as a site of black cultural formation and transmission. However, for me the organizing metaphor is not the ship but the captured bodies brought aboard slave ships and the ways those bodies, specifically male bodies, underwent processes of sexual and social cannibalization.

Traditionally, historical considerations of cannibalism in the context of European exploration and occupation of foreign lands focus on European ideas of natives (American and African) as cannibals. Take the 1503 decree of Queen Isabella of Spain that dictated that "no Indians under her dominion were to be hurt or captured."[30] However, "a certain people called 'cannibals' might be fairly fought and, if captured, enslaved, 'as punishment for crimes committed against my subjects.'"[31] This early distinction between "Indians" and "cannibals" would eventually give way to the thought that all Indians and Indian ways were heathen or subject to cannibalistic practices. Similarly, Europeans, generally speaking, believed diverse African groups, from one end of the continent to the other, a cannibalistic race.[32] Nineteenth-century Europeans and Americans promulgated the idea of the heathen African, which also implied cannibalism. Speaking of the Christian reformation of the African cannibal, Rev. Henry Ward Beecher defined heathenism in 1850 as derived "from idolatry, from fornication and incest, from infanticide and cannibalism."[33]

Today, a growing body of cannibalism scholarship has developed that spans the disciplines of literature, anthropology, history, philosophy, political economy, cultural studies, and postcolonial studies. In fact, cannibalism is said by many scholars "to be one the most important topics in cultural criticism today."[34] An exciting outcome of this emerging corpus of cannibalism scholarship is that it takes us beyond the Eurocentric master narrative of cannibalism into a complex arena that includes, for example, recent sophisticated work on African Mane and Azande customs and practices of cannibalism.[35] We now have a deeper understanding of the human sacrifice and consumption rituals of Aztec and other Meso-American people.[36] We also now have studies that excavate and analyze European legacies of religious, medicinal, and survival cannibalism and still other studies that locate the cannibalistic urge within the European Enlightenment itself—within the workings of the modern and postmodern European and American state.[37]

The postcolonial branch of contemporary cannibalism studies has been most helpful to my work. This branch has, more than any other, undertaken to unearth and analyze the cannibalism discourses that arose from colonial contact between Europeans and Africans and Native Americans. As I emphasized earlier, Europeans were not the only ones who understood the colonial encounter in terms of cannibalism. On both sides of the Atlantic, in Africa and the Americas, black and African people in the nineteenth century documented this culture in slave and travel narratives, political philosophy and treatises, newspaper articles, and sermons, among other types of documentation. For example, the famous 1839 slave insurrection aboard the ship *Amistad* occurred because the Mende revolt leader, Sengbe Pieh, and those who followed him feared that Spanish slavers intended to eat them.[38]

As I have demonstrated, the African belief that Europeans were cannibals was not uncommon. Importantly, such beliefs represented the captured African's first articulations of an intersection between themselves (their bodies, erotic life force, labor capacity, and exoticization) and the European's hunger for new land, physical and psychic contact with foreign others, and a perfect state of global dominion. The logic and incisiveness of those first African critiques of European cannibalism have accrued power and congealed into a number of contemporary African cannibal discourses. For example, in contemporary Sierra Leone, the land of those original Mende aboard the *Amistad*, cannibalism serves as a "politically charged hidden transcript" intended "to expose, discredit, and disrupt the imbricated relations of power at work in Sierra Leone during the late 1980s just prior to its descent into civil war."[39] Today, "in the context of postcolonial African political struggles, the language of inequality continues to revolve around the metaphors of eating and, by extension, cannibalistic consumption. The trope of cannibalism as a symbol for the economic exploitation, material accumulation, and violent coercion carried out by postcolonial elites has, in fact, come to dominate African political discourse."[40]

Because the examples of cannibalism that I use in the book range from figurative tropes to literal flesh eating to rituals of flesh taking and harvesting, I employ a cluster of terms that delineate the range of applications and cannibalism contexts that my study encompasses. The list includes the words "consume," "consumption," "social consumption," "appetite," "taste," "delectable," "delectability," "hunger," "ingestion," and "auto-cannibalism." I use the words "cannibalism" and "consumption" interchangeably: The phrase "a culture of consumption" might elsewhere appear as "a cannibal culture." I frequently use "consumption" as a modifier, as in "consumption rituals" and "consumption practices." I think that my preference for the word "consumption" has something to do with the word's rootedness in modern notions of market economies, commodities, consumer appetite, and so forth. While my usage is always particular and usually grounded in human-to-human exchanges, I always have in mind the affluent, ruling-class eighteenth- and nineteenth-century economies that make possible the consumption of the slave along with other traded commodities, such as liquors, spices, and foodstuffs from foreign lands.[41]

I use the words "taste," "appetite," and "delectable" mostly to refer to how the desire for the African slave or American black person had epicurean implications. This desire was less about literal consumption and more about the cultivated taste the white person developed for the African. Whites often satiated this taste and appetite through acts of violence, sexual exploitation, imagined ingestion of the black, or through staged rituals designed to incrementally harvest black spirit and soul. The delectability of the black person was of course a factor in literal flesh consumption, but my main point, which I explain at length in chapter 1, is that literal cannibalism always occurred within cultural, ideological contexts. The cultural contexts to which I frequently refer— the plantation, the slave ship, the general schooner, the African coastal town—were highly eroticized situations and locales. The words "delectable," "taste," and "appetite" bring together homoeroticism in these contexts with overlapping occurrences of consumption.

My use of the word "hunger" relates to the idea of auto-cannibalism. Auto-cannibalism, or self-consumption, involves people consuming themselves voluntarily or through external coercion. In many instances, the cultivation of literal and emotional hunger in the slave produced the opposite effect. The hunger for familial connection, for self and safety, and the ability to resist literal and spiritual consumption led to just that, resistance and self-reclamation in the slave. In the second part of the book, chapters 5 and 6, this idea of hunger takes prominence, as I delineate the numerous ways the slave resisted cannibalization and struggled mightily against the institutionalized urge for self-consumption.

The emphasis upon the economic and metastructural in contemporary cannibalism discourse, especially within the postcolonial branch, has tended to obscure the underlying erotic implications of cannibalism between Europeans and Africans. This body of belief and political philosophy tends to evade or stop short of addressing issues of sexuality, sexual power, desire, and same-sex eroticism. I foreground same-sex eroticism because it brings the focus to issues of desire, power, and gender formation and helps me establish cannibalism as an originary framework for the emergence of homoeroticism out of the transatlantic slave trade and plantation culture. At the juncture where homoeroticism and cannibalism intersected, a new type of cannibalism system— beliefs and practices—emerged. On the continent of Africa, encounters with white "Christian minister cannibals" expanded traditional western and central African cannibal beliefs to include the Church, mercantilism, and European imperialism as institutionalized venues of cannibalism and resource consumption. In the U.S. South, the complexity and newness of this cannibal system registered in legal and religious discussion about "Christian cannibalism" and an existent "cannibal jurisdiction" within southern legislative and geographic territories.

## Slavery as History and Memory

Much of contemporary scholarship on the African diaspora or the black Atlantic has tended to follow Gilroy's path, emphasizing routes of transmission instead of the roots of origins and cultural legacies. An unfortunate result of this approach to the black Atlantic is that, as Houston Baker Jr. notes, much of the "multilocational history" of specific diasporic communities gets erased or overlooked. In particular, Baker takes issue with Gilroy's mishandling of the history and legacy of slavery and bondage: "*The Black Atlantic* remains surprisingly abstract and indeterminate with respect to the very 'chronotype' the book claims as its analytical 'organizing symbol'—namely 'ships in motion across the spaces between Europe, America, Africa, and the Caribbean.'"[42] In fact, "after early mention, *ships* virtually disappear from Gilroy's work. They disappear as chronotypes, material vessels 'transplanting' black populations, dread transports of 'conquered' peoples to penal colonies of the Americas. *Ships*—as disciplinary and carceral 'holds' on the shackled black body—receive no extensive treatment in *The Black Atlantic*."[43]

As Baker does in *Turning South Again: Re-thinking Modernism/ Re-Reading Booker T.*, I also aim to "bring together ships and plantations."[44] For this issue of roots of cultural transmission is not simply a matter of revising or changing the master narrative from Eurocentric to African origins of black American culture. Rather, at stake in this debate over cultural origins is a deeper understanding of the ways in which, for example, the penal politics of slavery and chattel bondage speak to current political phenomena, such as the incarceration of black people and black men in particular; economic issues of racial reparations and the larger, systemic sedimentation of racial inequality; and issues of trauma and post-traumatic stress that affect the ideological and material aspects of black uplift politics and communities. To give a more concrete example of the contemporary implications of the cultural origins debate, in chapter 5 I examine how William Styron's historical novel *The Confessions of Nat Turner* occasioned the first-ever public debate on the subject of homosexuality in the context of slavery. This national debate, occurring in the 1960s, demonstrated how, for black people, the memory of slavery and questions of cultural origins attached to the slave ship had profound political implications rooted in the history and memory of slavery.

My transhistorical approach to slavery is informed, in part, by contemporary calls in African American cultural studies for the excavation of documented material on the subject of homoeroticism during slavery. Many black gay scholars in the 1990s saw their contemporary dislocation from black communities and political infrastructures as linked to a larger history of dislocation and silencing dating back, at least, to slavery. Charles I. Nero, for example, felt that 1980s Afrocentrists, Black Arts spokespersons, and Black Power advocates might have changed their ideas about black gays as threats to and pariahs within black families had they known that homoeroticism existed during slavery. Referencing a few antebellum court cases in which black men were persecuted for sodomy offenses, Nero wrote: "Although the evidence for homosexual practices among black male slaves is small, it does suggest that we do not exclude homoeroticism from life on the plantation."[45] Beyond these instances of criminalization, Nero concludes that additional evidence of homosexuality excavated from "diaries, letters, and narratives" would go a long way toward helping us to "revise our models of the black family and of homosexuality as alien to black culture."[46]

Intuitively, black gay men understood the issue of homosexuality during slavery as a complex phenomenon shaped by a number of factors, including the nation's unresolved relationship to the legacy of slavery, black liberatory ideology dating back to slavery, and, most importantly, the maintenance of traditional notions of family and community that originated in the eighteenth and nineteenth centuries. The legacy and memory of slavery had a powerful effect that left many black gay men feeling isolated from and rendered invisible within black communities. Joseph Beam said it first and best: "I cannot go home as who I am. . . . When I speak of home, I mean not only the familial constellation from which I grew, but the entire black community: the Black press, the Black church, Black academicians, the Black literati, and the Black left. . . . I am most often rendered invisible, perceived as a threat to the family, or am tolerated if I am silent and inconspicuous."[47] Beam's comments echo back through time to the threatening relationship between the homosexual Bayard Rustin and the Civil Rights movement, and, before Rustin, to the homosexual threat that Augustus Dill represented to *The Crisis* magazine and W. E. B. Du Bois. Both Rustin and Dill experienced scandalous public sex incidents in the 1950s and 1920s, respectively, that involved arrests and, in Rustin's case, widely circulated media attention. Both men, loyal and dedicated racial liberation advocates, were asked by key black figures to remove themselves from organizing centers of the Civil Rights and Reconstruction movements. As Philip Brian Harper has noted, the black homosexual functioned in the twentieth century as an index for black masculine anxieties. These ranged from the very personal and painful anxieties of lynching, castration, and the denial of civil rights to a larger set of anxieties rooted in historical erasure and cultural genocide.[48]

▲ Black gays in the late twentieth century found themselves in a double bind of history and memory, which had an unfortunate result: Black people equated their sexual identities with homosexual violation dating back to slavery. In response to this dynamic, such black gay scholars as Robert F. Reid-Phar, Darieck Scott, Nero, Marlon Ross, Charles Clifton, Dwight A. McBride, Harper, Lindon Barrett, and Ron Simmons, among others, took this opportunity to historicize their sexual identities and subject positions and to call attention to the ways in which black people, at least since the Reconstruction era, have conflated the legacy of homosexuality during slavery with a twentieth-century notion of the black faggot, or "Negro homosexual."[49] For example, Eldridge Cleaver associated anal sex between a white man and black man with a racial death wish extending back to slavery and with miscegenation. Cleaver conflated his contemporary understanding of the homosexual person with the particular and different ways in which homosexuality was thought of and configured in the context of slavery. Working with Cleaver's idea of the "Negro homosexual," Reid-Pharr asserts, in *Black Gay Man*, that "to be fucked in the ass by the white man is not simply to be overcome by white culture, white intellect, white notions of superiority."[50] Contradicting Cleaver, Reid-Pharr suggests that the act of anal penetration, at least in the realm of memory, "opens up space for the reconstruction of the black imaginary such that the most sacrosanct of black 'truths' might be transgressed."[51] Truly, the inability to creatively imagine homosexuality during slavery reflected a fundamental fear within the black collective of moving outside of the normative categories of masculinity, reproduction, pleasure, and family.

Elaborating on this point, Reid-Pharr notes that black people are most accustomed to thinking of black female violation during slavery because this theme "resonates with a long history of Black American literature and lore in which the licentious white man acts as the absolute spoiler of black desire."[52] Reid-Pharr's assertions are borne out in the heartrending depictions in black men's slave narratives and autobiographies of black mothers, daughters, and wives raped by white men or the whole lynching and raping dynamic wherein black men are the historical objects of lynching and castration and black women serve as the historical objects of rape. "The image of the white (Southerner) fucking the black man, however, throws all this into confusion," Reid-Pharr contends.[53] It did not occur to Cleaver or to many of his compatriots in the 1960s that a sexually receptive black man during slavery might have absolutely nothing to do, historically speaking, with a self-declared, cosmopolitan homosexual man living in the 1960s or 1990s.

In the twentieth century, our most prevalent examples of same-sex contact during slavery have tended to focus on anal rape and other types of sexual abuse, a fact that underscores this issue of memory or, more specifically, the failure and inability to imagine homosexuality in complicated ways during slavery. This was the problem that Nero had with Morrison's depiction of black men preferring sex with animals and performing forced fellatio on white prison guards in *Beloved*.[54] Deborah McDowell suggests that in order to see black masculinity during slavery in a more complicated frame we may have to revise our prevailing genealogy—our way of locating black male heroism and virility at the center of black uplift and liberation in the nineteenth century. Citing Douglass's slave narratives, McDowell focuses on his omission of his matrilineal legacy, suggesting that his gender, sex, and uplift politics derive from the female body—black female subjugation, mother hunger and loss, rape and sexual violation—as opposed to the genealogy of white male dominance and authority that Douglass foregrounds.[55] A black feminist, E. Frances White, has admitted that for her and many others the issue of homosexuality during slavery brings to the surface ambivalent feelings. Nevertheless, she encourages scholars of the African American experience to explore "the implications of homosexual rape and its relationship to heterosexual rape." Furthermore, she advocates that we inquire "with Morrison-like curiosity . . . why historians have presented the African American past as if the only sexual concerns that black men had during slavery were castration and whether they could protect (and, for some, control) black women's bodies."[56] Baker enacted just such a revision when he asserted, in *Turning South Again*, that "there existed a deeply homoerotic bond between Booker T. Washington and *all* white men—but in particular and most expressly between the Wizard of Tuskegee and General Armstrong."[57] Baker's comments, while speculative and cautious in his text, reflect a gradual turning within African Americanist scholarship toward the erotic and interior lives of black men during slavery.

All told, we have at the end of the twentieth century a collective call and move to excavate homoerotic materials and theoretical frameworks as a means of redefining and better understanding African American and larger American experience. *The Delectable Negro* responds to this collective call for a deeper, more useful understanding of homosexuality in the context of slavery by focusing on the nineteenth century as a moment in which black masculinity, racial identity, homoeroticism, and a distinctive American appetite for black male flesh and soul congealed. I concur with Maurice O. Wallace that still today too few critics and historians have pursued the problems and paradoxes inherent in black male enslavement.[58] Wallace's excellent and wide ranging study, *Constructing the Black Masculine: Identity and Ideality in African American Men's Literature and Culture, 1775–1995*, foregrounds sexuality, homosocial behavior, and black masculine anxiety as crucial social and theoretical frames for black masculine studies, focusing on the eighteenth and nineteenth centuries. His approach to the study of black masculinity marks a general shift echoed in more recent works that deal explicitly and implicitly with black masculinity in the nineteenth and early twentieth centuries, among them, *Turning South Again: Rethinking Modernism/Re-thinking Booker T.* (Baker); *Manning the Race: Reforming Black Men in the Jim Crow Era* (Ross); *Impossible Witnesses: Truth, Abolitionism, and Slave Testimony* (McBride); *Are We Not Men?: Masculine Anxiety and the Problem of African American Identity* (Harper); and *Conjugal Union: The Body, the House, and the Black American* (Reid-Pharr).

No study on black masculinity in the nineteenth century focuses on homoeroticism. This has partly to do with issues of material evidence that have been duly noted by scholars of the African American experience. Many have argued that there simply are not enough primary materials available to conduct such a study. Contrary, though, to these claims of absence, I argue that homoeroticism *did* exist among nineteenth-century black peoples, chattel or free, literate or nonliterate, though a number of factors have prevented us from being able to discern and engage with the subject of homoeroticism as it existed then. Most importantly, our contemporary framing of homosexuality has obscured our vision. In addition, the absence of an appropriate linguistic apparatus, the dearth of historical documentation, and the lack of theoretical models with which to excavate homoeroticism from extant historical documents have all contributed to a lack of substantive information on the subject of homoeroticism.

The extant materials on homoeroticism that I work with in this study include slave narratives, Works Progress Administration interviews of ex-slaves, advertisements for runaway slaves, neo-slave narratives, journals, diaries, novels, poetry, and historical fiction. Most of the materials that I work with are staples of African American literature and culture, such as the slave narratives of Harriet Jacobs and Frederick Douglass. Other materials, such as James L. Smith's slave narrative, advertisements for runaway slaves, and numerous articles from black newspapers published in the nineteenth century are additions to the archive. In this way, I have attempted to respond to the call for the excavation of materials on the subject of homoeroticism during slavery.

The chapters of the book conform to my theoretical framing of homoeroticism in the context of cannibal culture and as a derivative of African homosexual practices reconstituted in the Americas. Chapter 1, "Cannibalism in Transatlantic Context," opens with an examination of Olaudah Equiano's well-known slave narrative, *The Interesting Narrative of the Life of Olaudah Equiano, or Gustavus Vassa, the African, Written by Himself*. Equiano's narrative brings together the themes of homoeroticism and cannibalism. It gives ample examples of Europeans' and West Africans' beliefs about cannibalism in the context of young Equiano's romantic, chivalric relationship (formed aboard a slave ship) with a young white American lad from the slave-owning South. Scholars have tended to dismiss the depictions of cannibalism in the narrative. I treat them seriously and use them to establish an interconnection between cannibalism and chattel homoeroticism and to establish a transatlantic context for incidents of cannibalism and homoerotic interactions in U.S. plantation culture that I discuss in the second chapter.

In chapter 2: "Sex, Honor, and Human Consumption," I examine literal and symbolic examples of human consumption in the antebellum United States. I begin with a discussion of the above-mentioned *Essex* affair, which involved the consumption of four black men in the nineteenth century. Isolating issues of male secrecy, shame, and honor inherent in the *Essex* affair, I move to a broader discussion of the same issues in the slave narratives of black men who documented their social consumption. Finally, in the context of black male lives and voices, I look at the widespread nineteenth-century concern over whether the United States was becoming a cannibal nation. This debate, which occurred among the clergy, congressmen, judges, and artists, among others, centered upon slavery as an essentially consumptive institution.

The third chapter, "A Tale of Hunger Retold: Ravishment and Hunger in F. Douglass's Life and Writing," focuses on Frederick Douglass's depiction of human consumption as a phenomenon that ate away at the psyche and soul. None was more articulate than Douglass about how these dimensions of the consumption of slaves eroded one's ability to resist and strategize against slavery. His observations in this chapter provide a blueprint for how the slave struggled in mind, emotions, and spirit not only against social consumption but also against endemic mechanisms of starvation and hunger designed to break the enslaved person. Douglass's own hunger for self, familial and ancestral bonds, and civil status manifested as complex erotic ties to white men and cross-gender behavior. Douglass's gender-variant and homoerotic experiences provide an opportunity to think anew about nineteenth-century models of black masculinity as gender variant and tied to emotional/erotic urges.

The focus of chapter 4, "Incest and Human Consumption," is Harriet Jacobs's *Incidents in the Life a Slave Girl*. Jacobs's narrative depicts some of the more graphic scenes of human consumption ever portrayed in a U.S. slave narrative. She depicts masters, within the domestic realm, as epicures of black flesh, sex, terror, and institutionalized hunger and starvation. Focusing on Luke (a black man raped by his master) and Jacobs herself, I elucidate the intersections between incestuous plantation dynamics and the culture of human consumption. Both Luke and Jacobs are infantilized and form part of a genealogy of human consumption that, for the master and mistress, extends back to childhood and learned, sycophantic relationships with mammy figures, black uncle figures, and black playmates.

Chapters 5 and 6 look at the topic of human consumption from more contemporary perspectives. Chapter 5, "Eating Nat Turner," focuses on William Styron's novel, *The Confessions of Nat Turner* (1967). This novel, along with *Ten Black Writers Respond* (1968), the edited black response to the novel, marked the first time that the subject of homosexuality during slavery had received sustained, public debate. I focus on what many black intellectuals and activist called Styron's "homosexual" representation of and degradation of Nat Turner's life and revolutionary efforts. Other black male critics of Styron's novel accused him of effeminizing and cannibalizing Nat Turner. (As I have mentioned, Turner's corpse was treated in a manner that suggests it might have been consumed as medicine and dispensed as a component of pharmacological serums.) In this chapter, I explore homoeroticism and cannibalism as transhistorical phenomena, linking the consumptive history presented in chapters 1 and 2 to the political insurgence of the 1960s.

The final chapter of the book, chapter 6, "The Hungry Nigger," opens with an examination of the controversy surrounding the chain-gang oral sex scene in Toni Morrison's *Beloved*. Black male responses to this scenario and the novel in general have ranged from accusations of homophobia to a lambasting of Morrison's "valorization of black suffering" to reading the scene as a psychoanalytic encapsulation of black male erotic life on the plantation. I suggest that the profound usefulness of this scenario is in conveying how, at the end of the twentieth and beginning of the twenty-first century, we are still at a loss for language and appropriate metaphors with which to describe black male hunger within a plantation culture of consumption. Hunger serves in the novel as an index for a culture of consumption; for black male emotional loss, trauma, and need; and for a complex black male erotic life. I draw parallels between Morrison's novels and late-nineteenth-century neo-slave narratives. From Morrison's novel, I segue into a more formal theorization of what I call the "black male orifice." This section of the chapter takes into account the long-standing historical challenge of theorizing and thinking through black male erotic orifices, the anus and mouth in particular. Working with Baker's notion of the "tight place," I suggest that we need to ground these erotic regions, along with the notion of black men hungering, in actual historical places. To this end, I sketch a genealogy of the black male orifice that recuperates the Middle Passage, plantation slavery, and transatlantic slavery as homoerotic and erogenous zones of black male experience.

As a final prelude, I pose the question: What if the nineteenth-century cannibalism question and debate pointed in a direction of inquiry we desperately needed to resolve? And from this side of things, what if we in this contemporary moment have a responsibility to make sense of that question, tracing its outgrowths to our current political and social climates?

1

Cannibalism in Transatlantic Context

In the eighteenth and nineteenth centuries, Europeans did not understand the extent to which western and central Africans regarded them as cannibals and flesh harvesters. In an 1849 exchange between Augustino (an African-born slave) and the Select Committee of the House of Lords, Appointed to Consider the Best Means which Great Britain Can Adopt for the Final Extinction of the African Slave Trade, British interrogators questioned the African man regarding his belief in European cannibalism. British interrogators "could not understand what had put the idea into the slaves' heads that they were to be eaten. 'Are they eaten in their own country?' asked the British interrogator, as ignorant and suspicious of Africa as the new slaves were of the white world."[1] In an expected rhetorical maneuver, the interrogator places the onus of proof and explanation on the African man, Augustino. The British man is willing to believe that African cultural practices lend themselves to cannibalism, whereas he presumes that "civilized" European legislative processes, mechanisms of reason, and critical inquiry rise above such a cannibal accusation.

Had Augustino truly received the opportunity and felt compelled to explain the particular constellation of beliefs, social practices, human science, and perceptions informing the African's belief in white cannibals, members of the Select Committee would have learned more that day than they probably wanted to know about African notions of

Christian cannibalism, slavery as a process of human consumption, and sex and the consumptive appetites of whites from an African perspective. The British interrogator asks the African man to speak, to testify before this legislative body but then renders his voice and perceptual reality (what he might have said about white cannibalism) unspeakable. Rather than inquiring into exactly what Africans meant by eating and flesh consumption, Europeans and white Americans habitually applied to African persons and cultural practices generic theories of social ineptitude and cannibalistic hunger. For example, in 1839, American media proliferated with images of the Mende persons who had taken over the slave ship *Amistad*. A number of the Mende men had "pointy filed teeth" and emerged from the slave ship onto American shores wearing no clothing. According to Patricia A. Turner, white Americans equated the African men's pointed teeth and their nakedness with cannibalism: "This was an appalling and disturbing lack of modesty as far as white Americans were concerned. In their minds, it made sense that people who were ambivalent about clothing would be the kind to eat human flesh."[2] The Mende, though, had their own ideas about Europeans as cannibals. It was the fear of cannibalistic Europeans that inspired the Mende men to revolt, seize the slave ship, and attempt to sail the vessel back to Sierra Leone.

Firmly wedded to rigid notions of their own civility, Europeans have, for the most part, presumed themselves beyond accusations of cannibalism. As we see with the British interrogator, the belief in European supremacy determines the direction and outcome of the exchange; from the outset, the British interrogator interprets any insight Augustino would bring to the topic of Europeans as cannibals as evidence of African cannibalistic ways. In the context of hearings focused on the African person and on ending the slave trade, the last thing British magistrates wanted to discuss was the topic of an emerging European cannibal. They wanted to end the slave trade, absolve their nation of moral taint, and return the Africans to their original status of savagery, unless the civilizing efforts of missionaries and other such persons sent to reform the continent of Africa intervened.

Taking my cue from this exchange between the British official and Augustino, I explore in this chapter the correlation between the consumptive appetites of whites and the transatlantic slave trade. It is my contention that somewhere between European denial and African accusation a new species of civilized "white cannibal" was born. This white cannibal was unique to the Middle Passage and transatlantic slavery. In addition to literal acts of eating, carving, and cooking flesh, European and American whites developed a culture of cannibalism wherein daily acts of violence, religious conversion, slave seasoning and breaking, and sexual brutality all fed into the master's appetite for African flesh and souls. Many historical texts on the subject of slavery describe the importance of the process of "seasoning" for breaking men and women and making them into docile "slaves." Elaborating on the culinary connotations of the word "seasoning" (season: "to heighten or improve the flavor of food by adding condiments, spices, herbs, or the like"),[3] I link the physically brutal culture of seasoning to the parallel development of erotic appetites, tastes, and aesthetic longings for the black male. This broader understanding of seasoning is important, as it helps explain how institutional processes, such as Christian indoctrination, male fraternal love and bonding, and the acquisition of literacy facilitated the social consumption of the Negro and the creation of a high cultural premium upon African flesh.

The textual focus of this chapter is Olaudah Equiano's *The Interesting Narrative of the Life of Olaudah Equiano or Gustavus Vassa, the African, Written by Himself*. We recognize Equiano's text as a staple among transatlantic slave narratives. It was the first to document extensively the experiences and travails of an African (Ibo) child sold into slavery and shuttled among English, U.S., and Caribbean slave owners. What is still little acknowledged among scholars of Equiano's narrative is how his text documents at length the process of the slave's social consumption, focusing on culinary rituals, processes of flesh seasoning, and the hunger and appetites whites developed for blacks in the context of slave culture. Equiano's text is a useful touchstone for beginning this book-length discussion of homoeroticism and human consumption, as it brings together this culture of consumption with male fraternity and homoeroticism. Equiano's social consumption always happens in the context of intimate, homoerotic relations, a fact suggesting that intimacy and connection rather than abjection and disconnection might have best facilitated the slave's social consumption.

For the most part, our scholarly responses to African accusations of cannibalism have failed to penetrate the surface. This is the case even as the accusations against Europeans proliferate, arising from local patterns of thought and belief about cannibalism. Generally speaking, Africans taken by force from their home communities feared Europeans, whom they frequently thought of as "ministers of destruction," "magicians," and "flesh eaters." Ottobah Cuguano, a West African captured by English slave traders and taken to England, recalled the first time he saw whites: "We came to a town, where I saw several white people, which made me afraid that they would eat me, according to our notion as children in the inland parts of the country."[4] Joseph Wright of the Egba people of Nigeria fell into a deep depression when his kinsmen sold him as a slave to the Portuguese. At the root of his depression was the common belief "that the Portuguese were going to eat us when we got to their country."[5] Even worse by way of reputation than the Portuguese were the English, whom some African groups understood to be an even more vicious species of cannibal. After their capture by the Portuguese, Wright and his kinsmen come the next day upon an English man-of-war. He fully believes the Portuguese when they describe the English as the "real" species of cannibal: "They [the Portuguese] . . . told us that these were the people which would eat us, if we suffered them to prize us."[6]

Scholars of the transatlantic slave trade and the black experience have tended either to metaphorize or dismiss such examples as superstitious thought or unfounded indigenous terrors. Scholarship on the life of Ota Benga, a pygmy man brought to the United States in the late nineteenth century and displayed as an attraction in a zoo, exhibits these tendencies. Benga is described by his biographer as believing that "White Eyes" (white men) are cannibals, a fear ascribed mostly to superstition Benga and the equally "savage" Apache chieftain, Geronimo, shared. Benga, who is portrayed as prone to childish "pranks" and witchcraft, and his pygmy-based cannibal beliefs are thought to have no critical bearing upon the structures of U.S. imperialism and exotic consumerism.[7] Mia Bay situates African beliefs that Europeans were cannibals in a historical context that ultimately reinforces Western conceptions of reality and overlooks the social logic and human science behind African cannibal beliefs. She attributes such beliefs to "traditional African tribal animosities that placed the imputation of cannibalism on distrusted foreign peoples" and to the fact that "Africans taken by the Europeans [in the context of slavery] were usually never seen again."[8] Bay concludes that "African misapprehensions about white cannibalism" were not real. Rather, she finds them to be based in a distorted historical vision, a viewpoint easily corrected with "facts."[9] In "White Cannibals, Black Martyrs: Fear, Depression and Religious Faith as Causes of Suicide among New Slaves," William D. Piersen draws conclusions similar to those asserted by Bay. He also attributes African "misapprehension of white cannibalism" to several culturally limiting and determined factors. These include the fact that kin and kinsmen who were taken in the slave trade were never heard from again, coastal Africans' mistrust of foreign peoples, and the widespread belief among differing African groups that the more suspect tribes, such as the Ibo, Coromantees, Angolans, and Ibibios, were cannibals.[10] Such logic, while meant to be corrective, has ultimately reinforced the idea of the African as superstitious and lacking a civilized perspective on the world and humankind. Furthermore, such thinking presumes a historical trajectory in which beliefs and practices related to cannibalism are "pre-civilization," with civilization being characteristically European and associated with Western advancement.

We are not in the habit of thinking about slavery and consumption as coterminous realities. It seems such an unreal occurrence to those who know very little of the global history of slavery and human consumption. Carl O. Williams, extrapolating from observations of ancient Icelandic slavery, describes the slave master as the ultimate human parasite, one whose fundamental relationship to the slave is that of a consumer to a food source or commodity. He writes:

> This class of the lowly is the source from which the master class draws its livelihood and leisure. Thraldom [slavery] is a degree of cannibalism. It is a system of man feeding upon man. The master is a human parasite, who, by the right of might, has secured his fellow-men in the bonds of thraldom in order to feed upon them and to use them for the satisfaction of his appetites.[11]

According to Orlando Patterson, sexual desire and codes of masculine honor strongly informed this culture of human consumption described by Williams: "What the slave mainly fed was the master's sense of honor and his sexual appetite."[12] After methodically butchering and cooking a male slave over a roiling open fire, one Kentucky slave master reported to his wife "that he had never enjoyed himself so well at a ball as he had enjoyed himself that evening."[13] Such incidents proliferated throughout the slave-trading diaspora (especially in the Caribbean and the Americas), where carving, cooking, and eating of flesh served as punishments and conditioning rituals. Typically, masters derived feelings of pleasure and social empowerment from rituals of torture and consumption. Patterson, concurring with Williams and drawing upon analyses of slavery among "primitive Germanic peoples," observed also that slaves were "socially consumed" and that this process of consumption was endemic to "all other slave holding societies," both before and after European global expansion.[14]

Importantly, both Williams and Patterson foreground the erotic and, more specifically, the homoerotic desires of masters that shaped and informed master/slave relations. Masters received a sexual high or erotic charge from consumptive acts. Power and sex intertwined, with the slave's body and sex serving not only the purposes of pleasure and erotic fulfillment but also reinforcing the master's authority, supremacy, and dominance.

## Romancing the Cannibal

Equiano's *The Interesting Narrative of the Life of Olaudah Equiano or Gustavus Vassa* is today regarded as an exemplary specimen of African civilization and cultural production. Equiano is not the silenced and culturally determined Augustino, who speaks but is not heard. Instead, Equiano, an African-born, formerly enslaved man, managed to achieve literacy and pen his narrative, which is not only a vindication of his Ibo people, but a model of literature in the genres of the travel, slave, and exploratory narrative. While little substantive scholarship has been written on the topic, Equiano's text remains one of our most thorough and elucidative explorations of the European acting as a type of cannibal in the transatlantic context. In his travel narrative, Equiano describes a culture of cannibalism based in practices of cutting, harvesting, and cooking flesh. In keeping with Patterson's assertion, a homoerotic sexual appetite facilitates the African's social consumption in Equiano's narrative: Homoerotic desire serves as a means of tasting, ingesting, and cultivating an institutionalized appetite for African flesh. Furthermore, in Equiano's narrative, the institutions of Christian fraternity, chivalric homoerotic love, transatlantic mercantilism, and literacy all serve as means through which European and American white males cultivate high cultural tastes for African males and perpetuate metaphoric and erotic rituals of consumption.

Scholars of Equiano's life and work have categorized and studied *The Interesting Narrative* as a slave narrative, a travel narrative, and an autobiography. Though it fits into all of these categories, I approach the text primarily as a slave narrative. When Equiano penned his narrative, British abolitionist efforts were well under way. The interview between Augustino and representatives of the British Select Committee reflected the British government's determination to throw its full legislative powers behind the ending of the African slave trade. In the prefatory material to the narrative, Equiano includes a letter that he wrote to the British Parliament. The letter begins: "Permit me with the greatest deference and respect, to lay at your feet the following genuine Narrative; The chief design of which is to excite in your august assemblies a sense of compassion for the miseries which the Slave Trade has entailed on my unfortunate countrymen."[15] Equiano wrote with the intention of locating himself and his narrative within this national abolitionist conversation.[16]

Equiano's abolitionist sentiments and finely attuned awareness of English feelings of cultural superiority distinguished his text from narratives written by his peers. It is the perfect text for initiating a discussion of black male consumption in a transatlantic context, as it is "the prototype of the slave narrative" and prefigures representations of white cannibalism in the slave narratives published by black American men in the nineteenth century.[17] Henry Louis Gates Jr. has described Equiano's narrative as the "silent second text" of the *Narrative of the Life of Frederick Douglass*.[18] Following a marketing strategy established by Equiano, Douglass distributed his slave narrative on both sides of the Atlantic and received acclaim in U.S. and British abolitionist circles.

Equiano's narrative, like none written before or after, provides an early snapshot of black experience and identity as transatlantic. It is the story of a West African child sold into slavery, bartered among white

masters, and raised aboard schooners that traverse the Atlantic carry-
ing slaves and cargo from England to the Caribbean and then to the
United States. Equiano begins his narrative as an isolated and traumatized child whose overwhelming response to slave captors is fear and
terror. He fears he will be eaten. He fears the whites are cannibals. Equiano first raises his concern that the whites are cannibals after British
slavers purchase him and take him aboard the slave ship *African Snow*.
Secretly, the African youth questions his bonded kinsmen about the
whites: "I asked them if we were not to be eaten by those white men
with horrible looks, red faces, and long hair."[19]

The first section of his narrative documents his constant preoccupation with cannibalistic Europeans. His initial observations are only
confirmed by visions of boilers and African bodies chained together,
presumably waiting to be fed to the boilers: "When I looked round the
ship too, and saw a large furnace or copper boiling, and a multitude of
black people of every description chained together, every one of their
countenances expressing dejection and sorrow, I no longer doubted of
my fate, and, quite overpowered with horror and anguish, I fell motion-
less on the deck and fainted."[20] Even after the crew of the slaver and his
own kinsmen confirm for him that he is not to be eaten, Equiano's fears
persist. When the crew captures a shark and hoists it aboard the slaver,
he reports: "This gladdened my poor heart exceedingly, as I thought it
would serve the people to eat instead of their eating me."[21] Playing upon
his fears, the ship captain (also his slave master) would often threaten
to eat Equiano and his best friend, Dick: "He said he would kill Dick (as
he always called him) first, and afterwards me."[22] Equiano, later in the
narrative, reflects back on his "childish ignorance" and views of Europeans and corrects himself: "That fear, however, which was the effect of
my ignorance, wore away as I began to know them. I could now speak
English tolerably well. . . . I no longer looked upon them as spirits, but
as men superior to us [Africans]; and therefore I had the stronger desire
to resemble them."[23] Equiano strives to be and does ultimately become
an Anglo-African: "I soon grew a stranger to terror of every kind, and
was, in that respect, at least almost an Englishman."[24]

In this pivotal section of the narrative, Equiano seems to resolve
the issue of European cannibalism by attributing such perceptions to
his indigenous naïveté. Scholars have, for the most part, followed his

prompt, assuming that the issue of human consumption has no bearing on those portions of the narrative that follow chapter IV.[25] The remaining chapters in the narrative, chapters V through XII, depict his further cultural training and his sometimes harrowing, sometimes pleasant initiation into the ways of English civilization. I want to suggest, though, that the subject of cannibalism in the narrative is more complex than this. Later in the narrative, Equiano describes a culture of human cannibalism wherein whites perform as "human butchers" in order to satiate their appetites for African flesh, terror, and sometimes sex.[26] In the context of such occurrences, white men relate to Equiano as a delectable object who is not so much literally consumed as tasted, erotically desired, and cultivated as an object of male erotic needs and social stature. Patterson's idea of the master as a "parasite" who forces the slave to feed "the master's sense of honor and his sexual appetite" dictates Equiano's relationship to white men, who subject him to "both personal and institutional parasitism."[27]

Equiano first encounters white cannibalism through romantic love and companionship with a young white male shipmate. Richard Baker appears in Equiano's narrative and life as a type of young chivalric prince. Working off the stereotype of the African race as effeminate compared to the more masculine, martial nature of the Anglophone European, Equiano reconfigures the codes of chivalry by casting himself as a type of male princess and Richard as the saving prince. The Negro was, after all, thought of as "the Lady of the races," a more effeminate species compared to the Anglo Saxon.[28] As a specimen of the effeminate species, Equiano fits perfectly into the arms and racial mythology of his white suitor. Richard Baker is an American slave master, "a young lad" with an "excellent education" and a "most amiable temper."[29] It seems, in Equiano's eyes, unimportant that Baker owns slaves back in the United States: "Although this dear youth had many slaves of his own, yet he and I have gone through many sufferings together on shipboard."[30] Young Richard bonds quickly with Equiano in what the author refers to as a "friendship." Within the plantation culture from which Richard comes, "friendships" between young white and black males were always framed by the master/slave dynamic. The author makes no attempt to qualify his friendship; he does not refer to the young black slave boys who were used as nursemaids and made to play the roles of comrade, friend, and servile slave on plantations. Within the context of such plantation "friendships," young white boys developed and honed the skills of conqueror. Susan Snow, a former slave, recalls fondly that her young master would work in the fields with the slaves: "My young marster used to work in de fiel' wid us. He'd boss de Niggers. Dey called 'im Bud, but us all called 'im 'Babe.' Honey, I sho did love dat boy."[31] Snow romanticizes this white youth who practices the exercise of authority over black adults—adults who have raised him and labor for everything he will one day own.

Equiano's friendship with and ensuing romantic love for Baker is more complicated than Snow's maternal love. Richard civilizes the young African. Through Richard, Equiano learns that the "talking book" (the Bible) does not actually talk.[32] Rather, one learns to read this book and decipher the messages encoded therein. Richard helps Equiano move beyond his savage thinking and upbringing. At night, Richard and Equiano find comfort, warmth, and safety in each other's arms: "and we have many nights lain in each other's bosoms when we were in great distress."[33]

This theme of the saving, intimate embrace of a white youth is not unique to Equiano's narrative. The same year his narrative reached print (1789), a French author, Joseph Lavallée, published the novel *Le nègre comme il ya peu de blancs*. Lavallée's novel, an international phenomenon, appeared almost immediately in English translation. In the novel's dramatic opening scenes, the main character, Itanoko, escapes from an African prince who desires and uses him as a sexual object. Itanoko is swimming madly toward an offshore slave ship. The ship's officer pulls him out of the water, immediately remarking upon his beauty and physique: "This is the finest black I have ever seen," he says.[34] Itanoko is nude, and it is noted earlier in the translated English version of the text that he lacks "pudicity"—modesty concerning his genitalia. Musing aloud about his erotic feelings toward Itanoko, the ship hand imagines the captain as the luckiest man for having the choice of this African man to share his bed: "Zounds! Cries the officer on watch, with an energetic oath, that's the finest black I ever clapt my eyes on; how lucky is the captain, why fortune hunts him even in bed."[35] Itanoko, like Equiano, speaks in the master's tongue (French) and is instructed in Christian ways. Several men initiate him into these rites, but the most significant is Ferdinand, the ship captain's son. Itanoko feels an uninhibited romantic love for this youth, declaring that "nothing gave me so much pleasure as the sight of Ferdinand. Tall and finely formed, he possessed also an ingenious countenance, which ever attaches the heart in the first instance. I could not resist it."[36]

While Equiano labored to produce a work of nonfiction, he was not immune to the fictional conventions of sentimentalism and the European's romanticization of the African. Lavallée caters to these homoerotic hungers for the African's body. And the widespread popularity and translation of his novel in France, England, and the Americas attests to this social reality. The similarities between Equiano's work of real-life experience and Lavallée's fictional work are striking. These similarities reveal a culture of white sexual hunger for black flesh that was so widespread that a French man and an Anglicized African writing in different genres and from different geographic locales seized upon the same resonant themes and images. Beds, bedsides, and bedclothes are significant motifs that run throughout Equiano's slave narrative. At the bedside is where Equiano stages his most intimate religious conversion moments. The first moment involves himself and Richard lying in bed in an embrace and then praying together at bedside. Later in the narrative, Equiano will replicate this situation with an adult white Englishman and with a semi-clad Native American youth taken from the Caribbean. Richard teaches Equiano, an orphaned African child, to look to a symbolic white deity father for solace and comfort. The Christian principles of sacrifice and selflessness reinforce in Equiano a servile identification with the desires and hungers of white men. As kind and loving as Richard is, he ultimately conditions Equiano to better play the role of slave.

Months earlier, Equiano had lain below another ship deck in a scene of death and stink so thick that he could not breathe. Thinking back to that time, Equiano recalls that he had "scarcely room to turn himself." The heat sweltered and cooked. Babies carried onboard or born on the ship (it is not clear which) tumbled into tubs of feces and urine and almost suffocated. Everyone was dying, and many literally perished, "falling victims to the improvident avarice . . . of their purchasers."[37] The filth, thick air, and layers of bodies in that scene contrast sharply with the clean, open air in which Equiano lies in the young white slave master's arms. Equiano feels himself "chosen" by his young white companion, drawing upon the mythology of Christ and the myth of white innocence to convey to his readers Richard's kindness and altruism. Equiano describes Richard as "kind," "agreeable," and "faithful." Richard is safe and speaks kind Christian words, while the evil, worldly ship captain constantly threatens to eat Equiano. The captain relays his carnivorous messages through Richard, fondly referred to as "Dick" by Equiano: "He used often to tell him jocularly that he would kill and eat me. Sometimes he would say to me—the black people were not good to eat, and would ask me if we did not eat people in my country. I said, No: then he said he would kill Dick (as we always called him) first, and afterwards me."[38]

## Taste and Good Taste

The captain, of course, never eats Equiano, but his persistent references to Equiano's delectability are instructive. A better understanding of how taste itself is cultivated will help us understand how the ship captain's desire "to eat" Equiano belied a real, acquired taste for the enslaved African person. In *Consuming Passions: The Anthropology of Eating*, Peter Farb and George Armelogo note that tastes do not just emerge as full-blown realities; rather, they emerge from a complex of historical and cultural forces brought to bear upon a culinary object: "Cultural, historical, and ecological events have interacted," they write, "to cause frogs, for example, to be esteemed as a delicacy in Southern China but to be regarded with revulsion in Northern China."[39] They go on to describe how the acquired taste for a substance has to do with availability, the ease of culinary preparation, domestication that results in accessibility, nutritional value, cost, and the ability of said substance to reproduce itself efficiently, among other factors.[40] At this early stage in Equiano's chattel career, we can already place him neatly within this abbreviated list of things that constitute cultivated taste: He is isolated from his natal land, community, and language, rendering him entirely available. White males accomplish his domestication or recasting in a familiar cultural register through the conventions of chivalry, invocations of Negro effeminacy, and the implanting of Christian values. Culinary utensils, Christian ideology, English traditions of romance and affection, and ideas of Africa and Africans as heathens enable the cultivation and carving up of Equiano in the Eurocentric mind. And it goes without saying that the economic benefits of slavery translated readily into the currency of white male identity and acquired appetite that Richard (a child of the U.S. slavocracy) and the captain (an English slave owner and trader) enjoy.

Although Equiano the narrator emphasizes his enlightened, objective, and pristine relationships with white men throughout the narrative, this economy of taste reveals how thoroughly an acquired appreciation of the slave permeates and feeds into European ideologies and institutions used to condition the young slave. If Equiano is anything, he is nutritious fare, reifying and fortifying the social stature of Richard and the captain. Jean Anthelm Brillat-Savarin, expounding on the exponential potentials of taste, notes that "the number of tastes is infinite, since every soluble body has a special flavor which does not wholly resemble any other. . . . Tastes are modified, moreover, by their combinations with one, two, or a dozen others, so that it is impossible to draw up a correct chart, listing them from the most attractive to the most repellent."[41]

In Equiano's narrative, these multiple implications of taste inform the triangulated relationship among the young white male lover; the African beloved; and the hardened, cannibal-like ship captain. This triangulation of two white males erotically tied to Equiano recurs throughout the narrative. Traditionally, in English culture and literature, a white woman is the binding object of affection. Eve Kosofsky Sedgwick explains this dynamic: "Within the male-centered novelistic tradition of European high culture, the triangles . . . are most often those in which two males are rivals for a female."[42] Despite the metaphoric centrality of the female, the homoerotic attraction and rivalry between the men is often more powerful and determining: "In any erotic rivalry, the bond that links the two rivals is as intense and potent as the bond that links either of the rivals to the beloved: The bonds of 'rivalry' and 'love,' differently as they are experienced, are equally powerful and in many senses equivalent."[43] In this case, it is the delectable young Negro who serves as a different type of effeminate prize. Equiano's body and person mediate a subtle dynamic of rivalry and homoerotic chivalry played out between the captain and Dick. By asserting his power to eat and consume, the captain also asserts his phallic might and right of ownership. Dick, by virtue of his aristocratic class status, American civil identity, and interest in Equiano's humanity, represents something of an economic and erotic threat to the captain. And at the same time, these refined qualities in Dick, added to his youth, make him erotically appetizing to the captain. Triangulation serves to intensify desire. The special heart bond between Dick and Equiano excites the captain, who openly admits to the desire to ingest both of them. The picture of the white colonizers making Negro soup that I cite in the introduction clarifies the dynamic I am describing among the two whites and the black youth. In that picture, a commanding military officer, his attendant, and porter gather around a skewered Bakongo man. The missionary and explorer are implied, as military occupation would not be possible without the initial paving of the missionary and explorer. In Equiano's situation, his master and the captain of the ship is a naval officer. Dick is a devout Christian who also has a bit of the missionary's zeal. Both Dick and the ship's captain, Michael Henry Pascal, are emissaries of their respective states. Christianity, romantic friendship, British militarization, and U.S. slavocracy are all employed in the making of Equiano into a New World object of gastronomical delight.

Equiano portrays Richard as innocent, disconnected from the larger cannibalizing circumstances that have brought the two boys together. Richard has to stand apart if he is to serve as the young African's "kind interpreter," his reliable mediator into white ways and white culture. Equiano's genteel, kindly white readership had to identify with Richard, to see themselves in his kindness and altruism toward this slave, if they were to ultimately accept Equiano's transition from savage to noble gentleman. However, the captain, in his crude fashion, implicates Dick in the larger culture of African cannibalization. He anticipates the nineteenth-century American concern over "Christian cannibalism" and other forms of institutionalized consumption of slaves.[44] Richard is Christ-like, and for Equiano to experience Christian saving he will have to sacrifice himself, give himself over to this young savior. A part of this sacrifice involves accepting himself as heathen, denying his color and African features, and, through Richard and Christianity, learning to identify with and worship white masculinity. Much later in his narrative, Equiano will mark a turning point of spiritual growth and intellectual development with an increased admiration for white beauty and spirit: "I no longer looked upon them as spirits" he writes, "but as men superior to us; and therefore I had the stronger desire to resemble them: to imbibe their spirit, and imitate their manners; I therefore embraced every occasion of improvement."[45]

Equiano's relationship with Richard prepares him to encounter, later in life, Daniel Queen, an attendant aboard the ship *Aetna*. At this point in the narrative, the narrator has passed through the hands of several masters. When he is approximately thirteen years old, he is taken into service aboard the *Aetna* by his master, who is the ship's captain. Queen is a bachelor and a bit of a dandy, with a fine eye for dress and male couture. He is also devoted to biblical lore. Equiano's relationship with Queen centers on issues of taste and good taste. Queen instills in Equiano a more refined taste for English gentlemanly presentation and comportment. Through continued biblical studies, Equiano satiates his appetite for white spirit, which he will later apply to a Native American youth whom he attempts to colonize. Equiano and Queen, an African youth and an older white man, fall quickly into something of a Christian romantic relationship. On many occasions they, like Equiano and Richard, stay up "the whole night together" talking about European high culture and manners and the practice of those same customs in Equiano's homeland.[46] Equiano makes small, loving sacrifices on Queen's behalf: "Many things I have denied myself that he might have them; and when I used to play at marbles or any other game, and won a halfpence, or got any little money . . . I used to buy him a little sugar or tobacco, as far as my stock of money would go."[47] Thinking of Queen in a sweet manner, Equiano would purchase for him sweet things. Queen, in turn, would respond with the desire to remain forever close and bonded to the African youth: "He used to say, that he and I never should part; and that when our ship was paid off, and I was as free as himself or any other man on board, he would instruct me in his business."[48] Rendering his relation to Queen in the language of Christian romantic love, Equiano described how his "heart burned," how Queen treated him with "the greatest kindness," and the feelings of "tenderness" he imbibed from Queen.

In spite of his feelings of romantic and religious freedom, Equiano's relationship to Queen does not set him free. Instead, his ties to and

learning under this white shipmate reinforce a culture of social consumption. Equiano's relationship with Queen feeds the older man's
sense of nobility and moral sanctity. His homoerotic desire toward the
African youth reinforces in Queen the feeling of paternity, a paternity
that many on the ship acknowledge by sometimes calling the youth
after the elder man's name or referring to Equiano as the "black Christian."[49] Equiano and his white father/master relate through a paradigm
of human parasitism. The African's socialization, his training in English morality, religious values, and spiritual devotion temper the savage within and make him into something culturally palatable—desirable and beautiful—to Queen. Converting Equiano ennobles Queen.
And while Queen is not Equiano's documented master, he does play the
role of paternal figure and enjoys an incestuous relationship with the
youth that parallels the heavenly father/sacrificed son dynamic. Queen
is a surrogate for the white father God; Equiano, the child and ignorant
innocent, in turn plays the role of the sacrificial son. In this context, the
Christian doctrines of eating flesh and drinking blood, suffering, and
dismemberment take on a clandestine meaning that contradicts the
narrative of universal love and soul-saving that Equiano foregrounds.

The subtext of Queen's laborious instruction in Victorian manners,
customs, and religious values is the idea that Equiano comes from a
heathen land and is, fundamentally, a heathen subject. It is not, after
all, Equiano who instructs Queen in his indigenous customs and social
values. Queen, with missionary conviction and commitment, works to
convert Equiano through the promised love of a deific, white male figure. Equiano converts this Christian love into an imbibing and ingesting of whiteness to the extent that he makes sacrifices for this white
man who would rather instruct him in Christian morality than literally
free Equiano from the manacles of slavery.

As hard as Equiano the narrator tries to divorce the "kindness" of
Queen from the "cruelty" of his captain/master, he cannot. At the end
of this particular voyage, infuriated at Equiano's relationship to Queen,
the master violently sets himself upon Equiano: "He forced me into the
barge," the narrator recalls, "saying, I was going to leave him, but he
would take care I should not. I was so struck with the unexpectedness
of this proceeding, that for some time I could not make a reply, only I
made an offer to go for my books and chest of clothes, but he swore I

should not move out of his sight; and if I did he would cut my throat."[50] Equiano's training in religiosity and English etiquette make him even more of an acquiescing, ignorant slave. For he cannot see that the whole time he has rested under the wing and influence of Queen, the captain has watched and taken note. All the while, feelings of anger and betrayal have brewed in the captain. He is not only angry at the thought of losing his valuable commodity, he also feels betrayed by the slave's interest in and affection for Queen. Still fuming after the physical attack, the captain decides that as further punishment for his "betrayal," he will sell his young slave to a new master when they reach their destination, Portsmith.

All this time, Equiano has thought that his acculturation into English ways would ensure his freedom, his being manumitted from slavery. After the captain sells the African youth and formally introduces him to his new master (Captain James Dorian of the *Charming Sally*), Equiano tries to explain to his new master why his sale was illegal: "But I have served him [Pascal] . . . many years, and he has taken all my wages and prize-money, for I only got one sixpence during the war; beside this I have been baptized; and by the laws of the land no man has a right to sell me."[51] He invokes the statute of chattel law on his behalf, noting that he heard lawyers explain to his master that it was illegal for him to hold an African man who had undergone baptism. It gradually dawns on Equiano that his acculturation, instead of preparing him to be free of slavery, has prepared him for a final initiation into "a new slavery" more intimately tied to the appetites of white men and rituals and practices of flesh taking and consumption.

## Consumption under the "New Slavery"

The *Charming Sally* frequently transports slaves from Africa to the Caribbean. As a result, Equiano spends a significant amount of time in Barbados, Monserrat, and other parts of the Caribbean observing overseers, whom he describes as "human butchers" practicing their cruel trade.[52] One of the first narrated examples of this cruelty is a "negro man staked to the ground, and cut most shockingly."[53] His crime involved being "connected with a white woman who was a common prostitute." While staked to the ground, the overseer "bit by bit" cut off pieces of each of his ears, prolonging what was already a horrific and unbearable punishment.[54] It was common practice in the Caribbean to not only cut off the ears of slaves but to also broil them and make the slaves eat the broiled pieces as a punishment. Anglican missionary John Wesley documented this phenomenon in his *Thoughts upon Slavery*. He writes: "After they are whipped till they are raw all over, some put pepper and salt upon them; some drop melted wax upon their skin; others *cut off their ears, and constrain them to broil and eat them.*"[55] In this way, the slave was made an accomplice to his or her own social consumption. Such acts of auto-cannibalism (self-consumption) reinforced for the slave the interrelations among punishment; slavery as the slow, incremental death to body and soul; and the general culture of slave seasoning as a process meant to prepare the slave for all manner of consumption. In the 1700s, John Atkins, a surgeon in the British Royal Navy, recorded an insurrection that occurred aboard a slave ship. The captain and crew quelled the insurrection and as punishment made the captured African persons eat human body parts before murdering them: "Three others, Abettors, but not Actors, nor of Strength for it, he sentenced to cruel Deaths; making them first to eat the Hearts and Liver of one of them killed."[56] The correlation in this example between execution and death by consumption is noteworthy. Rosalind Shaw observes that among conflicting cultural groups in the colonial era, such acts of auto-cannibalism reinforced the militarized and legislative authority of a dominant group. "Not only do we consume you," the captain of the British Royal Navy conveys, "but we also make you consume each other."[57]

These incidents of auto-cannibalism punctuated a more subtle and pervasive reality of starvation and self-consumption. Within this new Caribbean context of slavery, masters frequently employed tactics of starvation, which ranged from the incremental loss of food to more blatant and debilitating forms of hunger. Early on, Equiano makes note of his master feeding a group of slaves well instead of starving them, as their own master frequently does: "My master often gave the owners of these slaves two and a half of these pieces per day . . . because he thought their owners did not feed them well enough according to the work they did."[58] Starvation is so endemic to slave culture that when Equiano's master rents the Ibo man out on jobs, he has to pay a white man to accompany him. The sole responsibility of this white man, whom he pays "from six to ten pisterines a day," is to make sure that those who rent Equiano feed him each day. "Once," Equiano recalls, "for a few days, I was let out to fit a vessel, and had no victuals allowed me by either party."[59] Equiano was made to literally starve for several days. Slaves treated thusly had less of a will to disobey and resist. Starvation ensured control and set the stage for the master to enact even more heinous forms of social consumption. Though not necessarily made to consume his or her own broiled flesh, the emaciated slave still embodied a condition of daily and incremental self-consumption. In commercial terms, the slave's emaciated body translated into the blood and flesh currencies of social stature, increased wealth, and spiritual dominion for the master. Quite literally, the master held within his hands the powers of life and death.

In another example from Equiano's Caribbean observances, the taking or harvesting of flesh is a regular occurrence. A particular nameless master has a reputation for cruel punishments: "He had not a slave but what had been cut, and had pieces fairly taken out of the flesh."[60] The idea of a human butcher seems to apply expressly to this individual. Equiano does not go into detail about what is done with the flesh carved out of individuals; that he leaves to the imagination. In the context of such occurrences, white men experienced a sense of deific power. Furthermore, Equiano makes a point of emphasizing that the master takes pleasure in this and other torturous activities, to which he has clearly given much thought.

It is easy to apprehend how such events conditioned and made humans into slaves. However, less ascertainable is the fount of meanings embedded in the master's pleasure taking. The choice of the word "pleasure" rather than "satisfaction" or "purpose," for example, cues the reader to the fact that this is an interchange of power, erotic energy, and soul. Following such brutal treatment, Equiano observed that many masters would "make slaves go on their knees, and thank their owners, and pray, or rather say, God bless them."[61] Plantation masters frequently cited Old Testament biblical references to devotees blindly serving their master. But this scenario, which draws upon biblical tenets, goes beyond simplified notions of morality, the typical roles of master and slave, and the master/slave relation. This scene brings into stark relief a moral problematic based in the spiritual and esoteric implications of a white man "gathering identity unto" himself "from the wholly available and serviceable lives of Africanist others."[62] For this type of religious rite, we do not have a fully developed linguistic framework. Nor do our typical understandings of the science of human interaction sufficiently account for the esoteric implications of the plantation master's *pleasure* taking.

The state of pleasure that Equiano describes connotes horror, abjection, and human vampirism. In this context of social death and energetic exchange, pleasure operates as 1) an organic unit, a life-sustaining energy readily bartered and exchanged during slavery; and 2) a process of internalizing and imbibing spirit and soul force. In *Rituals of Blood: Consequences of Slavery in Two American Centuries*, Orlando Patterson approaches this dynamic from the perspective of the enslaved person. Intersecting Christian theology with the consumption and sacrifice of slaves, he notes that the "slave and ex-slave had always been the major symbol of sin in Christian theology." Because "Christianity from its beginnings had identified the state of sin as one of enslavement to the flesh," it stood to reason that the "Afro-American slave or ex-slave was the perfect symbol of sin."[63] Patterson analyzes Jim Crow lynching rituals as ancient sacrificial rites, cannibalistic feasts, and attempts to feed a deity of terror and appetite usually referred to as "God." Though my interest, like Patterson's, centers on the ritual behavior of whites and the construction of deity, what I am more interested in are the specifics and moral implications of whites' creating themselves as deific agents. It was one thing for whites to draw upon Christian theology as a means of justifying their consumptive rituals and appetites and an altogether different matter for them to use Christian theology and social ritual as a means of feeding and sustaining self and social stature.

Africans throughout the continent frequently equated European Christianity with human consumption. In the Gambia it was thought that Christians ate human meat and that "all the slaves that they bought were carried away to be eaten."[64] Shaw records that in the Gambia at the turn of the sixteenth century, rumors of the European consumption of slaves identified the trade with "Christians" as a form of predation. Debunking the idea of the Gambians as ignorant, uninformed Africans, Shaw notes that "this was hardly a reaction of 'isolated' Africans to sudden commercial contact with the outside world." Rather, through observance of and sustained contact with Europeans, the Gambians had come to regard the slave trade as "a trade that fed the 'Christian' appetite for the consumption of humans—that was viewed as problematic."[65] In other words, the Gambians ascertained in Christian ritual and deity a process of soul harvesting and soul hunger that coincided with the bodies Europeans had also come to claim and transport. If we accept the conclusion of Europeans as soul and body harvesters, then we have to wonder how Europeans might have used, commodified, and ingested the very African souls that they consistently claimed did not exist. In Sierra Leone, an African typically regarded the white man as purchasing him either "to offer him as a sacrifice to his God, or to devour him as food."[66] Again, Shaw notes that persons from Sierra Leone and other regions viewed the slave trade as a "European ritual process that integrated the transport of African bodies across the Atlantic into a further set of transactions with the European's God."[67] The people of Niger even applied these notions of deity, deification, and consumptive practices to the slave ship itself, describing it as "some object of worship of the white man."[68]

These African-based perspectives bring into clearer focus how European practices of soul harvesting and human consumption coincide with the more obvious economic motivations of the trade. These observances bring us back to that seemingly obvious question: What exactly did Europeans want with African persons? What deity and processes of self-deification did the African's soul and body feed? We cannot readily access these types of considerations through the European's notion of their Christian practice; European Christianity advocates, at least overtly, the consumption of the divine, but not the consumption of another human being. The African-based perspectives of European Christian consumption inverts this logic, honing in on European religiosity, religious ritual, deity, and self-making as processes based in appetite and human consumption. When the African spoke of Christians as human consumers or of Christianity as a religion based in human consumption, what they were observing and articulating were the European's hungers, appetites, willfulness, glut, greed, and titillation all operating through an institutionalized context of spirit and soul edification. Africans, we might say, saw through the rhetoric of European spirituality to the real spiritual motivations informing the European's relationship to the slave trade. Europeans would insist that they had come to offer something to the African soul—to nurture, tame, and sustain this wild entity. However, what many African groups quickly ascertained, without the benefit of European literacy and theological learning, was that in fact the European had come to harvest and spiritually ingest them.

In presenting us with masters who buried their slaves alive and commanded their slaves to pray to and deify their persons, Equiano provides a glimpse into a Christian world that belied the European's pristine notions of religiosity and saving of the savage African other. Equiano, like so many of his peers and ex-slaves who would later pen their own narratives, attempted to describe and convey the reality of institutionalized consumption. He attempted to convey the extent to which European self-delusion and cultivated appetite for the African had thoroughly transformed institutions, such as Christianity, the law, literacy, and philosophy. In the section on the new type of slavery, Equiano makes reference to a Mr. Drummond, a Caribbean slave owner who owned over 41,000 slaves. Drummond, with little forethought, would cut off a "man's leg for running away." Equiano asks this Drummond, "If the man had died in the operation . . . how he, as a Christian, could answer for the horrid act before God?" Drummond replied that "answering was a thing of another world; what he thought and did were policy."[69] Even in the context of heinous abuse, Drummond invokes the lofty theological tenets of Christianity: a heavenly realm disconnected from the material world, the notion of delayed moral accountability, and a sense of deity removed from the immediate day-to-day actions of men's lives. In bringing up the topic of Christianity, Equiano encourages his reader to ponder the interconnections between Christian theological practice and Christian masters such as this, whom he frequently describes as "human butchers," flesh takers, and death dealers.[70] In deflecting the conversation onto the afterlife and a deity located elsewhere, Drummond evades the issue of his own self-deification and the larger question of exactly what type of deity his gluttonous, flesh-harvesting actions fed.

Equiano, for his part, resists at the same time that he reifies the common slave's institutionalized consumption. It is impossible to divorce

Equiano, whose narrative authority and spiritual validation derive from the deification of white males, from the plantation consumption scenes he relates. What saves Equiano from the fate of the common slave is his acknowledged difference. One master, he relates, "said he did not mean to treat me as a common slave. I told him I knew something of sea-manship, and could shave and dress hair pretty well; and I could refine wines, which I had learned shipboard where I had often done it."[71] By this point in the narrative, after his introduction to the new, more bru-tal form of slavery, Equiano understands well that only his usefulness and closer social proximity to affluent whites saves him from the con-sumptive fate of the common slave. Probably a combination of terror, rhetorical maneuvering, and genuine aesthetic appreciation of Europe-ans causes him to say: "I no longer looked upon them as spirits, but as men superior to us; and therefore I had the stronger desire to resemble them: to imbibe their spirit, and imitate their manners."[72] This seem-ingly casual statement, strategically placed in the text, signals Equiano's transition from heathen childish African to civilized Anglo-African adult. In order to gain greater authorial credence, Equiano professes to no longer believe that whites are "spirits" from a different realm of exis-tence, spirits who are cannibalistic agents of a cannibalistic slave trade. Driving this point home, Equiano even depicts himself as an enlight-ened consumer who has learned from the European to "imbibe their spirit, and imitate the manners."

How to lay claim to humanistic discourse and at the same time acknowledge cannibalism as a personal and social reality? This is the conundrum Equiano faced. In my later discussions of nineteenth-cen-tury figures who follow Equiano, this challenge of claiming a discourse of humanity that demonizes and makes heathens of black witnesses of white cannibalism recurs and presents an epistemic challenge. To stand before the high, European or American court of civilization, before the panoptic presence of the Interrogator, claiming enlightenment along-side white acts of human parasitism and cannibalism was incongruous.

In the end, Equiano's desire to survive by imbibing and imitating white ways results in his becoming parasitic and implicated in the proj-ects of white male deification and global occupation. The result of this cultivation is fully realized thirteen years later. Before embarking on a privately funded venture to the West Indies in 1775, Equiano encounters in London "four Miskito Indians" who had been taken from their homeland and brought to Jamaica "by some English traders for some selfish ends." The youths are described as "chiefs in their own country." The sponsor of the trip to Jamaica, Dr. Irving, is returning them to their West Indian homeland. In the meantime, though, we are pointed to the fact that while all of the youths are royalty—noble savages in their own right—there is one among them who was "the Musquito king's son, a youth of about eighteen years of age."[73] This youth, more than any of the others, draws Equiano's attention. Performing the role of surrogate Negro mother, Equiano feels it his divine duty to introduce this youth to his "well-beloved Master, Jesus Christ."[74] Taking the "heathen" youth under his wing, as he was taken by Richard Baker and Daniel Queen, Equiano instructs the boy in the English alphabet. They study religion and pray fervently together: "I made such progress with this youth, especially in religion, that when I used to go to bed at different hours of the night, if he was in his bed, he would get up on purpose to go to prayer with me."[75] Equiano makes a point of noting that the youth would kneel and pray "without any other clothes but his shirt," and that before he would eat his meals with any of the other men in the cabin "he would first come to me to pray, as he called."[76] An incestuous intimacy develops between the youth and his African instructor. The image of the youth semi-clothed underscores his vulnerability—an erotic availability to Equiano and to Equiano's well-beloved master, Jesus Christ.

His nakedness implies an infantile, trusting state; he presents himself to Jesus Christ as an innocent powerless child would present himself to an all-powerful nurturing father. In this case, though, the father is a slave master, an instrument of English imperialism and martial might. Equiano, as effeminate subject, is a natural counterpart to the father; he nurtures the youth in his stead. This undercurrent of violence and captivity in the context of Christian conversion is poignantly conveyed in an interchange between Equiano and the youth. Fascinated with Equiano's copy of John Fox's *Martyrology*, the youth asks him numerous questions "about the papal cruelties he saw depicted there."[77] Such poignant questions are punctuated by the fact that the native youths have been taken through trickery or lies (it is not clear which) from their native land. By this time in history, the English and other European groups had thoroughly occupied and colonized the Caribbean islands, and long before they had imported Africans to work on cane, tobacco, and rice plantations, they had decimated Native American populations. These groups had been systematically hunted and murdered in a style and heinous manner that often paralleled papal cruelties. In 1378, the pope sent inquisitors into the Waldensian valleys of northern Italy. Inquisitor Borelli had 150 citizens, including women and children, burned alive in Grenoble. In the same region, in 1400, citizens were chased from their homes in the dead of night by inquisitors on Christmas Eve. The following morning, strewn across the snow-packed hills, more than fifty children were found frozen to death in their mother's arms.

Equiano explains away such necessary cruelties in order to "make such progress with this youth, especially in religion."[78] When the young Equiano had been baptized in 1759 in a Westminster church, the presiding clergyman had given him a book titled *A Guide to the Indians*. European missionaries used this text, written by the bishop of the diocese of Sodor of Man, to assimilate Native Americans into the Christian faith and to justify genocidal actions taken toward native groups that did not conform and assimilate. This interchange between Equiano and the Miskito youth marks a pivotal moment for Equiano. At this crucial juncture, the roles are completely reversed. Where Equiano was once a self-described superstitious, infantile African, he paints himself at this point in his narrative as an enlightened gentlemanly Anglo-African. He describes the youth as a "poor heathen" and his tribesmen as emissaries of Satan.[79]

Equiano steps earnestly into the role of social pariah. He is not a fully endowed white British man. However, he is the European's chosen love, helpmate, and co-creator in the kingdom of European civilization. He serves as a middleman within this particular economy of Christian cannibalism. The Miskito youth ultimately rejects Equiano's advances. With the support of his clansmen, who tease him and inquire if the black missionary has "converted him to Christianity," the youth sees through Equiano, through the hypocrisy and irony of the moment: "How comes it," inquires the youth, "that all the white men on board who can read and write, and observe the sun, and know all things, yet swear, lie, and get drunk, only excepting yourself?"[80] His question insufficiently answered, the youth stays to himself for the duration of his journey back to his homeland, and Equiano never sees him or speaks of him again in the narrative following his return.

## The Slave Trade as Soul Trade

Within the closed circuit of Equiano's Anglo-African logic, it is difficult to get at how it might have been possible for the European to consume the African soul or, for that matter, to get at a systematized understanding of the esoteric purposes to which the energy of the consumed
body and soul might have been applied. Nineteenth-century American
whites, whom I discuss at length in the next chapter, also attempted
to apprehend the implications of "Christian cannibalism" but found
such a notion a philosophical and ontological impossibility. Equiano
comes from a world in which "man eaters" and witchcraft are components of a complex science of human behavior and moral interaction.
Just as Enlightenment discourses policed and ensured moral behavior
and a civilized populace, African witchcraft belief often maintained the
moral and individual center of a society. In actuality, witches or cannibals were not literal flesh eaters. They were individuals who drew off the
human life force, causing their victims to weaken physically, become
ill, and sometimes die. Anthropologist Wyatt MacGaffey recorded this
millennium-old belief in Central Africa. Through his field research in
the Congo in the 1960s, he learned that the Congolese had long associated the transatlantic slave trade with soul theft and witchcraft:

> In this aspect, therefore, witchcraft is similar, as a European would say, to
> slave trading. . . . It is not clear, however, that Bakongo make any distinc-
> tion between the two. Repeated contemporary references to nineteenth-
> century trade, the slaves in particular, show it is regarded as a trade in
> souls. Some of the techniques used are identical. Informants recall, and
> written sources confirm, that slave-catchers used to leave food so that
> hapless travelers, finding it and picking it up, might be seized for debt
> and sold; modern witches are supposed to leave money in the road for
> the same purposes.[81]

According to Bakongo cosmology, the soul is luminous, "like a shining star." The soul is the seat of good health, and when it is undisturbed,
the body flourishes. "The soul should be round, like the sun, but witchcraft attacks may cause it to crumble at the edges (*vezuka*), rendering
the body vulnerable. Witches may suck or draw off (*vola, hola*) all or

part of the soul, depriving all or part of the body of its inner essence, so that in a short time it will be seen to sicken or die."[82] Europeans who first encountered Africans questioned the nature and existence of an African soul. This was partially racial prejudice but also a reflection of the very different ways Europeans and Africans defined the nature and origins of the soul. Within European Enlightenment discourses, the soul was a lofty thing. A soul distinguished upright man from the animals who crawled on all fours. The soul was immaterial, connected to religion, and best cultivated within the higher realms of civilization. The iridescence of the soul was connected to white skin and the origins of the soul rooted in the sky—God descended from the heavens to breathe soul into Adam and Eve. According to Descartes, the difference between the human and animal soul was that the human soul granted mankind higher-order thinking and moral consciousness. In this philosophical and religious context, it would have been nearly impossible for the most well-intentioned European to see in Africans a soul categorically similar to their own.

The denial of the African soul would be the subject of philosophical and theological debate for centuries. However, a large portion of this debate went to justify a simple political end: profit and gain through the enslavement of humans. Europeans, among themselves, needed ideological justification for their heinous and vile mistreatment of Africans. When Africans such as Equiano, Cuguano, and Phillis Wheatley, among others, first argued their humanity to whites, they began always with this issue of the soul. Equiano's entire narrative is testimony and proof of the existence of a civilized soul. His initial desire to learn the Bible, his series of religious conversions, his romantic Christian friendships and the eventual missionary post he held in West Africa are all offered as evidence of a soul equal in moral aptitude and reasoning capabilities to that of Europeans. Yet the irony of Equiano's argument for his human soul was that he made it to imperialist institutions and an Anglophone society that had a fundamentally immoral relationship to Africans and Africa. None said it better than the English gentleman Charles Dickens, when he referred to the African "savage" as "something highly desirable to be civilised off the face of the earth."[83] Africans were brought to Europe and locked behind museum cages and bars. Europeans displayed their genitalia and scientists studied their harvested body parts.

Even when the English accepted Africans into society, it was under a mandate of racial cleansing. In the context of the Bakongo science of the soul, such demonstrations of European gluttony and knowledge-seeking belonged in the category of behaviors attributed to witches and cannibals.[84]

Still today in Sierra Leone the "conviction that slaves carried away in the Atlantic trade were eaten by Europeans persists."[85] This conviction had many strands of belief, which involved 1) the European sacrificing the African to his God; 2) the traded African serving as a literal food source for European slavers; and 3) the slave being used as a trade commodity between cannibals or witches. Not just European foreigners were accused. In Sierra Leone in the eighteenth and nineteenth centuries, it was common to find a powerful chief who had stepped "out of the bounds of moral human existence" accused of being a cannibal.[86] In such contexts, coastal Africans associated cannibalism with unhealthy social functioning; the cannibal was a person who fundamentally threatened the well-being of the community: Such persons were thought to literally and symbolically consume land, the ability to prosper and grow from the land, the people, and the very chiefdom itself, in the case of chiefs accused of cannibal behaviors.

Numerous African groups guarded against the emotional states of extreme anger, greed, envy, jealousy and hatred because such feelings were thought to have a cumulative, unseen power that acted negatively upon an individual and community. Usually a ceremonially sanctioned person who had the power to guard against cannibals in a community received training in a science of dream interpretation wherein cannibalism that occurred in dream/"spirit" was an indicator of imbalance in an individual and community. Europeans who first encountered Africans and later European colonizers stationed in Western and Central Africa habitually interpreted the African sciences of human cannibalism literally, going out to look for cannibals and for particular objects or slipping off skins that could be found only "in spirit" or in the dreamtime realm of emotional causation (a living, experienced domain that parallels what we today think of as the unconscious).

What differing African persons and groups universally recognized in Europeans whom they accused of being cannibals was a state of greed, gluttony, appetite, jealousy, and anger that had reached dangerous, unchecked psychic and spiritual proportions. To dismiss African observances that Europeans were cannibals as myth and superstition is to miss this very valuable and poignant insight into human capacity and immoral potential implicit in most indigenous African cosmologies and esoteric sciences of human consumption. It was not at all inconceivable, according to such a worldview, that slave masters could create themselves into deities and that slave ships that "gorged themselves until full" could operate as part of a larger network of institutions wired to a destructive human need for consumption.[87] This African notion of consumption under slavery as a fundamentally moral problematic overlapped with a similar concern voiced in nineteenth-century U.S. religious and political spheres. In chapter 2 I analyze the nineteenth-century U.S. cannibalism debate, which focused on slavery as a consumptive institution that was pervading and corroding American religious, legal, philosophical, and artistic institutions. Ironically, at the same time that Africans struggled to translate their understandings of European cannibalism, so too were white and black Americans beginning to craft a collective language and ideology of human consumption under slavery.

2

Sex, Honor, and Human Consumption

Lilburn Lewis, a Kentucky slave owner, owned a considerable number of slaves whom he "drove constantly, fed sparingly, and lashed severely," according to abolitionist Lydia Maria Child.[1] Lewis was a typical plantation owner whom most in the local community probably respected and looked to as a model wealthy citizen in terms of his treatment of his slaves. In 1826, he would commit crimes against his slaves that would cause his community to ostracize him and pursue legal restraint; he committed suicide while awaiting criminal trial. It is hard to say from the evidence if George, a young recalcitrant slave on Lewis's plantation, was a favorite or if Lewis consciously chose him, as many masters did, as the object of ritualized violence and as an emblem of his manhood and noble social stature. All we know for sure is that George, like many on the plantation, often went hungry, suffered the lash too often, and grew to despise and resist his condition of bondage. George provoked his master's penchant for punishment by frequently running away in addition to disobeying. Sent to the spring one day to collect water into "an elegant pitcher," George made the horrid mistake of letting the pitcher fall and standing by and watching as it "dashed to shivers on the rocks."[2] As punishment for George's transgression, his master bound him to a wooden plank and in the manner of a butcher quartered him with an axe and cooked his severed body parts and pieces of flesh over a billowing fire.

In preparation for this ritualized punishment, Lewis gathered all of the slaves on the plantation "into the most roomy negro-house," bolted the door, and told those assembled that "the design of this meeting was to teach them to remain at home and obey his orders."[3] The ritual begins with George's younger brother helping the master bind the slave to a wooden bench:

> George was called up, and by the assistance of his younger brother, laid on a broad bench or block. The master then cut off his ancles [sic] with a broad axe. In vain the unhappy victim screamed. Not a hand among so many dared to interfere. Having cast the feet into the fire, he [the master] lectured the negroes at some length. He then proceeded to cut off his limbs below the knees. The sufferer besought him to begin with his head. It was in vain—the master went on thus, until trunk, arms, and head, were all in the fire. Still protracting the intervals with lectures, and threatenings of like punishment, in case any of them were disobedient, or ran away, or disclosed the tragedy they were compelled to witness. In order to consume the bones, the fire was briskly stirred until midnight.[4]

Sometime in the early morning, an earthquake materialized and shook the slave shack, crumbling the walls and extinguishing the fire. This act brought an abrupt halt to the master's activities, and the "negroes were allowed to disperse, with charges to keep the secret, under the penalty of like punishment." Later that evening, Lewis's wife inquires into her husband's activities: "When his wife asked the cause of the dreadful screams she had heard, he said that he had never enjoyed himself so well at a ball as he had enjoyed himself that evening."[5] Lewis's response to his wife, as disturbing and incongruous as it is, puts this entire scenario into context. Contrasted against the plantation mistress and the domestic sphere, we see more clearly George's erotic significance to his master and the clandestine pleasure taking that the white man associates with his slave. The metaphor of the ball is significant insofar as one goes to a ball *with* someone. Lewis would, under normal circumstances, attend a ball with his wife, dancing with her, holding her close, smelling and touching her body. Instead, we have George as the unwilling feminized partner and conjugal mate; it is George whom the master touches, smells, violently lavishes with attention and care, and ingests with the same relish that he would hors d'oeuvre, fine music, or cocktails served at an open bar at a ball. George and his ritualized punishment reify and ennoble Lewis's white male identity. Powerful feelings of satiation, leisurely comfort, and pleasure accompany Lewis's cannibalization of George.

As parasite and consumer, the master takes in, imbibes George's essence; George's terror and the terror of all the slaves feed the master's authority and power. And we have to consider that in addition to emotional and spiritual consumption, the master might have literally ingested pieces of George's flesh. Literal consumption was such a taboo topic during the time period that even radical abolitionists such as Child evaded direct discussion of this topic.[6] When Child presented the facts of Lewis's case in *An Appeal in Favor of That Class of Americans Called Africans*, she made no comment about the literal implications of Lewis's flesh-quartering and -cooking ritual or about the significance of the secrecy that he continually reinforces through speech and act. This lack of comment from a woman who frequently noted the most extreme and disturbing implications of the slave master's cruelties, indicates how taboo was the subject of human consumption.[7] Understanding Child's tentativeness concerning the topic of human consumption gives us all the more reason to wonder about the literal implications of Lewis's cannibalistic ritual and the truth of what he really sought to hide through his constant reinforcing of silence and secrecy.

I begin this chapter with this graphic example of symbolic (if not literal) human consumption because it illustrates how there existed during slavery unspoken codes of white male honor and respectability connected to the consumption of the slave. Master Lewis reinforces the secrecy and clandestine nature of his actions by bolting the door of the slave cabin, threatening like punishment to those who "disclosed the tragedy they were compelled to witness," and excavating and secretly reburying George's bones after the earthquake has leveled the building.[8] Furthermore, his invocation of ball culture in his report to his wife clues us in to how he associated social esteem and finery with the cannibalization of George. A heinous and unspeakable bond of clandestine honor and pleasure taking binds Lewis to his slaves. As we see through events on the Lewis plantation, the most intimate sharers of the unknown secret were, in most cases, the slaves and the slave master, and the most reliable and enlightened witnesses were the slaves themselves. In slave narratives and ex-slave interviews, black persons correlated white consumptive appetites with southern codes of honor and nobility. Whites rarely acknowledged the comments made by blacks. All the same, these repressed black voices provide invaluable insights into debates about cannibalism in the nineteenth-century United States, the erotic and homoerotic implications of the consumption of slaves, and the unspoken codes of sex and honor that informed black male consumption.[9]

Orlando Patterson writes that "the master's sense of honor was derived directly from the degradation of his slave, beginning in childhood and continuing through life in his despotic exercise of power."[10] Elsewhere, Patterson emphasizes that the master generally camouflaged this association of honor with a master's relationship to the slave so as not to reveal "his dependence, his parasitism" of the slave.[11] John Hope Franklin posits honor as the most central defining characteristic of nineteenth-century southerner culture. "The honor of the Southerner," Franklin proclaims,

> caused him to defend with his life the slightest suggestion of irregularity in his honesty or integrity; and he was fiercely sensitive to any imputation that might cast a shadow on the character of the women of his family. To him nothing was more important than honor. Indeed, he placed it above wealth, art, learning, and the other "delicacies" of urban civilization and regarded its protection as a continuing preoccupation.[12]

Franklin describes a public culture of honor wherein chivalry, how one was regarded in society, upper-class status, courtship practices, and rituals of social etiquette all played a role in the performance of and the display of male honor. However, when it came to the topic of consumption under slavery, these public rules and displays of honor took on a clandestine, unspoken cast. Proponents of southern slave culture did their best to repress evidence of the slave master who would "rather whip a negro than sit down to the best dinner."[13] Such persons reveal the existence of an acquired taste for and a premium placed on Negro flesh that went against myths that blacks were tainted, disgusting, and untouchable. The example of the Kentucky slave owner Lewis exemplifies notions of etiquette, good taste, homoeroticism, and gender variance in shaping white masculinity on the plantation. Yet the slave-owning community to which Lewis belongs and Lewis himself both conspire to hide and contain, through legal reprimand and suicide, the reality of the master's feeding upon slave and ennobling self and society in the process. Numerous documented scenarios of this type confirm that plantation masters maintained, in large part, a clandestine culture of honor and sex based in the social consumption of the slave. Still, as prevalent as such examples are, the dominant narrative, on and off the plantation, continues to be that the consumption of slaves brought dishonor to self and community. Going against this common assumption, I strive throughout this chapter to decipher the implicit social codes that, as Patterson observes, translated the slave's degradation into the master's despotic honor and, more specifically, into consumptive appetites that reified and ennobled white masculinity on and off of the plantation.

Before we can understand and analyze this unspoken culture of honor associated with slave consumption, it helps to first understand how thoroughly a rhetoric of dishonor infused discussions of slave consumption in nineteenth-century America. Following this line of inquiry, I begin the discussion of consumption and dishonor by examining the prevalent nineteenth-century concern that the United States was becoming a cannibal nation. Clergy, congressmen, popular novelists, and northern abolitionists, among others, passionately debated the topic of the United States becoming a cannibal nation as a result of its condoning and legally sanctioning slavery. Implicitly, those who engaged in this discussion presumed that cannibal nationhood was a dishonorable thing. Concerned with returning to the nation a sense of honorable and noble purpose, discussions among white Americans rarely focused on the particular codes of honor within cultures of consumption on the plantation. Neither did such discussion focus on the social consumption of the Negro within the nation at large, a reality that fugitive and emancipated black persons consistently emphasized in their writings and speeches.[14]

This national discussion of black male consumption and honor frames my ensuing discussion of literal instances of human consumption. In the eighteenth and nineteenth centuries, a number of different instances of cannibalism at sea—cannibalism that took place following shipwrecks—occurred involving black men. Although cannibalism at sea was common in the eighteenth and nineteenth centuries, reported cases focusing on the consumption of black males were not. Cases that involved black men, like the above-mentioned *Essex* affair and incidents associated with the *Peggy* and the French *Tyger* still today evoke strong feelings of shame and dishonor among American whites and Europeans. These cases also illuminate how "the choice" made by whites to eat black men aboard ships coincided with ideologies of Negro inferiority and with the logic and practice of chattel bondage in the plantation South and other regions of the United States. By the nineteenth century, consumptive ideologies and practices on slave plantations had come to have a far-reaching influence, affecting even the consumption of blacks at sea. With such cases it was not just a matter of survival of the fittest at sea; rather, in these examples of consumption of black men, we see the culture and ideology of slavery strongly influencing the choice of whites to murder and eat black men. On the whole, American citizens regarded the consumption of black men at sea as dishonorable. I argue, however, that there existed in such acts an implicit code of honor that spanned from southern plantations to northern abolitionist communities. To support my discussion of survival cannibalism, I also examine numerous other examples of the ritualistic quartering, seasoning, boiling, and cooking of blacks that bestowed honor and social stature upon white men.

In the final section of this chapter, I examine the correlation among sex, honor, and human consumption. Throughout this chapter, as demonstrated through the Lewis plantation example, I presume an implicit interconnection among sex, honor, and human consumption. I make clear, though, in this last section of this chapter, how thoroughly homoerotic and homosexual desire shaped the master/slave relation and informed white male codes of honor. Erotic desire for the slave, as I argued in the previous chapter, frequently overlapped with consumptive appetites and practices. In the realm of the erotic, we get a clearer picture of the intimate ties between master and slave. Whites strove to conceal and hide this domain of intimacy, as it fundamentally contradicted the ideologies and brutal practices designed to reinforce the inhumanity of the enslaved and free black person. Drawing on the narrated experiences of ex-slaves who graphically depicted the hungers, tastes, and erotic desires of white men for black men, I demonstrate that the literal and metaphoric ingestion of black persons often coincided with white male sexual appetite, titillation, and erotic play. The scenarios I examine reveal, at the basest level of social interaction, how sex facilitates the honorific social status of white men and their dominion over the enslaved person. I close this section and the chapter with an examination of the Nat Turner insurrection. Following his execution, whites boiled Turner's flesh down to a liquid and allegedly ingested it as a medicinal substance. The erotics of taste, sexualized violence, and white male codes of honor coalesced in this incident, bringing into plainer view this hidden culture of the appetite and hunger of white men.

## Cannibal Nation

The social consumption of the enslaved person was such a concern in the colonial United States that senators, religious leaders, and abolitionists heatedly debated whether colonial America was becoming something akin to a cannibal nation. Among nineteenth-century abolitionists and other conscionable persons, the central issue was not the liberation and unburdening of the African soul but the moral implications for whites who were fast developing what many literally referred to as a "cannibalistic" hunger for black flesh. In the public domain, where this debate took place, whites regarded human consumption as a dishonorable act. Shame, national degradation, and widespread anxiety shaped the national debate, leaving no room for consideration of the secret codes of honor that white men maintained quietly among themselves.

Feelings of shame and national dishonor motivated Horace Mann to address the House of Representatives on February 23, 1849; the oration was published later as "Slavery and the Slave Trade in the District of Columbia." Speaking before his peers, Mann spoke of slavery as contagion, a rampant virus that "wounds our moral and religious sensibilities."[15] He offers an allegorical example of a clean, unpolluted northern statesman traveling to the District of Columbia and observing how slavery has tainted and corrupted the white citizens. In his allegory, he calls specific attention to the glorified purpose of white Americans as the "race of men whom God endowed with the faculties of intelligence." He describes the white American man as "despoiled of the power of improving those faculties" as a result of institutionalized slavery and makes reference to a dynamic of "honor and shame" impacting the lives of northern white citizens who condone slavery and the recapture of fugitive persons.[16]

It was difficult enough to convince whites at that time that the brutal treatment of the African person also had an effect on the African person's heart, emotions, and soul. Never mind trying, as Mann does, to bring the nation's and white statesman's attention to the subtle "motive and spirit" undergirding the relationship between master and slave. Missing the allegorical point, a Mr. Brodhead responds to Mann: "Would you advance the slaves to an equal social and political condition with the white race?"[17] A bit exasperated, Mann moves from this example of a white statesman to examples from English history, a discussion of race and skin color, biblical mythology, and additional legal statutes as a means of generating self-reflection in his audience. Finally, feeling that his point still had not been adequately conveyed, Mann asserts what he had perhaps all along meant to say: that U.S. slavery was a form of social cannibalism and that whites were becoming, unbeknown to themselves, the very cannibalistic types that they feared and projected upon every strange land and people they encountered: "It is as though a man should migrate from one of those South Sea Islands, where cannibalism is legalized, and where the public authorities, according to reports of travelers, not only condemn and execute a criminal, but dine on him after he is executed."[18] Mann also references cannibalism law and his sense of a "cannibal jurisdiction" that helps sustain this culture he describes. Not only does Mann accuse slave owners of practicing a type of symbolic (and perhaps literal) cannibalism, he also implicates northern states who, according to the practice of returning fugitive slaves to the masters, forego "cannibalism rights" but are nonetheless implicated in the appetite and principles of human consumption practiced in southern states.

In other domains of society, American citizens attempted to describe this appetite for human consumption that was cultivated in the context of slavery. The following year (1850), a concerned citizen published an editorial response to a letter defending slave-catching written by Daniel Webster in the widely distributed newspaper *The National Era*. The editorial applied the topics of slavery and fugitive law to the North. In particular, J. G. W., the author of the editorial, wanted the reader to understand the elusive moral implications of something he describes as "Christian cannibalism." The editorial begins:

> We are more pained than surprised, therefore, to find the great Massachusetts Senator [Daniel Webster] taking another step downward. . . . [H]e has published a very appropriate, and, we doubt not, very satisfactory . . . argument in support of the legal, moral, and religious obligation of slave-catching on the part of law-abiding citizens and Bible-loving Christians of the free states. It is a literary monstrosity which will make the fortune of the antiquarian who shall hereafter bring it to light, when Christian slaveholding shall have become as difficult of comprehension as *Christian cannibalism*.[19]

Many Christian slave-owning whites thought of themselves as rescuing Africans from a heathen land. Heathenism included, among other things, sexual licentiousness, incest, polygamy, and cannibalism. The idea of a Christian slaveholding cannibal or a northern, thoroughly Christian cannibal type was, as J. G. W. points out, inconceivable. It was a "literary monstrosity" that twisted the religious theologies, legal tenets, and rhetorical logic underlying church and state into monstrous forms. These looming monsters terrified many northern whites. In the Honorable Mr. Giddings, a member of Congress, this terror took the form of political anxiety and an outright declaration of white slave owners as cannibals: "All we can do," explains the Honorable Giddings, "is see that they [southerners] shall not disgrace nor degrade this Government . . . either by their slavery or their cannibalism. Our motto is, 'Keep your slavery, your disgusting barbarity, within your own States! Bring it not into this Hall, nor attempt to involve us in its burdens or its crimes.'"[20] Giddings imagines southern cannibalistic appetites as tainting the constitution of the North and spreading like a contagion into the moral core and implementation of the law.

George Fitzhugh, a political philosopher, southerner, and slave owner expanded the geography of this debate about cannibalism to include the North. In 1857, in *Cannibals All!: or Slaves without Masters*, Fitzhugh rehearses the typical narratives of Africans as heathen and slavery as a civilizing force in the African's life. He then makes broader, more reveal-ing arguments about the cannibalistic temptations inherent in the chat-tel slave system. Linking cannibalism to labor production, he writes: "To treat free laborers badly and unfairly, is universally inculcated as a moral duty, and the selfishness of man's nature prompts him to the most rigorous performance of this cannibalish duty."[21] The South, according to Fitzhugh, has risen above these temptations. Southern slave owners love, care for, and presumably want the best for their slaves. It is north-erners, asserts Fitzhugh, who are in danger of becoming cannibals; it is northerners who advocate a laissez-faire economics and ultimately unequal, unfair "consumption of the labor" of the disenfranchised working class.[22] Where southern slave owners "love" Negroes, Fitzhugh sees northerners as having "the aversion to negroes."[23]

In implicating the North in a capital-based system of human consump-tion, Fitzhugh hearkens back to ancient European legacies and traditions of human consumption that prefigure mercantilism and U.S. chattel slav-ery. These cannibalistic practices were, as Fitzhugh asserts, sometimes connected to aristocratic abuse and the profiteering interests of the busi-ness class. They figured in ancestral rites, religious practices, and burial rites. Edward Gibbon, relying on the authority of Saint Jerome, "reported that the Scots and Picts of pre-Christian England formerly delighted in 'the taste of human flesh' so that they attacked the shepherd rather than his flock 'for their horrid repasts.'"[24] Romans accused Christians of con-suming human blood in their rituals, a contested accusation that is still debated among contemporary scholars. A fifteenth-century German print depicts the murder of Simon of Trent, with Jewish rabbis assembled around his body harvesting his blood for consumptive purposes. There was a largely unremarked-upon strand of medical cannibalism practiced in Victorian and Renaissance Europe. This type of cannibalism involved mummifying the bodies of criminals and other persons so that the parts could be later ingested for medicinal purposes. Europeans brought this tradition to early colonial America, and in the eighteenth and nineteenth centuries, there were those who still maintained the practice.[25]

According to W. Arens, the forgetting of such legacies and the blan-ket consigning of human cannibalism to "faraway lands" and peoples has informed the mission of European global expansionism and occupation of other lands in essential ways:

> Much to our satisfaction, the discussion of cannibalism as a custom is normally restricted to faraway lands just prior to or during their pacification by the various agents of western civilization. Explorer, conquistador, missionary, trader, and colonizer all play their roles in the civilizing mission. Correspondingly, if the time is lengthened sufficiently back to the pre-Christian era, we permit ourselves a glimpse of this sort of savagery among our own forebears.[26]

Arens finds it noteworthy that as Christian-influenced European groups encountered "foreigners" in other lands, they consistently mediated this contact with myths and assertions of cannibalism. Accusations of cannibalism have served as a handy tool in the arsenal of conquest. Furthermore, the creation of Africans and Native Americans as cannibals has allowed European Americans to refashion themselves as anything but cannibalistic, erasing in the process their European legacies of cannibalism and their newly developed appetites and hungers for flesh in the New World. On this latter point, Arens says: "Cannibalism becomes the feature of the faraway or the foregone, which is much the same thing. In the way that the dimensions of time and space are interpreted, 'they,' in the form of distant cannibals, are reflections of us as we once were."[27]

This dichotomy of "them" and "us" is a crucial point of distinction that helps explain why the notion of white "civilized" cannibals brought to the mind and heart such strong feelings of dishonor, shame, and disgrace in nineteenth-century America. In a European colonialist mode of thinking, the presence of cannibalistic others marked a philosophical boundary, a threshold of human versus nonhuman experience. It helped Europeans and white Americans establish the rigid boundaries of the real, of the humane and inhumane, of chaos and temporal/spatial order, of honorable and dishonorable social status in the process of empire and reality building. "Cannibalism," according to Geoffrey Sanborn, "has functioned as . . . the ungraspable margin that limits and distort the 'objective,' and which is, precisely, the real."[28] To accept human consumption as a social reality and norm would have called for a fundamental rethinking of American civil identity and epistemic reality. Even more, it would have demanded of whites an acknowledgement of the deep and pervasive ways they had come to objectify the African and black person at the same time that they maintained intimate and acquired tastes for the black person's flesh, emotional presence, and soul in the nineteenth century.

## Eating Blacks at Sea

In the public domain and realms of debate, northern whites mostly sought out a means to excise the dreaded southern cannibal from the American landscape. The debate stayed in the realm of the ideological, with clergy, lawyers, congresspersons, and artists discussing the Negro's presence and his problematic social role in metaphoric terms. Ultimately, white men wanted to return to their persons and to the nation at large a sense of honor and nobility that they felt white southern slave-owning men had degraded through their consumptive appetites and social practices. The rhetoric of slave consumption as dishonorable grew out of these northern white desires and responses. However, I want to explore in this and later sections of this chapter the political/social reality of the consumption of slaves, which, contrary to popular notions of dishonor attributed to the consumption of human beings, took shape from unspoken codes of honor and white male social stature. Within this clandestine material culture of consumption, whites maintained emotional, affectionate, romantic, erotic, and disguised intimate ties with blacks that contradicted the commonly held notion that cannibalism was unnatural to civilized Westerners. According to Henry Bolingbroke's *A Voyage to the Demerary* (1807), "the reason westerns consider cannibalism to be unnatural is that 'it seems to be a principle of our nature, to be averse to devouring what has been an object of affection.'"[29] Scholars within cannibalism studies frequently cite Bolingbroke's assessment of Western aversion to cannibalism as a means of ameliorating any correlation between Western advancement and human consumption.[30] Yet the symbolic and literal consumption of black persons on and off the plantation contradicted Bolingbroke's idea, as consumptive acts often occurred in the most intimate and supposedly "loving" plantation contexts.

The love that motivated whites to consume blacks aboard the ship *Essex* did not fall into the category of romantic love. Rather, it was a peculiar brand of fraternal love, admiration, and honorific social status that motivated white men at sea to choose blacks as their ideal objects of consumption. In *Narrative of the Most Extraordinary and Distressing Shipwreck of the Whale-Ship Essex, of Nantucket* (1821), the first published account of the harrowing events that took place aboard the whaling ship, Owen Chase makes a point of emphasizing the inherent honor of ship captains, the respectable familial origins of young men such as himself, and the honor and respect that Nantucketers accorded men who worked in the whaling industry. Regarding the ship captain, he writes:

> Respect is due to the character and standing of a captain of a whale-ship, which those of the merchant service affect so much to undervalue. If the post of danger be the post of honour; and if merit emanates from exemplary private character, uncommon intelligence, and professional gallantry, then it is due to a great majority of the shipmasters of Nantucket."[31]

Commenting more broadly on men who work in the whaling industry, he says, "[A] Nantucket man is on all occasions fully sensible of the honour and merit of his profession; no doubt because he knows that his laurels, like the soldier's, are plucked from the brink of danger."[32] Elsewhere he writes, "The profession is one of great ambition, and full of honorable excitement: a tame man is never known amongst them."[33]

No one can deny the valor and honor that Chase, the *Essex* ship captain (George Pollard), and other crew members (Benjamin Lawrence, Gideon Folger, and Paul Macy, among others) displayed when their ship wrecked off the shore of Henderson Island on December 20, 1838. The quick-thinking captain had the crew immediately move all of the ship's provisions to three boats that had been left intact. He devised a plan for braving the sea and rationing their provisions while they searched for other whaling ships to rescue them. And even when the crew, having exhausted all of their provisions, resorted to human cannibalism, the captain still managed to maintain a semblance of order and cohesion reflective of the honor and respect accorded to him by his crew.

Given the emphasis upon honor and valor in Nantucket culture, it makes sense that the *Essex* incident would have registered in the

Nantucket community as a particularly shameful and dishonorable experience. As I have already noted, for America in general the idea of cannibalism brought to mind heathen and savage cultures. By this time in American history, Europeans had either conquered, mostly eradicated, or reformed the so-called savage cultures of Native America and coastal Africa. Nantucketers felt betrayed by Chase for even mentioning the subject of cannibalism in the public domain. According to Nathaniel Philbrick, "The last thing they wanted placed before the nation and the world was a detailed account of how some of their own men and boys had been reduced to cannibalism." In the early twentieth century, this stigma of shame and degradation remained. When asked about the Nantucket affair, the daughter of Benjamin Lawrence (the boat steerer aboard the Nantucket) replied, "We do not mention this in Nantucket."[34] The main reason for the silence concerning the *Essex* incident had to do in part with cannibalism, but more significantly with the fact that the first persons eaten from the *Essex* crew were African Americans. The captain's log reported that a

> black man, in one of the boats accompanying his, died on January 25, and was eaten. On January 23, a black man in the captain's boat died, and his body was shared for food between the crews of both boats. On January 27 a black man died in the other boat, and on January 28 yet another black man died in the captain's boat, both of whom were eaten."[35]

Human consumption at sea was not an unusual occurrence at the time. It *was* unusual, though, that the first four persons eaten among a crew of black and white men were black. Also questionable were the purported "natural" deaths of the black men from starvation and thirst. According to Philbrick, "It was also difficult for Nantucketers to explain why the first four men to be eaten had been African American."[36] More to the point, it was difficult for Nantucketers to explain how the black men had died or the racial logic informing their murder and consumption. It did not help that Nantucket had a national reputation as a Quaker town and a hub of abolitionist activity. Thought of as a people who protected and provided sanctuary for blacks, Nantucketers had a hard time accepting that members of their own community might have considered blacks expendable and, even more, consumable.

Late twentieth-century scholars have, for the most part, evaded these dynamics of shame and dishonor that informed the black men's consumption by the *Essex* crew. Rather than face disparities between abolitionism and human consumption, scholars have resorted to theories of luck and natural selection and even an invented pseudoscientific hypothesis that implicitly preserves Nantucket codes of honor and silence. In *The Cannibal Within*, for example, Lewis Petrinovich recounts how "the blacks" had "the bad luck to die first," completely ignoring the racial motivations informing the black men's deaths.[37] Accepting and elaborating on the natural death thesis, Philbrick attributes black deaths aboard the *Essex* to malnutrition. He writes: "It was likely that the African Americans had suffered from an inferior diet prior to the sinking." He adds to this hypothesis a late-twentieth-century "scientific study" that claims that "American blacks tend to have less body fat than their Caucasian counterparts. Once a starving body exhausts its reserves of fat, it begins consuming muscle, a process that soon results in the deterioration of the internal organs and, eventually, death."[38] In the final estimation, even Philbrick has to acknowledge the realities of racism and slavery ideology when considering the consumption of the black men. Setting aside his racially prejudiced and pseudoscientific hypotheses, Philbrick admits:

> Since there would be no black survivors to contradict the testimonies of the whites, the possibility exists that the Nantucketers took a far more active role in insuring their own survival than has been otherwise suggested. Certainly the statistics raise suspicion—of the first four sailors to be eaten all were black. Short of murdering the black crew members, the Nantucketers could have refused to share meat with them."[39]

Fortunately, we have the recorded observations of William Comstock. Comstock came closest to revealing the hidden racial reality behind the consumption of black males in the nineteenth century. Comstock revealed that although Nantucket stood as a stronghold of abolitionism, the community at large still maintained ideas of blacks as lacking humanity and as best suited to the roles of slaves and servants to white masters. These were some of the secret and unspoken thoughts that Nantucketers were unwilling to voice, for they revealed a world in which, contrary to popular rhetoric, the consumption and degradation of black men did in fact ennoble and reify white masculinity. According to Comstock, the fact that Nantucket was an abolitionist stronghold and a largely Quaker culture did not prevent ship captains and crews from treating blacks like beasts of burden. He writes in *A Voyage to the Pacific, Descriptive of the Customs, Usages, and Sufferings on Board of Nantucket Whale-Ships*: "An African is treated like a brute by the officers of their ship." Blacks were treated so badly that Comstock advised them to avoid Nantucket altogether: "Should these pages fall into the hands of any of my colored brethren, let me advise them to fly Nantucket as they would the Norway Maelstrom."[40] An 1807 visitor to Nantucket, agreeing with Comstock, wrote: "The Negroes, though they are to be prized for their habits of obedience, are not as intelligent as the Indians; and none of them attain the rank of [boat steerer and mate]."[41] These comments about the community of Nantucket reflect, within a broader cultural context, how European colonizers typically regarded "noble" Indian savages and "brutish" African types. Elsewhere in the nation during this time period, whites used this same logic to justify slavery and the general denigration of black persons in nineteenth-century American culture. As far as Nantucket was concerned, Nantucket ship captains had a reputation for being "Negro drivers." And Nantucketers themselves referred to the vessel that delivered potential black ship hands from New York City as the "Slaver."[42]

Comstock offers a different perspective on Nantucketers' feelings of shame and dishonor, helping us see how the consumption of the black men informed unspoken white male codes of honor. For the white men aboard the *Essex*, issues of group honor and masculine respectability informed their choice to kill and eat a black person before they would do so to one of their own. Such an act reinforced the black male's socially expendable status, his exclusion from white male honor and fraternity, his exoticization, and his brutishness, which whites linked to his supposedly inferior African ancestry. To have chosen a white man for consumption over a black man would have violated these codes of black dehumanization that implicitly informed white male honor and fraternity aboard the *Essex*.

Given the clandestine reality of racialized consumption aboard the *Essex*, one cannot help but wonder how many untold instances of black consumption at sea occurred under similar circumstances. To what extent has a larger history of black consumption at sea been altered or erased by whites who sought to conceal what they thought of as their shameful appetites and hungers for black male flesh? The *Essex* was neither the first nor the last white crew to engage in organized, ideologically justified consumption of black persons at sea. The American ship *Peggy* sailed from the Azores on October 24, 1765, bound for New York with a captain and crew of eight men, "one of whom was a Negro slave."[43] Only five days into their journey, the crew of the *Peggy* encountered a severe and disabling thunderstorm that lasted for weeks. The crew rationed all their food and water. When all their food was gone, they then ate leather, barnacles scraped from the ship's side, tobacco, lamp oil, and candles. The starving crew faced that dreadful decision: who to eat first among their crew? It appeared that the crew drew lots, with the result that the Negro was chosen as the first person to be murdered and consumed. In actuality, the white crew had decided before they drew lots that they would kill and eat the enslaved man. According to Petrinovich, "the lot had been consulted only for the sake of form" because "the black was proscribed the moment the sailors first formed their resolution."[44] Unspoken codes of superiority and group honor dictated the white crew's relationship to the slave. As a choice object of consumption, the black man reifies the bonds of fraternity, dominion, and right to life shared among the white men. In the choice to kill and consume the black man, the white men reinforced the premium value of white masculinity. The dishonorable and illogical act would have been to choose a white man over a slave. Such a choice would have violated the unspoken racial contract among whites and would have gone against the logic of the slave as an expendable, consumable object. The feasting that follows reinforces this white male bond in ideology and appetite: "One of the crew ate the liver raw, some of the rest of the body was cooked, and the remainder (cut up and referred to as 'steaks') was pickled, with the head and fingers thrown overboard."[45]

Curiously, in the *Peggy* incident, whites employ rituals of democracy and fairness to disguise for themselves and the slave the real nature of the social contract. The white men cast an arbitrary vote and allow all present seemingly equal participation. Yet the reality is that the white crew members cannot bring themselves to publicly admit the slave's expendable status, nor can they, for that matter, admit within the public domain how their masculinity and noble social stature take form and definition from the notion of the slave as consumable object. Such scenarios raise a number of unanswered questions: Why did the white men feel compelled to present an image of equal status with the slave? Why did they feel the need to hide their honorific social stature or to act outside of the extant master/slave, white/black power dynamic?

The empty lot-drawing ritual reflects the sense of dishonor that Americans associated with human consumption, at least publicly. Though isolated and days from civilization, the white crew cannot bring themselves to acknowledge the larger culture of black consumption; they cannot bring themselves to embrace, in a public and ritualized manner, the honorific and fraternal social bonds that the enslaved man's consumption reifies and sustains. If these white men, isolated and stranded at sea, could not bring themselves to claim the import and reality of black consumption, one can only imagine the depths of repression and silence within broader nineteenth-century American culture. Again, it should cause us to wonder: How many other blacks did whites consume at sea and how thoroughly have white Americans (and perhaps other groups of American citizens) repressed this social reality? In Nantucket, most of the white community agreed to maintain a tight-lipped silence concerning the consumption of a black man at sea. In addition to preserving white male honor, Nantucketers needed to preserve the integrity of their industry. If the truth about the consumption of black men was widely distributed, it would have affected their economy, their ability to recruit black ship hands. Because colonial-era whites had so much to lose (by way of property, repute, and livelihood), we should regard our acknowledgment of the *Essex* and *Peggy* incidents as only the starting point of a discussion that will, with the recovery of more precise historical evidence, deepen and complicate our understandings of the consumption of blacks at sea.

## The Meaning and Practice of "Seasoning"

In the public domain, whites, I have shown, either repressed the topic of human consumption or spoke of the consumed slave as a philosophical and moral issue. However, the slaves, having less to lose, described their enslavement as a form of appetite and epicurean hunger for black flesh that whites cultivated in the context of physical abuse, sexualized abuses, and all manner of daily master/slave relations. In John S. Jacobs's slave narrative, entitled "A True Tale of Slavery," he frequently described scenes he witnessed on the plantation in a language suggestive of consumption. He opened his narrative by describing the slave trader as a "human fleshmonger."[46] His own masters he describes as "hungry heirs" to a general "feast of blood."[47] This feast included black men who were hunted down and beheaded and slaves who were beaten so that their flesh was "like a steak."[48] One narrative contained in the massive collection *The American Slave: A Composite Autobiography* describes how male slaves were beaten and then "hanged up in the smoke house by their thumbs." [49]

Such punishment rituals were a form of seasoning. And seasoning usually involved breaking the will of a man or woman who was to be gradually conditioned to the life of the slave through physical and psychological torture. Lerone Bennett Jr. describes the process thusly:

> This process [of seasoning], whether it took place in liberal Brazil or harsh South Carolina, was a painful, mind-reversing operation in which two or three out of every ten died. In one form or another, every slave from Africa went through a "breaking-in" period. During this period, which varied from one to three years, the slave was taught pidgin English or French or Spanish. He got a new name and began to look at himself and others in a different manner."[50]

Seasoning is typically thought of as occurring at the point when the slave descends from the slave ship and is formally introduced into a plantation setting. Yet seasoning was a process that could and did occur throughout the career of the slave. Eli Coleman described a typical seasoning process that involved chaining a recalcitrant slave, who had already been introduced to the plantation, to a tree so that when he was finally released plantation life felt something like freedom compared with his more degraded condition. Coleman recalls: "So massa done put a chain round his legs, so he jus' hardly walk, and he has to work in the field that way. At night he put 'nother chain round his neck and fastened it to a tree. After three weeks massa turnt him loose and that the proudes' nigger in the world, and the hardes' workin' nigger massa had after that."[51]

*Webster's Encyclopedic Unabridged Dictionary* offers distinct yet overlapping definitions for seasoning that apply to the treatment of the black slave. I cite just two: "14. to heighten or improve the flavor of (food) by adding condiments, spices, herbs, or the like. . . . 17. to dry or otherwise treat (lumber) so as to harden it and render it immune to shrinkage, warpage, etc." Definition 17 is how historians and other scholars of slavery typically convey the purpose and outcome of seasoning, as a process that hardens or numbs the slave psychologically and physically to the brutality of his or her condition. The latter definition, while partially accurate, does not account for the ways seasoning rituals also cultivated the master or overseer. It was in the context of seasoning that the master developed certain appetites for the slave, learned to channel needs, pleasure, sport, and eroticism into the brutal treatment of the slave. At the same time that it numbed and hardened, seasoning also had the outcome of softening the flesh and, for the master, heightening and improving the flavor of certain types of interactions.

There was a distinct category of seasoning rituals that involved literally seasoning the human flesh. These rituals, which usually went beyond the bounds of normal punishment, provide evidence of seasoning as an epicurean process that prepared the slave for social consumption. I have already mentioned Virginia sport, which involved hanging a person up in the meat house after a beating and literally smoking the body. Often, a master would beat a slave until raw and bloody and then the master would apply the seasoning. For example, Wes Brady witnessed his master, following a beating, "take a brick and grind it up in a powder and mix it with lard and put it all over him [the slave] and roll him in a sheet."[52] Others frequently used, among other combinations, salt and pepper; vinegar, salt, and pepper; pepper and turpentine; and coal oil and turpentine. It was not enough to have slaves as a laboring commodity. Whites who enacted such heinous acts satiated cravings, took pleasure and delight in Negroes thusly treated, like master Tom, who "jus' bout had to beat somebody everyday to satisfy his cravin'. He had a big bullwhip and he stake a nigger on the ground and make 'nother nigger hold his head down with his mouth in the dirt and whip the nigger till blood run out and red up the ground."[53] Historians of slavery have typically described such acts as cruel and unnecessary forms of punishment. Yet the descriptors "cruel," "unusual," and "punishment" do not adequately define the "cravin'," the institutionalized hunger that often characterized the master's relationship to his slaves and, more specifically, to his male slaves.

James L. Smith's seasoning at the hands of a man to whom his master had rented him exemplifies how sex, brutality, and hunger all coalesced within the economy of slavery. In Smith's slave narrative, *Autobiography of James L. Smith* (1881), sexual and physical brutality converge. Smith's narrative offers a closer look into the sexual dimensions of white male rage, obsession, and desire for black men during slavery. As a youth, Smith works on the Mitchell plantation. One sunny morning, a ship captain comes to the Mitchell plantation to purchase grain. This man sees young Smith and admires his countenance. He wants to make the youth into a sailor, initiate him into the rigors and challenges of manhood at sea. Master Mitchell consents, and Smith, who has years earlier lost his mother and father, looks forward to a new environment, a temporary respite from milking calves and his other domestic chores in the master's "great house."[54]

Smith will soon learn, though, that his culinary responsibilities involve much more than food preparation. In addition to choosing the young slave to feed his physical hunger, the captain has also chosen Smith to fulfill other despotic hungers. One morning after the ship has docked in Richmond, Virginia, the captain and a shipmate go to town. The captain leaves Smith with orders to prepare his breakfast and have it ready upon his return. It is ice cold and raining fiercely outside. Smith asks the captain if he can cook below deck, away from the exposure to the elements, and the captain denies this request. The captain forces Smith to cook the fish in the caboose, which Smith describes as "a large black kettle set on the deck, all open to the weather, to make fire in, and supported by bricks to prevent it from burning the deck."[55] Try as he might, Smith cannot raise a fire strong enough to fry the fish as the captain likes. He decides to poach the fish and afterward pours them out into a dish and places them on the table, awaiting the captain's return.

The captain returns from town drunk. Needless to say, the cold poached fish fills the captain with "dissatisfaction and disgust." Anticipating the captain's response, Smith stood outside the captains quarters and "peeped through the cabin window, to see what effect the break-fast would have upon him."[56] The captain calls Smith to his side and demands an explanation. Smith tries to justify himself by telling the captain "that the rain and wind cooled my pan so that I could not fry the fish, and that I had done the best I could."[57] After hearing his expla-nation, the captain coolly and calmly directs Smith to remove all of his clothes and go stand on the deck in the freezing cold until he has fin-ished his breakfast.

The captain knows, even before leaving the ship, how difficult it will be to fry fish in the cold wind and rain. Even the most expert cook could not stand in the open air under such conditions and cook a fish, not to mention frying it to a well-done crisp. Smith is young, not yet a man. He is innocent; this is his first time living away from the planta-tion, and he is also physically disabled. Smith is perfect prey for this white man who makes ritual out of abuse and takes pleasure in a young terrified, trembling black man exposed to the freezing cold rain. This is not the first time that Smith will be commanded to strip, stand, or kneel as he waits for the captain to come and deliver punishment.

The colder Smith becomes, ridiculed by some of his shipmates and pitied by others, the hotter and angrier the captain becomes in his quar-ters. It is not clear whether he eats the fish or throws it into the waste pile. We only know that the captain emerges from his cabin with the "fierceness of his nature . . . roused."[58] Just as the fish is cold and coated by the rain, so too does Smith become cold and covered. The captain wants Smith to experience something of the cold disgust and dissat-isfaction that he, himself, tastes in the rain-drenched fish. A man who teaches through example, the captain restages the cooking scene. He has Smith stand in the freezing cold, basting and turning in the stares of crew members. Rather than a spatula, the captain gathers, in prepa-ration for Smith's punishment, the end of a rope, a phallic object in his hands. He waits in his cabin for the fires of his rage and desire to peak. Sex and good taste come together in the beating that is more of a styl-ized rape than a routine punishment. Smith describes the scene thusly: "There I was, divested of my clothing! He turned his fiery eyes on me when he came on deck; and, with a look of fierce decision on his face, (for now all the fierceness of his nature was roused,) he took a rope's end and applied it vigorously to my naked back."[59]

In *Ar'n't I a Woman?: Female Slaves in the Plantation South*, Deborah Gray White describes how semi-clad black women working in rice fields "nurtured white male notions of their promiscuity."[60] Frederick Law Olmsted, a northern white architect and abolitionist sympathizer, referred to black women working in flooded fields with their skirts "reefed up" around their waists as "clumsy," "gross," and "elephantine." He further described these women, who were focused on the task at hand, as "sly," "sensual," and "shameless."[61] White notes that the "exposure of women's bodies during whippings had similar consequences":

> Christopher Nichols, an escaped slave living in Canada, remembered how his master laid a woman on a bench, threw her clothes over her head, and whipped her. Another refugee remembered that when his mother was whipped, she was stripped completely naked: "Dey didn't care nothing bout it. Let everybody look on at it." Similarly, Henry Bibb reported a whipping where a woman's "naked quivering flesh" was "tied up and exposed to the public gaze of all."[62]

The captain responds to Smith as though he has intentionally prepared the unpalatable meal, as if he has committed a deliberate act of resistance like a slave who has stolen a pig or one who has sneaked away from the plantation at night. Within the general tableau of plantation violence, Smith's punishment registers as elaborate and extreme. A master or overseer might chastise and beat a slave for such an indiscretion, but the master usually administered such a beating with the clothes partially removed; they usually removed the shirt to get at the back. The captain has Smith remove all of his clothes and stand out in the open where all of the male crew members can laugh at and pity his nakedness. This gesture conveys the captain's sexual dominance over Smith, his familiarity with and mastery over every crevice and surface of his body.

Similar to Olmsted, who watches the black women working semi-clad in the rice fields with their skirts reefed up to their thighs, the captain reads sexual allure, brutal teasing, and masochism into Smith's labor. Smith thwarts his hunger, according to the captain's logic, because he wants to feel the captain's bite and taste, be penetrated and warmed by his violent embrace. Of course, these desires begin and end in the captain's mind. His desire for Smith is as impersonal as it is brutally painful and consuming. The captain leaves the ship unreasonable and disagreeable. Otherwise, he would have allowed Smith to cook below deck. He would have instructed other crew members to shield Smith from the rain and wind. In her discussion of rape and violence, White notes the connection between physical hunger and sexual brutality. She notes that the "man who whipped Henry Bibb's wife was often heard to exclaim that 'he had rather paddle a female than eat when he was hungry.'"[63] It seems the ship captain would also rather beat Smith than eat. Rather than have Smith prepare another portion of food, he thrusts "the fierceness of his nature" into the black youth. Furthermore, he forces Smith to participate. He makes Smith strip down, tremble in anticipation, and bear up under the biting cold. Smith's participation— his shame and degradation—make the trembling, raised flesh that rises to meet the captain all the more appetizing to the touch, all the more delectable.

A second horrid beating related by Smith also centers on eating and meal preparation. This time, after the captain has taken his meal, Smith serves him an after-breakfast pastry. The captain asks Smith why he has not made more tea. Smith replies, "I told him it was all out; he wanted to know why I did not make more tea; I told him I thought there was a plenty, it was as much as I generally made." The captain flies into a rage and challenges Smith for "daring to think." Again, he commands Smith to divest himself of all of his clothing and to go stand above deck naked, awaiting his arrival. At this point in the narrative, we are given to understand that the challenge—the command to strip and wait and the anticipation that ensues—are all a part of a sex/brutality ritual that the captain practices frequently. Every day, the captain finds reason to beat Smith. "The cat-o'-nine-tails had no rest . . . a day seldom passed on which he could find no occasion for its use," recalls Smith.[64]

The captain cultivates an aesthetic appreciation for Smith's naked, quivering flesh. Smith notes that the captain had a deep "love" for the "music" of the cat-o'-nine-tails. His taste for his delectable black subject transcends regular appetite. His taste for this Negro is a cruel parallel to the foundational tenets of Eurocentric culture and civilization. One thinks of music, poetry, the taking of an after-dinner dessert, and leisurely sport; these are practices of affluence and leisure culture that are all learned and based in an intangible sense of good taste. M. F. K. Fisher, a scholar of epicureanism, has developed a categorical list that explains the importance of and process of cultivating taste. A number of the items on her list are particularly relevant and help explain how the captain's cultivated taste for the Negro overlaps with and reinforces more traditional categories of Eurocentric taste. Fisher describes taste as "that one of our senses which gives us the greatest joy" because

> it recurs of necessity at least once every day, and can be repeated without inconvenience two or three times in that space of hours; (4) Because it can mingle with all the other pleasures, and even console us for their absence; (5) Because its sensations are at once more lasting than others and more subject to our will; (6) Because, finally, in eating we experience a certain special and indefinable well-being, which arises from our instinctive realization that by the very act we perform we are repairing our bodily losses and prolonging our lives.[65]

In Smith's brutalization, there is frequency; a compound combination of pleasures; an apparent lasting, aesthetic resonance that remains with the captain like music; and a sense of well-being that arises from some instinctual source. The Negro serves, in this context, as a symbol and hallmark of civilization, taking his place alongside musical appreciation, philosophy, and even the ability to reason. The ship captain chastises Smith for thinking, for "daring to think" outside of his useful role of sexual object, delight, and masochistic morsel. French political philosopher Montesquieu observed: "It is impossible for us to assume that these people [Africans] are men because if we assumed they were men one would begin to believe that we ourselves were not Christians."[66] Montesquieu's comments reveal a correlation between European institution making in the colonial context and the unmaking of the humanity of the African and black person. The captain's social stature and honorific role aboard the ship takes form and shape from Smith's denied humanity, the denial of Smith's innate abilities to think and reason.

When the captain finally arrives after finishing his breakfast and tea, he puts Smith down on his knees in a position more blatantly sexualized then the first one Smith relates: "When he did come he put my head between his legs, and while I was in this position I thought my last days had come; I thought while he was using the cat-o'-nine-tails to my naked back, and hearing the whizzing of the rope, that if ever I got away I would throw myself overboard and put an end to my life."[67] The captain places Smith between his legs in a position simulating an animal on all fours. He positions Smith's head below his genital region and gives himself ample access to Smith's back and buttocks.

Holding Smith in this manner between his legs, the captain beats him almost into unconsciousness. Smith feels that he wants to die: "The captain punished me so much that I was tired of life."[68] He jumps overboard and almost drowns. The captain relishes Smith's struggles between life and death. Reaching up for help, Smith sees the captain: "He sat perfectly at ease, or composed on the deck looking at me, but making no effort to help me."[69] This, finally, is the prize and revelation. The peril of Smith's soul and the tormenting of his spirit feed the captain. A parasite, the captain feeds upon the terror and loss of self Smith experiences. Only because Smith is his host—a vital source of his manhood, livelihood, and honor—does the captain finally draw the young black man up to the surface. This scene calls to mind a similar one relayed by Olaudah Equiano. Equiano describes a master who, after punishing his slaves, would then have them "get into a long wooden box or case he had for that purpose, in which he shut them up during [his] pleasure. It was just about the height and breadth of a man; and the poor wretches had no room when in the case to move."[70] This master placed his slaves in a coffin. This type of punishment, like that which Smith undergoes, the master used to emphasize the slave's socially dead status. It was a method of emptying out and making the person into an "*instrumentum vocal*—perfectly flexible, unattached, and deracinated." In this way, the master reinforced for himself and "to all members of the community [that] the slave existed only through the parasite holder, who was called the master. On this intersubjective level the slaveholder fed on the slave to gain the very direct satisfactions of power over another, honor enhancement, and authority."[71]

Smith makes the captain a man, rather than the captain's making him the same. When the captain first leases the young boy from the plantation, he tells him that he intends to make him into a sailor and a man. In truth, Smith is a type of food source to the captain's white masculinity. The captain reinforces Smith's infantile state by stripping him down, parading him before crew members, and not allowing him to express an intelligible thought. Domination of the black youth ensures the captain's supremacy.

Smith, we can say with certainty, undergoes a change through this process of the captain's making him into a slave, a slave being the opposite of a freedom-possessed man, a slave being, in a Hegelian sense, a sycophantic personality that takes identity from the deific power of the master. All of this to a great extent we know or have seen analyzed. But what does it mean, to alter the Hegelian dialectic, for the slave to be a type of food and the master a cannibalistic social agent? Stretching the dialectic even further, what does it mean when the nature of the "consciousness that exists for itself" is consumption, human consumption on the levels of sex, psyche, and soul?[72]

These questions take on greater significance and importance when addressed to members of the ruling southern aristocracy. Importantly, the captain was cruel and hungering, but he was only a middleman on the human food chain. The more refined epicurean appetite for the Negro's body and person existed among the ruling class, among the slave owners and their progeny. Edward A. Pollard was a white journalist from Virginia who was raised on a plantation. Pollard, a defender of slavery, declared the southern Negro the most loveable of creatures "in his place." In "Black Diamonds" (1859), he writes to a friend of returning to Virginia after traveling all over the world: "I have seen the hideous slavery of Asia. I have seen the coolies of China 'housed on the wild sea with wilder usages,' or creeping with dejected faces into the suicide houses of Canton. I have seen the Siamese slave creeping in the presence of his master on all-fours—a human quadruped."[73] Pollard is addressing "C," a "Northern acquaintance who was presumably awaiting enlightenment on the true condition of the Negro slave."[74] Pollard tells Mr. C that after all this traveling he looks forward to getting back to the southern institution, to "the evidences of comfort and happiness on the plantations of the South."[75] And to better illustrate the "comfort" and "happiness" that he imagines, Pollard presents C with the image of an "unadulterated negro" serving on the train car that is taking him back to the South. In poetic and emotionally compelling imagery, he writes about the black man: "He looked like *home*. I could have embraced the old uncle, but was afraid the passengers, from such a demonstration, might mistake me for an abolitionist. I looked at him with my face aglow, and my eyelids touched with tears. How he reminded me of my home—of days gone by—that poetry of youth."[76] Another southerner, Basil Lanneau Gildersleeve, thinking back to slavery before emancipation, wrote that "the poetry of life will still find its home in the old order."[77] This idea of slavery and the bonded Negro as poetic cultivation profoundly shaped the imagination of southern slave owners. For Pollard, the Negro serves as an emblem of home. He is a signpost of sorts: a marker of affections, beauty, nobility, and the innocence that the white southerner associates with his childhood. The Negro is also a separating line between comforting familiarity and the danger, uncertainty, and fatigue that foreign environments inspire.

Pollard compares this Negro man to the "warm, wide hills of my sweet home."[78] This is not simply a Negro man of which he speaks but rather a delectable thing, a personal familiar, an acquired taste and set of sensibilities. The Negro is as natural and permanent as the landscape, as aesthetically pleasing and necessary to the cultured citizen as poetry. The Negro is the institution of family and home and simultaneously an evaporative nothing, a non-entity to this southern white gentlemen who might just as soon lynch his object of affection were the black man to step outside of "his place."

For the Negro, this was dangerous territory indeed. It is as if whites brought to bear upon the Negro's person generations of European cultivation and institution building. Like poetry, a learned art and acquired taste, the taste and hunger for the Negro was learned, rooted in repetition and practice. The Negro that Pollard speaks of was a familiar home territory, a safe space in and through which white men could feel, play, lust, rage, and, finally, make themselves at home. This type of Negro whites naturalized and romanticized much as they romanticized "the natural landscape" of the Americas after seizing it from murdered and systematically contained Native Americans.

Booker T. Washington poignantly experienced this institutionalization of the Negro, and he documented it in *Up from Slavery: An Autobiography* (1900). In 1879, on a stopover visit in the nation's capital, Washington witnessed the town go into a furor over a "dark-skinned man" checking into a white hotel. The town intended to lynch the man until they found that he was from Morocco and therefore "not an American Negro."[79] In another instance that took place that same year, Washington was transporting a Native American youth who had a similar complexion to his own to Washington. Aboard the train, a dinner server informed Washington that the Native youth could enter the dining car but that he, a Negro of the same complexion, could not. In both the hotel and aboard the train car, we see the Negro serving as a utilitarian object that helped define social places, determine the interior and external margins of society, and mark the boundary between domestic and international terrains. The Moroccan man and the American Negro have the same hair texture, skin color, and phenotypic features; the only difference between the two men is a process of cultivation and domestication rooted in white tastes, comforts, habits, perceptions, and social needs.

During and beyond slavery, blacks have associated the type of Negro Pollard described with femininity, but more specifically with a nurturing, maternal male role. Trudier Harris describes a black man who plays a nurturing role as grandmotherly. Analyzing the issue more deeply, she notes that this "grandmotherly" type black man

> approaches the mammy figure in the extent of his concern for the white
> person who is in his care. His primary goal is to soothe . . . the precious
> "child" whose welfare rests in his hands. To comfort the child, the grand-
> mother must show him that the danger which threatened him is no lon-
> ger real because grandmother has control over the boogieman.[80]

The black man plays this role for Pollard, who wants to hold him/be held by him and feel a returned sense of safety within domestic shores, after having traveled throughout the strange and unsafe world. The black male grandmother-type figure reproduces the national identification and internal and external sense of geography of the white male. This he/she figure also reproduces the white male-child as father, master, owner, and kind paternal family member.

Like the difference between wild and domesticated game, the more appetizing Negro was one whom whites had domesticated, made into a type of pet whom they could work, romanticize, brutalize, or socially consume. Ex-slave Jim Allen, speaking to a WPA interviewer, admitted that he was his master's pet: "Did we have good eating? Yes ma'm, old Marster fed so good, *fer I was his pet*. He never 'lowed no one to perster me neither. . . . As I done tol's you, I was Marse Allen's pet nigger boy. I was called a stray. I slep' on de flo' by old Miss an' Marse Bob."[81] Another man named Pet Franks was given this name by his master. His master and the master's family conditioned him to be their domesticated object on the plantation. Interviewed years after slavery, he revealed: "I knows all 'bout slav'ry an' de war. I was right dere on de spot when it all happened. I wish to goodness I was back dere now, not in de war, but in slav'ry times. . . . I do 'members hearin' 'bout slaves on other places gittin' whipped sometimes. I guess Niggers lak dat wished dey was free, but I didn' want to leave my white folks, ever."[82] Allen and Franks reinforce plantation whites' sense of themselves as moral and benevolent; they deify their masters and whiteness in general and learn to participate in their consumption into the southern plantation body politic.

The slave master's taste and appetite for the Negro encompassed a range of cultural registers and social milieus. With Jim Allen, the master more explicitly draws upon the correlation between black person and animal, referring to the black man as a type of domesticated "pet" and "stray" creature. The parasitic master, in this instance, feeds his sense of authority and social stature through the diminishment of and animal-like treatment of his slave. Likewise, Pollard and Gildersleeve reveal, through a poetics of Negro consumption, a learned art of cultivating the Negro to fulfill white hungers, fantasies, imaginings, and deeply seated emotional needs. Even with the legal freeing of the enslaved population, Washington cannot escape what I describe as the institutionalization of the Negro, the Negro as vacuous and emptied-out social entity, a template upon which the white man and white culture inscribes its humanity and social reality.

This range and diversity of examples gives us a context for and a means to better understand in James L. Smith's narrative the references to musical appreciation, the captain's construction of Smith as an entity that does not reason and think, and the captain's choosing of Smith as a host meant to feed and reify his social stature and honorific standing among the members of his crew. We cannot fully appreciate the captain's scripted rituals of food and flesh consumption if we do not understand as well how a process of learned, cultivated aesthetic appreciation whets

and slakes his appetite. As well, we cannot fully interpolate the significance of the captain's rage at Smith's daring to think if we do not understand how the captain imagines Smith as domesticated creature, as pet
to his desires and needs, as a safe and home-like space that nurtures and
sustains. We should understand ritualized human consumption of the
type that Smith undergoes as a reified and highly stylized example of a
much broader and more pervasive phenomenon. Long before we get to
Smith's concrete example, whites had constructed a social reality and
set of conditions in which social consumption can occur. We should
not think of consumption simply as acts that momentarily occur but as
an already existent set of philosophical and social conditions that operate prior to and following acts of literal and ritualized consumption.

## The Taste of Nat Turner

In the final section of this chapter, I want to more concretely deal with
the topics of taste and flesh cultivation that emerged from Smith's abuse.
Nat Turner's life and political legacy represents one of the most graphic
documented cases of white cultivated tastes for the Negro manifest-
ing as literal consumption and the harvesting of body parts. The literal
consumption of Turner alongside the sexualized consumption of Smith
offer a fuller picture of white hunger for black flesh and sex coinciding
with white male codes of honor and self-glorification.

The themes of white male nobility, a cultivated appetite for the Negro,
and human consumption all informed the life and legacy of Nat Turner.
As a result of the controversial nature of Turner's memory and legacy,
in his hometown of Southampton, Virginia, there exists to this day no
memorial to commemorate his life and his efforts to free enslaved persons of the region. Outside the historical society in the center of town,
there is a colonial-era house that stands on a raised brick foundation
behind a sign that reads: "This is the last house on the killing spree
of Nat Turner and his men."[83] Whites regard Turner, in local lore and
memory, as the murderer of whites and their babies; as a twisted, sexual
deviant; and as a depraved example of criminal insanity. In antebellum
America, whites even went as far as to depict Turner and his accom-
plices as murderous cannibals who hungered for white flesh. In Harriet
Beecher Stowe's fictional rendering of the Turner revolt in *Dred* (1856),

she has a black male insurrectionist say: "When the Lord saith unto us, 'Smite,' then will we smite. We will not torment them with the scourge and fire, nor defile their women, as they have done with ours! But we will slay them utterly, *and consume them from off the face of the earth*."[84] Even among the most well-intentioned white abolitionists, the harsh reality of unmitigated black male violence and retribution conjured racist images of African cannibals engaged in human consumption. From abolitionist tract to court records to the journals and correspondence of U.S. statesmen, this notion of Turner and his soldiers as cannibalistic held sway. For example, Governor John Floyd of Virginia described in his diary a cannibalistic scenario that had been conveyed to him through written transcripts of court trials: "Through out this affair," he noted, "the most appalling accounts have been given of the conduct of the negroes, the most inhuman butcheries the mind can conceive of, men, women, and infants, their heads chopped off, their bowels ripped out, ears noses, hand and legs cut off, no instance of mercy shown."[85] Floyd paints the image of Turner and his men killing and then tearing open, ripping through, and harvesting a white person's body parts.

Whites from the North and South, of both abolitionist and slave-holding sentiments, contrived to paint an image of Turner as cannibalistic and, more importantly, as a dishonorable and self-hating man. In *History of Virginia, from Its Discovery and Settlement by Europeans to the Present Time*, Robert R. Howison describes Turner as "small and somewhat feeble in body, but of shrewd and enthusiastic mind."[86] Newspaper accounts from the time proliferated with misinformation designed to discredit and dishonor Turner's efforts. In *The American Beacon*, they had Turner admitting to cowardice and fanaticism: "He [Nat Turner] acknowledges himself a coward and says he was actuated to do what he did, from influence of fanaticism, he says the attempt originated entirely with himself."[87] *The Petersburg Index*, reporting on the Turner insurrection over thirty years later, described the black revolutionary thusly: "Nat Turner came out of the Dismal Swamp starved at last, and was taken and hung as a monster black fiend, and history has passed him as a murderer on the gallows."[88] Whites had to dishonor Turner, disfigure him, and make of his person and legacy a monstrosity. Such a strategy of character assassination deflected attention away from the real, brutal circumstances of slavery that initiated Turner's revolt and the incidents of literal consumption that informed the execution of Turner and the treatment of his corpse.

After Turner was captured, he was hung, skinned, and bled and his body was boiled down to grease. Blacks of the region around this time swore off the consumption of castor oil. According to William Sidney Drewry, a late nineteenth-century historian, "The famous remedy of doctors of antebellum days—castor oil—was long dreaded for fear it was 'old Nat's grease.'"[89] Drewry and others have referred to such beliefs as an "older prejudice" common among "older darkies."[90] Even younger, more liberal historians, such as Scot French, have labeled black concerns over consuming Nat Turner as "folk belief."[91] For the most part, scholars have shied away from the question of what Southampton whites wanted with Nat Turner's grease. In contrast to the rhetoric of Turner as a monstrous and unpalatable figure, it helps to know that during that time period, white men associated honor and nobility with unspeakable acts of violence and consumption perpetrated against black bodies. General Eppes, for example, described the treatment of black persons as "revolting—inhuman and not to be justified" and characterized by "acts of atrocity."[92] Perhaps the general had in mind individuals like the following black man whom whites shot, quartered, and beheaded for no reason at all, except that he knew nothing about the Turner insurrection: "'He told 'em he didn't know anything about any insurrection. They shot several balls through him, quartered him, and put his head on a pole of the fork of the road leading to the court.' (This is no exaggeration, if the Virginia newspapers may be taken as evidence.)"[93] The Turner insurrection brought out in whites, in particular in white men, a violently stoked appetite and rabid hunger for black flesh. Unspoken codes of honor and vengeance drove whites to quarter, burn, maim, and behead blacks, whom they saw as having violated the sacred provinces of white masculinity, white family, and the innocence embodied in murdered white babies.

In this context of unchecked violence, there was nothing to keep plantation whites from first murdering and then tasting and ingesting Turner. Yet since slavery Southampton whites have made a mockery of black observations of white cannibalism and denied the same observations made by whites. In a 1931 editorial, J. S. Musgrave cites from a history text that documents the consumption of Turner. The excerpt reads:

"Nat's body was boiled up, his oil saved and sold for a long period as a panacea for all ills and known as 'Nat's grease.'"[94] Musgrave refers to these documented observations as "pure, unalloyed bunk."[95] He retreats into a typical mode of white denial, yet when one thinks about the boiling down of Turner's flesh in an inquiring manner, it makes sense to ask: For what purpose did whites use his liquefied flesh? Was it used to cook food, oil the body, for ingestion as medicine, or for some other domestic use? Working from a largely unrevised notion of the folk, scholars have failed to see the inherent layers of inquiry in the folk's refusal to eat Nat Turner. It would have been so much simpler to hang, bury, or burn the body. Why go through all of the effort involved in bleeding the corpse and boiling down the flesh? Why preserve the liquid flesh of one so hated and feared? Why behead him and secretly preserve the skull?

Ironically, we find the suspicions of the folk validated and archived in Eurocentric hegemony and legacy. The treatment of Nat Turner's body might possibly date back to Renaissance and early American societies. Under the auspices of "Medical cannibal" (the practice of preserving and ingesting body parts for medical purposes), Europeans preserved and ingested blood, skin, and other body parts. According to Shirley Lindenbaum, it was common for Renaissance and Victorian era "Europeans [to] ingest human tissue, usually that of an executed criminal, as a supposed medicine or tonic."[96] Rev. Edward Taylor was a New England practitioner whose "Dispensatory" included remedies made from human blood, heart, flesh, and other parts of the human body meant to be "'took,' or ingested." In this practice, which Taylor brought over from England, the body parts were usually obtained from criminals hanged for various crimes. It was commonly thought that the best parts came from "artificial mummies" who had died a violent death.[97] Not surprisingly, one cannot readily find such information in general inventories of medical supplies in the early American colonies or within the contents lists of apothecaries.

Southampton whites and others involved with the Turner insurrection wrote to deny this European legacy of the consumption of criminals and, more specifically, of Turner as a nutritional substance. With intention, whites have reconstructed the narrative of Turner's consumption through metaphors of the Negro as disgusting and tainted and through references to the grotesqueness of the Negro body and soul.

Governor Floyd described the Turner affair as leaving him "with a bad taste in my mouth." Days later, he again uses gastronomical metaphors to describe his visceral response to Turner's insurrection: *Eleventh day*: I hear nothing this morning from below. I do not feel so badly as yesterday. I had more appetite to-day and not so bad a taste in my mouth."[98] Governor Floyd gives the impression of Turner and Turner's violent actions inspiring disgust at the levels of gut and taste. Yet as I have demonstrated throughout this chapter, the consumption of black persons, on literal and metaphoric levels, reified and restored in whites a sense of honor and ennobled social stature (not to mention that Turner likely served as a nutritional substance to the whites who used his body in that manner). Governor Floyd's personal and sentimental recordings obscure the easy and seamless translation of white male rage after the Turner insurrection into literal appetite and hunger for black flesh. I cited earlier the example of the black man who was tortured, beheaded, and had his head hung on a pole for not admitting to information about the Turner insurrection. Rare and honest white citizens from the time period described the treatment of blacks in the region following the insurrection as "a Reign of Terror"—that is, white-inspired terror.[99]

What better way to annihilate the threat of one's terror (I'm speaking of white terror here) than through consumption, a permanent taking in of that which horrifies, that which embodies the threat of self- and communal annihilation? Governor Floyd's response to the "taste" of Turner, though one of revulsion, indicates that whites had all manner of appetite-based responses to Turner. The governor's outrage, terror, and sense of violated honor take the form of abjection. In others, similar sentiments generated the opposite effect, leading whites to rape, pillage, behead, and castrate blacks. Tasting and ingesting Turner in this context of retribution and erotic violation would have represented for white men the ultimate erotic and satiating act. Rather than projecting their desire—through the violation of black bodies, communities, and homes—white men could, through the oral ingestion of Turner, experience at first hand a taste of the terror, fascination, hatred, and death wish that they felt toward the black liberator. Given this fuller explication of the autoerotic and necrophilic implications of the consumption of Turner, it makes better sense that whites would, still today, deny and attempt to suppress black accusations of white appetite for and consumption of Turner. That consumption reveals too much, takes us too deep (for the comfort of most) into the interior reality of white males' hunger and the death drive they fixated upon the Negro.

For at least two generations, the entire Southampton black community stopped using castor oil. This gesture of communal solidarity and fear of consumption of a black man is arresting for what it conceals and also for what it reveals (through a communal gesture of silence and knowing). What more did these historically silenced persons know, when did they definitively begin to know it, and at what cost do we continue to deny the basis of their knowledge and the implications of their resistance?

3

A Tale of Hunger Retold

*Ravishment and Hunger in F. Douglass's Life and Writing*

Frederick Douglass described slavery, more eloquently than anyone else has, as a cannibalistic institution. In images striking and poetically reso-nant, he depicted slavery in the *Narrative of the Life of Frederick Douglass, an American Slave* as a personified "stern reality, glaring frightfully upon us,—its robes already crimsoned with the blood of millions, and even now feasting itself greedily upon our own flesh."[1] Slave traders he thought of as "human flesh-mongers."[2] In the context Douglass described, slave own-ers cultivated consumption, hunger, and starvation at all levels of social interaction. If it was not Aunt Katy, the cook on one plantation, who was literally starving Douglass, then it was a master punishing a hungry slave for stealing molasses by making him drink gallons of it until he sickened, engorged on the sweetness. Such examples proliferate in all of Douglass's works, including *Narrative* (1845), *My Bondage and My Freedom* (1855), and *The Life and Times of Frederick Douglass* (1881). To my knowledge, lit-tle scholarly analysis exists of the culture of consumption depicted in Dou-glass's narratives. This is striking, considering that in Douglass's narratives and in the slave narratives I discussed in previous chapters, such refer-ences abound—not to mention those slaves who were literally consumed and the catalogue of flesh-cooking, consumption rituals, and habitual flesh-taking that formed a part of the larger archive of consumption.

Building on the findings of earlier chapters, I want to move beyond acknowledging and arguing for cannibalism as a social reality for the enslaved person to the particular ways that the male slave resisted and internally wrestled with this dominant hunger and appetite. In this chapter, I examine three different ways that Douglass wrestled with consumption at the hands of others and self (the two acts often occurring simultaneously). First, I examine how mental and emotional consumption coincided with coded instances of rape at the hands of an overseer. Sexual and spiritual consumption overlap, especially in Douglass's first two narratives, providing insight into how he understood sex, at least abusive sex, as one way white men attempted to consume him. Also in this first section, I introduce the topic of incest. The most formative sexual encounters that shape Douglass's life and structure his narratives have to do with the incestuous treatment of an aunt, his mother, and himself. This topic of incest takes on increased importance as Douglass attempts throughout his life to work through sexually laden kinship ties with white men.

The second thing I consider is a condition of mother hunger that characterized much of Douglass's life. The fear of social consumption, the hunger for family, for civilized lineage, for safety, physical satiation, and for paternity showed up often in Douglass's writing as mother hunger. Even in his relationships with white authoritative figures and heads of state, this mother hunger emerged as erotic desire, affection, and the need for care and intimacy.

Lastly, I apply the framework of male effeminacy developed in the previous two chapters to Douglass himself. Alongside his heroic male identity, Douglass described himself as playing the role of male concubine and male daughter to the plantation system and to certain white male authority figures. Douglass depicts this role mostly as negative, but I focus on how from a reproductive, procreative perspective, this role strikes a balance in his life. For out of a dangerous, potentially self-consumptive hunger, he gives birth to the central statutes and tenets of the U.S. republic. This hunger and desire, combined with Douglass's intellect and stoic reserve, inform his vision and unique contributions of genius to American culture.

For the most part, scholars of Douglass's written work have overlooked the proliferation of references to appetite, multiple layers of hunger, and consumption in his three narratives. David Van Leer, an exception to this trend, calls attention to a section from the *Narrative*

that highlights "the horrors of cannibalism, dismemberment, and execution." In his cursory treatment of cannibalism in Douglass's *Narrative*, Van Leer describes such occurrences as "imaginative" acts and
as part of a "fictionalizing moment" in Douglass's text.[3] Importantly,
rather than treating Douglass's claims as real, Van Leer metaphorizes
and fictionalizes the race leader's observations. Van Leer analyzes textual and literary conventions such as the Gothic and sentimental traditions informing Douglass's style and choice of images. The deeper pre-
sumption underlying Van Leer's observations and I believe fueling the
inattention to this topic in Douglass's writing is the notion that cannibalism has nothing to do with Enlightenment, with myths of American
progress, and with nation-making in the nineteenth century. It is, to
put it bluntly, inconceivable to most that cannibalism was an implicit
aspect of slave culture and, more broadly, of American race/caste systems based in the sycophancy of slavery.

   Still, Douglass depicts the slave institution as cannibalistic and
he gives us also a telling glimpse into the manner in which he internally resisted and wrestled with the reality of his social consumption.
Describing the slave condition as one of consumption and self-consumption, Douglass describes slavery in the *Narrative* as a condition of
"starvation, causing us to eat our own flesh."[4] In *The Life and Times of
Frederick Douglass*, he describes himself as enmeshed in webs of "soul
devouring thought" that reinforce the fact that he is a slave.[5] Douglass
parallels the material reality of cannibalism with interlocking ideologies of cannibalism that allow the master to consume the slave in body
as well as in spirit and thought. Douglass's observations affirm Carl O.
Williams's understanding of slavery as a highly stylized, institutionalized form of cannibalism. Williams describes thralldom (slavery) as a
degree of cannibalism, wherein the master is a human parasite who, by
the right of might, has secured his fellow man in the bonds of thralldom in order to feed upon him for the satisfaction of his appetite.[6]
Further elaborating on the erotics of this libidinal hunger, Orlando Patterson notes that "what the slave mainly fed was the master's sense of
honor and his sexual appetite, for the economic role of the slave was
quite marginal among most of the continental Germanic tribes."[7] Germanic slavery, differing from U.S. chattel slavery, was less economically
driven and more of a domestic variety, which served to highlight the

interpersonal connections between master and slave. Though U.S. slavery was economically driven, this tie between the hunger and sexual appetite of the ruling class also applied to it. Perhaps even more so, as the exoticization of the "African type" and early racial codes heightened white titillation at the thought of black flesh.[8]

In the nineteenth century, allusions to the consumption of and flesh hunger for black males proliferated in American culture. However, black men such as Douglass often alluded to this culture through subtle references to manhood and black male bodies exotically exposed before whites. In an 1854 speech delivered by the racial liberator before an audience of educated white males, Douglass debated the subject of black humanity. An ethnologist by the name of Mr. Grant who was present at the meeting distributed scientific statistics and studies as proof "against the humanity of the negro."[9] A master elocutionist, Douglass used the stark example of himself—his powerful rhetorical capabilities, his "face," and "his entire physical conformation"—to refute Grant's argument.[10] Turning to the assembled audience, he demanded of them: You "judge between me and that gentleman [Mr. Grant]. Am I a man?"[11] This exchange and especially Douglass's closing reference to his manhood calls to mind a more notorious contestation over gender that occurred the following year, in 1851. According to Dana Gage's synopsis of the Ohio Women Right's convention, Sojourner Truth towered, had a commanding air about her, and consistently drew attention to the problem and plight of black womanhood through her oft-repeated question "Ar'n't I a woman?"[12] Cognizant of the biblical arguments against black humanity, Truth used references to biblical women to authorize her voice and the fact that she could labor as much "as any man" to reset the premium of the burden and labor of black females. On a separate occasion, at a meeting Truth convened in Indiana in 1858, the female itinerant preacher found herself challenged outright as a man and not a woman. Before removing herself backstage to undergo a breast exam by white women present at this event, Truth masterfully exposed the undercurrent of sexualization, incest, and the desire for access to black female bodies that was fueling her accusers. She invited them to suck at her breasts, offered to reveal her bosom before all persons assembled, and compared the men present to white babies sucking at the breast of a plantation nursemaid.[13] Importantly, Truth's references to suckling, tasting, and ingesting allude to the social consumption of the black female caregiver.

Issues of sexual access, physical exposure, and rape also informed Douglass's presentation, but he deflected "audience attention from the 'feminine' exposure of his body (taking off his shirt to reveal his scars)" by drawing their attention to "the 'masculine' display of his face," voice, and intellectual prowess.[14] Navigating through undercurrents of exposure/concealment, secrecy/revelation, Douglass offers his visage and commanding posture as a "'standing accusation' against the slaveholder fathers and their concealed sexual crimes."[15] Douglass was well aware that whites, even abolitionist whites, took pleasure and gratification in seeing black bodies exposed. In *My Bondage and My Freedom,* he observes that John A. Collins, general agent of the Massachusetts Anti-Slavery Society, would often introduce him as a "graduate from the peculiar institution . . . *with my diploma written on my back*."[16] He found himself consistently referred to as a "brand new fact," "property," "chattel," and a "thing" by abolitionists.[17] Collins and others would habitually caution Douglass against speaking with too much education in his voice: "Better have a *little* of the plantation manner of speech than not," they chided; "'tis not best that you seem too learned."[18] The irony of having to speak in this manner, from the so-called slave body, is that the most visceral truths pertaining to consumption and sexual maltreatment remained obscured. White men did not have to own up to their subtle phallic references and anxieties and their desires for a nurturing, consumable black male, phallic object. (I will come back to this connection among black masculinity, nurturing, and white male appetite as it recurs in Douglass's relations with white men.)

The naked, unintelligible slave body served as fodder for the white imagination. It allowed whites to entertain the idea of the Negro as the lady of races, as passively subject to the more aggressive will and ways of the European. It also reinforced the idea of the slave as infantile.[19] In relationship to abolitionist William Lloyd Garrison, Douglass wrote that he stood "something like that of a child to a parent," which hearkened back to Douglass's infantile relationships to cruel parental plantation masters.[20]

I place Douglass alongside Truth as a way of illuminating how they each had to negotiate an idea of black humanity linked ideologically and historically to issues of gender variance, sexual (homosexual) abuse, white appetite, and incestuous kindred relationships to white masters and their plantation progeny. In contrast to Truth, Douglass and black men in general dealt with such issues through diversion: They drew attention away from their bodies and their sexuality. Am I a man? Ar'n't I a woman? Each question informed the other and as questions rather than statements revealed a sense of gender instability both Douglass and Truth felt. We still do not know what to do with the reality of Truth's sexual molestation by one of her plantation mistresses or, more broadly, with the complex ways white women desired, hated, abused, and sexually lusted after black women on the plantation.[21] In the case of Douglass, who masterfully manipulated the desires and expectations of the white men in his audience, questions of effeminacy, sexual abuse, and sexual transgression form a template. Not speaking about these topics, titillating and chastising his male listeners with this common knowledge, make possible Douglass's claims to heroic masculinity.

Scholars of Douglass's life and work have tended to focus upon and emphasize the male aspects of Douglass's genealogy—his relationships to Garrison and Wendell Phillips; his relationships to Auld, Covey, and Sandy from the plantation; his depiction of his maternal legacy as the Egyptian pharaoh Ramses II. We should never forget that Douglass, a master linguist, always spoke in code. He always spoke to both sides of a gender fluidity that lay at the root of his epistemology and rhetorical self-fashioning. Given this fact of Douglass's rhetoric, I want to move, momentarily, into the murky, unstable regions of the question "Am I a man?" because I think that we have tended to presume too much about the fixity of Douglass's manhood. We have presumed too much, I feel, about Douglass's internal investment in being "a man," especially when he consistently employed female modes of speaking about sexual violation, personal mythology, and genealogy in his writing.

In addition to recording a masculine genealogy of experience, Douglass wrote to situate himself within a sublimated genealogy of female experience. As evidence of this female genealogy, I want to turn briefly to the notorious Aunt Hester scene first recounted in Douglass's *Narrative* and referenced in his last two autobiographies. Deborah McDowell has written that Douglass's graphic depiction of his aunt's abuse puts "him into a voyeuristic relation to the violence against slave women, which he watches, and thus enters into a symbolic complicity with the sexual crime he witnesses."[22] Likewise, Van Leer has interpreted this scene as marking the impenetrable boundary of Douglass's manhood. He writes: "As a male he is shut out from a knowledge of this uniquely female experience."[23] McDowell and Van Leer, each in different ways, presume a boundary of masculinity marked by female abuse, Van Leer suggesting even that Douglass was not sexually abused and was never subject to the struggles of sexual dominance that define his aunt's existence.[24] While I do not want to dismiss valid points that do speak to Douglass's overt self-fashioning and performing of masculinity for his reader, I want to insert a third reality. And that is that Douglass narrates Hester's graphic abuse because he intimately understood it and because it was the only way that he could reference his own struggles over sex, against sexual consumption, and against the master's quest for sexual dominance over the male slave's body.

The brutality and trauma of Douglass's narrative literally begins with the Hester scene. Up to that point, Douglass gives general information—a description of where he grew up and the details of his family life. A few pages into the narrative, the author assails us with the image of the aunt hanging from a meat hook in the kitchen: "After crossing her hands, he tied them with a strong rope, and led her to a stool under a large hook in the joist, put in for the purpose. He made her get upon the stool, and tied her hands to the hook. She now stood fair for his infernal purpose. Her arms were stretched up at their full length, so that she stood upon the ends of her toes."[25] Douglass alludes to the brutalizer's absence of "pure morals" and "virtue." In his depictions of the master's cursing of Hester, frequently calling her a "d----d b----h," and his outrage that she would go to see her lover from another plantation, Ned Roberts, Douglass gives us just enough information to understand the master's sexual motivations. While Douglass probably could have, he does not take from his memories a literal instance of rape. Slaves, male and female, never depicted the graphic details of rape. They alluded to it often, but out of concern with decorum and preserving the sensibilities of their readers, they never provided graphic sexual details.[26] By giving us a torture scenario laden with sexual tension (and the implicit understanding that Anthony has raped Hester in the past), Douglass brings us more immediately into the layered and complicated meanings of slave life. In this world, physical brutality is often informed by sexual violence and the dynamics of sexual domination.

Also important is the undercurrent of incest. Captain Anthony, the slave master, is Douglass's father, which Douglass knows at the time he pens the narrative. It is possible that Anthony's father raped Hester's mother, resulting in a kinship tie between the captain and Hester. Her "noble form" and "graceful proportions," unparalleled "among the colored or white women" of the neighborhood, allude to her mulatta racial status.[27] Douglass does not give enough details for the reader to know her exact parentage. One thing that we know from slave history, though, is that incestuous behavior on many plantations was generational, a pattern of behavior that the son learned from the plantation father or overseer. Hester may have had a blood tie to Anthony; she may have been the daughter of his father, his uncle, or some other male relative. If Hester and Anthony did share a blood tie, then the prospect of Douglass, cowering in the closet, fearing that he too might undergo the same type of punishment, takes on added meaning. He is not just speaking a child's terrors. Rather, he is honing in on the ways that this dynamic of sex and brutality unveils a dynamic of incest.[28]

Literally and metaphorically, then, Hester embodies a female genealogy for Douglass: a genealogy characterized by the body so debilitated and abused that it cannot speak, by incestuous desire, by the ritual sport of abuse, by gender ambiguity, and, most importantly, by the spectacle of white male appetite and hunger. It is no coincidence that Hester's beating takes place in the kitchen and that Anthony, like the master who beat Henry Bibb's wife, seems as though he would "rather paddle a female than eat when he was hungry."[29] Hester is hung up on a meat hook. Her pooled blood and flesh particles commingle with sites of food preparation, with the whole enterprise of feeding and sustaining life on the plantation.

Hester brings into focus the multiple meanings of plantation torture and the difficulty of interpreting the scars and pain that result. As I showed earlier, in the example with Douglass speaking about black humanity before an all-male audience, Douglass maintained a poignant awareness of the ways in which the naked, exposed body could work against him, diffusing his claims to representative manhood. The difficulty of speaking about the body, as I demonstrate earlier, shaped his early encounters with proprietary abolitionists.[30] Early on in his public speaking career, Douglass refused abolitionists and the audience they generated access to his body. Touring throughout Europe with Garrison, before the publication of his first narrative, Douglass replaced his body with that of his cousin Henny: "Douglass frequently employed his cousin Henny to act out the role of female victim as an ancillary to his antislavery speeches, while also displaying ostentatiously a variety of whips, chains, and other tools of slavery, so as to make manifest the violence of a system that was often described elsewhere in more euphemistic terms."[31] Douglass does exactly what McDowell asserts; he uses the mother and the female body as the vehicle that ensures his speakerly authority. In this way, the mother/woman's silence precipitates the male/son's ability to speak.[32] Henny shows, embodies, and demonstrates slavery, but it is Douglass who narrates and translates the body. He performs this same narration and translation on behalf of Hester. The effect of this gesture is that within the larger culture, Douglass comes to embody slavery, to take on the role of "paradigmatic slave," a gesture that was "part of linguistic convention and a general cultural tendency to privilege maleness."[33]

Douglass was not the only black male author from his time period to use black female sex and torture in this manner. Francis Foster notes that from William Wells Brown's character of "Clotel to [Alex Haley's] Kizzy, our most frequent images of slave women are as victims of illicit sexual intercourse and as childless mothers."[34] According to Foster, the reason black men gravitated to such depictions of black women during slavery and after is that the selling of children and the raping of women were actual events and the genre of the slave narrative defined women in terms of manners, morals, and motherhood. Anticipating McDowell's observations, Foster sees black men during slavery using female sex and abuse to foreground their manhood and natural paternal rights.[35] Foster's observations show that Douglass's use of the black female was not an individual occurrence. Rather, it was symptomatic of a culture of nineteenth-century black masculinity and slave narrative rhetoric.[36]

McDowell writes of a "latent grammar" operating beneath Douglass's "descriptions of the mother." McDowell refers mostly to Douglass's effacing of his maternal legacy and using black maternal figures in his narratives to advance his claims to rugged individualism and self-made genius.[37] While this is true, there is also another implication of this latent grammar, and that is that Douglass consistently writes of black female abuse and sexualization in order to locate the unspeakable dimensions of his own sex and embodied knowledge within this latent framework. As scholars, we have tended to read Douglass's narratives at the levels of rhetorical performance, convention, and sign. If rhetoric is the cumulative effect of oration, then grammar parses the finer units and the even finer components of these that enable this effect. A grammatical reading of Douglass's life and work begs that we draw closer, paying greater attention to mechanics—to details of body proximity, nuance, subterfuge, and male and female modes of speaking.

Taking the idea of grammar literally, we should know that it is from women, such as Sophia Hugh, that Douglass first gains the rudimentary structure of the language: She teaches him the letters of the alphabet, to spell words of three or four letters, and to pronounce words from the Bible.[38] It is her husband, Mr. Hugh, who breaks in on this opportunity for Douglass and forbids his wife to continue instruction. Ironically, from Master Hugh's lecture forbidding his reading, Douglass receives his first "decidedly antislavery lecture."[39] Sophia's gesture toward teaching the rudiments of the language and her husband's negative response teach Douglass the first rules of the social grammar: inversion and subterfuge. He will apply these tools when he goes on to trick young boys into teaching him English by challenging their intellects, exchanging food for grammar lessons, and mimicking the letter system used to mark crates at the ship yard. Moreover, in the second narrative, *My Bondage and My Freedom*, Douglass reveals that his mother could read and attributes his love of reading and the creative means of acquiring literacy to her: "I am . . . happy, to attribute," he says, "any love of letters I possess . . . *not* to my admitted Anglo-Saxon paternity, but to the native genius of my sable, unprotected, and uncultivated *mother*."[40] As with Hester, Captain Anthony sexually violated Douglass's mother, perhaps even subjected her to the same manner and style of abuse. The text of the page and the text of the female body are coterminous. For Douglass, learning to read and speak the written word would always intersect with speaking from, around, and through sexual abuse and sexual consumption, lending an entirely different interpretation to McDowell's notion of a "latent grammar" informing Douglass's engagement with the black mother/woman.

## Male Daughter

Scholars have had a challenging time deciphering Douglass's public letter written to his former slave master, Thomas Auld, in 1848. William
S. McFeely, the Douglass biographer, refers to the letter as "one of the
strangest pieces in the literature of American slavery."[41] What makes
this letter so strange is the fact that Douglass speaks vicariously through
the voice and body of a young white daughter. Added to this, he alludes
to a relationship—a very intimate, erotic relationship—between himself and his former master in this female voice. One gets the sense of
Douglass and his former master as estranged natural enemies on one
hand and, on the other, as intimate sharers of a deep, binding secret.
When one thinks about this letter written by Douglass as a coded way
of speaking about his own rape, his own body through female metaphor, it does not appear strange at all. Instead, it serves as an example of
how Douglass's overt grammatical gestures were oftentimes informed
by latent, inverted references to his own sex and sexualized treatment.
The occasion for writing the letter is the anniversary of Douglass's
emancipation. Celebrating himself in his own venue, the *North Star*
newspaper, Douglass gives his own synopsis of his liberation and what
it means to him, three years removed from a life of bondage. Addressing Auld in 1848, he writes:

> Sir—The long and intimate, though by no means friendly, relation which
> unhappily subsisted between you and myself, leads me to hope that you
> will easily account for the great liberty which I now take in address-
> ing you in this open and public manner. . . . I have selected this day on
> which to address you, because it is the anniversary of my emancipa-
> tion. . . . How, let me ask, would you look upon me, were I, some dark
> night, in company with a band of hardened villains, to enter the pre-
> cincts of your elegant dwelling, and seize the person of your own lovely
> daughter, Amanda, and carry her off from your family, friends, and all
> the loved ones of her youth—make her my slave—compel her to work
> and take her wages— . . . more and still more horrible, leave her unpro-
> tected—a degraded victim to the brutal lust of fiendish overseers who
> would pollute, blight, and blast her fair soul—rob her of all dignity—
> destroy her virtue, and annihilate in her person all the graces that adorn

the character of virtuous womanhood! I ask how would you regard me, if such were my conduct?[42]

What has stuck many as immediately strange is Douglass's slipping between a speaking "I" and a speakerly "her," essentially his easy transition between his black male body and voice and the voice and body of a young white plantation mistress. In particular, for McFeely, most strange is "the fantasy of the rape of Amanda, the daughter of Thomas and Lucretia, whom Douglass remembered both as a child Auld cherished and as one who had been a kind of young friend."[43]

Others, reading against the grain of the letter, have hinted that Amanda is a metaphor for Douglass's own ravishing at the hands of white men.[44] I agree with this perspective and feel that what Douglass attempts to convey through this letter are the powerful ways in which he and Auld share a union in body and soul, the fact that they share "a terrible calamity" that has made them both "kin."[45] Were Douglass, hypothetically speaking, Auld's daughter, such acts committed against him by Auld and other men of his class would qualify as acts of incest.

Keeping the letter to Auld in mind and returning to the *Narrative*, we find a direct correlation between the sacrifice of the daughter to "the brutal lust of fiendish overseers" and "the rape" of Douglass at the hands of the slave breaker Covey. A short time after being sent to Covey, Douglass is given the responsibility of herding the oxen. While standing at the gate to Covey's plantation, the oxen grow excited and rush through the gate, tearing their cart to pieces and almost crushing Douglass against the gate. A livid Covey discovers his demolished property. In his anger, he orders Douglass to strip down nude in preparation for a beating: "He ordered me to take off my clothes. I made him no answer. . . . He repeated his order. I still made him no answer, nor did I move to strip myself. Upon this he rushed at me with the fierceness of a tiger, tore off my clothes, and lashed me till he had worn out his switches, cutting me so savagely as to leave marks visible for a long time after."[46] Douglass makes much of the pleasure and excitement that Covey receives from such seasoning rituals. The suggestive nudity, the tearing into flesh, the physical climaxing, and the wearing out of lash and clothing all suggest a type of sexual violation.

In *My Bondage and My Freedom*, references to ravishment recur. In another instance, among many, Covey tears into Douglass even more viciously, causing Douglass to proclaim: "Had I escaped from a den of tigers, I could not have looked worse."[47] After this beating, Douglass escapes from Covey with the intention of going to Auld, showing him the horrific proof of his condition, and seeking his intercession: "I had begun to hope that my master would now show himself in a nobler light than I had before seen him. But I was disappointed. I had jumped from a sinking ship into the sea; *I had fled from the tiger to something worse.*"[48] In this passage, we have a direct correlation between the master who prostitutes his daughter to the "brutal lust of fiendish overseers" and Auld himself. Whereas Covey is true to his nature, bloodthirsty and predatory by virtue of his vocation and temperament, Auld is an altogether different animal. The letter makes clear that what makes Auld even more reprehensible, more immoral than Covey, is the fact that there is a blood tie, a clandestine kinship that binds him to Douglass. Covey's crime is rape, but Auld's is incest. He takes the ultimate pleasure and gain from Douglass's violation, the breaking of his slave reinforcing his genteel southern standing, his authority and affluence among plantation-owning peers.

Covey makes delight and sport of Douglass. He tortures him at least once a week for six months: "The reader has to but repeat, in his own mind, once a week, the scene in the woods, where Covey subjected me to his merciless lash, to have a true idea of my bitter experience there, during the first period of the breaking process through which Mr. Covey carried me."[49] Following this passage, and in numerous places throughout Douglass's narrative, he insinuates that much worse than what he can describe occurred on Covey's plantation. "I have no heart," he admits, "to repeat each separate transaction. . . . Such narration would fill a volume much larger than the present one. I aim only to give the reader a truthful impression of my slave life, without unnecessarily affecting him with harrowing details."[50] Up to this point, I have suggested that sexual violation is metaphorically present in Douglass's narrative, but I think it important to consider that Douglass may have in fact been literally raped. For what could be more harrowing in description than the blood-soaked scenes that he describes? What details, missing from all three volumes of his autobiographies, could fill additional volumes?

A genre of short story and novels about slaves that became popular at the end of the eighteenth century is implicitly referenced in Douglass's narratives. In this tradition of writing, Europeans and white Americans graphically depicted the rape of enslaved males through language and metaphors similar to those used in Douglass's narrative. Joseph Lavallée's *Le nègre comme il ya pue de blancs* (*The Negro As There Are Few White Men*) is a perfect example of this tradition. Lavallée, a French Montesquian, published *Le nègre* in 1790. That same year other authors translated the text into English and serialized it in magazines in England and the United States. The protagonist of Lavallée's novel, Itanoko, is a West African man captured by French slavers off the Gold Coast of West Africa and taken into slavery. Lavallée's text was a highly sexualized treatment of the African and European colonial relation. Ship hands consistently remarked upon Itanoko's physicality and imagined themselves bedding the African. His nakedness and the size of his genitalia are noted. Itanoko engages in a romantic friendship with the ship captain's son. The ship captain intends to sell Itanoko "into a position of sexual service," but before selling him, cannot restrain the desire to sample the slave himself. Itanoko describes Urban, the white slaver, as a "ravisher," a "perfidious ravisher" who was "struck by my comeliness."[51] Urban feels compelled to "violate what is most sacred among men."[52] Itanoko describes his rape in animal-like metaphors, saying: I "bore resemblance to a man, who, weary with struggling with a *tiger*, that threatened his life, would fall into a voluptuous sleep, between the clutches of the monster."[53] John Saillant described Itanoko as a prototype for the "black man who appeared between 1790 and 1820 in antislavery narratives, essays, and poems . . . deserving benevolence but denied it by his white masters." "This sentimentalized 'poor negro,'" he clarifies, "on American soil, became an eroticized 'friend,' echoing the homoeroticism of classical martial virtue as well as gesturing toward nineteenth-century blackface and its interracial homoerotics."[54]

Douglass, as disenfranchised friend and one abolitionists ally with, definitely writes as a "sentimentalized poor negro." Furthermore, Itanoko's allusions to struggling with a tiger cast light on the sexual implications of similar details in Douglass's narrative. Even if Douglass did not read Lavallée's story (though it is possible that he did, either in American serialized form or during his time spent in England with Garrison), abolitionists read the story in serialized form in U.S. magazines.[55] Douglass wrote to a community of readers on both sides of the Atlantic that would have implicitly understood his allusions to that most unspeakable outrage—male rape. Furthermore, it was common within the U.S. sentimental tradition to refer to rape through animal metaphors, such as tigers and wolves. In *Red Rock* (1898), Thomas Nelson Page describes the rape of a white woman by a black man as "a single tiger-spring," as "black claws" sinking into a "soft white throat."[56] Abolitionists and the larger educated American readership would have immediately recognized Douglass's numerous references to rape and been able to read between the lines of the *Narrative* to ascertain that Douglass had probably been raped by Covey or other males in the plantation community.

Hazel Carby makes a useful point regarding how we think about rape on and off the plantation and at different moments in American history: "Rape . . . should not be regarded as a transhistorical mechanism of women's oppression but as one that acquires specific political or economic meanings at different moments in history."[57] Carby refers here to the need to distinguish the political import of black women raped on plantations from black women raped during the Reconstruction era in the South as a means of economic and social control.

Her statement, though, applies also to the subject of male rape. We have tended to regard rape as happening only to biological females. In black uplift discourse, the phallus and castration of the phallus are always emphasized. Yet what does it mean that Douglass, reticently in his first narrative and more directly in his second and third narratives and in his letter to Auld, calls our attention to the subject of male rape?

I find that what we get, in part, through Douglass's depictions of rape is his understanding of rape as definitionally linked to a culture of consumption. From Hester being tempered and flesh tendered in the Anthony kitchen to perpetrators depicted as tigers and wolves, Douglass emphasizes how rape and sexual violence are a means of satiating a cultivated white appetite for black flesh. Southern slavery apologist George Fitzhugh explained the political economy of slave consumption in the following manner: "The use of an article is only a proper subject of charge when the article is consumed in the use; for this consumption is the consumption of the labor of the lender or hirer, and is the exchange of equal amounts of labor for each other."[58] Thought of as an object of labor, as labor itself, in the mind of many slave owners, the slave could be completely consumed with no moral repercussions. Rape in this context serves as an index for a larger culture of consumption, the sex act being a means to take self from the slave and ritualistically consume this taken self.

This subtext of sex and consumption lends an entirely different meaning to constant references to female rape in black male writings. Surely it tells us something about the nature and confines of black masculinity in the nineteenth century, specifically about the impossibility of translating black male sexual abuse into usable political currency. The raped black female/emasculated black male dyad aside, black men among themselves held each other to a strict code of masculinity that entailed never being sexual subjects and defining their masculine relationship to one another through black female violation. Writing to the tribe of black husbands and fathers, in *Walker's Appeal . . . to the Coloured Citizens of the World*, David Walker implored: "Oh! my coloured brethren, all over the world, when shall we rise from this death-like apathy?—And be men!!"[59] Walker implicitly defined black manhood as the ability to protect wives and mothers from rape and other forms of abuse.[60]

For men like Douglass and Walker, the subjects of female rape and the larger institution of slavery linked implicitly to the issue of social consumption. Walker never lived as a slave. He was born to a free mother and an enslaved father in Wilmington, North Carolina. Yet he understood slavery as fundamentally a system of appetite and consumption. In *Walker's Appeal*, he writes: "They keep us miserable now, and call us their property, but some of them will have enough of us by and by—*their stomachs shall run over with us; they want us for their slaves, and shall have us to their fill.*"[61] For Walker, social consumption is equal to social death, "a death-like apathy."[62] The outcome of black persons continually fed into the glut of slavery is that they will cease to exist, literally, psychologically, and spiritually. Already in their death-like apathy, Walker finds that black men have faded from their lives and from natural agency. Walker invokes the female body as womb and vessel of racial continuity, subtly connecting this aspect of black female anatomy to social consumption: "(viz. we cannot help the whites murdering our mothers and our wives)," he says.[63] He ties racial continuity to the female anatomy. Black male rape, the particulars of black male consumption, and black male reproductive capacity do not figure into Walker's cosmos. In this worldview, the black woman symbolizes body and sex and the black male embodies the opposite values—reason, action, and virility. The black male does not have a reproductive capacity, and he also has no strongly defined interiority.

Douglass writes within a similarly closed circuit, alluding to himself as erotically consumed but finally positioning himself outside this dynamic through his notorious battle with Covey, his acquired literacy, and his eventual escape from slavery. The letter written to Auld and Douglass's descriptions of ravishment at the hands of Covey, though, disrupt this genealogy and urge us to rethink this idea of the feminine as external to black male experience. Might the allusions to himself as daughter and as sexually vulnerable be indicators of a regenerative capacity, an ability to regenerate self that elided the larger culture of sexual and psychic consumption? Along this same line, might Douglass have revealed (at the same time that he concealed) how his master related to him and saw him as a daughter or as a feminized sexual conquest? Whites were fond of referring to him as "the only perfectly pronounced and complete specimen in the world of his color, kin and kind."[64] As a youth, the race leader carried a newspaper clipping around that described him in romantic terms as a uniquely American creature, a natural outcome of the fated American experiment: "Mount Caucuses [and] the mountains of the Moon were joined with our Indian wilderness to mix the strain of blood from three races in his veins and produce a peculiar individuality with no antecedent or copy of his traits."[65] Evoking at once savagery, the feminine allure of the natural world, and the danger of colonization (of occupying a foreign territory), this article served as a reminder that Douglass's masculinity was an open-ended question that could be just as easily deployed by the state and the abolitionist cause.[66]

This discussion picks up many of the themes of male rape that I earlier elucidated, the ways in which and reasons that black male rape has remained a categorical impossibility and therefore impossible to speak about. On political and rhetorical levels, the subject of black male rape has always implied much more than the sex act or sexual preference. Douglass's letter and, in his personal narrative, his abuse under Covey convey the subject of male rape as layered through with issues of black/ white kinship, gender variance and ambiguity, and the conundrum of same-sex reproduction. Naturally, when we have thought about the

rape of black women during slavery we have thought in terms of progeny or reproductive capacity. Our limited concepts of black male biology and interiority have inhibited our thinking on the topics of black
male emotional and erotic life and, more specifically, black men having
the ability to generate life. A part of what I am urging and will reinforce
in the next section of this chapter is that we expand our notions of black
experience and cultural formation to include black men as agents of
reproduction, sexual subjectivity, and effeminate values, among other
categories of experience.

## Mapping Mother Hunger

In the final phase of this chapter, I want to dwell more fully upon the
idea of the black male interior. The themes of emotional, psychic, and
spiritual hunger have historically constituted female domains of experience. Within nineteenth-century rhetoric, men do not speak, at least
overtly, in terms of hungering, needing to be filled emotionally or otherwise. It is like an undiscovered, mysterious land, this region of black
male interiority that we suspect exists but that we have little concrete
evidence of, few artifacts with which to verify its existence. In Douglass's
writings, mother loss and mother hunger (the desire for the mother, the
desire for an intimate familial touch, to know one's origins and tribal
legacy) serve as emotional guideposts that help us to understand where
and how Douglass hungered and from where within himself he transformed this potentially self-consuming hunger. In my final analysis, I
read this mother hunger, beyond the physical loss of his mother, as a
fecund place within Douglass's self from which he gives birth to the
promise of the republic, himself as masculine icon, and all of the emotional and psychic hungers that he carries out of slavery.

Although he sees very little of her, Douglass's mother leaves an
imprint on his emotions and memory that will later permeate and
shape his masculine identity and internal landscape. In the *Narrative*,
he recalls that in spite of the risk of death and the threat of potential
beatings, his mother frequently traveled miles to visit him at night:

> She made her journeys to see me in the night, traveling the whole dis-
> tance on foot, after the performance of her day's work. She was a field

hand, and a whipping is the penalty of not being in the field at sunrise, unless a slave has special permission from his or her master to the contrary—a permission which they seldom get.[67]

As an infant, Douglass cannot be aware of the hardships and fatigue that his mother undergoes to be with him. The four or five times that he sees her he feels only her warm comfort. They communicated very little during these nightly rituals: "She was with me in the night. She would lie down with me, and get me to sleep, but long before I awaked she was gone."[68] And long before Douglass could awaken as an adult man to the great pains and obstacles his mother overcame to see him, she dies: "Death soon ended what little we could have while she lived, and with it her hardships and suffering. She died when I was about seven years old, on one of my master's farms, near Lee's Mill." [69] Adding to the pain of this loss is the fact Douglass was not allowed "to be present during her illness, at her death, or burial."[70] A pattern of loss and unrequited need is set in Douglass.

Plantation culture and masters cultivated this emotional and natal hunger. Such hunger, arguably more than physical acts of torture, conditioned slave psyches and bodies for larger acts of social and literal consumption. In the *Narrative*, Douglass describes how he, his sister Eliza, and his Aunt Priscilla were kept in a state of perpetual hunger and starvation: "A great many times have we poor creatures been nearly perishing with hunger, when food in abundance lay mouldering in the safe and smoke-house, and our pious mistress was aware of the fact; and yet that mistress and her husband would kneel every morning, and pray that God would bless them in basket and in store!"[71] In addition to starving Henny, Auld would frequently tie her up and whip her as pre-course to taking his meals: "I have known him to tie her up early in the morning, and whip her before breakfast; leave her, go to his store, return at dinner, and whip her again, cutting her in the places already made raw with his cruel lash," recalls Douglass.[72] What makes Henny so delectable to the master is the fact of her "being almost helpless."[73] Henny has no parents to protect and look out for her. Burned during a childhood accident, she has little use of her hands. Her state of deprivation slakes Auld's appetite and causes him to choose her, above all others, as the object of his morning and evening meal-taking rituals. Later in life, Douglass would experience a no less cruel form of starvation conditioning at the behest of Mrs. Lucretia Auld, the female head of the plantation. Often Mrs. Auld forced Douglass to sing for his food beneath her bedroom window: "When pretty severely pinched by hunger, I had a habit of singing, which the good lady very soon came to understand as a petition for a piece of bread. When I sung under Miss Lucretia's window, I was very apt to get well paid for my music."[74] Making Douglass perform in the age-old role of the romantic singer, Mrs. Auld seemed to imagine him courting her or titillating her with his hungering pleas. She no doubt took pleasure in such remonstrations, which she encouraged and rewarded with food.

Many on the plantation implicitly understood this culture of hunger and deprivation as it was acted out in daily relations. Aunt Katy, the cook on the Anthony plantation, would frequently punish Douglass for a slight or an offense by making him "go all day without food."[75] Douglass would often fight the dog for scraps of food and bake stolen pieces of dried corn in the fire. Such acts of starvation wounded Douglass most deeply in his heart and soul. He writes of trying to keep his spirits up but eventually going out behind the kitchen wall to cry. Surprising Aunt Katy one day, Douglass's mother visits and witnesses her starving him. His mother has words with Katy. "That night," he says, "I learned as I had never learned before, that I was not only a child, but somebody's child. I was grander upon my mother's knee than a king upon his throne."[76] For Douglass, the worse starvation involved being emotionally cut off from and made to hunger for his mother's love and care. His mother literally and spiritually saves him from self-consumption (starvation) by affirming and feeding his sense of self. For that was the danger and underlying intention of the culture of consumption, to imprint slaves so deeply with hunger that they came to relate to themselves as essentially commodities and to also consume themselves with a litany of "soul devouring thought" and behaviors reinforced by the master's hungers and tastes.[77]

Despite the oppressive intentions of masters who facilitated this culture of hunger, enslaved persons often found the will to invert this structure, using their own hunger as a means of resistance and survival. The graphic example of Lavinia Bell conveys a sense of hunger as the will to survive. As punishment for running away from the plantation, Bell's master leaves her to hang in a tree by wire threads that cut into her flesh. She suffers starvation and the devouring presence of birds and other animals of prey. After days left in this condition, Bell makes a strategic choice; she attempts to tear out her eyes and eat them.[78] Douglass experienced such survivalist aspects of hunger as tied to the memory of and loss of his mother. Mother hunger informed his relationship with white male authority figures and heads of state. In the context of this hunger, white men took on maternal significances and roles in Douglass's life. This deep yearning for the feminine, in some instances, brought the same out of Douglass, who depicted himself and the heroic male figure as giving birth to the values and central tenets of the republic. Operating out of an essentially feminine praxis of survival, Douglass turns a potentially devouring legacy of slavery and emotional state of loss and longing into a self that is gender ambiguous and imbued with a regenerative capacity.

One of the last places one might expect to find residues of Douglass's mother loss and child need would be in his adult relationships to white men. From the mythic battle with Covey on, Douglass would have us believe that he approaches and quickly passes beyond the temporal and psychic territory of slavery. But even at the end of the *Narrative,* as Douglass intently pores over issues of the abolitionist newspaper *The Liberator* and prepares himself to enter fully into the abolitionist speaking circuit, he admits: "I felt myself a slave, and the idea of speaking to white people weighed me down."[79] Nine years later, white abolitionists would oppose Douglass's wish to start his own paper, referring to him as "a slave . . . assuming to instruct the highly civilized people of the North."[80]

These contemporary eruptions of slavery differed from the personal, sacred ways that Douglass carried slavery in his heart and mind. In a letter written to Harriet Tubman in 1868, Douglass refers to her and John Brown as consigned to his "sacred memory" of slavery.[81] The sacred memory of slavery arose from a tender place in Douglass connected to his mother. Remarking on the death of his mother and the fact that he was denied permission to attend her funeral in *My Bondage and My Freedom,* he stated that

> scenes of sacred tenderness, around the deathbed, never forgotten, and which often arrest the vicious and confirm the virtuous during life, must be looked for among the free, though they sometimes occur among the slaves. It has been a life-long, standing grief to me, that I knew so little of my mother; and that I was so early separated from her.[82]

This sacred, maternal memory is connected to feelings of safety, the relieving of the slave child's suffering, and a longed-for home space. When he felt in this way toward white male allies, such as Garrison, John Brown, and President Abraham Lincoln, Douglass usually also romanticized these men, describing them as perfect examples of "beauty."[83] Douglass reenacts this need for home and safety in *The Life and Times of Frederick Douglass*. Approximately ten years after Douglass has bested the brutal Covey, the race leader reaches yet another milestone in his quest for masculine identity. President Abraham Lincoln invites him to a party at the executive mansion in honor of his reelection. Douglass feels overwhelmed with the presence of the elite there and enthralled by the power of this historic moment. He writes: "I had for some time looked upon myself as a man, but now in this multitude of the elite of the land, I felt myself a man among men."[84] Although under much different circumstances, this is another instance from Douglass's life when the presence of white men, of white male power and civilization, bring on an epiphany in the race leader. This newly discovered sense of manhood is only magnified by the presence of the white female friend, Mrs. Dorsey, who has agreed to accompany him on this journey. Hand in arm, the black Douglass and the white Mrs. Dorsey approach the entrance to the White House.

At the entrance, Douglass's momentary reverie quickly shatters. The policemen stationed at the door to the president's mansion inform him that they are "to admit no persons of [his] color" and just as abruptly take him by his arm and order him to stand back.[85] Suddenly, Douglass is outside. No longer a man among men, the officers (as policing extensions of the state) remind him of his "nigger" social status. No wonder the black men he invited refused his invitation. Used to such treatment from whites in low and high places, they did not look forward to such "discomfiture," as they described it.[86] Undaunted by the officer's racism, Douglass and his ally refuse to leave. A passerby recognizes Douglass and rushes within to inform President Lincoln of his guest's detainment at the door.

Lincoln immediately sends word to allow Douglass entrance to the mansion. Douglass and his companion are escorted into the spacious East Room of the president's mansion. Douglass is taken aback by the luxuriousness of the scene, the bounty and plenty reflected in the architecture, the drink, the suited and gowned personages, the food, and the fraternity. He recalls "a scene of such elegance such as in this country I had never witnessed before."[87] Lincoln restores Douglass's masculinity and Douglass in turn responds with a description of Lincoln as rising "like a mountain pine high above all the others" gathered in that East Room. Seeing Lincoln stirs deep feelings in Douglass. Lincoln counters his feelings of outsiderhood, of isolation with his "grand simplicity, and home-like beauty."[88] Lincoln's eyes and mouth move Douglass to poetic description: "His eyes had in them the tenderness of motherhood, and his mouth and other features the highest perfection of a genuine manhood."[89] Douglass's childhood dreams and maternal hunger are mapped onto the larger American dream and the White House as home. Longing after and eulogizing Lincoln's maternal bosom, Douglass asks: "What are sweet of peace, what are visions of the future?" Like his very own laboring mother, Douglass finds in Lincoln's face a "blending of suffering with patience and fortitude."[90] Douglass even romanticizes the president's lips, imagining them as perfect, aesthetically pleasing, and the most genuine specimens of manhood.[91]

A part of what made Lincoln so attractive to Douglass was the president's apparent commitment to freeing enslaved persons. Both Tubman and Brown of sacred memory sacrifice their lives for enslaved persons. It is something of the slave in Douglass, the one who has had to constantly battle for freedom and a place to rest, who sees finally in Lincoln the maternal bosom, an emblem of a final resting place. He relates to Lincoln as a romanticizing male child, a male-to-female romantic object. Lincoln is in turn depicted as male patriarch, as maternal figure, as fecund female earth. The undercurrent of mother hunger blurs gender boundaries and causes Douglass to transfer to Lincoln a measure of unrequited love and feelings of mother loss. Descriptions of Mrs. Lucretia Auld years earlier on the Auld plantation prefigure his descriptions of Lincoln. Mrs. Auld, he writes, "had bestowed upon me such words and looks as taught me that she pitied me, if she did not love me."[92]

In a related instance aboard a steamer, Douglass encounters Edward Marshall, a California congressman. He describes Marshall in terms that are both deific and evoke the natural world. The catalyst for Douglass when describing Marshall in this manner is a racist incident aboard the steamer. The captain orders Douglass to be physically removed from the dining room. Marshall rebuffs the steward with eyes "full of fire."[93] Douglass sees "lightning flash" and imagines this saving individual as a deity of the sky with "golden hair and fiery eyes" whose voice "resounded like a clap of summer thunder."[94] In this instance, Douglass casts himself in the more effeminate role, describing Marshall as "chivalrous," "gallant," and possessed of "generous and manly qualities."[95] Not coincidentally, Marshall has just come from Kentucky, where he visited his black mammy. "I was nursed at the breasts of a colored mother," he admits.[96]

Both Lincoln and Marshall intervene on behalf of the freed slave. Their allegiance to abolitionism evokes in Douglass romantic feelings that range from the maternal cast to a glorification of the white male as the emblem of the natural world and the natural order of things. Marshall does not take on the sacred significance and emotional complement of the black mother. Instead, black mother as emblem of infantile hunger (the white man nursing at the black woman's breasts) is cause for shared affection between the two men.

Douglass was in a phase of his life when he believed that proximity to black nobility and empathy could change whites. He would realize, though, after finding out about Lincoln's support of the Fugitive Slave Act of 1850, that northern whites had used him and the enslaved person's cause to further their nationalist and other political aims. At the undraping of a bust carved in Lincoln's honor years later, Douglass would describe Lincoln not as a caring, valiant romantic object but as one who had betrayed his love and affections. Speaking before hundreds of white persons at this honorary occasion, Douglass regrettably reminds those gathered of Lincoln's hypocrisy and willingness to sacrifice black people. He says:

> He was ready to execute all the supposed guarantees of the United States Constitution in favor of the slave system anywhere inside the slave states. He was willing to pursue, recapture, and send back the fugitive slave to his master, and to suppress a slave rising for liberty, though his guilty master were already in arms against the Government.[97]

Lincoln's willingness to send a fugitive slave back to his master was most painful to Douglass, who was himself an escaped slave. In this public address, Douglass speaks about how he, as a representative of the slave experience, felt betrayed by one he was so willing to love, admire, and seek solace in. Speaking to his white fellow citizens, Douglass admonishes:

> First, midst, and last, you and yours were the objects of his deepest affection and his most earnest solicitude. You are the children of Abraham Lincoln. We are at best only his step-children; children by adoption, children by forces of circumstances and necessity. To you it especially belongs to sound his praises, to preserve and perpetuate his memory, to multiply his statues.[98]

Douglass speaks of white people as children—Lincoln's true children—and of black people as stepchildren. This statement hearkens back to the problematic issue of kinship between white and black men during slavery. Douglass is a free man, a man of agency and affluence, but still the historical problem of relatedness and all of its emotional and sexual implications bear down upon him in the present.

It is during slavery that the orator first develops the habit of romanticizing and identifying himself with the white male aristocracy. When he leaves the Covey plantation, he contrasts Covey's membership in the demeaned overseer class to that of a Mr. Freeland. Freeland acts toward him with the "sentiment of honor," a "sense of justice," and a "feeling of humanity."[99] Mr. Freeland belongs to that class of slaveholder admired and affectionately thought of by the slaves: "Slaves were not," Douglass notes, "insensible to the whole-souled qualities of a generous, dashing slave-holder, who was fearless of consequences, and they preferred a master of this bold and daring kind, even with the risk of being shot down for impudence."[100] Following this logic of aristocratic refinement, one can understand how Douglass found in Lincoln the perfect embodiment of the ennobled father figure.

In reality, Lincoln's response to black people ranged from repulsion to exotic fascination. He enjoyed minstrel culture and had minstrel troupes come to the White House to entertain him and also was known to attend shows when he visited Chicago.[101] Most whites presumed that white blood gave the Negro higher intelligence, beauty, and more evolved sensibilities. The very high cultural standards that Douglass used to distinguish himself from the base Negro are the same standards that make him attractive to and ultimately dispensable to the president. By calling attention to their kinship bond, Douglass reveals how deeply intertwined issues of relatedness between black and white men with the subject of nation formation are for him.

Lincoln fails, as the father-mother figure, to live up to Douglass's natal and maternal expectations. And he confirms in Douglass the permanence of his orphaned, homeless social status. As maternal caretaker and sustainer of the central tenets of the republic, Douglass expects that Lincoln will give rebirth to the slave, not just freeing him in word from slavery but birthing him into a social and political body that cancels out the social death of slavery. By the time Douglass makes the speech before the Freedmen's Monument and begins years later to work on *The Life and Times*, he had seen Reconstruction efforts go drastically awry. The Freedman's Savings Bank fiasco, the stealing of land promised to freed persons, and the erection of Jim Crow laws served as indicators of how the nation seemed intent on keeping the slave buried—freed from the coffin of slavery but socially dead in all other respects.[102]

Driven by the need for a collective rebirth of himself and the masses of black people, Douglass would ultimately locate this regenerative capacity in himself. Mother hunger—the sense of being orphaned from the nation, the desire for intimate belonging, and his own personal legacy of sexual violation—would fuel and defines Douglass's attempts at self- and national rebirth. Beginning to realize an interconnection between the rebirth of the nation and personal rebirth, Douglass broke from white abolitionists. In opposition to predominant abolitionist views, Douglass became "convinced that there was no necessity for dissolving the 'union between the northern and southern states.'"[103] He felt that the vote was power and that the "Constitution of the United States not only contained no guarantees in favor of slavery, but, on the contrary, it is, in its letter and spirit, an anti-slavery instrument, demanding the abolition of slavery as a condition of its own existence, as the supreme law of the land."[104]

Breaking from abolitionists and feeling more freed from his slave past did not mean that Douglass did not have to contend with white male desires, with white male appetites within a culture of consumption. If anything, Douglass understood better how the plantation was as "a little nation of its own" and how the nation operated in many respects like the plantation.[105] Douglass came to a much fuller understanding of the plantation as an incestuous household/nation and the larger republic as a social grave and promise of stillborn birth. As I argued earlier in this chapter, throughout history black men have typically imagined this dynamic of birth and domesticity in their writings in oppressive female terms. Douglass does this in all of his autobiographies, through depictions of black women raped, especially his mother and his aunts. But what I want to draw our attention to is how this potentially fecund space was also depicted in his fiction and nonfiction writings as a male womb-type space, a regenerative space with capacity to give birth to self, nation, and a transformed citizenry. The idea was that if Douglass and black men like himself could give birth to the nation, then they could, on terms of their own, finally exist. It was a homosocial maternity that Douglass conceived that still largely excluded women and black female maternity on practical, feminist levels. Still, this gesture toward embodying his hunger for liberty and social acknowledgment points us to entirely new ways of thinking about racial legacy and black masculinity in the nineteenth century.

*The Heroic Slave*, Douglass's only published fictional work, teems with references to black male fecundity. Published in 1852, this text, in title and storyline, continues what would be Douglass's lifelong project of elevating and glorifying the heroic black male figure.[106] The hero of the story, Madison Washington, is a composite figured based partly on the leader of the revolt aboard the slave ship *Creole* and President George Washington. The story opens with the narrator having the reader "peer into the dark," a dark pregnant with liberty and the legacy of Patrick Henry, who "led all the armies of the American colonies through the great war for freedom and independence."[107] We are told that someone is "enveloped in darkness" and then taken into the searching dark, only to "return from the pursuit like a wearied and disheartened mother, (after a tedious and unsuccessful search for a lost child)."[108]

This maternal darkness takes on human form a few pages into the story when from the darkness Washington steps with "arms like polished iron;" a face "'black, but comely'"; "a brow as dark and as glossy as the raven's wing."[109] At the beginning of the story, it is Washington who prays in the darkness, who draws into his speaking John Listwell, a northern white man who feels compelled to stop, descend from his horse, and listen. Listwell (whom we might also think of as Listens Well), we learn, had "long desired to sound the mysterious depths of the thoughts and feelings of a slave."[110] As his eye catches hold of Madison in the shadows, he "tremble[s]" with terror and excitement. Washington's prayer titillates Listwell, who receives his remonstrations as a type of erotic climax: "He did not have to wait long. There came another gush from the same full fountain; now bitter, and now sweet."[111] Afterward, Washington takes on "a glow to his countenance" and teems with a "hope of freedom [that] seemed to sweeten . . . the bitter cup of slavery."[112] The fact that Washington ruminates on his wife, Susan, in the darkness and experiences anguish at the thought of having to leave her to escape north further highlights the clandestine, erotic sharing that Listwell experiences. He experiences Washington, and through Washington, the passion the enslaved man feels for his wife.

This copulating in the mysterious, impregnated dark results in a rebirth for Listwell. Washington leaves the pine forest and begins his trek North to freedom, but his white interloper is forever changed: "From this hour I am an abolitionist," he swears to himself; "I have seen enough and heard enough, and I shall go to my home in Ohio resolved to atone for my past indifference to this ill-starred race, by making such exertions as I shall be able to do, for the speedy emancipation of every slave in the land."[113] For all of its representational problems, which I will attend to shortly, this scenario is a striking break from the historical tradition of representing the black female body as the dark, chaotic interior of black experience. It is a unique moment through which we can imagine and begin to think about a politics of black male interiority and hunger. Moving beyond images of white males ravishing his body in the past and controlling the terms of erotic engagement, Douglass scripts a homoerotic interchange that is mutually beneficial. According to P. Gabrielle Foreman, at the time that Douglass pens his story, he "is acutely aware that white men are the only reader-citizens imbued with legal standing as witnesses; they are his only politically embodied readers; the only ones, that is, with a 'vote.'" So as a way of harnessing this political power, "Douglass attempts to seduce white male readers."[114]

Seduction is the means to constructing a new genealogy of American nativity based in the copulation of the black and white male. The character of Washington combines several strands of American radicalism in one person. He is a reference to the black plantation insurrectionist and to the founding revolutionary fathers of America, specifically George Washington and Patrick Henry. Before the House of Burgesses in 1775, Henry stated in his "Liberty or Death" speech: "Three millions of people armed in the holy cause of liberty, and in such a country that which we possess, are invincible by any force which our enemy can send against us."[115] This mandate for national security and fortitude remained unfulfilled in Douglass's mind with the continuance of slavery. Referencing the Henry speech in *The Life and Times*, he writes: "It was a great thing to achieve American independence when we numbered three millions, but it was a greater thing to save this country from dismemberment when it numbered thirty millions."[116] Douglass imagines the heroic male slave as the receptacle of the unrealized national vision Henry espoused.[117]

Douglass unites in his "womb" the opposite and contradictory forces of white paternity and black maternal legacy. Henry and Washington represent something of Douglass's own whiteness, his lifelong problematic relationship to white male paternal figures. Taking their seminal visions into himself, while problematic, is for Douglass the only choice if he is to make peace and home of an America plagued by white male immorality. Choosing to be a receptacle acknowledges as well the political reality of black people effeminized and eroticized by whites. Douglass's choice does not ameliorate the stigma and challenges of assuming a feminine posture. Rather, it serves as an example of one black man crafting agency and negotiating complex, fluid notions of gender at the same time that he experiences himself as circumscribed by these ideas.

There is a passage in *My Bondage and My Freedom* where Douglass refers to his mother as resembling an Egyptian pharaoh. He writes: "There is in 'Pritchard's Natural History of Man,' the head of a figure— on page 157—the features of which so resemble those of my mother, that I often recur to it with something of the feeling which I suppose others experience when looking upon the pictures of dear departed ones."[118] Some have questioned why Douglass chose to represent his mother with the image of a male pharaoh.[119] This is an important question, considering that in the same volume there are images of "Hindoo" women and northern and southern African types that would have been more appropriate and accurate examples of Douglass's mother.[120] If we think, though, of the image as a meshing of Douglass's maternal legacy with the reformation of the U.S. empire, then it makes sense. Douglass recasts his mother as ancestral figure and bridge to an ancient African royal lineage. By depicting his mother as Ramses II, not only does he ennoble her, he also establishes, by virtue of his bloodline, his natural right of claim to the American legacy.

This image of a male mother presented in the second and third installments of his autobiography reinforces how emotional natal needs confounded prevailing nationalist gender politics. Douglass's consistent move to externalize his natal hunger is instructive. It seems that implicitly he understood that in order to not be consumed by feelings of loss and the sense of emotional and spiritual dislocation that threatened him from without, he would have to actualize his emotional needs, his hungers. In the image of the male mother and his depictions of the fecund heroic male, we are shown how hunger facilitates a deeper grounding in geography and place and enables him to locate himself in history and in the context of national reformation. The heroic figure embodies Douglass's idea of the constitution as an essentially antislavery document. He conveys his ideas of "suffrage for black men" through this heroic male who is male and female, a combination of women's suffragist politics and male slave abolitionist strivings.[121] His hunger is male and female, or perhaps better understood as a cauldron of self and experience that syncretize the two. Hunger is power, or at least the means to accessing power encased within the discourse of nation. David Leverenz has noted that Douglass's "entrepreneurial" notion of manhood meant "not freedom so much as dominance and the fear of humiliation."[122] As I have argued throughout this chapter, there was no humiliation deeper or more unspeakable than the sexual humiliation suffered by one man at the hands of another. Black men found the femininizing outcomes of such abuse untenable, as they translated neither into the preferred dominance over nor access to the entrepreneurial benefits of American capitalism.

Yet the idea of Douglass as fecund and the image of the male mother suggest that things were not quite so simple. The image of the male mother is a syncretic figure that adds up, ultimately, to more than the sum of its parts. For example, while the male mother is a new emblem of the nation, it is also a deeply personal metaphor for Douglass, who himself/herself gives birth to this symbol of the new. The male mother is a coded representation of the ways that male-male relations for Douglass took form from a fluid sense of gender and the consistent goal of whites to make the male slave into an effeminate relational object.

From the framework of the male mother, we see that Douglass was aware of and acted from a place of gender indeterminacy or fluidity. If we acknowledge this complex facet of his self-awareness and representational politics, then we must also acknowledge a broader understanding of who Douglass was and what he means to us in the present. In the 1960s and 70s, historians and activists sought to recover Douglass "from the dark nineteenth-century past as the tradition's very own Representative Man."[123] At the end of the twentieth century, cultural critics and feminist scholars such as McDowell, Charles Clifton, and Foreman began to unpack Douglass's heroic masculinity and suggested a more complicated genealogy or genealogies of Douglass's masculinity and personal legacy. I am advocating that our newer scholarship on Douglass integrate and apply the complex vision we now have of his person and contribution. We should see him simultaneously as a heroic male; a male daughter; a fecund, birth-giving male; a male child who was raped; a striving and self-serving patriarch; and an ennobled father of black letters and liberation. If I had to choose a more central motivation fueling these multiple, overlapping, and intersecting identities, I would choose hunger over and beyond reason, falling back upon the female genealogy of hunger and consumption evinced in Douglass's maternal relations and in his own embodied feminine sensibilities. Hunger, as I am thinking of it, is logical, reasoning, and strategic. It is also embodied, sensate, and intuitive. Hunger is a mediating, alchemical ground, a point from which Douglass consistently translated what was felt and desired into reasoned action, rhetorical performance, and civic belonging (as problematic as this always was). It is out of Douglass's hunger and in response to forces that threatened to consume him that he dreamed, envisioned, and embodied a nation as complex, unresolved, and revisionary as himself.

4

Domestic Rituals of Consumption

David Walker, a major black abolitionist figure, acknowledged the capacity of slavery to consume black bodies and souls. In *Walker's Appeal*, Walker depicts a plantation reality where black men suffer emasculation. They can neither protect their wives and children nor can they themselves escape the all-encompassing power of whites whose malicious hunger, Walker says, "gnaws into our very vitals."[1] Walker describes the consumptive process as fundamentally an attack on male potency and phallic assertion: "They (the whites) know well, if we are *men*—" he says, "and there is a secret monitor in their hearts which tells them we are—they know, I say, if we *are* men, and see them treating us in the manner they do, that there can be nothing in our hearts but death alone, for them."[2] To Walker's thinking, docile and acquiescing black men are more easily consumed. He advocates instead the virile, radical black male. This male, he predicts, will glut and violently over-flow the consuming machine.

Nineteenth-century black male abolitionists tended to agree with Walker; they felt that only male virility and a strong paternal role could save black people from social consumption. I noted in chapter 3 how images of human consumption haunted Frederick Douglass. He described slavery as a living entity that wore "robes already crim-soned with the blood of millions, and even now feasting itself greed-ily upon our own flesh."[3] Everywhere Douglass turned he saw slavery literally and psychically consuming black people. In the battle between Covey and Douglass, we get Douglass's version of black male might and gladiator-like potency winning out over the white male parasite determined to suck all vitality from the slave. Another black abolitionist, John S. Jacobs, described slave owners and traders as "hungry heirs" who partook daily of a "feast of blood."[4] Jacobs's most painful memories of slavery center upon his emasculated and socially consumed father. He writes:

> To be a man, and not to be a man—a father without authority—a husband and no protector—is the darkest of fates. Such was the condition of my father, and such is the condition of every slave throughout the United States: he owns nothing, he can claim nothing. His wife is not his: His children are not his; they can be taken from him, and sold any minute, as far away from each other as the human fleshmonger may see fit to carry them.[5]

White abolitionists documented incidents of black children literally boiled alive, butchered, and fed to open fires.[6] They debated and deliberated about whether or not America was becoming a cannibal nation. Black men, though, as Jacobs demonstrates, strove to convey the private effects of human consumption. By situating these factual and philosophical considerations in the context of their personal demise, black men demonstrated how the culture of consumption robbed them of their masculinity, destroyed familial units and ties, and portended the literal extinction of the race.

Black men had good reason to worry about literal annihilation. Across the nation, whites predicted the extinction of and extermination of the Negro. For example, Midwestern economist George M. Weston predicted in 1857 that "when the white artisans and farmers want the room which the African occupies, they will take it not by rude force, but by gentle and gradual and peaceful processes. The Negro will disappear."[7] Others, of the religious persuasion, felt that "an inherited capacity for Christian persuasion . . . guaranteed the survival of the white race, and the lack of it condemned the Negro to extinction."[8] Where whites foresaw and depicted clean and innocent processes of natural selection, black men saw bloodshed and gluttonous consumption. William Wells

Brown described a man named Walker, "a Negro speculator, who was amassing a fortune by trading in the bones, blood, and nerves, of God's Children."[9] Solomon Northup, a free black man illegally captured and sold into slavery, linked the "gastronomical enjoyments" of whites and their entitlement to processes of consumption that involved starving, raping, and emasculating slaves.[10] In emphasizing black male virility and paternity, black men sought to counter this national death wish toward the Negro, which they experienced as intrinsically tied to their social consumption.

In this chapter, I want to complicate this idea of black male paternalism and radical insurgence as a final solution to social consumption because what such an assertion tended to imply was that only radical, paternal-type men could overcome or escape consumption. Along with radical black masculinity, black men emphasized traditional structures of the black family, reproduction, gender, and sexuality. As an example, the natural counterpart to the virile, insurgent black father was the black mother, whom most conceived of as the mistress to and caretaker of black civilization. In response to slavery's habit of consuming black people in body and soul, David Walker advocates the restoration of black female maternity and reproductive power. The regeneration and sustenance of the race resides in "mothers who bore the pains of death to give birth to us" and within "wives, whom we love as we do ourselves."[11] While this framing of the black male's social consumption was a useful uplift strategy, it limited then, and still does today, what we can know about the complex culture of consumption and the myriad ways black men resisted and grappled with the reality of their social consumption.

The textual focus of this chapter is Harriet Jacobs's slave narrative, *Incidents in the Life of a Slave Girl, Written by Herself.* The narrative offers many examples of literal, psychic, and erotic consumption. From slaves whose flesh is literally cooked to others fed alive to machines to still others starved into sexual submission and erotically consumed by masters, Jacobs depicts a shocking and haunting tableau of consumption and violence. Like her male contemporaries, Jacobs conceives of institutionalized consumption as a process that erodes familial ties, makes black men into "heathens" and "brutes," violates black female chastity, and is antithetical to the black uplift project. For her, the natural antidote to the culture of consumption she graphically depicts is black male virility, intelligence, and uplift spirit. In the narrative, men such as John Jacobs (her brother), Peter (a man who helps her escape), and her embattled father fulfill this role. She frequently refers to these men as "intelligent, enterprising, and noble hearted."[12] These men form a natural complement to the black maternal politics informing the narrative. It does not matter that she never successfully couples with a black man, that her father's loss of his wife contributes to his death, or that men must suffer torture and death to secure only a few fleeting moments with wives and children.[13] Such tragic losses underscore how slavery isolates loved ones from one another and makes individuals vulnerable (through the disruption of male/female conjugal unions and familial support systems) to processes of social consumption.

Jacobs structures her uplift politics around stereotypic nineteenth-century dyads of thought and experience, the most central dyad being the black maternal figure and the insurgent or suffering patriarch. On the one hand, this central male/female pairing and its outgrowths (male virility/sacrificing maternity, safety/familial union, chastity/racial continuity) enabled a politics of black survival. And on the other hand, this rigid male/female dynamic prevented access to deeper realities of black male experience, to black erotic life, and to a fuller range of black male survival strategies within a culture of consumption. Someone like Luke, a slave Jacobs depicts as sexually brutalized and socially consumed, has nothing, in Jacobs's presentation of him, to do with racial uplift, with an ennobled nineteenth-century black masculinity, or with black female sexual politics under slavery. Luke does not fit into the traditional male/female dynamic because he does not affect outright resistance, he is subject to his master's homoerotic desires, he registers as sexually ambiguous, and he undergoes a sustained and ritualized process of social consumption. According to the prevailing nineteenth-century discourse of manhood, Luke is not a man. And if we go along with Jacobs's interpretation of his life and circumstances of consumption, we can easily write him off as a casualty of white hunger and appetite.

In making Luke one of the focal figures of this chapter, I intend to argue the opposite of Jacobs's presumptions. I feel that Luke is a different type of representative black man who, because he does not fit neatly into prevailing gender and sexual dynamics, offers a nonconforming and complicated understanding of black male sensibility that we do not get from those black men who have come to us through history as representative race men. Rather than presuming that he is simply an example of emasculation and white parasitism, I ask exactly how Luke qualifies as a man and in what ways his gender and sexual variance necessitate a more complicated understanding of black masculinity in the nineteenth century. Furthermore, going against the nineteenth-century logic of the black paternal and maternal pairing, I draw numerous parallels between the lives of Luke and Jacobs. Jacobs also experienced homoerotic abuse at the hands of her mistress and had experiences that did not conform to norms of gender and sex. When we look at Jacobs and Luke relationally, we get a different picture of black maternity and crucial dimensions of black female sexuality that we have tended to overlook or misrecognize come into focus.

In the conclusion of the chapter, I theorize on the largely undertheorized topics of gender and sexual variance in the context of slavery. Drawing mostly upon black feminist scholarship, which has undertaken to correct narratives of black people as lacking gender and sexual identities under slavery, I challenge us to rethink the theoretical and material potential of transgenderism, gender variance, and sexual fluidity in terms of black cultural production. These fluid categories of sex and gender, I argue, are crucial to formulating a deeper, more complicated understanding of black interior life and black political praxis generated in the nineteenth century.

## Deciphering Black Male Rape

On the subject of parallels and pairings, I want to begin my discussion of Luke by drawing our attention to a common and consistently invoked nineteenth-century pairing. I am thinking of the dialectic between the liberated, freedom-seeking black man and the so-called slave. As noted earlier, David Walker consistently grounds his rhetorical claims to manhood in the dynamic of man versus brutish slave. Speaking to enslaved brethren, he asks: "Are we men?" and then later affirms that "we are men, and not brutes."[14] Elsewhere in *Walker's Appeal*, he proclaims: "Oh! my coloured brethren, all over the world, when shall we arise from this death-like apathy?—And be men!!"[15] The natural counterpoint to Walker's appeal to manhood is the slave. Rhetorically speaking, without the slave there could be no liberated black man, as they each mutually defined and demarcated the threshold of the other. In terms of consumption, Walker regarded the slave as a natural by-product of the culture of consumption. Like slabs of meat, slaves *are made* through acts of "butchering, and murdering," their flesh seasoned and tendered through cruel acts of self-consumption. Walker describes how "a son [might] take his mother, who bore almost the pains of death to give him birth, and by the command of a tyrant, strip her naked as she came into the world, and apply the cow-hide to her."[16] Such initiatory acts make a man into a slave, according to Walker, and render him vulnerable to the consumptive urges of whites who gorge and satiate themselves upon such twisted acts of violence.

Walker's conception of man versus slave reflected general abolitionist thought. A popular abolitionist image conveys this dialectic. The widely used antislavery emblem was a manacled slave kneeling in supplication. The caption to this image read: "Am I not a man and brother?"[17] "How could a man be both manly and a slave?" argued abolitionists, who believed that slavery unmanned and systematically consumed black men.[18] Black activist Maria W. Stewart, speaking before a group of black Bostonians in 1831, admonished: "O ye fearful ones, throw off your fearfulness. . . . If you are men, convince [whites] that you possess the spirit of men." To Stewart's thinking, "real" black men overcame their fears and were assertive in the world, acting as brave "sons of Africa" able to draw upon their noble heritage.[19] Whereas Africa signified under slavery heathenism and the loss of a cultural legacy, manhood makes possible the transformation of even Africa into a noble and enlivening landscape.

The general tide in abolitionist rhetoric was toward manhood and away from a deeper, more complicated meaning of the slave.[20] For example, in his bold assertions of black manhood, Walker countered Thomas Jefferson's ideas of the black slave as heathen, akin to the orangutan, and "in reason much inferior" to the white man.[21] Walker does not complicate the reality of slave experience by exploring how a man could be a man and also be sexually violated and lacking in paternal authority or, for that matter, a slave and also a noble and reasoning human being. Instead, he relies upon a dichotomy wherein manhood transcends all of the negative, unseemly connotations of enslavement. In consistently positioning manhood over slave status, black abolition- ists tended to reinforce a false dichotomy in which manhood always represented the good and discerning path toward freedom. The condi- tion of the slave, on the other hand, embodied the most depraved and unspeakable aspects of black experience.

Douglass gives us an example of these unspeakable dimensions of slave experience in his first slave narrative. After witnessing the brutal beating of his Aunt Hester, Douglass lets on that this is not the worst of what he will see or what he will be forced to participate in. He has not words, he says, to describe the sensations and awareness that accom- panies his brutal initiation: "It was the first of a long series of such out- rages, of which I was doomed to be a witness and a participant. It struck me with awful force. . . . It was the most awful spectacle. I wish I could commit to paper the feelings with which I beheld it."[22] Douglass never describes this scenario, which recurs in his later narratives, in graphic detail, nor do we ever glean from Douglass's other published writings deeper insight into the secret, unspeakable world to which he refers. In chapter 3, I demonstrated how the legacy and ontology of the slave car- ries over, continues beyond the temporal freeing of the slave. I contend that it is the slave (in Douglass) who is essential to understanding the limitations, horizons, and potentials of the free and emancipated man.

I reference this distinction between man and slave because it is crucial to understanding why Jacobs chose to narrate Luke's story of explicit male sexual violation in the first place. Jacobs's narrative is, at least on the surface, a story about black female violation and the recu- perative powers of motherhood. In the preface to the slave narrative, Jacobs makes clear that she writes on behalf "of the condition of two millions of women at the South, still in bondage, suffering what I suf- fered, and most of them far worse."[23] Black male sexual violation did not figure into Jacobs's gender and sex politics, which might explain why scholars have had very little to say about Luke or why Jacobs chose to tell his story. For the most part, scholars of Jacobs's narrative have either ignored the subject of male rape or misrecognized it. P. Gabrielle Fore- man refers to Luke as a rare example of "homosexual abuse to which male narrators rarely, if ever, admit," but does not himself analyze the import and significance of Luke to the larger narrative.[24] Anne Bradford

Warner cites Luke as a terse example of slave vernacular, making no reference to his sexual treatment.[25] Jean Fagan Yellin, the preeminent Jacobs biographer, painstakingly tracks down all manner of minute detail and historical fact from Jacobs's narrative but leaves untouched the subject of male rape and the broader implications of homoeroticism on the plantation.[26] Maurice Wallace offers the most insightful understanding of Luke and sodomy belief of the time period. Luke's master suffers, according to Jacobs, from "excessive dissipation."[27] Wallace traces this malady to the medical science of the period: Excessive dissipation and palsy were "the consequences of sexual perversions including masturbation and sodomy, for which the usual prognosis was progressive dementia."[28] Using the terminology of the time period, Wallace helps us understand how Jacobs's reading of Luke's master as demented and sexually strange coincided with medical notions of sodomy as an illness of the mind and body.

What Luke meant, though, as an outgrowth of his master's sexual illness has little to do with the politics of why Jacobs chose to tell his story. Two centuries earlier, a New Netherland court executed Jan Creoli for committing sodomy upon the body of Manuel Congo. The court defined both Creoli and Congo as sodomites, black sodomites. The reason their stories were told had to with the preservation of Christian morals and values; both blacks were "condemned of God . . . as an abomination."[29] Elsewhere in the colonies, separate sodomy legislation for blacks would affirm how, in the minds of whites, the black sodomite was a natural outgrowth of African heathenism and innate immorality.[30] We cannot separate a sexual interpretation of Creoli, Congo, or Luke from larger institutionalized conceptions of the Negro as sexually licentious and amoral. The reasons Jacobs chose to tell Luke's story would have differed greatly from the political aims of the Christian state. Yet I use this state example to demonstrate how moral, political, and state-making ideology inform the depiction of black sodomites or raped black men in the colonial United States. Questions of intentionality direct us to the political utility behind colonial-era depictions of black male homoerotism.

Jacobs's motive in telling Luke's story takes on even greater import when we recall that black people on the whole did not write about male rape or homoerotism. Of the hundreds of thousands of pages of narrative, testimony, recorded speeches, and liberationist tracts written by black men, we have yet to recover overt depictions of male rape or homoeroticism. For black women, such a topic was even more taboo, as it suggested sexual licentiousness and a knowledge of sexual matters that most women disavowed. Jacobs knew these rhetorical/sexual politics well. A master of rhetorical strategies, she single-handedly revised the conventions of the slave narrative, the sentimental novel, and the uplift tract to construct a unique and singular document about black female liberation and womanhood under slavery. For such a woman, the telling of Luke's story had profound political import that we can access only partially through sexual interpretations of his master and his treatment under his master.[31]

Thinking about Jacobs's intentionality in terms of the man/slave dialectic, Jacobs can entertain certain elements of Luke's sexual abuse and personal history because he never, within the schema of her narrative, enters into or threatens the sacred precincts of manhood. Most of the scholarship on Jacobs's narrative focuses, quite appropriately, on the centrality of motherhood and on Jacobs's frequent appeals throughout the narrative to the cult of true womanhood. Alongside her claims to femininity and motherhood, though, Jacobs intended her narrative to document the parallel plight of black men, which she understood to complement her model of the black woman as nurturer and sustainer of the race. For example, in a chapter titled "The Slave Who Dared to Feel Like a Man," she documents at length the parallel struggles of her brother, Benjamin, to sustain an embattled sense of manhood. Luke's story, on the other hand, takes up approximately two-and-a-half pages of the narrative and focuses on his sexualized treatment, his folk-like ignorance, and his lack of moral perspective. Where Benjamin complements and provides a parallel to his sister's story, Luke represents the extent to which the chattel institution can unman an individual. In terms of the man/slave dynamic, we might think of Luke, according to Jacobs's logic, as the perfect embodiment of the slave. Of all the male slaves depicted in the narrative, Luke's sexual violation marks him as the most depraved, the most degraded, and the most apt object of the male unspeakable.

Long before we get to Luke, a "poor, ignorant" depraved specimen of manhood, Jacobs drops hints and suggestions that dictate how we are to read and interpret Luke's lack of manhood. The first of these hints comes in chapter VIII of the narrative, titled "What Slaves Are Taught to Think of the North." Jacobs begins by commenting on the deceptive tricks of masters. One master describes to his slaves the horrible and impoverished circumstances of free life. "A slaveholder once told me," Jacobs recites, "that he had seen a runaway friend of mine in New York, and that she besought him to take her back to her master, for she was literally dying of starvation; that many days she had only one cold potato to eat, and at other times could get nothing at all."[32] According to Jacobs, many of the "general mass of slaves" believe such lies, which results not only in their physical bondage but also in the enslavement of their minds and sensibilities. Black men, under such circumstances, do not understand "that freedom could make them useful men."[33] Nor do they understand, according to Jacobs, how freedom could "enable them to protect their wives and children."[34] Subtly, Jacobs argues against the belief that the Negro was innately heathen. She admits that the black man in slavery is a "heathen" but blames this state on the absence of proper Christian training, the denial of the paternal role, and the inherently heathen nature of the institution of slavery. Jacobs navigates a fine line between the "innately heathen African" and her New World African American heathen who is, unlike his ancestors, a victim of circumstances.[35]

The slave is heathen, either by ancestry or circumstances. And "the man" walks free of ideological as well as literal shackles. Heathen black men, or slaves, by definition could not protect their wives and children; they were "sneaky," ignorant, and susceptible to the mental suggestions of their masters. "Some poor creatures have been so brutalized by the lash they will sneak out of the way to give their masters free access to their wives and daughters. Do you think this proves the black man to belong to an inferior order of being?" Jacobs responds to her own question a couple of lines later: "I admit the black man is inferior." In contrast to the inferiority of the slave, Jacobs first chooses for herself a free black man whom she desires to marry. Her master does not allow this union, so she later chooses an erotic relationship with a white man who does not own slaves. Compared with these chivalric models of manhood, Jacobs finds enslaved men "an inferior order of beings."[36]

Not only can Luke not protect a hypothetical wife or child from abuse, he cannot protect himself from the sexual licentiousness of his master. Luke's unnamed master chains the black man to his bed. Having fallen "prey to the vices growing out of the 'patriarchal institution,'" Luke's master perpetrates "the strangest freaks of despotism."[37] Jacobs leaves it to her reader to imagine the details of these sexual acts but does make clear in her references to the "patriarchal institution" and the master's "degraded wreck of manhood" how thoroughly unmanned is Luke in the process of his enslavement. She uses the term "patriarchal institution" elsewhere in the narrative to refer to masters who sexually violate black women on the plantation. Luke's master treats him like a black woman. Jacobs does not go so far, however, as to label Luke as feminine or womanly. Her politics of black womanhood do not allow for feminine or womanly men.

Instead, she references his feminine nature through allusions to the master's sexual dominance and implicit comparisons with other black men who presumably avoid Luke's fate. For example, Jacobs describes Peter, the black man who assists her in her final escape, as a "brave," "enterprising, noble hearted man [who] was a chattel!"[38] Technically speaking, Peter is a slave like Luke. However, the author casts Luke as "poor, ignorant, [and] much abused," even after she encounters him, following his escape, in the North. Within Jacobs's paradigm of masculinity, black men fall into one of two categories, "man" or "slave." In the above-mentioned chapter titled "The Slave Who Dared to Feel Like a Man," she focuses on the evolution of her brother, Benjamin, from slave to man. The culminating moment of Benjamin's manhood is the prototypical physical battle between slave and master. One day the master tries to whip Benjamin. "He resisted. Master and slave fought, and finally the master was thrown. Benjamin had cause to tremble; for he had thrown to the ground his master—one of the richest men in town."[39] In pursuit of his manhood, Benjamin flees the plantation, his master captures him, he escapes again, and finally he achieves permanent free status in the North. Physical combat, literal escape, and longing for a lost paternal figure typify the journey of the real man that Benjamin represents.

Luke, by comparison, does not flee from his abuser, nor does he engage him in a warrior-type physical battle. Instead of depicting Luke as brave, enterprising, and intelligent, Jacobs depicts him as defeated and degraded—a slave who dares not to feel or act as a man. Just because Luke is sexually violated, though, does not mean that he is not brave, enterprising, or intelligent. His escape from slavery indicates that on some level he maintained a reserve of bravery and enterprise that allowed him to outsmart local patty rollers and slave catchers. Yet to allow Luke this complexity would necessitate looking more deeply at the erotic tie between master and slave and, on Jacobs's part, working from a politics of black womanhood that did not depend upon dichotomies of ennobled man versus emasculated slave.

In her presentation of Luke, Jacobs implicitly draws upon plantation codes of black masculine shame and self-blame. According to James Oliver Horton and Lois Horton, "Among the slaves, men who refused to submit to the master's authority were accorded respect. . . . 'Them as won't fight,' reported Lewis Clark, 'is called Poke-easy.'"[40] This unspoken honor code helps explain the sparse historical record regarding male rape. Admission to rape, more than any other act I can think of, would have called into question a black man's honor. Luke's master had greatly diminished physical strength. He had to call in the constable to administer beatings for him. According to the unspoken black male code of honor, Luke represented a least-respectable model of black masculinity, if he registered as a man at all.

In contrast, black women could undergo rape and still emerge from such circumstances as honorable, contributing members of the race. In the context of racial uplift, both black men and women bartered in black female violation. For black men, it represented the greatest measure of their emasculation and for black women, such as Jacobs, the reality of rape informed her politics of black womanhood and motherhood. Trudier Harris offers a useful assessment of the gender politics of rape during and following slavery. Her explanation helps us understand why Luke has no gender identity outside of the ambiguous sexuality of the slave. Though raped black women, she contends, "were psychologically warped," their sexual violation does not lead "to a subtraction from their persons." The implicit reference here is the castrated or emasculated black male. She continues: "No matter the father of her children, she still was able to fulfill—in spite of the conditions under which the fulfillment was carried out—her traditional role as woman within the society, that of bearer of children. The black male, on the other hand, could only envision his worth in intangible ways."[41]

Harris raises several illuminating and useful points. First, she points to an implicit sexual politics within black uplift ideology. According to these politics, black people have historically identified black women with the womb, with reproduction, while they have identified black men with the penis or phallic agency. After slavery, lynching and castration came to symbolize black masculinity and male violation. The raped wife and maternal figure, examples of which proliferate in slave narratives and abolitionist writings, came to signify the defilement of black womanhood. Luke's sexual violation does not fit neatly into either of these categories. We do not know exactly how his anus and penis were used in the context of sexual abuse. And as far as transcending his sexual violation, his rape does not reap children, the ultimate sign of female accomplishment. The only access to gender and sexuality for Luke and for black men in general is through the black woman. If he can have the black woman, possess her, and protect her, then he is a man. If not, he is devoid of manhood. In Jacobs's version of this equation, black men had neither gender role nor sexual identity outside of their main role of protecting and complementing the black woman. In this equation, black male sexual violation is, in and of itself, a zero factor: Black male gender roles mean nothing in relationship to black or white men.

When we speak of the absence of historical examples of male rape, we are implicitly referring to a worldview in which the rape of black men had no cultural currency, had neither psychic nor political import. And so in order to tell Luke's story, Jacobs has to work through an alternative constellation of signs and social meanings. Framing Luke as a slave makes his articulation possible. The slave was already understood in the negative, as the opposite of all the positive and sustaining characteristics of the heroic black man. Where the heroic black man stood apart from the relational and affectional ties that endeared and bound black men to whites (either through escape or frequent acts of resistance), the male slave was erotically available as caretaker, nursemaid, uncle, and domesticated servant. The correlation between Luke and slave status, I am suggesting, should inspire us to look anew at the discursive implications of *the slave* within antebellum black liberationist discourse. Rather than presuming, as we commonly do, that black people on the whole adopted Victorian attitudes about sexuality, it might be more correct to assume that black people maintained complicated understandings of the slave's life and being as intrinsically sexualized. Among his numerous meanings, Luke is an indicator of a realm of sexual experience and discourse that nineteenth-century gender and sexual norms only obscure.[42]

## The Master Epicure

We might recover some of the discursive potential of the slave through a deeper exploration of hunger and consumption on the plantation. The culture of consumption constituted a complicated terrain wherein the slave effected resistance, often occupied a gender- and sexually variant status, and constituted self through violent and coercive homoerotic ties to the master. The category of slave in such contexts was essentially fluid and informed by a larger dynamics of plantation incest, relational ties between whites and blacks, and, most importantly, the white person's cultivated hunger for black flesh and soul. Before inserting Luke into the context I am describing, let me first explain the centrality of sex and human consumption within Jacobs's narrative.

Jacobs depicted scenes of consumption more gruesome than those documented by any of her contemporaries. The only woman to come close to horrors that few wanted to confront was Lydia Maria Child. Child penned the introduction to Jacobs's narrative and wrote the widely read *An Appeal in Favor of That Class of Americans Called Africans* (1833). *An Appeal* was a groundbreaking abolitionist tract that documented the horrors of slavery and depicted Africans as having a cultural legacy and an innate moral character. At the age of thirty-one, Child was hailed as the best-known woman writer in America.[43] However, after the publication of *An Appeal*, "most of the Beacon Street homes that had once welcomed its author were henceforth closed to her. The Boston Athenaeum canceled her membership. Sales for her books declined, and subscriptions to *Juvenile Miscellany* dropped off so sharply that the magazine ceased publication in 1834."[44] Many had come to know Child as a paragon of female virtue and domestic cultivation. Part of the reason for her ostracization stemmed from her graphic and what some considered "licentious" and "unsexed" depictions of slavery. One illustrated page in the text features sketches of more common torture devices—the "iron cuffs," "iron shackles," "thumb-screw," and "speculum oris"—and detailed explanations of how each device functioned. Prefiguring Jacobs's depictions of consumption, Child describes a ten-month-old baby boiled alive aboard a slave schooner. In one of the most graphic depictions of plantation violence from the era, Child describes the literal butchering and cooking of a recalcitrant young slave on a Kentucky plantation. Adding insult to the injured, "delicate" sensibilities of her readers, Child alludes in *An Appeal* to the fortunes of Bostonians "made by the sale of Negro blood," advocates for the legalization of marriage between persons of different colors, and argues against Massachusetts's support of the Fugitive Slave Law.

As a result of her own painful social ostracization and with an eye toward preserving Jacobs's female respectability, Child recommended that Jacobs compile all of the incidents of flesh consumption and references to human cannibalism in one chapter of the narrative. In the chapter from the slave narrative titled "Sketches of Neighboring Slaveholders," Jacobs depicts bodies literally consumed by vermin, literally cooked, or having cooked iron things applied to their flesh. Masters starve their slaves, do not allow them to breastfeed their young, and in other ways introduce bonded persons into the consumptive machinery of slave culture.

The idea of slavery itself as a living and consuming thing is difficult to imagine. However, Jacobs brings this reality to life by depicting scenarios of consumption that involve machines, shackles, and mechanical contrivances. As punishment for trying to escape, one slave was "placed between the screws of the cotton gin, to stay as long as he had been in the woods."[45] The cotton gin was then "screwed down, only allowing him room to turn on his side when he could not lie on his back."[46] The master's placing of the slave literally between the screws of the cotton gin, at the point at which the cotton feeds into the machine, makes even more graphic the consumptive relationship between chattel person and machine. What follows, while the man is positioned thusly, emphasizes his master's feeding of him to the machinery of slavery:

> Every morning a slave was sent with a piece of bread and bowl of water, which were placed within reach of the poor fellow. . . . Four days passed, and the slave continued to carry the bread and water. On the second

morning, he found the bread gone, but the water untouched. When he had been in the press four days and five nights, the slave informed his master that the water had not been used for four mornings, and that a horrible stench came from the gin house. The overseer was sent to examine into it. When the press was unscrewed, the dead body was found partly eaten by rats and vermin. Perhaps the rats that devoured his bread had gnawed him before his life was extinct.[47]

As I have noted earlier, slaves consistently referred to slavery as a consuming, bloodthirsty institution and slavers as human butchers and the like, but incidents such as this one applied concrete images and scenario to a reality that we have tended to largely dismiss as metaphoric or a residue of the slave's traumatized imagination. For example, in her slave narrative *The History of Mary Prince, a West Indian Slave* (1831), Mary Prince makes constant reference to slavery as a process of butchery and to slaves as butchered meat. Describing herself on the auction block, Prince laments: "I was soon surrounded by strange men, who examined and handled me in the same manner that *a butcher* would a calf or a lamb he was about to purchase."[48] Later in the narrative, she describes her transition from one master to another as "going from one butcher to another."[49] While those who study slavery have been willing to acknowledge the authority of slaves to speak "on the subject of 'what slaves feel' about the morality of slavery,"[50] we have yet to fully grant this acknowledgment to the disturbing reality and moral implications of slave consumption.[51]

In addition to the cotton gin punishment, Jacobs records other systemic processes of consumption. On a neighboring plantation there lived an extremely wealthy man who owned upward of "six hundred slaves, many of whom he did not know by sight."[52] In response to slaves' frequent stealing and eating of hogs, this master developed a mode of punishment that entailed the culinary preparation of flesh. Of his many styles of punishment, "a favorite one was to tie a rope round a man's body, and suspend him from the ground. A fire was kindled over him, from which was suspended a piece of fat pork. As this cooked, the scalding drops of fat continually fell on the bare flesh"[53] Typically, in the kitchen of the plantation big house a piece of pork fat served as seasoning in, say, a pot of beans or stew. Within a modern-day soul food repertoire, collard greens are still prepared in many kitchens with pork fat or ham hock, a tradition that stems back to slavery.

This practice, which makes no sense to our contemporary, largely sedentary and non-agrarian society, was a means by which slaves could avail themselves of desperately needed fat and sustenance that they would need to draw upon during backbreaking field labor.[54] Pork meat was typically associated with starvation and hunger under slavery. "Hog stealing reached such proportions that in 1748 Virginia decreed the death penalty for a third offence."[55] Aware of the premium placed on pork meat by the starving slave, this master's punishment was doubly cruel, as it punished the slave first for simply hungering and, second, with the scalding, liquefied flesh that he would otherwise consume as nourishment.

Rather than the typical process of fattening up a food source, the inverted man conveys how starvation and hunger induction make the slave ready for consumption. The master demonstrates that the slave is an emotional and physical food source by situating him within an inverted cooking scenario; the master situates the slave below the cooking fire and the scalding grease used to season and temper his flesh. In another less graphic example, Jacobs depicts what happens to a man on a plantation caught stealing food. His master chains him to a tree, beats him, and then starves him to the point of visible emaciation: "If a slave stole from him [the master] even a pound of meat or a peck of corn, if detection followed, he was put in chains and imprisoned, and so kept till his form was attenuated by hunger and suffering."[56]

These larger systemic examples of consumption took on more intimate, erotic connotations within the domestic sphere of the plantation, where social death rather than literal death was the preferred outcome. Orlando Patterson's description of the master as human parasite feeding his "sense of honor and his sexual appetite" through the slave is borne out in the Jacobs narrative.[57] Jacobs describes her own master, Dr. Flint, as possessed of a "restless, craving, vicious nature."[58] Flint habitually "roved about day and night, seeking whom to devour."[59] In Jacobs's life, Flint's hunger takes on a sexual significance that involves his consistently propositioning her for sex, inviting her to be his concubine, writing notes that spell out explicitly his sexual intentions, and physically abusing her when she does not acquiesce.

Slave masters sustained the systemic aspects of consumption that I have outlined on emotional and psychic levels through cultivated tastes, socially sanctioned appetites, and high cultural values attributed to the enslaved person's consumption. In Jacobs's narrative, this culti- vated sensibility and personality takes the form of masters who play the role of "epicure."[60] *Incidents* provides many examples of masters who are epicures of certain types of punishments, sexual brutality, physical brutalization, and much more. Incidents of graphic human consump- tion were, in Jacobs's mind, symptomatic of a broader ideology of flesh tasting and sexual/erotic hungers that the master cultivated in himself. In Flint, this cultivation of flesh hunger and sexual appetite stems back to childhood and the social consumption of the black mammy. Jacobs describes Flint as "an epicure." She means this in the traditional sense of this word: a person who has specialized, cultivated knowledge in the arts, food, or some other specialized area. The context of this statement is Flint's scrutinizing of every single dish that comes out of the main kitchen. In addition to these typical meanings of the word "epicure," Jacobs also uses the word to refer to Flint's cultivated knowledge of slave consumption. The cook "never sent a dinner to his table without fear and trembling." If a dish was not sufficiently prepared Flint would have this woman whipped or "compel her to eat every mouthful of it in his presence."[61] Literally, Flint would take the food and "cram it down her throat till she choked."[62] Gorging and starvation define the cook's existence, whom Jacobs describes as a "poor, hungry creature."

The brutality and calculation of Flint's epicurean punishments know no end. In another incident, the house dog dies after barely consum- ing a plate of "Indian mush" prepared by the cook: "He refused to eat, and when his head was held over it, the froth flowed from his mouth into the basin. He died a few minutes later."[63] Of course, Flint blames the cook and compels her to eat this mess, which sickens her but satis- fies her master. Operating out of a traditional idea of the mammy cook, Flint expects the black woman to have no needs, no appetites. Not only does she cook food, she "*is* food; she/it is the ever-smiling source of sus- tenance for infants and adults."[64]

The cook/mammy represents Flint's appetites, tastes, and hungers, which extend beyond the table into the flesh and the maternal urges of the cook herself. Jacobs further elaborates this interlinking of black maternity with white male appetite through scenes in which the master compels the cook to starve her newborn infant as punishment for her indiscretions: "This poor woman endured many cruelties from her master and mistress; sometimes she was locked up, away from her nursing baby, for a whole day and night."[65] On the surface, Flint operates as a patriarch, as an authoritative figure with the power to chastise and infantilize his female slave. At a deeper level of social meaning, Flint plays the role of a sycophantic child whose hunger and impulses compete with those of the bonded child. Adult whites such as Flint grew up within a plantation reality that conditioned them to think of black women as endless fonts of nurturing and sustenance. This expectation, according to Deborah Gray White, originated in the mythology of the mammy, whom whites thought of as "the woman who could do anything, and do it better than anyone else. Because of her expertise in all domestic matters, she was the premiere house servant and all others were her subordinates."[66] Jacobs recalls whites referring to her grandmother as "mammy."[67] White women were generally thought of as ennobled mothers, but mammies (a degraded model of motherhood) had to bear the stigma of enslavement and still compassionately mother white babies before their own. Jacobs's grandmother had to do this, replacing Jacobs's mother at the breast with the daughter of the master, whom she nursed until weaned.

Keeping this correlation between maternal nurturing and human consumption in mind, I want to turn now to Luke. Luke's master is also an epicure: He acts upon infantile urges, develops a cultivated taste for Negro flesh, practices a type of sexual consumption, and is a parasitic personality. I mentioned Flint's epicurean appetites in advance of those of Luke's master, because Flint, as the model consumer in the narrative, serves as the prototype of the master as epicure. We cannot fully grasp the import of Luke's sexualized treatment apart from this larger context of Flint's hunger for and his process of glutting and starving the black mother. Neither, I intend to show, can we fully understand the implications of female maternity, female consumption, or black female sexuality in Jacobs's narrative without considering Luke's paternal/maternal relationship to his master. Within the psychology of white males in the antebellum South, homoerotic desire for black men and fantasies of maternity coalesced. In the culture of blackface minstrelsy, Eric Lott interprets the female roles (performed, at the time, solely by white men) as a cover for black maleness. Her typically jutting protuberances and general phallic suggestiveness bear all the marks of the white-fantasized black men who loomed so large in racialized phallic scenarios. It makes perfect sense that castration anxieties in blackface would cojoin the black penis and the woman. . . . Another referent for whites of Lacan's threatening (m)Other, Franz Fanon argued, is precisely the black male.[68]

If Luke is anything, he is a sign and source of the type of nurturing and constancy that a mother provides. Luke's master returns to the plantation from the North completely incapacitated. The white man returns "deprived of the use of his limbs," "bed-ridden," and often so weak that he could not perform his daily tortures of Luke.[69] He is like a helpless infant who has to depend upon Luke for his sustenance and well-being. Jacobs observes: "The fact that he was entirely dependent on Luke's care, and was obliged to be tended like *an infant*, instead of inspiring any gratitude or compassion towards his poor slave, seemed only to increase his irritability and cruelty."[70] As we have seen with Flint and the cook, the satiation of the master's hunger is typically infused with cruelty and sadism. Denying the cook's maternal responsibilities, equating her with something animal-like, and making her eat from the dog's dish all serve a singular purpose. These actions serve to feed Flint's twisted, infantile understanding of the black mammy as an endless font of nurturing and sustenance.

In Luke, we have another example of the slave nurturing and sustaining the psychic and emotional well-being of the master. For Luke's master, making Luke go about half-clothed in a day shirt reinforces childhood memories of plantation life. Luke is often "not allowed to wear anything but his shirt, in order to be in readiness to be flogged," and "a day seldom passed without him receiving more or less blows."[71] Frequency and access increase the master's pleasure and well-being. He finds pleasure and erotic climax in the context of punishment, often whipping Luke "till his strength was exhausted."[72] Luke's rear parts serve as erotic spectacle, as he is often made to bend down, bend over, and turn around half-naked. Sam Anderson, an ex-slave, tells a WPA interviewer: "In slavery time we wore shirts, I wore a shirt 'till I was ten years old and these shirts were split up the side and when we ran they would sail out behind."[73] Ruling-class whites were in the habit of seeing the slave's exposed body under these gowns. If the gowns sailed out behind, there was nothing to inhibit frontal view of genitalia. Duncan McCastle, at the age of fifteen, had never worn a pair of pants.[74] You had young adults with well-developed bodies running around the plantation (sometimes into their twenties) fully exposed to whites. Perhaps Luke's master sought to recreate recollections of mature younger slaves dressed as half-clad infants. Perhaps he drew from mental snapshots of same-aged playmates made to go about half-clad. Either way, dressing Luke in just a day shirt evokes a childhood reality of half-dressed slaves. It reinforces Luke's position of "child" and his master's position of parasitic adult child.

In Luke's master, we have an extreme example of the master's epicurean refinement manifested as blatant self-consumption. Over time, the punishing arm of the tyrant "grew weaker, and was finally palsied."[75] He devolves into a "degraded wreck of manhood," which does nothing to abate his sexual hunger or prevent the "freaks of despotism" that he perpetrates against Luke.[76] It is not enough to simply think of Luke's master as an isolated, freakish occurrence of "sodomy," "despotism," or sexual hunger. Rather, we should understand him as emblematic of the slave child's sexual vulnerability overlapping with the nurturing of white children on the plantation. In our scholarly treatments of plantation sexuality, we have tended to emphasize the sexual hungers and desires of masters and mistresses as evidence of adult sexuality, but the rituals and appetites of Luke's master originate from childhood experiences.

Connecting this notion of child sexuality to the topic of plantation rape, we readily acknowledge that white men raped black women and that children learned such behaviors from their parents. Yet we rarely speak to the myriad ways in which all white children on the plantation learned to eroticize and desire the slave.[77] Harriet Beecher Stowe's young Eva, cared after and chivalrously admired by Tom, belied an insidious sexual reality in which children learned to associate the nurturing presence of mammies, toms, and uncle figures with incestuous sexuality and unrestrained appetite for the Negro. Stowe conceives of Eva as an angelic source of spiritual nourishment, a Christ-like supper that Tom, Patsy and even Eva's father gratefully and mournfully consume. In reality, though, little Miss Eva literally fattened on the emotional and spiritual nourishment received from black nursemaids and

attendants. "Miss Sara," for example, a real-life version of the Eva character, "pined and sickened" and almost died when her father sold Mary
Reynolds, her personal slave. The local doctor orders Miss Sara's father
to buy back Mary and when he does, "Miss Sara plumps up right off
and grows into fine health."[78] What medical terminology can we use to
accurately describe this process of need and racialized consumption?
What manner of child is this—so early conditioned to desire and pine
for black presence and care? Neither food, medicine, nor the promise of
other material delights add flesh and well-being to the child. Only the
return of and psychic repossession of her slave makes Miss Sara plump
in a manner that defies medical science and our prevailing understandings of the energetic exchange between master and consumed slave.

Luke's master is at base a helpless "infant."[79] Yet his punishment of
and sexual treatment of Luke reinforces the opposite reality. He dresses
Luke like a plantation child, repeatedly chastises and punishes him for
crimes he does not commit, and physically lowers him to a subservi-
ent position that allows the incapacitated master to feel larger and more
powerful. As a means of further binding and humiliating the young
black man, he chains Luke to his bedside, reinforcing in Luke the feelings of limitation, needfulness, and captivity that the master himself
feels. Generally speaking, whites like Luke's master cultivated a diverse
range of rituals and ideologies designed to mask their own infantile
hungers. The fame of Samuel A. Cartwright, a leading New Orleans
physician, rested upon this inversionary mode of thinking. Cartwright's
"Report on the Diseases of and Physical Peculiarities of the Negro
Race" (1851) refers repeatedly to Negroes as "children" and "newborn
infants" dependent upon the parental care of slave owners. Cartwright
attributes contrived "medical diseases" such as "drapetomania" (the
phenomenon of blacks running away from captivity) and "dysesthesia
Aethiopis" (a fatigue and resulting stupor from which neither punishment nor the threat of death could wake the slave) to the childlike
nature of the Negro.[80] Any person subjected to backbreaking labor from
sunup to sundown would naturally, at some point, succumb to fatigue.
Cartwright describes this natural response to abuse and exhaustion as
an African-based disease.[81] Such systematized and ritualized practices
of self-delusion and inversion made right (in the white mind) a twisted
system of consumptive human relations.

Earlier in this chapter, I described the master who habitually inverts his slaves, hanging them by their feet below a boiling fire and flesh-cooking grease. I also described the slave who was literally fed into the cotton gin so that body and machine merge into one gruesome image of rot, consumption, and death. Such examples of systematized consumption take on an even more disturbing hue and significance within the domestic spheres of the plantation. While the rope, gurney, and metal gear constitute the external machinery of consumption, Luke's example helps us see some of the internal machinery—infantilization, childhood fantasies, nurturing, and parentage—fueling the larger culture of consumption. More of our intellectual energy needs to go toward analyzing childhood and the ideological infrastructure of childhood in slavery. When it comes to the topic of consumption under slavery, we cannot thoroughly engage this subject if we do not, from the outset, construct a teleology of the master that extends back, at least, to early childhood. For it means something entirely different to think about Luke's master as an adult child who is eroticizing and sexualizing Luke (who is himself infantilized and made to play the role of paternal caregiver).

This way of thinking about Luke and his master disrupts conventional understandings of genealogy, sex, and relational dyads. Rather than regarding Luke as *the slave* and the white male as *the master*, we have Luke playing the role of child and adult and the master playing the roles of adult child and ruling-class adult. Through the discourses of sodomy and excessive dissipation, we know that Luke's master masturbated himself and probably Luke. We know that he probably either received or perpetrated anal copulation; in his weakened condition it was probably Luke who was made to anally penetrate the master. But what we cannot know when we think solely in terms of sodomy is, for example, how anal penetration might have fed the child impulse (the impulse to be nurtured) in the master or how such an impulse indicated a genealogy of appetites and hungers extending back to childhood. To extend this exploration of childhood, nurturing, and maternity even further, it could have been that acts of anal copulation (or other sexual acts) reinforced in the master the role of nurturing parent (paternity and/or maternity). Ruling-class whites habitually thought of themselves as bettering slaves through bondage and "love," "care," and "compassion" extended to the slave in the context of the most heinous punishments and psychological abuses. Cartwright summed up this sentiment among whites. Correlating discipline and the childlike nature of the Negro, he writes: "Although their skin is very thick, it is as sensitive, when they are in perfect health, as that of children, and like them they fear the rod."[82] Continuing these observations, he writes:

> They resemble children in another very important particular; they are very easily governed by love combined with fear, and are ungovernable, vicious and rude under any form of government whatever, not resting on love and fear as a basis. Like children, it is not necessary that they be kept under the fear of the lash; it is sufficient that they be kept under the fear of offending those who have authority over them."[83]

The layers and overlapping implications of what Luke means complicate and invert gender norms. Did Luke represent a masculinized or feminized child in the psychic world of the master? Did the master imagine himself as mothering and/or fathering Luke through daily, ritualized beatings? Did Luke understand himself as cast in the role of man, woman, mother, father, husband, wife? Did he signify none of these or all of them in some combination? Was he chosen for particular male or female characteristics? Did his body parts and orifices (mouth and anus) represent only pleasure and pain, or were they also construed as sexual organs, female entrances, a womb?

I bring up all of these possibilities—the combinations of bodies, body parts, and gender and sexual implications—to clarify a point: When we talk about the invisibility of homoeroticism in the context of slavery, we are implicitly talking about norms of gender, sex, and so forth that inhibit our seeing. I mention David Walker at the beginning of this chapter who, in his fiery *Appeal*, correlated the consumption of black people under slavery with the saving powers of motherhood: "They keep us miserable now," he laments, "and call us their property, but some of them will have enough of us by and by—their stomachs shall run over with us; they want us for their slaves, and shall have us to their fill."[84] Black men should rise up out of "abject servility" and "be men" protecting their "wives and mothers," writes Walker. Where slavery literally consumed the race, motherhood and the black female womb had the power, in Walker's mind, to resuscitate and reconstitute the race. Using Ralph Ellison's *Invisible Man* as a reference, Trudier Harris describes the derogatory implications of the "black male grandmother," a figure from slavery and Reconstruction. Harris describes Bledsoe, the Booker T. Washington-like character from the novel, as "Grandmotherly Bledsoe." She says that he "approaches the mammy figure in the extent of his concern for the white person who is in his care. His primary goal is to soothe Norton [the wealthy white man] as the precious 'child' whose welfare rests in his hands. To comfort the child, the grandmother must show him that the danger which threatened him is no longer real."[85] Examples of the Walker and Harris variety proliferate within African American history and letters.

Walker's notion of the saving black maternal womb and Harris's idea of the black male grandmother have much to do with Luke and the topic of homoeroticism during slavery. Yet in a commitment to a dyadic mode of thinking (masculinity/femininity, consumed/not consumed, infant/adult), we have tended to overlook the interconnections and overlaps. Luke's master is as much a representative of "the patriarchal institution" as he is a by-product of conventions of sentimentality tied to motherhood and maternity. Luke gives birth to his master's dominion and psychic stability at the same time that the master births Luke—makes meaning of his life and person—within a consumptive framework. The discourses of hunger and human consumption also have a constructive function. At the same time that they proscribe and delimit black bodies in Jacobs's narrative, they allow us also to think more broadly about homoeroticism as an index for inversions, body disfigurements, and transgressions of gender and sex norms that recur throughout Jacobs's narrative.

## Hunger and Gender Inversion

I have attempted to demonstrate, up to this point, that when we talk about male rape and, more broadly, homoeroticism during slavery, we are implicitly addressing power in the forms of gender, sex, and corporeality. The opened-ended nature of Luke's example (the resolute meanings we can never fully achieve from his body, sex, and gender) presents both a challenge and a number of theoretical potentials. We can marshal these potentials and apply them to a broader understanding of motherhood, consumption, hunger, and resistance in Jacobs's narrative and nineteenth-century American culture in general.

Luke's incomplete story and the incomplete record of homoeroticism within the historical record coincides with a relentless drive within African American history and letters to achieve completion, or at least to convey completion at the levels of gender, sex, and body.[86] It is as if, this whole time, we have striven against the possibility of a body that is part machine and part corporeal entity. I am referring to the body meshed into the cotton gin, the body that is part machine, part rot, part torso. In Luke, this threat of disfigurement takes the form of reversed paternal/child roles and body parts that are so disfigured that we can ascertain their shapes and shadowy forms only through discourses of filth, despotism, and a restraining, sentimental silence.

What would it mean, though, to think about Jacobs in particular and black womanhood and maternity more broadly as incomplete frameworks? What I mean here by "incomplete" is this: What if they did not fully and neatly facilitate ideas of racial uplift or of female reproductivity as saving? What if Jacobs did not construct black femininity to complement the sufferings and subjectivity of black male patriarchs? More broadly, what would be that model of black femininity that did not respond, that did not correct, ideas of black taint and licentiousness? Through these questions, what I am attempting to convey is that in rendering, say, Jacobs's personal genealogy as a political response, albeit to repressive forces, we miss out on her hunger, we miss out on a fuller understanding of her sexuality (as opposed to her reproductive capacity). Jacobs's sexuality, above and beyond the significance of motherhood and reproductive capacity, has become increasingly more important to ascertain. Yet her sexuality (outside of maternity) is rarely given full treatment within black feminist and feminist scholarship more broadly. What would it mean to break open, pry apart, and hold in a kind of suspended animation the very infrastructures that have allowed us to pursue our relatively complete understandings of maternity, female genealogy, and sexuality, for example, in Jacobs's narrative and in slave culture more broadly?

In terms of infrastructures, what comes most readily to mind is the logic of gender and sex operating through recollections of sexual abuse in Jacobs's narrative. Summing up this system, Jacobs writes: "It makes the white fathers cruel and sensual; the sons violent and licentious; it contaminates the daughters, and makes the wives wretched."[87] To break it down further: Jacobs plots sons on the plantation as coming under the "unclean influences" of their fathers. This leads them to rape young black women. Daughters hear of their father's sexual indiscretions, which leads them also to rape and violate. The daughters'

> curiosity is excited, and they soon learn the cause. They are attended by the young slave girls whom their father has corrupted; and they hear such talk as should never meet youthful ears, or any other ears. They know that the women slaves are subject to their father's authority in all things; and in some cases they exercise the same authority over the men slaves.[88]

And wives, as more or less helpless victims, respond wretchedly to their husband's inattentions. In the narrative, a good example of this is Mrs. Flint's crimsoning and weeping as she has Jacobs relate to her all of the lurid details of her husband's sexual advances.

Missing from this matrix of sexual desire are any references to homo-eroticism. In presenting this dynamic, Jacobs presumes that the father's desire runs one way—from male to female—and that all other desires conform to this rule. With Luke, though, we have a clear example of this not being the case. Luke's master embodies a genealogy of white male desire that runs across, betwixt, and between gender and sex norms. In Luke, the master satiates maternal as well as paternal needs— the young slave representing nativity, homespace, and a site of pastoral pleasure. Luke's body and body parts traverse feminine as well as masculine physicality. Not to mention the master, who simultaneously plays the roles of needy child, parasite, and adult tyrant.

Jacobs's narrative is the story of black maternity and womanhood. It is a story centrally concerned with evasion and pursuit: the master pursuer and the enslaved young woman who constantly evades her pursuer. In order for the narrative of pursuit to work, gender and sex have to stand still while a framework of erotic desire stemming from the plantation master takes center stage. Ironically, Jacobs reifies the white male paternity that she seeks to displace and from which she endeavors to disentangle herself through a sexual logic in which the master is always the central node, giving meaning and motility to all other erotic desires on the plantation. Through this model, we can never get at or make sense of Dr. Flint's playing the role of male mother to Jacobs or his wife's simulating "mock intercourse" with the young slave girl. Such fluid expressions of gender complicate and challenge our base presumptions about the master's "masculinity" and belie an altogether different framing of desire. And even if we were to accept that the patriarch was the center and that daughters raped black men, that still does not account for the erotic dynamics between white women and their black female nursemaids, mammies, aunties, and playmates. Before black men, white women had access to black women and black girls. They learned to eroticize and sexualize black women and girls in ways that often had little to do with the sex drives of fathers and brothers. This is not to say that white women did not rape and entice black men on the plantation; they did. But what I am most concerned with is how Jacobs and history on the whole have tended to overlook the most obvious and more primary level of erotic interaction for white women: the relationships between white and black women.

More and more texts are emerging that document the relationships among women on the plantation (between white and black women and between black women in their own communal settings). However, from general studies such as Elizabeth Fox-Genovese's *Within the Plantation Household: Black and White Women of the Old South* (1988) to Marli F. Weiner's *Mistresses and Slaves: Plantation Women in South Carolina, 1830–1880* (1998) to Deborah Gray White's focus on the black female in *Ar'n't I a Woman? Female Slaves in the Plantation South* (1985), the subject of eroticism among women on the plantation remains largely untreated. I mentioned in the previous chapter on Douglass that the only text that I know of to make overt reference to sexual dynamics between women on the plantation is Nell Irvin Painter's *Sojourner Truth: A Life, A Symbol.* Offering some insight into why black women at the time said virtually nothing about sexual abuse at the hands of women, Painter writes:

> Truth had two motives for keeping secrets by the time she told her story. Having come through a libel trial in the mid-1830s, she was concerned about her credibility. She also feared that because what had happened to

her was "so unaccountable, so unreasonable, and what is usually called so unnatural," readers who were "uninitiated" would not believe her.[89]

Connecting the uninitiated of the past to the uninitiated of the present, Painter confirms that "then, as now, the sexual abuse of young women by men is deplored but recognized as common. Less easily acknowledged, then and now, is the fact that there are women who violated children."[90] We can only speculate about the extent to which shame and the emphasis upon "reason" and "nature" have kept from us these deeper realities of black female experience. White women speaking about the hard facts of slavery risked being thought of as sexually licentious or, even worse, as "unsexed."[91] For black women, the risk was even greater as whites de facto linked their sexuality with African wilds, physical disfigurement, and the "horses, dogs, and other domestic animals" to which Thomas Jefferson compared blacks in his *Notes on the State of Virginia*.[92]

In Jacobs's own life, her grandmother serves as an object of white female desire, eroticization, nurturing, and consumptive appetites. Long before Dr. Flint comes into the picture, marrying Jacobs's mistress, selling her grandmother, and pursuing the young Jacobs as his concubine, Mrs. Flint has learned from elderly women in her family about the erotic utility of and serviceability of the black woman. The scene that culminates this history is another bedroom scenario that calls to mind a number of the dynamics that play out in Luke's abuse. Jacobs's mistress, like Luke's master, confines the younger black woman to a room adjoining her bedroom. As with Luke, expectations of sacrifice and service fuel sexualized brutality. And also, similar to the Luke scenario, appetite and hunger enable a fluid sense of gender and sexuality.

Let me describe the significant details of the scenario before correlating it further with Luke's abuse and an overarching dynamic of black female consumption. Motivated by jealously and humiliation, Mrs. Flint takes Jacobs into her bedroom. Her actions, according to Jacobs, are a knee-jerk reaction to her husband's sexual pursuit of the young slave girl. She pulls her aside, hands her a Bible and says, "Lay your hand on your heart, kiss this holy book, and swear before God that you tell me the truth," the truth being that Jacobs has not succumbed to the sexual advancements of Flint.[93] At this point in the narrative, Mrs.

Flint, consumed by her erotic obsessions, comes to fixate on Jacobs. She imagines Jacobs as a seductress, assumes her guilty before the young woman can prove her "innocence," and then wants all of the sordid details, which cause Mrs. Flint to alternately blush, weep, groan, and moan. She seems to blame Jacobs for her degraded state.

Jacobs imagines Mrs. Flint as a by-product of her husband's desire. She paints her as powerless and pitiable. Yet it is my contention that Mrs. Flint is the perfect portrait of what Morrison has described as "the reckless, unabated power of a white woman gathering identity unto herself from the wholly available and serviceable lives of Africanist others."[94] The deeper issue, within the confessional confines of the bedroom, is not Flint's pursuit of Jacobs or vice versa, but the utter powerlessness of this white woman who receives neither love, devotion, nor any semblance of affection from her cruel, predatory husband. Jacobs does her best to render the white woman in a pitiable, compassionate light in this particular moment, but everywhere else in the narrative suggests that her situation is endemic to the culture of consumption. These facts I will take up shortly.

For the moment, we have Mrs. Flint convinced that Jacobs tells the truth regarding her husband. To thwart his sexual schemes, she takes Jacobs "to sleep in a room adjoining her own."[95] Jacobs imagines in her mistress a saving presence. However, her feelings of safety and saving are short lived, as Mrs. Flint begins a nightly vigil that terrifies the young girl and causes her to fear for her life.

> Sometimes I woke up, and found her bending over me. At other times she whispered in my ear, as though it was her husband who was speaking to me, and listened to hear what I would answer. If she startled me, on such occasions, she would glide stealthily away. . . . At last, I began to be fearful for my life. It had been often threatened; and you can imagine, better than I can describe, what an unpleasant sensation it must produce to wake up in the dead of night and find a jealous woman bending over you.[96]

Deborah M. Garfield finds the positioning of the women's bodies sexually suggestive. She refers to the mistress as performing "mock-intercourse" with Jacobs.[97] Garfield describes Mrs. Flint alternately as a "stand-in for her husband," a type of male "impersonator," and enacting a "role-reversal" that stems back to Flint (the patriarch and motivating figure within the incestuous plantation household). Garfield explains Jacobs's motives for her depiction of this scenario as an attempt "to replicate the sexual act and to block her reader from its reality." This scenario, according to Garfield, is yet another example of Jacobs's following Child's instruction and foreclosing sexual details that would offend and taint her female reader. The bottom line? "Mrs. Flint's imitations are still grounded in her husband's physical and discursive presence."[98]

My only problem with Garfield's provocative analysis is that it denies the deeper meaning of Mrs. Flint's erotic proximity, *her* sexual fantasies about Jacobs, and *her* sexual agency independent of her husband. Garfield's analysis adheres religiously to the schema I referenced earlier of erotic desire originating in the white patriarch and informing that of the son, daughter, and wife. The meaning of the mistress's transgendered behavior is for Garfield an esoteric occurrence that underscores how "in the master-slave dialectic . . . roles can be mystically exchanged in narrative but never permanently escaped."[99] In other words, the specter of the master's hunger and desire is always present, animating and acting through his wife, who inexplicably takes on his voice and sexual appetites. All this perceived effort, though, to disguise Dr. Flint's desire and presence makes no sense, given, as Painter points out, that the sexual abuse of women by their masters was a commonly noted occurrence. I submit that what has truly mystified and defied articulation has been female sexuality under slavery and, in particular, erotic ties between black and white women.

Painter's comments about Sojourner Truth's situation apply as well to Jacobs, which is that to call attention to the homoerotic interests of white mistresses would have undermined the ethos of black women's claims to motherhood and womanhood. The motherhood and womanhood even of the plantation mistress had to remain pristine and inviolate if the thesis of patriarchal desire as the primary corruptor of female innocence was to apply. In the reality that Jacobs foregrounds, white women did not corrupt white women or learn to eroticize black women through primary relations with mammies and other caretaker figures. Painter notes that "less easily acknowledged, then and now, is the fact that there are women who violate children."[100] Yet with the plantation

conceived of by whites as a "household" and blacks always as infantilized and eroticized "infants," how could the mistress not find herself
seduced by this sex/power dynamic that was reinforced everywhere
around her? As Morrison asserts, how could she not hunger, become
reckless, and learn through osmosis "the process of gathering identity
unto herself" from the completely available and expendable resource of
the female chattel slave?[101] Beyond the basic issues of sex and violation,
Morrison finds in the white mistress/female slave dialectic "the coordi-
nates of an intensely important moral debate."[102]

Morrison's observations call to mind the nineteenth-century debate
about Christian cannibalism. Such a notion did not easily translate into
concept and terminology. By the late 1800s, white identity on the plantation was so deeply wedded to unspeakable practices of consumption
that whites themselves *could not see* and therefore *could not name* the
specter and terror of the emerging white civilized cannibal. Even the
idea of child molestation forwarded by Painter does not convey the
dynamic overlay of consumption upon sex, of consumptive hungers
driving the erotic interchange between Mrs. Flint and Jacobs.

We cannot separate Mrs. Flint in the bedroom, acting as both master
and mistress, from Mrs. Flint the parasite and consumer practiced in
the methodology of slave consumption. Mrs. Flint was well versed in
the language and ideology of consumption. She threatened her slaves
with skin peeling and pickling.[103] She spit in all of the pots after the cook
had finished the big house meal in order to prevent the cook or any
other slave from "eking out their meager fare with the remains of the
gravy and other scrapings."[104] She rationed out the food and starved her
slaves as a means of maintaining psychic and emotional control. Providing further insight into her character, Jacobs observes: "Mrs. Flint,
like many southern women, was totally deficient in energy. She had not
strength to superintend her household affairs, but her nerves were so
strong, that she could sit in her easy chair and see a woman whipped,
till the blood trickled from every stroke of the lash."[105] Mrs. Flint lacks
power and vitality yet strongly demonstrates these traits in the context
of the torture and subjugation of black females.

For women like Mrs. Flint, the plantation was a spiritual and emotional wasteland. Such women hungered and even starved for the affections and attentions of their husbands. They learned to harden and

deaden themselves to physical and psychological abuses and further-more, in the context of such brutalities, developed a method of nurtur-ing and sustaining themselves by drawing upon the erotic and psychic energy of black women. In the bedroom scenario, Mrs. Flint takes Jacobs into her "special care." She channels her sexual frustration regarding her husband, her "jealousy" and "hatred," into nightly vigils, into rituals of erotic interchange that usually end with whispers and Jacobs's awaken-ing to the woman leaning over her "in the dead of night."[106] Jacobs feels an unnamed terror: "At last," she says, "I began to be fearful for my life. It had been often threatened. . . . Terrible as this experience was, I had fears that it would give place to one more terrible."[107] Sex and consumption fuel Dr. Flint's constant threats against Jacobs's life. Similarly, with Mrs. Flint, the threat of death co-mingled with sex, so that we cannot know for sure if the "terrible act" that Jacobs imagines is molestation and rape at the hands of the mistress, the mistress beating her to death, or death by some other heinous, unspeakable means. The point is that we do not have to know the particulars to understand how thoroughly interwoven is this moment with same-sex eroticism and with a socially sanctioned white female hunger and appetite.

Jacobs locates the roots of all this in the good doctor and in plan-tation patriarchy. However, the problem with Dr. Flint's desire (male, patriarchal desire) as the glue that holds all of this together is that his example overshadows and inhibits our access to more central domestic operations. More specifically, I am thinking of the intimate female-cen-tered ways in which a woman such as Mrs. Flint learns to objectify and erotically consume a black woman slave. Replacing Flint with someone like Jacobs's grandmother would take us a lot further in recovering Mrs. Flint's learned practices of social consumption. Aunt Marthy (Jacob's grandmother) does not stand out in the narrative as someone who suffers from social consumption. As Jacobs struggles for her life, this elderly black woman is free, a land owner and property owner, and is considered an upstanding member of the community. In her goodness (of moral character and domestic practices), Aunt Marthy seems to be in no way connected to the cruelty, meanness, and consumptive urges of Jacobs's mistress.

Aunt Marthy is the typical good grandmother from black antebel-lum experience. Moses Roper describes in his slave narrative how his grandmother comes into the slave cabin and saves him in childhood from the murdering knife of the slave mistress.[108] In Douglass's narrative, the caring, sustaining black grandmother replaces the absent mother.[109] So, too, in Jacobs's narrative does the grandmother come to represent the whole of black maternity. She, even better than the mother, helps establish racial continuity, maternity, and female virtue as inherent phenomena. Both Jacobs and her editor/benefactress, Lydia Maria Child, seized upon the idea of "The Good Grandmother" as a way of refuting northern white women's ideas of black women as bad, unclean, and natally dead. Child even published an excerpt of Jacob's narrative under the title "The Good Grandmother" in her 1865 text *The Freedmen's Book*.

Jacobs's grandmother fits the typical role of the mammy figure: a nurturing black woman beloved by all "who could do anything, and do it better than anyone else. Because of her expertise in all domestic matters, she was the premier house servant and all others were her subordinates."[110] Whites in the community refer to the grandmother as "Aunty" and "mammy."[111] Underlying all of the goodness and affection associated with the mammy was an undercurrent of cruelty and self-sacrifice from which young white women, such as Mrs. Flint, benefited. For it was implicitly understood that, unlike that of the Jezebel, the role of the mammy displaced "sexuality into nurture and transformed potential hostility into sustenance and love."[112] Devoid of sexuality, the mammy served as a font of nurturing. She was the perfect emotional playground, the perfect vehicle through which young white women could work out and practice their need, their sexual hostility, and other types of aggression.

Mrs. Flint learns in the suckling stage of her development this utilitarian purpose of the mammy figure. Years and generations later, it still pains Aunt Marthy that while nursing her female child she had to take "her own baby from her breast to nourish his wife [Mrs. Flint]."[113] Even when Mrs. Flint is dismissive of Jacobs's grandmother, not greeting her when she passes her in the street, the black woman, because of her abiding maternal feelings, cannot completely disconnect from the white woman. Jacobs relates that such public treatment "wounded my grandmother's feelings, for she could not retain ill will against the woman whom she had nourished with her milk when a babe."[114] Jacobs's grandmother and

Mrs. Flint have an entirely different expectation of the maternal bond that binds them. Mrs. Flint's nurturing in infancy is intrinsically tied to the starvation of and emotional denial of the slave. Her spitting in pots, denying food to her cook and her cook's children, are gestures that reflect the dominion of her white womanhood and the kindred tie that she has learned from her mother, her aunts, and at the breast of Aunt Marthy.

Mrs. Flint's mother, while more subtle and refined in her appetites, maintains rituals of social consumption that devolve upon the black mammy figure. By the time we encounter Jacobs's grandmother in the narrative, she is a free woman. Her freedom from slavery is not so much given as it is earned through backbreaking labor and sacrifice. She does her plantation chores as well as additional baking, washing, and other jobs in order to save up money to purchase her freedom and that of family members. Before her mistress dies, the elderly white woman borrows $300 from Aunt Marthy to purchase a silver candelabra. She promises to pay the money back and to free Aunt Marthy upon her death. She never pays the money back and only frees the black woman after she has died and has no further use of her. Her will and testament reflects her promise to free Aunt Marthy, but Dr. Flint does not honor the will. Instead, he puts the grandmother up for sale at a private auction. Adding insult to injury, he also keeps the silver candelabra as part of his personal cache of precious household wares. Jacobs paints a classic sentimental scene around the selling of her grandmother:

> When the day of sale came, she took her place among the chattels, and at the first call she sprang upon the auction-block. Many voices called out, "Shame! Shame! Who is going to sell *you*, aunt Marthy? Don't stand there! That is no place for *you*." Without saying a word, she quietly awaited her fate. No one bid for her. At last, a feeble voice said, "Fifty dollars." It came from a maiden lady, seventy years old, the sister of my grandmother's deceased mistress. She had lived forty years under the same roof with my grandmother; she knew how faithfully she had served her owners, and how cruelly she had been defrauded of her rights; and she resolved to protect her.[115]

Miss Fanny purchases the black woman for the extremely low price of fifty dollars. Jacobs casts white women such as Miss Fanny and her sister in the role of protectresses, as honorable, keepers of their word, good, conscionable, and ladylike. The author has little to say of the silver candelabra purchased with the money saved by an enslaved woman to purchase her freedom and that of her children. For the sake of her white female readership, Jacobs emphasizes instead the good intentions of the deceased mistress and the system of self-sacrifice and reward that ultimately secures the freedom of Aunt Marthy. Flint serves as a type of pressure valve through which Jacobs filters all of the contradiction and irony of the grandmother's predicament. He is the executor of the elder white woman's will, he keeps the candelabra, and he advertises the selling of Jacobs's grandmother.[116] Flint fits seamlessly into this role, since we have already come to associate him with greed and extreme sexual appetite.

Yet we should not too hastily separate the refinement and good taste of Aunt Marthy's mistress from the social consumption of the black mammy. If Flint is a despot and pariah, then it is his wife's affluence and her deceased grandmother's wealth that infuses and animates his desires. By law, Jacobs and her children belong to Flint's wife. While Flint is brash and blatant (his appetites and devouring nature pronounced throughout the narrative), the consumptive drives of the deceased white mistress remain cloaked in finery and social affluence. The silver candelabra serves as an emblem of her good taste, an article recognized in the domestic sphere as beautiful, tasteful, and feminine. In this way, the grandmother's labor and state of enslavement feed into and sustain this white woman's self-esteem and domestic virtue. The characteristics of self-sacrifice and self-negation typically ascribed to the mammy facilitate this white woman in fulfilling her fantasies of material well-being and social finery.

Jacobs's configuration of the goodly black grandmother and the beneficent white female does not readily reveal the ties of consumption binding the black grandmother to her mistress. In Jacobs's version of her history, she encourages us to perceive no connection between the acquired high cultural tastes of Mrs. Flint's grandmother and Mrs. Flint's starving her of slaves and hovering over Jacobs at night in a sexually suggestive manner. The nursing of the young white mistress in infancy apparently has nothing to do with the institutionalized starving of the black woman's children on the plantation. To clarify, I am not suggesting that we replace the "good" with the "bad," recasting Mrs. Flint's grandmother, for example, as the bad white woman who does not free her slave and steals the money the black woman has saved to purchase her freedom. What I am urging is a more complex understanding of the good, of the fact that we cannot divorce a white slave mistress's good intentions from the spiritual depravity and practices of social consumption that shaped her.[117]

I have no doubt that Mrs. Flint's mother cared deeply for Aunt Marthy. Neither do I doubt the affections of the larger white community, whom she supplied "with crackers and preserves" and who "respected her intelligence and *good character*."[118] The whites who yell out "Shame! Shame! Who is going to sell *you*, Aunt Marthy? Don't stand there! That is no place for you" have grown up at the nurturing breast and spoon of Aunt Marthy.[119] Like the well-shined silver candelabra, she is a familiar and valued fixture in their emotional and psychic worlds. They imagine her as surrogate mother, familiar, and relative, and hence, the spectacle of the black woman on the auction block shocks them. Mary Prince, a black woman who experienced slavery around the same time, likened the auction block to the butcher block. Standing for auction, as I have mentioned once, she recalls: "I was soon surrounded by strange men, who examined and handled me in the same manner a butcher would a calf or a lamb he was about to purchase, and who talked about my shape and size in like words—as if I could no more understand their meaning than the dumb beasts."[120] The whites imagine Aunt Marthy as separate and apart from the economy of human consumption that Prince describes. What they seem to not realize, though, is that their regard for the mammy's self-sacrifice and over-brimming goodness serve only to oil and ease the machinery of consumption.

What I am attempting to tease out through this auction block scene is the difference between the institution of consumption and the intimate human ties that fueled and enabled this system. It was one thing for whites to construct gurneys and rope ties or to literally feed a slave into a machine, such as the cotton gin. And it was an altogether different matter for them to feel, as one Kentucky slave master felt, a sense of enjoyment and completion in the consumption of the slave. We have already observed that, after literally butchering and cooking his slave's quartered body over an open fire, this Kentucky slave owner reported to his wife that "he had never enjoyed himself so well at a ball as he had enjoyed himself that evening."[121] I am not equating the whites gathered around the auction block with the heinousness of this particular slave master. This man was more insane than most and later committed suicide. Yet his example of acquiring a taste for the Negro is instructive. It demonstrates, in the extreme, how whites within a culture of consumption could not help but develop tastes, affections, and high cultural values rooted in the chattel slave. I see little difference between the Kentucky slave owner who associates the butchering and cooking of flesh with ballroom refinery and the whites gathered around the auction block associating sacred maternal feelings with a black woman who is at base an "owned object," a utilitarian repository of their infantile memories and needs.

It is the good in these whites and not the bad that completes the circuit (the logic of need and self-denial that undergirds mechanisms of consumption). Without the intimate, feel-good tie between the mammy and her white progeny, there could be no psychic and spiritual consumption. And without ideological and symbolic structures intended to validate the mammy's consumption, there could be no sanity in this essentially inverted reality—which is why, getting back to the bedroom interactions between Mrs. Flint and Jacobs, we need different structures of erotic desire, gender, and intimacy to help us make a broader sense of slave experience within this essentially unstable and hunger-driven context. We cannot get from here to there (to an understanding of the masculine mistress or of Jacobs's fears of death and sexual violation) through models of gender and sex that always privilege the patriarch and the male/female conjugal union as natural and originary states.

Mrs. Flint does not simulate masculinity, as some have suggested, nor does she simulate the master's erotic desire and dominion. She *is* masculine. She is aggressor and predator. She comes naturally by a "restless, craving, vicious nature" that causes her to rove about, like her husband, "day and night, seeking whom to devour."[122] Her masculine drive originates in the domestic sphere, a fact that goes against usual ways of thinking about the feminine as linked to the domestic realm and about masculinity as originating within the male body and the male sexual drive. Describing Mrs. Flint as whispering in her husband's voice and adopting his erotic mindset is as close as Jacobs can safely come to asserting that Mrs. Flint is male, acting male, seeming to her senses and sensibilities to be male. Such discussion of a male type of female was risky, as it could be easily used to support commonly held notions of women as hungering and disfigured and black women, in particular, as sexually knowledgeable, monstrous, and devouring. Social conventions limited Jacobs, as did her reliance upon a pristine, untainted model of womanhood. However, these discursive limitations upon Jacobs need not restrict our exploration of gender variance in the narrative.

Mrs. Flint's masculinity makes greater sense when we think about her through the ideology of slave consumption. Mrs. Flint's "male behaviors" serve as an index for appetite and consumptive capacity. Jacobs understands slavery as sexual ravishment and sexual ravishment as a process that facilitates the consumption of the female slave. She lays out this ideology when she speaks of Dr. Flint as hungering and devouring and as one who consistently channels these appetites into acts of sexual domination.[123] More than anything, Mrs. Flint hungers like a man, a fact that shocks and terrifies Jacobs as she lies beneath her mistress in the dead of night. Only through this deeper understanding of and contextualization of masculinity can we understand how impor- tant and intrinsic hunger and consumption are to the white female's gender and domestic identity. We might even say, in a way that scholars up to this point have not allowed, that hunger and appetite are constitu- tive of gender and sex within the plantation context. Does hunger then come before sex and gender, or do the former categories come before the latter? It is a question that merits extensive examination beyond the purview of this study. I point out the correlation between hunger and gender categorizations only so that we might understand how the mas- culinity of the mistress is a significant point of fact. As opposed to being a male mask, the mistress's "male identity" is more a reflection of an intrinsic consumptive capacity that we cannot otherwise get at within the lexicon of nineteenth-century gender roles.

Not just in Mrs. Flint but in other slave owners we find hunger depicted as fluid, mutable, and able to conform to myriad social con- ventions. In other parts of the narrative, Jacobs documents plantation mistresses who taunt and pursue their female slaves with the "might of a man."[124] Even Flint does not operate out of a strict sense of patriar- chal authority. At one point, he writes to Jacobs in the guise of a slave mistress. He wants her to voluntarily return home after having escaped from the plantation. He entreats: "The family will be rejoiced to see you; and your poor old grandmother expressed a great desire to have you come, when she heard your letter read. In her old age she needs the consolation of having her children round her."[125] Adding another layer of sentimentality to his maternal voice, Flint describes an all-night vigil at the bedside of Jacobs's dying aunt: "Could you have seen us round her death bed, with her mother, all mingling our tears in one common stream, you would have thought the same heartfelt tie existed between a master and his servant as between a mother and her child."[126] Flint manipulates the consumptive currency of the black mammy. He plays upon Jacobs's mother loss and mother hunger, hoping to entice her back through her unrequited needs. Explaining the correlation between emotional and physical starvation and sexual ravishment, Jacobs reveals that "the slave girl is reared in an atmosphere of licentiousness and fear. . . . When she is fourteen or fifteen, her owner, or his sons, or the overseer, or perhaps all of them, begin to bribe her with presents. If these fail to accomplish their purpose, she is whipped or *starved into submission to their will.*"[127]

When we figure hunger centrally into the equation of gender and sex in the narrative, what we presume to know about certain normative realms of experience gives way to a fluid uncertainty. How are we to make sense of masters who speak in the voices of young mistresses? And to what extent can we rely upon a patriarchal model of consumption when women such as Mrs. Flint's grandmother anticipate and enable the consumptive passions of her son-in-law, Dr. Flint?

## Male Mothers and Female Masters

I began this discussion of gender variance and the master's epicurean hungers with the example of Luke. By beginning with Luke and an exploration of his gender and sexual ambiguity and then tracking similar findings in Jacobs's life and circumstances, my intention was to denude us of certain binary logics and relationships: man/woman, black female abolitionist/white female abolitionist, master/mistress, and reproductive/neutered, among others. In response to my own question about how to make sense of Flint as a male grandmother and the inherently "masculine" appetites of Mrs. Flint, I think that we need to begin from an implied zero ground: the unstable sex, gender, and corporeality of the slave. In the context of Jacobs's slave narrative, the Flints' gender fluidity rests upon the bedrock of gender and sex presumptions attributed to the body and person of the slave. Both Jacobs and Luke, I have labored to prove, embody this central dynamic of gender and sex instability in their relationships to abusive masters and within same-sex erotic scenarios that defy normative schemas of gender and sex formation. The master/slave dynamic, as fruitful as it is, can take us only so far in understanding how gender variance and gender fluidity have historically operated in the lives of enslaved persons.

What I have had in mind this whole time is Luke and Jacobs together constituting a new and dynamic field of possibility. For they are not just anonymous actors in Jacobs's narrative, but historical antecedents to "Sapphire," who "enacts her "Old Man" in drag"[128] and to Trudier Harris's conception of the black male mammy who services white men on the plantation and during the Reconstruction era.[129] In the slave past and still today, the gender-variant dyad of black male-and-female functions as an antinode of black experience, that dynamic that we have privately and silently acknowledged but have disavowed in all ways in the public domain. Hortense J. Spillers has, quite astutely, identified the politics of *gender differentiation* as central to black subject making in the New World. Spillers conceives of the captivity in Africa and the Middle Passage as "a *theft* of the *body*—a *willful and* violent . . . severing of the captive body from its motive will, its active desire."[130] She also equates this theft of the black body with the loss of gender identity for black people in the New World: "Under these conditions, we lose at least *gender* difference *in the outcome*, and the female body and the male body become a territory of cultural and political maneuver, not at all gender-related, gender-specific." In the absence of gender specificity, of distinctive categories of gender, Spillers finds the enslaved black body functioning in European and white American imaginations "as a category of 'otherness,' the captive body translat[ing] into a potential for pornotroping and embod[ying] sheer physical powerlessness that slides into a more general 'powerlessness,' resonating through various centers of human and social meaning."[131] Who can contest Spillers's spot-on analysis of gender ambiguity coinciding with white American conceptions of black animality, disfigurement, sexual taint, and the clandestine "pornotroping" that has characterized white erotic access to black bodies under slavery? Colonial-era whites constructed "black," "slave," "chattel," and "African" to mean qualitatively nothing and virtually anything. These indeterminate categories whites then mapped onto black, male, and female bodies in overlapping and indiscriminate ways. Spiller's well-stated point is that this gender ambiguity mapped onto Negroid bodies helped concretize the exclusion of African Americans from the humane categories of mother, father, statesman, son, daughter, citizen, and so forth.

The challenge, though, with what Spillers describes as the political imperative to differentiate between genders is that within African Americanist scholarship, this gender politics has contributed to a theoretical aversion to gender and sex instability. We have yet to fully develop or recover the ability to see black culture as positively constituted through a fluid gender and sex dynamic. For example, in *Ain't I a Woman: Black Women and Feminism*, bell hooks conceives of "the masculinization of the black female and the . . . de-masculinization of the black male" as primarily dysfunctional experiences that can only reveal to us "the dynamics of sexist and racist oppression during slavery."[132] hooks, keeping to a strict understanding of black demasculinization as the loss of the phallus, of phallic might, asserts that "while black men were not forced to assume a role colonial American society regarded as 'feminine,' black women were forced to assume a 'masculine' role."[133] hooks's rigid conception of gender forecloses, from the outset, any consideration of men such as Luke, who were effeminized and made to play a range of social roles that transgress normative gender roles. Angela Y. Davis, in her pioneering scholarship on black women's roles during slavery, locates the idea of the genderless black female in plantation labor practices: "Expediency governed the slaveholder's posture toward female slaves: when it was profitable to exploit them as if they were men, they were regarded, in effect, as genderless."[134] Davis also equates the genderless black woman and female masculinity with the negative intentions of the master and the sense of the genderless black women as lacking power and social agency.

Michelle Wallace has linked black cultural workers' long-standing aversion to gender and sex fluidity to 1980s radical black sexual politics.

Describing the black homosexual as descending from black women raped during slavery, she writes: "The black homosexual is counter-revolutionary (1) because he's being fucked and (2) because he's being fucked by a white man. By so doing he reduces himself to the status of our black grandmothers who, as everyone knows, were fucked by white men all the time."[135] As with hooks, Wallace conceives of sexual variance within radical black experience as a reflection of "the dynamics of sexist and racist oppression during slavery."[136] How unfortunate that association with black female sexual violation under slavery would render black men in the late twentieth century counterrevolutionary. This is exactly what I am talking about, the clear need that we see demonstrated in Wallace's commentary for a sex and gender politics that would allow the contemporary male homosexual to positively embody the powerful legacy of the sexually violated grandmothers under slavery. As it stands, during the time of Wallace's writing and still today, black men who embody the sexual genealogies of the black mother and grandmothers suffer misrecognition and demonization within most arenas of black radical activity and thought.[137] Trudier Harris, whom I quoted from earlier, excavates the reality of the black grandmotherly or mammy-like figure only as a means of demonstrating black men's emotionally emasculated relationships to white men, stemming back to slavery.

In calling our attention to Luke and Jacobs as a prototypical, historically resonant pairing, I had in mind the implicit gender-variant pairings that have informed the logic of Harris, hooks, Davis, or Spillers, who each, in her own way, construes gender variance and instability as a negative state to be corrected or transcended. In her discussion of gender, Spillers describes a transgendered Sapphire switching gender roles with her father: "'Sapphire' enacts her 'Old Man' in drag, just as her 'Old Man' becomes 'Sapphire' in outrageous caricature."[138] hooks pairs the improbable black male effeminate with masculinized black women on the plantation. Harris's notion of the black male mammy parallels black female powerlessness. It is the masculine connotations implied in the mammy role and black women in general that lends itself to donning or dragging by black men under slavery. Then there is Wallace's notion of black men who enact the sexual roles of raped maternal figures from slavery. Wallace also invokes, as a parallel structure, the masculinized

black woman from the plantation. In a largely unacknowledged manner, these gender- and sexually variant pairings have operated and continue to operate at the nexus of our conceptualizations of black bodies,
sexes, gender expressions, and so forth that emerged out of slavery.

As a pairing, Luke and Jacobs help us see the positive outcomes
of theorizing gender fluidity. The variance and fluidity of Luke and
Jacobs enable them to survive within a culture of human consumption.
Luke's role of the male mammy facilitates his resistance to his master
and reveals to us, in stark fashion, the deeper, often unseen dynamics
of incest and emotional hunger charging the relation between master
and slave. Although Jacobs provides ambiguous information about his
erotic proclivities, we can and should still speculate about the ways in
which, perhaps, Luke's erotic desire for men or for a specific man may
have sustained him and made him resistant to his master's desires to
erotically partake of and consume him. Likewise, with Jacobs, in maintaining so vehemently the narrative of her pursuit of motherhood, we
have largely overlooked how an aggressive sexuality and masculinized
female economy of reproduction defined her relationship to reproduction and her children. Perhaps, then, her pursuit of coital pleasure and
the children that resulted are better thought of as expressions of her
resistance to social consumption. Of course, if we follow this line of
thinking, we have to think about Jacobs in all sorts of sexually knowledgeable and therefore unsexed capacities. In additional to her sexuality, there is also the genealogy of Jacobs's gender and black maternity,
which I have already explained as rooted in the notion of male mistresses and "masculinized" white female appetite and aggression. It is
time for us, as forward-thinking scholars of slavery, to get beyond our
theoretical aversions to gender and sex variance under slavery. I have
attempted to clarify, through the example of a variant Luke and Jacobs,
that we still have much labor to do in the way of formally excavating
and beginning to analyze the import of the gender-crossing, sexually
fluid pairing.

5

Eating Nat Turner

Most people do not readily associate Nat Turner, the heroic figure and slave insurrectionist, with the themes of auto-cannibalism (self-consumption), white male consumptive desires, or homoeroticism. These themes, however, strongly informed how Southampton, Virginia, whites punished Turner and treated his corpse after his public lynching. In the nineteenth century, the white press throughout the country reported that Turner had "sold his body for dissection, and spent the money on ginger cakes."[1] Many papers reported that Turner "feasted on" these sweet ginger cakes "before his own execution."[2] This was an erroneous assertion, as slaves did not own themselves and therefore had no agency to barter and trade in their own flesh. More than anything, this ginger cakes story reflected the psychology of whites who needed to convince themselves that black men such as Turner somehow consented to and were complicit in their social consumption. This linking of consent to black self-consumption was a common idea that found its way into lynching ritual practices in the late nineteenth and early twentieth centuries. In 1934, whites made Claude Neal, whom they lynched in Jackson Country, Florida, eat his cut off penis and testicles. James McGovern relates the details of the Neal lynching in *Anatomy of a Lynching*: "After taking the nigger to the woods about four miles from Greenwood, they cut off his penis. He was made to eat it. Then they cut off his testicles and made him eat them and say he liked it."[3]

Making Neal eat his own sexual organs, as grotesque as this was, was only a by-product of an even more disturbing reality of white hunger and power. The cutting off and forced eating of the penis was a reflection of white male oral fixations upon black male virility and black men as a sexual threat. In a different erotic scenario, the white men might have taken the black penis into their own mouths or anuses, but in the absence of such imaginative privacy, they use the black male body as a type of puppet through which they grope, grapple with, and ultimately subdue their hungers for black male flesh and sex. On the level of ritual, it is not enough to simply desire and want to consume Neal; the ritual is not complete until he eats the evidence of white desire, swallowing his debasement and degradation along with white hunger and erotic fascination.

Many whites feared that Turner would literally rise from the grave and rebone himself. This is how some have explained the gruesome cannibalization of Turner after his death.[4] William Sydney Drewry, a member of the Southampton community, documented in *The Southhampton Insurrection* (1900) the exact methods of punishment and postmortem abuse of Turner's body. According to Drewry, after Turner was executed, his body was "delivered to doctors, who skinned it and made grease of the flesh. Mr. R. S. Barham's father owned a money purse made of his hide."[5] This desire to literally possess Turner's flesh and make use of his body calls to mind the homoerotics of the Neal scenario, with Turner's flesh serving as fetish and symbol of corporeal possession. The money purse made of Turner's skin and the grease made from his boiled-down flesh convey the limitless consumptive uses of the slave and the myriad ways in which the ruling class could satiate unspoken desires and tastes for Negro flesh. Blacks of the Southampton community further complicated this erotics of taste through accusations that whites ingested Turner's boiled-down flesh as a medical substance, as I discussed earlier. William Styron brought all of this suppressed homoerotic and consumptive history to the fore with the publication of *The Confessions of Nat Turner* (1968). Styron's *The Confessions* and the debate that surrounded it clarified, like no moment before had, why black people have maintained a tight-lipped silence on the subject of homoeroticism under slavery. Homoeroticism, especially in the context of Turner's legacy, brought up for black people in the 1960s unspeakable issues of white consumption of blacks, sexual objectification, bestial treatment under a white regime, and the inconceivable topic of auto-cannibalism (blacks made to eat one another and themselves during slavery). The 1960s was a moment when the legacy of black consumption under slavery culminated around the activist platforms and ideologies of the Civil Rights and Black Power Movements. The subjects of slavery, homosexuality, and cannibalism took front-page prominence in newspapers and journals, editorials, speak-outs, and mediated conversations between blacks and whites.

In this chapter, I use the black radical 1960s to further illuminate the myriad social, spiritual, political, and moral implications of white hunger for and consumption of the black male during slavery. Issues of memory and temporality figure prominently in this chapter and drive my desire to understand the emotional and psychic forces that accrued around Turner's person, lending his life a mythic and transhistorical significance in the 1960s. Some of the black men who responded collectively to Styron's novel in the widely read *William Styron's Nat Turner: Ten Black Writers Respond* accused Styron of institutionalized cannibalism, of attempting to eat Nat Turner. These black men referred to the legacy of white cannibalism that I discuss in earlier chapters. In this mid-twentieth-century moment—characterized by political activism, black self-determination, and anti-apartheid efforts at home and abroad—black people powerfully linked individual and institutional consumption of "the Negro" to a negative understanding of homosexuality and effeminacy. The implicit homoerotics of flesh tasting and the particulars of white culinary appetite for black flesh congealed in this moment. One thing that was clarified through this union and in the context of national debate was why, during and beyond slavery, it has been so difficult for black people to talk openly about homoeroticism and, furthermore, to talk in complex ways about the linkages among black male gender formation, intimacy patterns originating in slavery, same-sex desire, and racial uplift.

In this chapter and through Turner's legacy, I broach the issue of why so little evidence and analysis of homoeroticism during slavery has "survived." By referencing the antebellum cannibalism debate, discussions of resistance and revolt during slavery, and the charged, pivotal 1960s, I ground this idea of homoerotic survival in political and social context.

Because what this 1960s moment reveals, among its many startling revelations, is how homoeroticism in the context of black experience has always been embedded in issues of black nation formation, liberation politics, and the legacy of literal and metaphoric black consumption. In the second portion of the chapter, James Baldwin emerges as an important mediating figure and filter for my discussion of homoeroticism and black cultural formation in the 1960s. As friend of Styron and nationally acknowledged black activist and artist, Baldwin found himself in the uncomfortable position of speaking as a black and homosexual person who understood the import of blacks and whites breaking their historical silence concerning the homoerotic legacies of slavery. Rather than disavowing Styron's use of Turner's memory, Baldwin felt it necessary that white artists such as Styron be allowed to work through their fears of and fixations upon the black revolutionary. Baldwin saw Styron confronting black people with a disturbing but necessary vision of a shared racial history and feared that black people would, out of their terror at the past and mistrust of white people, miss out on this historic opportunity to dialogue and confront the past. At base, Baldwin advocated for a model of black homoeroticism that incorporated and transformed the trauma of the past. I resuscitate Baldwin's model and correlate it with the visions and racial uplift politics of the same black male race leaders who denied and denigrated his person and vision.

## The Negro Homosexual Problem

W. E. B. Du Bois's powerful framing of the Negro problem has gone down in history as one of the most formative premises of the beginning of the twentieth century. This question literally haunted the lives and social strivings of black people in the nineteenth and twentieth centuries. For it was emancipation, the acquisition of the vote, and the desire to own property and contribute as a full member of society that made the Negro problematic. This was not a static problem. Rather, it was the outgrowth of cataclysmic, dynamic social change. The Negro problem and the Negro's emergence into full, protected citizen status were two sides of the same coin. Acknowledging the twentieth-century importance of this problem, I would like to propose a slight amendment to its scope. In the 1960s a newer, more complicated version of this problematic emerged onto the national scene, and that was the problem of homosexuality within black experience. From the antebellum period on, this problem had percolated and boiled beneath black family structures, racial liberation and uplift, and icons of male heroicism and valiance. In 1967, this bedrock gave way to the lava underneath, and what had long remained unspoken in the mainstream took on frightening voice and form.

The occasion for this eruption was the publication of Styron's *The Confessions*. Styron described the novel in the "Author's Note" as "a meditation on history."[6] Styron took the title of the text directly from Thomas R. Gray's interview with Turner, "The Confessions of Nat Turner" (1831), which Gray published after Turner was executed. The novel explores the specifics of Turner's upbringing and his relationship to his kinsmen. Special attention is given to the topics of his parental lineage, his life on the plantation as a "house slave," his early childhood interactions with and feelings toward his enslaved kinsmen, his acquisition of literacy, and his lifelong mission of enlightening his fellow men. It culminates, of course, with the Southampton insurrection. In keeping with the confessional format of the original "Confessions," in the novel, Turner tells his story to a fictional Gray, a court-appointed attorney who visits him while he awaits execution and records all the minutiae of his life. Widely reviewed and well received, Styron's novel received the Pulitzer Prize in 1968 and was translated into at least five different languages—German, Spanish, and Italian among them. Even before its publication, the New American Library paid $100,000 for the paperback rights. The Book-of-the-Month Club set a personal record by offering $150,000 for the novel.[7] Styron could not have known that his novel would become a lightning rod for racial controversy. He was not the first nor would he be the last to revisit the memory of Turner in order to make sense of his life for a present generation.[8] The publication of Styron's novel collided with a number of other historical forces to produce an explosive effect: Malcolm X was assassinated on February 21, 1965; on March 31, 1968, Lyndon Johnson announced that he would not run for reelection; four days later Martin Luther King Jr. was assassinated; and approximately a month and a half later, Styron received the Pulitzer Prize for a novel that, in the minds of many, denigrated the memory of King and other black freedom fighters and revolutionaries.

All of these historical occurrences set the stage for the Black Power era and marked a time of increased black militancy, which Turner's revolution legacy perfectly embodied. Unlike those who struggled during the 1940s or 50s, blacks at this moment in history grew more vocal about the connection between their radical efforts and historical recovery efforts and were therefore not willing to allow Styron or any other white person to continue to appropriate and determine the meaning of their radical heroes from the past.

In an essay review of the novel, Oliver Killens felt moved to correlate King's death with that of that other "valiant freedom-fighter," Nat Turner. Concerning Styron's depiction of Turner, he notes: "It reveals more about the psyche of the 'southern liberal' Styron, direct descendent of ol' Massa, than it even begins to reveal about the heart and soul and mind of black revolutionary Nat Turner." He goes on to correlate the popular reception of Styron's novel with the death of King: "Black brothers and sisters, be not deceived by the obscene weeping and gnashing of teeth by white America over the assassination of our great black brother and Messiah, Martin Luther King. They loved him not, or he would still be here amongst us. They understood him not. Our Martin was a revolutionary, and they did not dig him; therefore they destroyed him."[9] Black people felt themselves assailed from all sides, in the present moment by white racist institutions and ideologies and in their memories of the past, which they felt that whites like Styron had stripped from them and distorted. Blacks felt that Styron had written his own white liberal southern confession rather than anything that approached Turner's motivations, convictions, and interior struggles.

To be fair, it was not entirely Styron's fault that the media and the conservative mainstream artistic community had lauded his novel and positioned him as an authentic scribe of Negro male psychology and historical experience.[10] Had he not received so much attention and been hailed as a true, insightful perceiver, his document and his historical methodology would have probably received little attention from black people. But his accolades mirrored too closely the violent racial reality of the 1960s. That same year, 1968, Columbia, the university that administered the Pulitzer, acted in a racially prejudiced manner toward the black Harlem community, moving to violently contain student civil disobedience efforts.[11] In 1963, a white assassin had gunned down Medgar

Evers, the field secretary for the NAACP, in his Mississippi carport. The Nation of Islam, with the rumored assistance of the, U.S. Secret Service, had assassinated Malcolm X in 1965. That same year a six-day insurrection began in the Watts section of Los Angeles.[12]

Amid this national furor, Styron's novel and notoriety led to the resurrection of the most contentious and racially charged aspects of Turner's legacy. In November of 1968, Styron received a letter from one Robert B. Franklin in Elkhart, Indiana, describing how he had come to possess Turner's missing skull. "I have in my possession a skull," he begins,

> which I believe to be that of Nat Turner. . . . The skull was given to me by my father who inherited it from his. My grandfather was a doctor who practiced in Richmond, Virginia, around the turn of the century. The skull was given to him by a female patient whose name is not known. She claimed to have gotten it from her father who was a physician in attendance when Nat Turner was executed.[13]

Turner's missing skull had long been a sore spot for black people living in and outside of the Southampton, Virginia, community. The beheading of Turner coincided with the boiling down of his flesh and the use of his skin parts to make the notorious money purse. Franklin's letter to Styron only confirmed long-standing black suspicions that whites had literally and socially consumed Turner's body. Whether or not Franklin actually possessed Turner's skull (a fact that remains today unproven by medical science), his safeguarding of the skull and treating it like a cherished family heirloom demonstrates that well into the late twentieth century, the possession of Turner's cannibalized body had social and historic significance for whites.

This issue of whites consuming Turner's body influenced late nineteenth- and mid-twentieth-century black resistance communities and their practices. The nineteenth-century question of Turner's consumption reared its head in the twentieth century in a way that redefined the issue of black consumption under slavery and lent an even greater import to the disappearance of Turner's body. In the 1960s, such concerns took on a political edge that is documented in the above-mentioned *Ten Black Writers Respond*. Apart from its critique of Styron's novel, *Ten Black Writers Respond* is a singular historical and cultural document that is a touchstone for the numerous debates that surrounded the novel. I intend to address Styron's novel shortly. Before analyzing the novel, though, I want to spend a bit of time on *Ten Black Writers Respond*, because the range of activist, scholarly, and psychological perspectives contained therein provides a frame for my later readings of homoeroticism and consumption during slavery. The individuals published in *Ten Black Writers Respond* help us understand how time and memory altered the cannibalism debates that I present in earlier chapters, and they also clarify how a more contemporary language of consumption and same-sex eroticism evolved from slavery-era debates about cannibalism.

The subject of cannibalism during slavery was difficult for black people to talk about in the 1960s, in some respects even more difficult than it was for black people who lived through slavery. This difficulty had in part to do with Turner's dismemberment (his missing skull and the coveted money purse made of his skin) and the fact that he never received a complete burial. Moreover, this torture and social consumption of Turner constituted an unresolved realm of racial trauma that black men had not yet begun to forthrightly address. In an essay from *Ten Black Writers Respond*, "The Failure of William Styron," Ernest Kaiser chastises Styron for writing an article that gives the explicit details about cooking and consuming Turner's flesh: "Examples of bestial descriptions in his article," writes Kaiser, "are his unnecessary, gruesome explanation that the doctors skinned Nat Turner's dead body, after he was hanged along with 17 other Negroes, and made grease of his flesh; and the lurid details in his novel of the killings of whites by Negroes."[14] Kaiser spoke for most of the black men in the edited collection who simply could not bear such descriptions of Turner, which they claimed violated Turner in body as well as in cherished memory. In a moving letter to Harriet Tubman in 1868, Frederick Douglass described a domain of African American memory reserved only for the most hallowed, self-sacrificing revolutionaries. He writes: "Excepting John Brown—of sacred memory—I know of no one who has willingly encountered more perils and hardships to serve our enslaved people than you have. Much that you have done would seem improbable to those who do not know you as I know you."[15] For Douglass, what makes

John Brown sacred is his commitment, his sacrifice, and his willingness to die for black liberty. In his 1907 biography on Douglass, Booker T. Washington also invoked this idea of sacred memory, seeing in Douglass the noble embodiment of all black struggles during slavery: "The life of Frederick Douglass is the history of American slavery epitomized in a single human experience. He saw it all, lived it all, and overcame it all."[16] In Douglass, Washington saw what was "greatest" in the race as well as the potential for "a high destiny."[17]

It was this spirit of commitment to the sacred memory of Turner that inspired the distinguished activist/scholar John Henrik Clarke to compile and edit *Ten Black Writers Respond*. The idea was to hold persons such as Brown and Turner in their best light, to emphasize the aspects of their lives that could inspire and ennoble future generations. In his introduction to the collection, Clarke emphasizes the connection between the sacred memory of Turner and the political climate of the 1960s: "The contributors to this book collectively maintain that the distortion of the true character of Nat Turner was deliberate. The motive for this distortion could be William Styron's reaction to the racial climate that has prevailed in the United States in the last fifteen years."[18] Clarke goes on to position H. Rap Brown and Stokely Carmichael, two Black Power proponents, as direct descendants of Turner's legacy. Some of the titles of the essay compiled in the anthology reveal the feelings of the sacred and personal ownership black men associated with Turner's memory: Vincent Harding's "You've Taken My Nat and Gone," Lerone Bennett Jr.'s "Nat's Last White Man," and Charles V. Hamilton's "Our Nat Turner and William Styron's Creation" are examples.

The image of Turner as consumed by whites did not fit into this model of the sacred black heroic figure. In his analysis cited earlier, Kaiser links the cannibalization of Turner to emasculation, effeminacy, and larger moral issues confronting the nation. He points out how Styron's argument builds upon the "fraudulent and untenable thesis of Frank Tannebaum and Stanley M. Elkins," which was "that American slavery was so oppressive, despotic and emasculating psychologically that revolt was impossible and Negroes could only be Sambos."[19] Styron has admitted in an interview that the text that most influenced his thinking about slavery as an institution and the slave's psychology was Elkins's *Slavery*.[20] Kaiser briefly entertains the issue of cannibalism in the white author's writing only to point out how "lurid," "bestial" and "morally wrong" are Styron's perspectives.[21] Kaiser's remarks reveal how black people repressed and did not discuss certain painful issues, such as this issue of human consumption. It was painful for blacks and strategically risky to publicly broach subjects that might add fuel to white misconceptions and attempts to emasculate black men in the past and the present. Only twenty years earlier, ethnologist Melville J. Herskovitz had published *The Myth of the Negro Past* (1941) as a way of refuting strongly held beliefs that the Negro had no cultural legacy, came from a land of heathens and cannibals, and benefited from his bondage in America.[22] Styron's novel proved that for many whites all of the revised black history and documented anthropological proof in the world could not dissuade them from the idea that the African was innately ignorant and destined to subservience to the white male. Kaiser paraphrases Gertrude Wilson of the *New York Amsterdam News*, who explained the connections between Styron's *Confessions* and contemporary racial apartheid in the following manner: "The book is so popular with whites because it proves that if Negroes retaliate against injustice by violence, they will be quelled by violence. The book also gives, she says, the blessing of history for continued violence against Negroes."[23] The rampant church bombings, lynchings, and assassinations of the 1960s supported Wilson's assertions. Styron's novel only exacerbated the myths and social fictions that fueled this institutionalized violence against African American persons.

## Equating Black Consumption with Homosexuality

Kaiser's unwillingness to talk about the topic of cannibalism did not make it any less relevant to or have less of an impact on all of the ten black men who responded to Styron's novel. In fact, what happened as a result of the compounded pain of the past and the threat of social consumption and racial annihilation in the present was that black men approached discussions of Styron's novel in order to liberate the voice of the people and at the same time reinforce historical silences. Their general approach tended to diminish the emotional aspects of their masculinity, foregrounding a negative image of homosexuality, and left the issues of white consumption and black self-consumption to

fester in the black imagination and soul. The ten black male contributors coupled cannibalism (overtly and covertly) with homoeroticism
and effeminacy. For these black men, homoeroticism became a way
of circumventing and projecting their experiences and pain onto certain "effeminate" black men: the consumed black man these black men
equated with the homosexual man. Homosexuality served as a means
of containing certain unwieldy and historically difficult topics pertaining to black masculinity, such as the need for intimacy, gender variance,
sexual and emotional vulnerability, and violation. It was as if, in this
very powerful and discursive moment, threads that had been all along
winding through history wove together in a manner that illuminated
the past as much as they clouded and blocked full access to its complicated meaning.

Vincent Harding, in distinction from the other nine authors, foregrounds a connection between the consumption of Turner and the contemporary consumption of black men. Rather than chastising Styron
for speaking about Turner's cannibalization, as does Kaiser, Harding
openly accuses Styron of attempting to cannibalize Nat Turner: "Now
this is precisely what William Styron fails to do with the world and
words of Nat Turner. He has been unable to eat and digest the blackness, the fierce religious conviction, the power of the man."[24] Harding
draws upon the antebellum legacy of the black heroic figure as imper-
meable, steeled, and inviolate to prove his point. It is Turner's "power
and driveness," his "liberating truth" that makes him impervious to
the jaws and appetites of whites—"those who have neither eaten nor
mourned."[25] Harding writes the truth. Styron's Turner appealed to the
general media, to highbrow white literate communities, and to institutions that awarded and sanctioned literary greatness. Styron's Turner
appealed to white desires for a palatable black radical figure diminished
in all of his complexity and transhistorical powers.

Harding's thinking about black male consumption reflected traditional models of black male virility, literacy, and enlightened consciousness. The counterpoint to the virile, powerful figure in Harding's essay
(and in most of the essays the other black men wrote) was the effeminate, homosexual, and therefore emasculated black man. Where radical
individuals such as Turner, Martin Luther King Jr., and George Jackson
could not be eaten, the assumption was that a Luke (a raped black man

depicted in the Harriet Jacobs slave narrative), a James L. Smith, or a contemporary James Baldwin could be consumed. Harding's discussion of homosexuality in the novel begins with Brantley, "a social outcast among whites" and a "personally repulsive homosexual whose specialty seems to be the molesting of young boys."[26] Brantley is, in Harding's view, the typical white male parasite of the parasitic master/slave relation. It is disturbing to Harding that "Styron alone chose to create such a pariah-like personality for the one white man who is drawn to Nat Turner's religious teachings."[27] This is a perfect example of Styron's attempt to make palatable the "fierce religious conviction" of the heroic black figure, Styron's use of homosexuality and Christian-sanctioned incest to turn Turner into a consumable subject. In the previous chapter, I discussed how there is an undercurrent of historical truth to this dynamic between black and white men during slavery. It would have been, of course, inappropriate for Harding, in his defensive posture, to invoke this history. It would have only added grist to the white mill of consumption he was attempting to deconstruct. Still, his easy conflation of homosexuality with consumption and black male virility and power with immunity to consumption perpetuates silences and unspeakable domains of black male experience extending back to slavery. I intend to discuss these more thoroughly, but for the moment let us explore more deeply how other black writers in Clark's compilation perpetuate Harding's correlation of homosexuality, emasculation, and sexual taint.

Loyle Hairston also equated emasculation with homosexuality: "William Styron," writes Hairston, "triumphantly reduces his slave to a religious celibate—a kind of self-castration. Poor Nat Turner's only sexual experience is—alas!—a *homosexual* one!"[28] Lerone Bennett Jr. accuses Styron of "emasculating Nat Turner" by depicting him as "an impotent, sex-crazed celibate who masturbates every Saturday in the carpenter's shop" and as one who has "a homosexual encounter and a detailed white fantasy life."[29] Concurring with Bennett, psychologist Alvin F. Poussaint offers further insights into Styron's psychological motivations:

> I think Styron's selection of "factual" and psychological material speaks for itself. It speaks for itself again when we read that the closest our black rebel comes to a realized sexual experience is through a homosexual one with another young black slave. What is the communication here?

Naturally, it implies that Nat Turner was not a man at all. It suggests that he was unconsciously really feminine.[30]

From these and other observations there emerges a complicated picture of homosexuality as understood in this context. We could begin with just the use of the word "homosexual." Most black men in the collection use the word "homosexual," which had no currency during the antebellum period, to describe "Styron's Turner," while Styron himself does not actually use that word in his novel. The use of the word speaks to a conflation of historical time periods, the conflation of twentieth-century psychological discourses of sexual deviancy with same-sex behavior in all of its variations in the context of slavery. On the one hand, the use of the word "homosexual" conveys a lack of historical consciousness and historical specificity on the part of the black men. On the other hand, this word, as a reflection of 1960s racial politics, does accurately convey how the legacy of slavery fed into contemporary understandings of homosexuality in the context of black experience.[31] In the minds of many of these men, the state was a virile, predatory white man that had long preyed upon and sought to instill in black men an effeminate, sexual availability. Late twentieth-century scholars of sexuality, responding to the use of the words "homosexual," "faggot," and "effeminate" by the black male writers, have tended to refer to the group as "homophobic" or as maintaining "homophobic assumptions."[32]

This easy conflation of the past with present (of an effeminate man during slavery with a homosexual man in the present) reflects the extent to which this historical era marked yet another recalibration of the meaning and application of the history of slavery. Ron Eyerman writes in *Cultural Trauma: Slavery and the Formation of African American Identity* that "every twenty to thirty years individuals look back and reconstruct a 'traumatic' past."[33] One could plot the publication of Styron's novel, the assassinations of Malcolm X and Martin Luther King Jr., and the publication of *Ten Black Writers Respond* on a twenty-year cycle dating from the Emancipation Proclamation. The year 1965 marks the fifth twenty-year cycle following the end of slavery, or the 100-year anniversary of emancipation. At stake for so many black people were not just the historical facts of the experience but also the power to control and interpret the meaning and historical significance of the legacy of slavery. Poussaint and others made extensive references to historical texts about slavery written by white men. Herbert Aptheker's *American Negro Slave Revolts* was an exemplary text for its ample depiction of the spirit and practice of revolt that pervaded slave life. Many black persons considered Thomas A Bailey's *The American Pageant: A History of the Republic* a prejudicial text that infantilized and diminished Turner's contributions. Most of the ten black men considered Stanley M. Elkins's *Slavery*, a text that directly informed Styron's portrait of Turner, to be a strongly white-influenced text, even though Elkins was African American. More than anything, black men and women felt strongly compelled to protect the image of the black family, black masculinity, and black motherhood and womanhood as sustained in the context of slavery. Within this recreated and imagined context, there was no room for a complicated understanding of homoeroticism during slavery.

In her critique of Styron's novel, Alice Walker emphasized how Styron depicted Turner as loving a white woman and how he uses homosexuality to strip Turner of his revolutionary spirit and power:

> A slave revolutionary who revolts simply because he cannot have the woman he loves, if he loves her (and there is no proof that Nat loved anybody white), denies that there was anything about slavery itself to make him revolt. Revolts are made, but rarely from the love of one adolescent enemy female whom one lovingly stabs and then beats over the head with a fence post, until she is dead. Besides, if Nat were really a homosexual, as Mr. Styron implies, why should he bother?[34]

June Meyer (better known as June Jordan) interpreted *The Confessions* as an attack on Turner's masculinity and that of black men in general. In her 1967 review, published in *The Nation*, she wrote: "There is a man who exists as one of the most popular objects of leadership and legislation and quasi-literature in the history of all men. There lives a man who is spoken for, imagined, feared, and criticized, pitied, misrepresented, fought against, reviled and loved, primarily on the basis of secondhand information or worse."[35] Meyer's review speaks to the longstanding systematic use and consumption of the black male. Meyer critiques both Styron and those who favorably reviewed his novel for taking Turner out of context, depicting him as disconnected from black family and community. The black women and men who reviewed *The Confessions* overtly and covertly assumed a relationship between the black family during slavery and black male virility. Sex and gender they also conflated with homosexuality, made out to equal effeminacy. Many blacks linked homosexuality to castration and the recent history of black men who had been lynched and black women who had been raped in the Jim Crow South and in the North. Homosexuality, in its metaphoric power, had an exhaustive function: It is equated with the absence of family, hatred of black people, estrangement from one's kin and culture, and all of those horrific aspects of black experience about which black people would rather not speak.

On the surface, at least, I do not disagree with these black men and women. I think their analysis regarding historicity and the diminishment of black communal ties was mostly correct. Styron's novel was historically inaccurate, depicting Turner as raised by whites rather than the black parents and grandmother Turner spoke about in his original "Confessions." Styron depicts aspects of Turner's sexual life that are not validated in any documentation coming from the time period, and Styron's exhaustive probing into the racial hatred and self-hatred of Turner clearly reflected something in his own psyche and white identity that he felt compelled to project onto Turner. Black men were put on the defensive by both the novel and by the institutions (literary production, the media) and individuals who supported Styron as an authentic interpreter of black historical experience. Many black men, like Bennett, felt that Styron was waging a literary war that paralleled the contemporary political and police state war against black men: "He wages literary war on this [Nat Turner's] image, substituting an impotent, cowardly, irresolute creature of his own imagination for the real black man who killed or ordered killed real white people for real historical reasons."[36] In such embattled situations, black people have had to historically adopt strategic postures. They have had to adopt a perspective of themselves, the race, and their history that white people could not "eat and digest." That was the irony of this moment. Black people invoked the cannibal discourse that could have freed up and complicated black male perspectives on everything from social consumption to homoeroticism only to defend black masculinity and black culture. Black men were not interested in, nor capable of dealing with, the complex legacy of cannibalism and homoeroticism that so powerfully shaped their responses to Styron's novel.

One black man did have a fairly clear and nuanced understanding of the danger and potential of this moment: James Baldwin. Indeed, Baldwin predicted that Styron's novel would be a "storm center." In an interview for *Newsweek*, he acknowledged: "It'll be called effrontery. . . . Bill's going to catch it from black and white. . . . It's a very courageous book that attempts to fuse the two points of view, the master's and the slave's. . . . It's important for the black reader to see what Bill is trying to do and to recognize its validity."[37] In preparation for his novel, Styron read Baldwin's writings and spoke extensively with the black author about black experience. Styron credited Baldwin with breaking down his greatest racial prejudices: "Jimmy broke down the last shred of whatever final hangup of Southern prejudice I might have had which was trying to tell me that a Negro was never really intelligent."[38] Baldwin encouraged Styron, which might partially explain why he was not invited to contribute to *Ten Black Men Respond*.[39] Generally speaking, black people felt confused by and disapproved of Baldwin's support of Styron. As part of his response to Styron, Harding also critiqued Baldwin. Harding's comments to Baldwin begin to broach an area that was largely unexplored in the national debate, and that is the feelings, emotions, secrets, and common history that Styron's novel brought up for black men in relation to one another. Harding, in so many words, refers to Baldwin as a race betrayer: "Nevertheless, as with all tragedy, the deepest level is to be found within us—black us. And it was perhaps symbolized by one of our most important artists, James Baldwin. For it was Baldwin who praised his friend's work highly, Baldwin who saw himself in Styron's Turner, and Baldwin who dared to say, 'This is the beginning of our common history.'"[40] In the *Newsweek* interview, Baldwin actually refers to Styron as constructing "our common history." Harding strongly disagreed with this statement:

> Surely, it is nothing of the kind. In spite of Baldwin's largest, kindest hopes, Styron has done nothing less (and nothing more) than create another chapter in our long and common agony. He has done it because we have allowed it, and we who are black must be men enough to admit that bitter fact. There can be no common history until we have first

fleshed out the lineaments of our own, for no one else can speak out of the bittersweet bowels of our blackness.[41]

The fact is that Baldwin, in a most ironic and painful way, was right. Styron, I think rather unconsciously, wrote out of a shared historical consciousness of slavery. And part of the disavowal and swearing off of this tie by Harding and other black men had to do with black men being neither ready nor able to face the painful legacy of objectification, incest, and infantilization between master/patriarch and slave. Black men were not ready to look at how their institutional consumption in the 1960s originated in slavery-old processes of cannibalization. So many powerful unexamined emotions, such as hatred, love, desire, and need, undergirded the historical relationship between black men and white men.

## A Slave Kiss

I'll now turn to the novel as a vehicle for exploring this issue of "common history," as Baldwin conceived of it through Styron's text. Rather than dealing with the black/white homoerotic dynamic, I want to examine a scene in the novel that deals with same-sex eroticism between two young black men, Nat Turner and his boyhood friend, Willis. The riverside scene in *The Confessions of Nat Turner* is a tender, disturbing, and complex depiction of black male need and desire. I say this, knowing full well that black scholars at the time expressed feelings of disgust and betrayal about this scene. They referred it as simply "masturbation," "homosexuality," and a depiction of Nat Turner as a homosexual.[42]

We are introduced to Willis as an orphan. His mother dies from a "lung complaint," which brings the youth to the attention of one of Turner's former masters. In his depiction of Willis as motherless and fatherless, Styron, who failed on many historical counts, captured a true reality of slavery. So many young black boys during slavery found themselves without mother and father as a result of the auction block, disease, and violence. Nat observes Willis working and is enraptured by "something irresistible" in the youth, his "gaiety," his "innocent, open disposition," his song that accompanies his work. In the novel, Turner describes Willis as "a slim, beautiful boy with fine boned features, very gentle and wistful in repose, and the light glistened like oil on his smooth black skin."[43]

Ever since meeting Willis, Turner has worked diligently to convert the "heathen" Willis to "the truth of Christian belief."[44] Willis believes in omens and conjuring. He wears a mojo, or fetish, of his own construction. Willis has decorated his mojo fetish "With the long hairs from the cock of a bull that had died of the bloat he had tied up three fuzzy patches on his head, to ward off ghosts; the fangs of a water moccasin he wore on a string around his neck, a charm against fever."[45] This scene has an eerie historical familiarity, this relationship between the black enlightened subject and the black heathen, the decorous, literate speech of Turner contrasting against the guileless, obscene ways of the folk. Frederick Douglass constructs a similar dynamic between himself and Sandy, a root-working black elder. He refers to Sandy and all slaves who believe in conjure like Sandy as "the more ignorant slave."[46] In his preparatory research for his novel, Styron read the slave narrative of Frederick Douglass and numerous others. And it could have very well been from Douglass's narrative or that of another slave that Styron first gleaned an understanding of this dynamic between enlightened and heathen slave.

Returning to the text, Turner and Willis sit at the riverside one weekend fishing and enjoying each other's company. Both boys typically "went fishing together on Saturdays and Sundays."[47] This particular weekend will change the course of their relationship and history itself. This is the fateful weekend when they will kiss and masturbate one another. Shortly after their arrival, Willis pricks his finger with a hook or the sharp spine of a fish. Instinctively he cries out, "Fuckin Jesus!" Turner, a devout Christian with a missionary's zeal, swiftly "rapped him sharply across the lips, drawing a tiny runnel of blood." Turner punctuates this act by proclaiming to the shocked Willis: "A filthy mouth is an abomination unto the Lord!"[48] Turner's violent response to Willis calls to mind nineteenth-century black missionaries who traveled all the way to Africa to civilize and save so-called African heathens from extinction.[49] Black culture has been, if anything, a long uphill battle against the heathen without and within. Styron exploited this theme for his own ends, but there is still this truth at the heart of this scenario, a truth made all the more complicated and disturbing when intermingled with the theme of homosexuality.

After Turner strikes Willis, a whirlwind of emotions grips the two. Willis affects "a broken, hurt look."[50] Turner is, in turn, overcome with emotion: "I felt a pang of guilt and pain at my anger, and a rush of pity swept through me, mingled with a hungry tenderness that stirred me in a way I have never known."[51] This hunger and rush of feeling gives way to touch and forbidden warmth. Turner describes Willis's eyes as "brimming with tears," then flashes onto "the moccasin fangs gangling at his neck, bone-white and startling against his shiny bare black chest":

> I reach up to wipe away the blood from his lips, pulling him near with the feel of his shoulders slippery beneath my hand, and then we some-how fell on each other, very close, soft and comfortable in a sprawl like babies; beneath my exploring fingers his hot skin throbbed and pulsed like the throat of a pigeon, and I heard him sigh in a faraway voice, and then for a long moment as if set free into another land we did with our hands together what, before, I had done alone. Never had I known that human flesh could be so sweet.[52]

Willis is Africa in the flesh. He is the African infant compared to Turner, who plays the role of the enlightened, paternal Negro, a type of New World black missionary. Styron depicts homoeroticism as a complex affair shaped in part by discourses of African exoticization, Negro socialization, and Christian indoctrination. As I mentioned earlier, black reviewers and commentators accused Styron of exoticiz-ing and further indoctrinating black men in this scene. Poussaint read this scene as the psychological disfigurement of Turner and, as well, his emasculation. Referring to this Willis/Turner scene, he asks: "What is the communication here?" His response, as we have seen: "Naturally, it implies that Nat Turner was not a man at all."[53] Poussaint's observations are complicated. For they speak to homosexuality used, in this instance, to dislocate Turner from his natal origins and as a tool to "get inside" of Turner in order to expose the erotic and sexual confusion underlying his revolutionary politics. Styron uses and, I would agree, abuses the idea of homosexuality in this instance.

Styron's depiction of the Willis/Turner dynamic speaks to a historical dialectic between black men dating back to slavery. As mentioned ear-lier, one can see the seeds of Willis and Turner in Frederick Douglass's depiction of the more African-like, elderly Sandy and himself in his first slave narrative. He describes Sandy as believing in conjure. Sandy takes him out to a wooded area to recover "a certain root," which, according to Douglass "would render it impossible for Mr. Covey, or any other white man, to whip me."[54] As with Turner, it is not the root (according to Douglass) that sets him free, but his life-or-death struggle against the slave breaker Covey that returns his lost manhood to him. Douglass and Sandy do not actually kiss, but they are nevertheless bound by the very same cord of heathen versus civilized, infantilized versus manly black man that binds Turner to Willis in the novel. The nineteenth-century black religious leader Alexander Crummel thought of the African heathen as licentious, someone to be civilized off the face of the planet. In essays and speeches he imagined the African heathen as seductive, wielding the same power and sinful allure that Willis wields over Nat. W. E. B. Du Bois, a protégé of Crummel, described the Negro of the South as tainted with African beliefs and heathen practices:

> The Negro has already been pointed out many times as a religious animal,—a being of that deep emotional nature which turns instinctively toward the supernatural. . . . He called up all the resources of heathenism to aid,—exorcism and witch-craft, the mysterious Obi worship with its barbarous rites, spells, and blood sacrifice even, now and then, of human victims. Weird midnight orgies and mystic conjurations were invoked, the witch-woman and the voodoo priest became the centre of Negro group life, and that vein of vague superstition which characterizes the unlettered Negro even to-day was deepened and strengthened.[55]

Du Bois romanticizes, even eroticizes, the very black folk that he seeks to liberate from the emotional and spiritual clutches of American history. As a lettered Negro, Du Bois's experiences and sense of self are counterbalanced by the heathen sensibility contained in the body and social practices of the unlettered Negro. Du Bois feels seduced by and is at the same time repulsed by this Negro whom he describes as bloodthirsty, sexually licentious, massive and erotically overpowering, and even cannibalistic in his urges and rituals.[56] In his review of Claude McKay's novel, *Home to Harlem* (1928), Dubois more explicitly coupled his idea of something heathen in the folk with homosexuality and sexual abandon in artistic culture of the Harlem Renaissance.[57] Such evidence at least hints at something much deeper than the offense-taking that characterizes black people's knee-jerk response to the Willis/Turner scene in Styron's novel. Perhaps a deeper fear of recognition is operating, for a real acknowledgment of something "essentially black" in the Willis/Turner dynamic would necessitate a rethinking of constructs such as the color line and problematics such as the Negro problem as having been from their inceptive moments imbricated with a black homoerotic discourse.

I think this might have been some of what Baldwin was trying to get at through the double implications of "our common history." Where others saw void and absence—nothing of nation, community, or the black self in homoeroticism—Baldwin saw homoeroticism as being, in some ways, most representative of racial experience. An example from Baldwin's book-length essay *No Name in the Street* illustrates this point. Baldwin has come from a self-imposed exile in Paris to the U.S. South to observe and report on the civil rights conditions there. He interviews children who are integrating schools and their family members, black ministers, white sheriffs and governors, among other persons, in each city he travels to. At one point in his observations, at a loss for examples to explain the incestuous thread that binds white men to black men in the South, Baldwin relates the experience of being sexually groped by a drunken white state official: "I realized that I was being groped by one of the most powerful men in one of the states I visited. He had got himself sweating drunk in order to arrive at this despairing titillation. With his wet eyes staring up at my face, and his wet hands groping for my cock, we were both, abruptly, in history's ass-pocket. It was frightening—not the gesture itself, but the abjectness of it."[58] The broader implications of this secret desire for black male flesh—black male cock—are that black people in the South are at the mercy of men such as this who pull and press the levers that run Jim Crow machinery. This white man "was one of the men you called (or had a friend call) in order to get your brother off the prison farm. A phone call from him might prevent your brother from being dug up, later, during some random archaeological expedition."[59]

Baldwin demonstrates how homosexual desire is seamlessly intertwined with the legacy of American slavery and black civil identity in the South. It was even conceivable to him that were it not for the migration of black men out of the South post-emancipation, the entire region might have become "an absolutely homosexual community," wherein white male desire for black men was more open and socially acceptable.[60] There is a fluid correlation in Baldwin's mind between this white man reaching for his "cock" and the castration of black men in the context of lynching rituals, the black exercise of the right to vote, school integration, and the over-incarceration of black men on chain gangs and in jails. Baldwin's sexual encounter counters the idea that if "a black man were doing the fucking" of a white man, then his manhood remained intact and he could be considered revolutionary, a notion that many Black Power advocates silently entertained.[61] State-sanctioned racial oppression, as this scenario demonstrates, pairs well with homoeroticism. The homosexual oppression of black men overlaps with and feeds seamlessly into larger systems of racial oppression. And to say just a bit more about the sexual implications of this scene, just because the white man was reaching for Baldwin's penis does not mean that the man sought sexual penetration. He may have wanted to penetrate Baldwin; he may have wanted oral gratification—one way or the other. I could speculate endlessly about the sexual particulars of this scenario, but what we know for sure is what Baldwin himself finally clarifies, which is that "it is absolutely certain that white men, who invented the nigger's big black prick, are still at the mercy of this nightmare, and are still, for the most part, doomed, in one way or another, to attempt to make this prick their own."[62] No matter what form the sex takes, the white man's power will not be compromised. Having access to "big black prick," Baldwin infers, is constitutive of the state-sanctioned power of the white official that he encounters.

A number of scholars have experienced frustration at Baldwin's slippery relationship to and outright rejection of a homosexual identity and politics. However, this excerpt from *No Name in the Street* clarifies how Baldwin sees homosexuality, in terms of black experience and black male identity formation, as "buried" or "methodologically disguised" in racial logic, in the history of slavery, and in the psychological workings of the southern racial ideology.[63] For Baldwin, homosexuality does not and cannot ever exist as something isolated from racial formation. Bryan R. Washington, agreeing with this last statement, notes that in

Baldwin's writing and overarching cosmology of race and sex, "black-ness and homosexuality . . . are not simply coterminous; they are virtu-ally interchangeable."[64] The encounter between himself and the white official helps us better understand why Baldwin would support Styron's freedom to imagine and inhabit Nat Turner (in all of the lurid homo-sexual implications of that habitation), for how else were the unspeak-able fantasies and suppressed homosexual desires of southern white men going to be exposed and potentially exorcised?

This subtle level of discourse was lost upon and completely ignored in the prevailing black commentary and debates that centered on Sty-ron's novel. There was the general opinion that Styron was construct-ing a white, southern, neo-slave-master's version of black American history. Most viewed James Baldwin's contention that Styron was con-structing "our common history" as at best a misguided perception and at worst as white apologist sentiment. Still, there is a solid ethos inform-ing Baldwin's statement. As a black homosexual (who was not afraid to speak publicly about being groped by a white man), Baldwin occupied a unique position that allowed him to understand how desire and sexual-ity transcended and confounded racial thinking. In his essay "Down at the Cross: Letter from a Region in my Mind," Baldwin refers to whites and blacks as having to come together as lovers in order to achieve America's loftiest ideals and transcend the prison of racial ideology:

> Everything now, we must assume, is in our hands; we have no right to assume otherwise. If we—and now I mean the relatively conscious whites and the relatively conscious blacks, who must, like lovers, insist on, or create, the consciousness of the others—do not falter in our duty now, we may be able, handful that we are, to end the racial nightmare, and achieve our country.[65]

For black men, the problem with this idea of the lovers, in partic-ular homoerotic lovers in Styron's novel, was not so much the image of homoeroticism but the twisted spectral pleasure that whites took in Styron's depictions of black sexuality. Killens, from *Ten Black Men Respond*, likened the white review community, journals, and the Pulit-zer Prize committee itself to whoremongers. Recording his feeling after reading a review of the novel in *The New York Times Review of Books*, he

writes: "I had this uncomfortable feeling that a hoax was being perpetrated against the American reading public. I also had the uneasy feeling, even worse, that the reading public dearly loved it. Like a whore
being brutally ravished and loving every masochistic minute of it."[66]

Killens had justification for feeling the way that he did. In the 1930s,
psychologists and sexologists from Sigmund Freud to Richard Krafft-
Ebing documented that some Europeans achieved sexual arousal
through romanticized images of slaves. Krafft-Ebing, who coined the
term "masochism," includes in his compendium on sexual pathology
the following letter from a self-diagnosed masochist (Case 57): "Even
in my early childhood I loved to revel in ideas about the absolute mastery of one man over others. The thought of slavery had something
exciting in it for me, alike whether from the standpoint of master or
servant. That one man could possess, sell or whip another, caused me
intense excitement; and in reading 'Uncle Tom's Cabin' (which I read
at the beginning of puberty) I had erections."[67] In her study of masochistic desire, Marcia Marcus lists the childhood books that provided
materials for her own adolescent masochistic fantasies: "There were the
books about boarding school, in which small boys slaved for the bigger
boys. . . . There were books about the initiation rites of exotic people.
There was Uncle Tom's Cabin, and other books about black slaves in
America."[68] From the antebellum period, critiques of Stowe's novel by
white southern men revealed how these men themselves associated sexual "license and impurity" with the novel and often read into many of
its scenes a "pornographic" subtext.[69] These men, themselves titillated
by the novel, wanted to limit and ultimately prevent its distribution.

When it came to slavery, the concepts of love, intimacy, and desire
between white and black men had been for the longest time shot through
with violence, with white erotic voyeurism, and a precarious politics of
white empathy and sentimentalism. Baldwin understood this legacy. He
found Stowe's novel, for example, to be riddled with sentimentality, the
type of sentimentality that is an excuse for "violent inhumanity," "the
mask of cruelty" that made objects of the slave among both abolitionists and plantation owners.[70] Baldwin even goes as far as to link Richard Wright's Bigger Thomas with Stowe's Tom, asserting that "Bigger is
Uncle Tom's descendant, flesh of his flesh, so exactly opposite a portrait
that, when the books are placed together, it seems the contemporary

Negro novelist and the dead New England woman are locked together in a deadly, timeless battle."[71] Bigger Thomas rapes a white woman and obsesses over white femininity as symbol and prize. Stowe, on the other hand, obsessed over black male virility while domesticating it, packaging it, and emotionally mastering it so as to ward off the unspoken threat of the black beast, the rapist. Baldwin understood how this legacy of black men, fixated either upon white women or white men, had prevented black men from developing more complex models of masculinity and of black male sexuality. For *Ten Black Men Respond* was just that, a response to white representations of and appetites for blackness. It was black men primarily engaged with white men and white institutional structures at the expense of a more private, long-overdue discussion of these same issues among black men.

Styron's novel presented Baldwin with the perfect opportunity to publicize and mediate the subject of homoerotic connection between black and white men and among black men during slavery. In a *Newsweek* interview, Baldwin acknowledged his identification with Styron's Turner: "'Yes,'" he admitted, "'I think there's some of me in Nat Turner. . . . If I were an actor, I could play the part.'"[72] Baldwin would have cause to rethink this statement when, months later, he served as mediator when blacks protested against efforts in Hollywood to make Styron's novel into a film. This statement is loaded with double meaning; it can be read, as many black men read it, that Baldwin was something of a template for Styron's Turner. It also reads as a gesture toward revising the slave past. Baldwin, as person and symbol, impressed upon black people in this moment the possibility of an entirely different script of revolutionary masculinity during slavery.[73] This statement clarifies how the term "our common history" referred to black/white relations on the surface and beneath the surface, to the repressed and denied historical presence of the black homosexual in a genealogy of black radicalism extending back to slavery.

Needless to say, black men received Baldwin's speech and actions across a great divide. While he envisioned a new radical genealogy and pushed, through Styron, for a model of antebellum resistance that included homoeroticism, most black men were still stuck on homosexuality as a derivative of white decadence and as the sexual exploitation of black people. Killens, as a representative of this black constituency, linked white desires to the black homosexual person. He depicts whites as whoremongers. He effeminizes whites and recuperates, in a small way, some of the stolen legacy of black masculinity. He plays upon the Christian dichotomy of the chaste virgin and the filthy whore. Not only is the pristine black revolutionary virtuous and free of such taint, he is also virile, according to Killen's logic, hence the white "whores'" hunger for and pleasure taken in the black male's sexuality in Styron's text. Killens attempts in this way to recuperate black masculinity and flip the Christian and moral script on the very whites and white institutions that claim an unquestionable moral position. The idea of whoredom definitely struck home and made a powerful point, but it was a point that cut both ways.

Within 1960s radical culture, black men applied this same paradigm of the virgin/whore to black lesbians, black women who coupled with white men, and black women who asserted themselves in myriad ways, refusing domination by black men.[74] Killens's representation of white sexual appetites as whoredom carried over as well into descriptions of black homosexuals as whores, carriers of filth, and race betrayers. It is no coincidence that Cleaver refers to Baldwin and to Negro homosexuals in his *Souls on Ice* (published the same year as *Ten Black Men Respond*) as whores and objects of white masochistic desire:

> Many Negro homosexuals, acquiescing in this racial death-wish, are outraged and frustrated because in their sickness they are unable to have a baby by a white man. The cross they have to bear is that, already bending over and touching their toes for the white man, the fruit of their miscegenation is not the little half-white offspring of their dreams but an increase and unwinding of their nerves.[75]

Like the whore of Killens's imagination, Cleaver describes the Negro homosexual as a "sychophant," an "automated slave," and one who looks to the white man as his "Big Daddy," or pimp in the marketplace of white desire. A number of scholars have noted the significance of Cleaver's comments insofar as they reflected a radical black ideology that equated homosexuality with a racial death wish.[76]

Bearing the weight of such an attack, Baldwin understood better than any other how white desire, even in the radical black imagination, had intrinsic ties to the metaphoric and real presence of the black homosexual. When Killens spoke of white whoredom, he was already and implicitly speaking to a sexual framework in which females and effeminacy were suspect and in which the Negro homosexual could, at a moment's notice, serve as a substitute for the body and person of the black female. Long-held assumptions inform Killens's and Cleaver's statements; there is the assumption that black homosexuality originates in the brutality of slavery, the idea that the black male phallus is the only true measure and means of racial continuity, and the idea that black homosexuality is always suspect by virtue of its connection to whiteness.

Holding firmly to these assumptions for reasons of political strategy and the desire to forget what Kaiser refers to as the "bestial" and "lurid details" of slavery resulted in the missed opportunity among black men to speak openly and honestly about their historically charged erotic relations to white men. Black men also missed the opportunity to talk about homoeroticism—same-sex intimacy, need, love, and desire—among themselves. Baldwin did not publicly claim a homosexual identity; in fact, he publicly disavowed the labels of "homosexual," or "gay" to define his person and art. When called upon to speak on behalf of the race, Baldwin habitually adopted the voice and posture of the angry, emasculated black patriarch: "*Protect your women*: a difficult thing to do in a civilization sexually so pathetic that the white man's masculinity depends on a denial of the masculinity of the blacks. *Protect your women*: in a civilization that emasculates the male and abuses the female, and in which, moreover, the male is forced to depend on the female's bread-winning power."[77] Baldwin was "well aware of the dangers of—indeed, the 'price of the ticket' for—trying to synthesize his racial and sexual identities."[78] As Dwight A. McBride points out, "his efficacy as a race man was—at least in part—dependent on limiting his public activism to racial politics."[79] Baldwin calls upon a dynamic within the black collective conscious that is as old as slavery—the image of the lynched or emasculated black man and the raped, sexually violated black woman. This dynamic foreclosed a number of other configurations, such as black men sexually violated by white men, black men during slavery who played nonpatriarchal roles, and black men who, for whatever reasons, did not sexually reproduce the race.

## The Legacy of the Black Fathers

Although Baldwin did not claim a homosexual politics, he found himself in a historic moment that desperately needed a politics that linked
homosexuality with race and with a legacy of black male sexual violation and sexualization stemming back to slavery.[80] In the corpus of his
work, especially in texts such as *The Fire Next Time*, *Go Tell it on the
Mountain*, and *No Name in the Street*, Baldwin lays some of the ground-
work for this sexual politics that was never fully realized in the context
of the Black Power movement. The example that I cite earlier, of his
being sexually fondled by a white state official, demonstrated Baldwin
organically theorizing out his sexual subjectivity, a politics of abuse and
white homosexual desire that had an effect upon the entire race and the
cause of the Civil Rights Movement. Because Baldwin saw himself ultimately as "a witness to the truth," as one whose most valuable tools were
his experience and person, in much of his writing, Baldwin encodes his
racial/sexual politics in his experience, especially those experiences
finely attuned to the intimate, unspoken regions of male intimacy and
same-sex eroticism.[81]

Differing from the popular homosexual politics of the day, this blueprint of black sexual politics linked homoeroticism to the memory and
legacy of slavery, expanded the meaning and expressions of black masculinity, and maintained a critical stance toward patriarchal institutions
that perpetuated domineering models of black masculinity. In the essay
"Down at the Cross" from *The Fire Next Time*, Baldwin records a meeting between himself and the honorable Elijah Mohammed, leader of
the Black Muslims. Baldwin recalls being frightened upon receiving the
summons from the leader to come to his house for dinner: "I was frightened, because I had, in effect, been summoned into a royal presence."[82]
Baldwin is also afraid, perhaps more afraid, of the tension this meeting
inspires in himself "between love and power, between pain and rage."[83]
In the leader's home, Baldwin awaits the elder black man while Mohammed's devotees attend to him before dinner. Baldwin experiences the
meeting as tense and framed by much unspoken history shared between
the two men. Ruminating to himself on the Muslim's belief that whites
are devils, Baldwin thinks: "For the horrors of the American Negro's life
there has been almost no language. The privacy of his experience, which

is only beginning to be recognized in language, and which is denied or ignored in official and popular speech."[84] More specifically, Baldwin empathizes with Mohammed's own tragic history, which involved seeing his father hanged before his eyes: "His father's blood rush[ed] out," and as Baldwin has heard it, Mohammed saw this same blood "rush down, and splash . . . down through the leaves of a tree, on him."[85] On a trip to Georgia years earlier, Baldwin had wondered at how the red clay of the earth had "acquired its color from the blood that had dripped down from these trees," lynching trees. He thinks of Willie McGhee and Emmett Till and the host of unnamed black men lynched for supposedly violating white southern women.[86] Slave narratives are rife with examples of sons made to witness the momentary and long-term demise of their fathers. Many slaves, like John Jacobs, located their genealogy in "a man—a father without authority—a husband and no protector."[87] Baldwin acknowledges the right and responsibility of both he and Mohammed to claim and interpret this legacy of black male emasculation.

Mohammed, on the other hand, privileges his relationship to the legacy of the fathers over that of Baldwin. He equates Baldwin's homosexuality with whiteness and with having strayed from the race. He seeks to convert the invert before him and, in the posture of a paternal figure, he expresses concern for Baldwin's salvation, his safety in the white world, and his confusion about what it truly means to be responsible to one's ancestral inheritance. Baldwin leaves Mohammed's home with strong feelings of longing, unrequited need, and abjection: "I felt very close to him, and really wished to be able to love and honor him as a witness, an ally, and a father. I felt that I knew something of his pain and his fury, and, yes, even his beauty."[88] Baldwin had come from a religious family. His father, a minister in the Baptist church, was a man who inspired in him intense feelings of love, resentment, and competition.[89] Through his father and by virtue of his own ancestral connections to the South, Baldwin had just as much right as Mohammed to make of the legacy of paternal pain that united them.

The contestation over the meaning of the unspeakable past dictated Baldwin's interactions with Mohammed and, a decade later, strongly influenced his relationship to the black men of *Ten Black Writers Respond*. Elijah Mohammed and the black men from Clarke's edited collection maintain one narrative of paternal pain, familial role, gender,

and sexuality and Baldwin, by virtue of his erotic and tribal relationship
to the black fathers, maintains another. At stake here are, in part, central questions of racial origins: Where do black people and, in particular, where does black masculinity come from? What is the ideal image
of this masculine identity and what does this image of black manhood
have to do with a larger racial liberation project? Mohammed and others draw upon a century-old model of black masculinity originating out
of violent, emasculating black/white relations. However, Baldwin shifts
the discussion of this violence away from a black/white dynamic to a
deeper terrain—the interior world of longing and pain perpetuated by
and shared among black men.

In his first novel, *Go Tell it on the Mountain*, Baldwin situates the origins of black masculinity in a racial mythology dating back to the first
contact between Europeans and coastal Africans. The Curse of Ham is
a myth of racial origins that deals with incest, homoerotic desire, and
slave legacy between black son and father. The Curse of Ham is one of
the oldest racial mythologies used by whites to justify their inhuman
treatment of the African and black American. The curse involves a son
(Ham) looking upon the naked body of his father (Noah). As a result
of looking at or touching his father—it is not clear which—the descendants of Ham are to be slaves. During slavery, black men interpreted the
curse in a number of different ways: as an explanation of their infantilized relationship to white slave owners, as an explanation for why
they descended from the tribe of Cush rather than the tribe of Canaan
(the cursed son), and as a way of talking about the introduction of white
blood into an African lineage. Curiously missing from most discussions
of the curse is a reference to its overt homoerotic implications—the son
looking upon the father's nakedness and responding with desire or even
erotic touch.

Baldwin explores the homoerotic implications of this racial mythology through the characters of John (the son) and Gabriel (the father) in
*Go Tell It on the Mountain*. Baldwin reenacts the Curse of Ham by having John, while scrubbing his father's back in the bathtub, look down
upon his father's nakedness as Ham had originally done to Noah:

Yes, he had sinned: one morning, alone, in the dirty bathroom, in the
square, dirt-gray cupboard room that was filled with the stink of his

father. Sometimes, leaning over the cracked, "tattle-tale gray" bathtub, he scrubbed his father's back; and looked, as the accursed son of Noah had looked, on his father's hideous nakedness. It was secret, like sin, and slimy, like the serpent, and heavy, like the rod. Then he hated his father, and longed for the power to cut his father down.[90]

As with Turner and Willis from *The Confessions of Nat Turner*, religion frames the tense relationship between John and his father. Gabriel, who sits in the bathtub, is a deacon in their local Harlem Baptist church. Gabriel "was called" to the ministry as a youth and practices a type of southern Christianity that dates back to slavery. It is in the context of desire for and hatred toward his father that John attempts to understand larger questions of racial origins and the grander cosmic meaning behind the enslavement and dislocation of Africans. Referring even more directly to the biblical curse in his blood, he laments: "This, and not that other, his deadly sin, having looked on his father's nakedness and mocked and cursed him in his heart? Ah, that son of Noah's had been cursed, down to the present groaning generation: *A servant of servants shall he be unto his brethren.*"[91]

Baldwin's use of and representation of homosexuality in *Go Tell It on the Mountain* goes far beyond sex act and contemporary homosexual politics. What the scenario between John and his father speaks to is the intrinsic way that homoeroticism has, from the very beginnings, figured centrally in the mythic, originary landscape of African American experience. While blacks have worked hard to construct a mythology of the race based in the male/female conjugal union and Adam and Eve as mythic gender prototypes, Baldwin exposes a different racial genealogy rooted in the homoerotic interchange between father and son and between black male compatriots and brothers.

This other unspeakable homoerotic legacy was an even more painful and raw wound for black men. For how could black men talk about need, desire, and eroticism among themselves without also talking about the numerous ways, in the context of slavery, in which such intimate ties had been denied, violently circumvented, or routed through the body and person of a white master, overseer, or some other ruling-class white? In so many ways, this history was repeated in Styron, whom whites billed as an authentic and authoritative interpreter of black male experience and motivations. The other "homosexual" scene in Styron's novel that stirred up a great amount of controversy focused on Ethelred T. Brantley, an assistant plantation overseer. Harding describes Brantley as "a social outcast among whites . . . a mentally retarded, personally repulsive homosexual whose specialty seems to be the molesting of young boys."[92] Brantley is attracted to Turner's preaching, which has the effect, according to Harding, of diminishing the personal charisma and visionary message of Turner in the novel. Styron does paint a despicable picture of Brantley: His face is pock-marked and he exudes a flatulence that smells "like air from a swamp bottom." Added to all of this is the fact that he is a confessed child molester.[93] As I note in earlier chapters, it was not unusual for the homoerotic appetites of the overseer to spill over into the punishment of enslaved persons. And while I agree with Harding that Styron does attempt to use Brantley to diminish the power of Turner, there is also the real and largely unexplored sexual history between overseers and male slaves. This history is present in the violent interchange between Douglass and Covey, but what black scholars such as Harding have preferred to emphasize is the violent exchange, the fight unto liberty or death, instead of examining the complicated ways slaves had to negotiate the homoerotics of plantation life.

By simplifying the debate into two types—the black man who was virile and could not be consumed and the black man who was effeminate, tender-fleshed and could be consumed—we have missed out on a deeper understanding of the ways homoeroticism has permeated black liberation discourse. When I first cited Harding's comments on cannibalism at the beginning of this chapter, I told only part of the story—the part of the story that concerned white appetites for consumption. However, it was not as simple as I initially suggested, that only white people wanted to consume, ingest, and be filled with black male essence. Black men wanted this too, however for entirely different—and sacred—reasons. Harding upbraids and severely criticizes Styron for cannibalizing Turner. In the same breath Harding speaks of Turner's message, his virile word, and his masculinity as something that black men such as himself can eat, Turner's body and words going down as "sweet as honey." He likens Turner to Ezekiel from the Bible, "Ezekiel who was forced to eat the scroll with the Lord's words, to fill his stomach with the terrible oracles of God."[94] In Harding's articulation, "fierce religious conviction,"

"power," and "liberating truth" tenderize black male flesh into a nour-
ishing source ingested and integrated into the black spiritual collective.
In her essay "'Where, By the Way, Is This Train Going?': A Case for (Re)
Framing Black (Cultural) Studies," Mae G. Henderson comments upon
the Oedipal, flesh-eating dynamic between black sons like Harding
and their symbolic fathers (W. E. B. Dubois, John Henrik Clarke, and
George Washington Williams). "Harding," she writes, "constructs the
origins of Black Studies in a narrative which fashions an Oedipal tale of
black 'sons (especially with Westernized training)' who 'seek to devour
their fathers.'"[95] Black Studies served as an intellectual counterpart to
Black Power activism and community-based organizing. What black
feminists and so-called homophile figures such as Baldwin were painfully aware of was how this dynamic of the chosen black son excluded
women and homosexual men as representative voices of black experience. As Henderson points out, black men sanctioned, institutionalized
even, the homoerotic triad among black father, son, and Western (white
male) tradition. In his *Beyond Chaos: Black History and the Search for
the New Land*, the document to which Henderson's comments refer,
Harding makes reference to the character of Trueblood from Ralph
Ellison's novel *Invisible Man*. He romanticizes Trueblood's raping of his
daughter, the black female sexual orifice bonding Trueblood and the
white man (Mr. Norton) in an erotic tryst: "Mr. Norton realized that
Trueblood had struggled with some of the same demons which he had
sought to escape. It was then that Norton exclaimed in wonder, 'You
have looked upon the chaos and are not destroyed.'"[96] The black man
and white man feel unified in their fear, objectification, and use of the
black female's body—her vagina. Trueblood projects his own feelings
of emasculation, sexual violation, and economic disempowerment onto
the black female body.

The more central problem here, though, is black male interiority, the
black male orifice. The black female body is and always has served as
a convenient, all-too-familiar tabula rasa for working out confusions,
aggressions, instabilities, and a host of other masculine anxieties. If we
replace the female body with that of the male, the essay's reference to
chaos takes on new meaning: chaos as the black male anus, chaos as
the black male mouth, chaos as the metaphysical, the quantum conundrum of a black male orifice that devours and consumes as easily as it

might constitute and reify masculinity. In the section that follows this discussion, Harding talks of the same blackness that he associates with Trueblood and the black fathers as something that he "in the darkness" touches and gropes with erotic longing: "As we handle our blackness, we are tempted to fondle it, to worship it, to lie down in its beauty and sleep a long black sleep of rapping and joy."[97] The sentence that follows this one clarifies its referent to the phallic might of black revolutionaries, such as "brother Fanon and our fathers."[98] Under the guise of revolution, of racial uplift, and racial unity, Harding's observations reveal a powerfully charged domain of black male experience wherein the consumption of and groping of the phallus, sons eating fathers and fathers eating sons, and a general erotic sharing among black men is the norm. It is a painful mythic and social reality that Harding imagines, in which "hurt is necessary, for it grows at once out of the nature of the struggle and out of the natural tendency of the sons (especially with Westernized training) to seek to devour their fathers."[99]

Harding writes against a legacy of consuming blacks, tasting them, and making them into delectable objects of white phallic authority. For that is the ultimate tragedy and failure of paternal figures such as George Washington Williams, Booker T. Washington, and even Carter G. Woodson, that they function as delectable Negroes who have so deeply internalized the palate of the white fathers that they cannot help but feed their male progeny—in body, soul, and essence—to the insatiable hunger of white America. For example, Williams, the author of the first full-length historical treatment of black people in the Americas, *History of the Negro Race in America, 1619–1880* (1885), advocated black assimilation into the body politic: "The Colored people had always displayed a matchless patriotism and an incomparable heroism in the cause of Americans."[100] Williams glorified the white male body of persons such as Thomas Jefferson, John Adams, and Abraham Lincoln; he also glorified the tenets and law of American democracy. Contrary to Harding's glorification of the black male body and in particular the phallus, Williams's primary romantic affection is toward the white male, for whom the state is an extension of his authority and power to either annihilate or consume. As a devouring black father who has an appetite spurred by his loyalty to the drives and palates of the white fathers, Williams is a figure that the black sons must devour if the race is to survive.

In addition to casting black history and collectivity in a traditional gender framework that threatens to undermine the intervention he is attempting to make, what also occurs within Harding's tableau of eat or be eaten is that so much complexity and differing meanings of appetite and consumption get obscured. The general sexual violation of black men during slavery does not figure into Harding's analogy. According to Harding, this history and the figure of the sexually violated black man literally represents the threat of black male virility being "devoured by inverted sexuality."[101] The ultimate psychic and social threat of the effeminate or raped black is not only that he can take in sex, hunger for and desire it in his interior, but also that he has, in addition to this hunger, the capacity to castrate, bite, chew, and disappear into a teeming chaos the continuity and vital essence of the race.

Harding's glorification and eroticization of the black male phallus demonstrates how homoeroticism was intrinsic to black cultural formation in his formulations. Whereas the invert—who resonates too closely with historical notions of black men as unclean, as unchristian, as licentious, effeminate, unbounded, and insane—is the figure that has been most difficult to incorporate into the body politic. In *There is a River: The Black Struggle for Freedom in America*, Harding refers to Malcolm X as "'the shining black prince' of the Northern movement."[102] King was also often referred to in this way by black men. Black people worshipped both men, saw them as beauty itself, and both radiated a seductive air of rest and long-awaited joyfulness. Harding romanticizes the seductive virility of blackness and its hidden phallic implications; so too does he romanticize female rape, incest, and white male fascination with women raped on the plantation.

This dynamic calls to mind the contradictory words and actions of Eldridge Cleaver. On the one hand, Cleaver could lambaste Baldwin as a virile Negro homosexual, a race traitor, and so forth and on the other hand show up at a party with Huey P. Newton, run into Baldwin at the party, and engage Baldwin in a long passionate French kiss. Newton recalls: "In 1967, Cleaver was invited to a special dinner for James Baldwin, who had just returned from Turkey, and he in turn invited me. When we arrived, Cleaver and Baldwin walked into each other, and the giant, six-foot-three-inch Cleaver bent down and engaged in a long, passionate French kiss with the tiny (barely five feet) Baldwin."[103]

Another example from the Civil Rights era is King, who engaged in frequent sexual escapades with white and black women in scenarios that involved him and other black men having sex in the same room and switching female partners and doing who knows what else. King clearly loved sex and exhibited an uninhibited aspect of his sexual nature. Yet King folded under pressures from within the movement to publicly distance himself from Bayard Rustin (the openly homosexual strategist and organizer of the March on Washington) and to not allow Rustin to speak at the March on Washington. All of which brings me to the question: What are we really talking about when we talk about homoeroticism in the Civil Rights and Black Power eras and, in particular, in the context of slavery? How are we to make sense of Harding's idea of the sacred consumption of the black fathers alongside the glorification of black female rape and the demonization and misrecognition of homoeroticism during Harding's time and in the context of slavery?

What Harding understood as sacred consumption was partially that, but it was also part of something larger, more complicated, and disturbing. Douglass, for example, was painfully aware of those aspects of the slave experience that were "causing us to eat our own flesh."[104] In his slave narrative, Douglass referred to the legacy of violence and terror that had caused many slaves to remain frozen in terror and apathetic to their bonded status. He referred to the constant haunting presence of "grim death," a catchall term for the range of horrid deaths that resulted from desperation, nihilism, and soul murder.[105] Douglass understood self-consumption as a process of turning in upon the self, a natural response to the physical and spiritual starvation endemic to the culture of slavery.

Fixated on the idea of the valiant heroic black man who is impervious to consumption (except consumption in a sacred way), we have remained transfixed by those final, determining words: "You have seen how a man was made a slave; you shall see how a slave was made a man."[106] Especially in the 1960s, most black people accepted the battle as the index of black masculinity largely without question. Yet what I have been attempting to elucidate throughout this chapter are more subtle levels of warfare and resistance that defy simplistic dyads: consumed/not consumed, effeminate/masculine, race man/not race man. As mightily as black people have struggled to fend off the reality of

Nat Turner's consumption, the fact is that he was most likely literally consumed. And in the meantime, our analytic, historical, psychic, and political tools have been insufficient to the task of analyzing how his consumption was possible, how it might in fact be ongoing, and how we, in the present moment, are implicated in the legacy of Turner's consumption.

6

The Hungry Nigger

At the end of the twentieth century, black gay men began to bravely articulate and embody a suppressed history and politics of the black, male orifice. For example, Essex Hemphill's brazen anal-erotic manifesto, "Loyalty," marked a historic moment in black sexual politics and cultural recovery. Tracking an epistemology of the anus rooted in black Christian ideologies and faith practices stemming back to slavery, Hemphill writes:

> For my so-called sins against nature and the race, I gain the burdensome knowledge of carnal secrets. . . . A knowledge disquieting and liberating inhabits my soul. It often comforts me, or at times is miserably intoxicating with requisite hangovers and regrets. At other moments it is sacred communion, causing me to moan and tremble and cuss as the Holy Ghost fucks me. It is a knowledge of fire and beauty that I will carry beyond the grave. When I sit in God's final judgment, I will wager this knowledge against my entrance into the Holy Kingdom.[1]

Hemphill writes against the normative logics of nature and race, founding his complaint within the taboo, interior regions of the male anus. The anus functions here as a vehicle of erotic coupling, as a site of knowledge apprehension, as a means of existential inquiry, and as a central ground of racial formation. Religiosity and saving (of one's

self and community) figure centrally in black epistemology and experience.[2] Through the sacred idea of and sacred relationship to his anus,
Hemphill builds upon a legacy of black people using their bodies and
body parts since slavery to reconfigure the precincts of the sacred and
humane.

For example, as I have noted, Sojourner Truth at strategic moments
in her oratory career referred to her breasts and her womb in public
speeches. This referencing of her body parts had a dual effect: First, it
allowed her to make claims to the spiritual and maternal authority of
women from the Bible; and second, it facilitated her challenge to the
stereotype of the masculinized black woman.[3] In "The Confessions of
Nat Turner," recorded by Thomas R. Gray, Nat Turner too experiences
the Holy Ghost as a mediating and corporealized presence: "And from
the first steps of righteousness until the last, was I made perfect; and
the Holy Ghost was with me."[4] Hemphill experiences the Holy Ghost
as anal penetration and a resultant sacred "bloodshed," and Turner also
experiences the Holy Ghost as blood physically manifested in the natural world: "I discovered drops of blood on the corn as though it were
dew from heaven. . . . And now the Holy Ghost had revealed itself to
me, and made plain the miracles it had shown me."[5] Though Hemphill
was not a slave, feelings of captivity and the erasure of his humanity
motivate him to articulate a praxis of anal/spiritual liberation that has
clear antecedents in the itinerant and radical black Christian systems
that Turner and Truth embody. In revising these traditions to include
the black male anus, Hemphill encourages a rethinking of deity, corporeality, and black cultural formation in the past and the present.

With another eye toward racial revisioning, Ron Simmons, in the
same decade as Hemphill, challenged the sexual hypocrisy of the Black
Arts Movement, focusing in particular on Amiri Baraka's homophobia and formulation of a negative anal sexual politics. "Perhaps," writes
Simmons, "it is the homosexual desires Baraka had as an adolescent
and young adult that motivate his homophobia."[6] Simmons traces Baraka's malice and violent disposition toward "the faggot" to the author's
vexed experiences with anal sex. Baraka admits these experiences to a
hooker named Peaches after failed attempts to achieve erection: "I'm
sorry. I'm fucked up. My mind is screwy, I don't know why. I can't think.
I'm sick. I've been fucked in the ass."[7] The penis and the anus represent

for Baraka two opposing nodes of black experience. In his poetry, political writings, and plays, Baraka associates the phallus with male/female coupling, racial solidarity, and black male heroicism. The anus and anal copulation, on the other hand, represent the erosion of black male prowess and sexual vigor and the breakdown of racial solidarity. Simmons also traces these negative implications of the anus and of black gay identity to the ideologies and political praxes of other Afrocentric thinkers and leaders, such as Haki Madhubuti, Louis Farrakhan, Ben-Jochannan, and Molefe Asante. Ultimately, Simmons writes to revise historical misrepresentations and to reclaim the anus as a site of "liberation of black people."[8]

Other black gay scholars and artists have staked out claims similar to those of Simmons and Hemphill, arguing for a broad understanding of the anus and the black male oral cavity as viable sites of eroticism and black cultural formation. Gary Fisher, for example, recovers the black male oral cavity as a complicated site of slave history, historically based trauma, sexual play, and racial formation.[9] Robert Reid-Pharr also sketches a genealogy of "'civil' American race talk" extending back to "the debauchery of the [slave] master" who has left a "raw milk smell of cum on the breath" of both the antebellum "nigger" and the contemporary "black." Charles I. Nero correlates anal sexual activity between two black men on a plantation in the eighteenth century to the need to rethink, in the past and the present, "our models of the black family and homosexuality as alien to black culture."[10]

Black gay men, writing at the end of the twentieth century, demonstrated the culturally challenging and historically problematic nature of the eroticized black male orifice. Through their personal sexual politics and appeals to a broader racial political platform, they argued for the need to rethink the genealogy of the black male orifice, to reexamine its political import, to decouple the orifice from black gay bodies and sex practices, and to begin, in the most creative ways possible, to locate black self-fashioning and cultural formation within the eroticized male interior. As I have argued throughout the book, the black male interior has constituted a highly undertheorized yet impacting region of black experience. By grounding this notion of the interior in eroticized regions of the male body, black gays have begun collectively to blueprint a way for us to finally and fully begin to inhabit and theorize this idea of the black male interior. Hemphill's luscious taking of the Holy Ghost into his anus and Fisher's correlating of oral sexual hunger with slave ancestry and Hegel's philosophy of the master/slave dialectic each serve as examples of a rich interior terrain existing just beyond the erogenous threshold. Each artist depicts the black male interior as an erogenous and culturally relevant structure rooted in the body's emotional and spiritual needs.

What I want to hone in on and make more explicit in this chapter is the historical tie between the black male orifice and a largely unspoken politics of interiority. The eroticized anal and oral orifices, in and of themselves, have not constituted a problem for black cultural formation. In fact, black people have, to useful ends, imagined these regions of the male body as surface structures, as demarcating and indecipherable zones of experience. This mode of imagining has facilitated, for example, black men and women of the 1960s equating same-sex practices with seeds of a racial death wish implanted during slavery. For example, W. E. B. Du Bois construed Augustus Dill, the black man arrested for having tearoom sex in the 1920s as a threat to black uplift and the dismantling of the historically laden color line. In firing Dill (a devoted cultural worker) for his arrest and expressing disdain toward tearoom sex, Dubois reinforced ideas of the homoerotic anus and mouth as dangerous corporeal regions that were antithetical to black experience.[11] From these twentieth-century examples we get a sense of the anus and oral cavity depicted in racial uplift contexts as racial gravesites and terrains of experience existing beyond the boundaries of blackness. Such modes of thinking reinforce the notion of the black male erotic interior as empty, as unspeakable and unknowable, as uninhabitable and fundamentally antithetical to black experience.

Bringing together the slave past with the present, I use Toni Morrison's *Beloved* to initiate a discussion of black male interiority in slave history and within the collective black memory of slavery. Focusing on what many have referred to as the "male rape scene" in the novel, I point out some of the limitations and inaccuracies of the term "rape." Rape names acts of sexual violation in the novel but obscures realities of black male sex and sexual appetite. Furthermore, rape, as most conceive of it, gives no indication of the rich interior and emotional life that precedes and follows the sexually violating act. These surface-level and more contemporary readings have also involved equating male rape and eroticism during slavery with contemporary black gay identities and sexual politics. Even black gay men, I suggest, are guilty of transposing the historically specific implications of the black male orifice in slave contexts into contemporary registers of gender and homosexual understanding.

As a solution to this tendency to erase historical specificity and to shine over the depth and rich metaphorical implications of the anus and oral cavity, I suggest that we read the black men in Morrison's neo-slavery novel as suffering from a condition of institutionalized hunger. The black men in Morrison's novel suffer under the same culture of hunger and human consumption that I have documented throughout this book. In Morrison's novel, this culture of hunger takes the form of staged "breakfast" scenarios, forced oral sex in the context of "breakfast," and "hungry niggers" who symbolize the compound experience of racial and sexual degradation. However, the difference between Morrison's hungering black male figures and, say, a Luke or a James L. Smith, is that they bring us to a much clearer and immediate understanding of black male erotic hunger as an index of internal need, self-awareness, alternative gender expressions and social roles, and longing for ancestral and ancient pasts.

From this discussion of Morrison's novel I segue into theorizing the black male interior space. My thinking along these lines is helped by Houston Baker Jr., who has written of this interior space as a "tight spot," or "tight place." The "tight place," as Baker thinks of it, is a place of hunger and black male desire, a zone of homoerotic contact between black and white men, and a site of black masculine anxieties that date back to slavery. Though sexually suggestive, Baker's model does not formally ground this terrain within the male anus and oral cavities. Advancing upon Baker's claims, I ground this idea of the tight place in the homoerotic experiences of black men during slavery. In particular, I look at how anal and oral sexual contact between black men on the plantation served as a means of reconstituting African cultural legacies, self- and communal identity, the memory of and loss occasioned through the Middle Passage, and nonnormative modes of gender expression. Rather than interpreting the anus and mouth as flat, utilitarian surfaces, I encourage and model a process of inhabitation, of theoretically embodying the black male interior. Only from the perspective of the inside, I attempt to show, can we ascertain the rich, fecund, and reproductive potentials of the black male orifice.

## The Rape/Hunger Dialectic

At the end of the twentieth century, the subject of slavery emerged in the hearts and imagination of Americans with haunting acuity. A cluster of novels about slavery, or neo-slave narratives, appeared at this time: Sherley Anne Williams's *Dessa Rose* (1986), Gayle Jones's *Corregidora* (1975), Charles Johnson's *Middle Passage* (1990), Randall Kenan's *A Visitation of Spirits* (1989), Octavia Butler's *Kindred* (1979) and *Wildseed* (1980), and, of course, Morrison's *Beloved*. In the visual arts, the work of Michael Ray Charles, Beverly McIver, Renee Cox, and Kara Walker all dealt with racial stereotypes, the historical memory of slavery, the recovery of slave memory, and issues of racial typing and demonizing originating in slavery. On a grander scale, films such as *Sankofa* (1993), *Amistad* (1997), and Jonathan Demme's *Beloved* (1998) brought the subject of slavery to the big screen and reintroduced the topic into the collective imagination.

In this context of remembering and recovering the legacy of slavery, the notion of the black male erotic interior emerged as a recurring and haunting problem for black people. Black people expressed this concern over black male inner life through a range of cultural registers. These included Trudier Harris's notion of nurturing male mammy figures, Alice Walker's depiction of male rape and coercion in a contemporary plantation in *The Temple of My Familiar* (1989), and Michelle Wallace's interlinking of black male rape with black grandmothers raped during slavery. The fear of rape at sea experienced by the black male protagonist in Charles Johnson's *Middle Passage* conveyed a general black male anxiety regarding issues of black male sexuality during slavery and on the plantation. Finally, as I have already described, there was, within Black Nationalist spheres, the equating of the male anal and oral cavities with racial dissolution and a death wish stemming back to slavery. These various considerations of black male inner life, though problematically fixated on male rape during slavery, signaled black people as, in a positive way, attempting to inhabit and more deeply embody the legacy of slavery. Morrison has suggested in an interview that the movement of black people away from the trauma of slavery has resulted in the abnegation of certain moral responsibilities: "I think Afro-Americans in rushing away from slavery which was important to do—it meant rushing out of bondage into freedom—also rushed away from the slaves because it was painful to dwell there, and they may have abandoned some responsibilities in so doing."[12] In other interviews and writings, Morrison has linked the legacy of slavery to contemporary U.S. fascism, the demonization of black single mothers, and the presence of black people as haunting specters in early American literature.[13] Slave experience, she insists, cannot be forgotten because it continues to have a real, determining impact on the present.

This legacy of memory is even more complicated and difficult to manage when it comes to the subject of black male sexuality, violation, and homoeroticism in the context of slavery. What we see, from one end of the twentieth century to the other, is a pattern and geography of black migration that charts how black people have had to and have chosen to leave behind the issues of black male sex, sexual violation, and sexual ambiguity. Leaving behind, though, does not necessarily imply never returning to, especially when memory and trauma are experienced as cyclical. According to sociologist Ron Eyerman, the memory of slavery has always reemerged in the collective black psyche in a cyclical manner. Since emancipation, the memory of slavery has served as a container of important historical and contemporary events for black people. He writes: "Without the means to influence public memory, blacks were left to form and maintain their own collective memory, with slavery as an ever-shifting, reconstructed reference point."[14] Regarding the transhistorical significance of slavery for differing generations of black people, Eyerman clarifies: "Slavery has meant different things for different generations of black Americans, but it was always there as a referent."[15]

As I have pointed out, at the end of the twentieth century, the meaning of the slave experience expanded to include homoeroticism and, more specifically, the topic of male sexual violation. I speak of rape and homoeroticism together—as a unit—because as Nero and others have pointed out, there has been, at least since the Reconstruction period, an unspoken correlation within the black imagination between all forms and expressions of homoeroticism during slavery and the subject of black male rape. Over time—and across cycles of memory—the pain, trauma, and terrifying consideration of black male rape has overshadowed the distinct and complex ways that homoeroticism impacted and shaped the lives of black men during slavery.

I dealt extensively with the topic of male rape in earlier chapters, but I come back to this theme again in this chapter as a way of more directly naming and more fully exploring the haunting specter that the topic of male rape has become. At this point in the cycle of slave memory that Eyerman delineates, rape operates as a phenomenon that overshadows the historical reality of the past. In terms of the black male interior, rape, though a real and disturbing historical occurrence, functions as a screen that keep us from accessing black male emotional and erotic life in a complex way.

Morrison's depiction of black male rape in *Beloved* is rare in the annals of slave history and neo-slave literature written about the slave's condition. Morrison's depiction of black men made to perform oral sex on white chain gang leaders contradicted these myths of black paternity and stimulated scholars at the end of the twentieth century to reconsider the significance and meaning of black male rape under slavery. Before considering the import and various meanings these scholars have attributed to male rape, let me first describe and briefly analyze the rape scenario depicted in *Beloved*.

The scene in question begins with black men awakened at dawn by the sound of buckshot and then, one by one, let out of their cages and made to kneel before the white chain gang leaders.

> When all forty-six were standing in a line in the trench, another rifle shot signaled the climb out and up to the ground above, where one thousand feet of the best hand-forged chain in Georgia stretched. Each man bent and waited.
>
> Kneeling in the mist they waited for the whim of a guard, or two, or three. Or maybe all of them wanted it. Wanted it from one prisoner in particular or none—or all.
>
> "Breakfast? Want some breakfast, nigger?"
>
> "Yes, sir."
>
> "Hungry, nigger?"

"Yes, sir."

"Here you go."

Occasionally a kneeling man chose gunshot in his head as the price, maybe, of taking a bit of foreskin with him to Jesus.[16]

This scene, unlike any other in the novel, has occasioned among scholars a crisis in definition and meaning. According to E. Frances White, the black men in the chain gang experience "homosexual rape" at the hands of white chain gang leaders. White conflates contemporary homosexual practices and identities with the sexual treatment of black men during slavery. Noting her own ambivalence toward the topic of "homosexuality" under slavery, White offers the following explanation of why the topic is so disturbing and best classified as a homosexual act:

> Homosexuality has already had such bad press—why add to that by pointing to instances in which it would be seen as sordid and despicable? Admittedly, the acknowledgement of heterosexual rape during slavery does not make most people think that the entire institution and various practices of heterosexuality need to be condemned. . . . But, of course, homosexuality and heterosexuality are not parallel and equal constructions: The latter depends on the former for its claim of normalcy.[17]

While White, quite appropriately, sees the privileging of "heterosexual rape" and heteronormativity under slavery as problematic, she adds to the problem by conflating the identities and interior lives of the black and white men on the chain gang with a contemporary same-sex politics. Her commentary calls to mind Hazel Carby's very useful comments regarding the historical and political specificity of rape. Referring to the distinction between the institutionalized rape of black women on the plantation and rape used as "an instrument of political terror, alongside lynching, in the South," Carby clarifies: "Rape itself should not be regarded as a transhistorical mechanism of women's oppression but as one that acquires specific political or economic meanings at different moments in history."[18] In this case, White uses the notion of homosexual rape to bridge a contemporary understanding of homosexual subjectivity with the particulars of black men made to undergo oral rape under slavery. White conceives of rape as a "transhistorical mechanism" and in the process flattens out the historical and cultural particulars of black men raped during slavery. She seems to ignore, for example, the implications of Morrison's choosing to depict oral rape over some other form of violation or penetration. Additionally, particular valences of power and self-glorification are invoked in the black men forced to kneel, take in semen, and verbally acquiesce to their abuse.

White was not the only one to conflate past and present sexual politics in her treatment of Morrison's chain-gang scenario. Nero, the black gay critic, refers to Morrison's treatment of the black men on the Sweet Home plantation as homophobic. In particular, Nero takes issue with Morrison's failure to imagine erotic sexual ties among black men on the plantation and within broader slave culture:

> Although deprived of sex with women, Sweet Home men were capable of enormous restraint and for sexual relief they either masturbated or engaged in sex with farm animals. . . . Morrison's description of the restrained Sweet Home men does a great disservice to the complexity of men's lives. Her description reinforces a false notion of a hierarchy of sexual practices in which masturbation is a substitution for intercourse. Morrison's description is homophobic because it reveals her inability to imagine homosexual relationships among heroic characters. By implication, sex with farm animals is preferable to homoerotic sex.[19]

Nero's complaint, more broadly, is that Morrison imagines homosexuality as the most degraded sexual option for black men on the plantation. While he does not directly mention the chain-gang scene, this scene, which merges sexual violation with homoerotic desire, forms part of the homophobic tableau that Nero finds Morrison's imagination informed by. Nero's point concerning the failure of black people and black women in particular to imagine homoerotic ties among black men during slavery is well taken and reflective of larger historical dynamics that he documents: "At best," he writes, "our understanding of the sexuality of our slave ancestors is fragmentary. We need to uncover more and reread diaries, letters, and narratives to gain a greater understanding of the sexuality of our forebears. At the very least, we need to revise our models of the black family and of homosexuality as alien to black culture."[20] I fully agree with Nero's historical analysis and call for historical revision but want to challenge the casual manner in which he, like White, draws correlations between contemporary homosexual politics and the particular and local circumstances of same-sex behavior practiced by black men under slavery. The emphasis upon sex and sex practice obscures, among other things, the ways that gender, gender-variant behavior, and social roles played by black men on the plantation might have shaped their erotic lives. To see Morrison simply as homophobic is to overlook these epistemological and material considerations. In addition, the designation of homophobia obscures the long-standing historical problem that the topic of black male rape has represented to black people.

Morrison's imaginative failure is part of a much larger network of imagining and remembering slavery that dates back to slavery and the first slave narratives written by black women. From Harriet Jacobs to Pauline Hopkins to Alice Walker and Morrison, black women have throughout history maintained an imaginative fixation upon the specter of black male violation. This fixation, as Nero asserts, has worked to obscure the deeper emotional and erotic realities of black men under slavery. Still, I do not believe that the solution is to completely abandon the topic of male rape for a more pristine, "freer" dimension of black male experience on the plantation. If anything, the consistent historical preoccupation with black male rape indicates the importance of beginning, as Carby suggests, to unearth a deeper, more particularized understanding of black male sexualization, sexual violation, and interior response to sexual brutality.

Darieck Scott's treatment of the chain-gang scene in Morrison's novel comes closest to what I am suggesting in the way of unpacking and particularizing black male rape. After rehearsing the details of the scene, Scott moves to analyze the powerful reactions of African Americans to the scenario:

> What is at stake in the intense reactions to *Beloved*'s chain-gang episode, I think—reactions both convergent with and divergent from the homophobia and heterosexism of the dominant culture in the United States—is the very manliness of black men as a matter of fact and history: What is in jeopardy is African Americans' own investments in the "truth" of black manhood.[21]

Scott's observations call to mind Sojourner Truth's oft-repeated antebellum inquiry: Ain't I a woman? However, in this instance the question becomes—shrouded in historical silence, shame, and gender ambiguity—Ain't I a man? Ain't I a heroic and noble man? Thinking about this very personal statement in a broader, more historically sweeping context makes one wonder, at this late juncture of black arrival, if it is possible to recover any usable vestiges of manhood and honor from something as unspeakable and unpalatable as "the breakfast." Scott refers to the oral ingestion of semen and the spectacle of black men made to watch, retch, and perform as "the breakfast." We are prepared to encounter anything and everything else in a scenario of this nature, he notes, but the notion of taking breakfast; the image and idea are too incendiary.[22]

What I would like to suggest, though, is that we when we think about "the breakfast" in the broader context of consumption and institutionalized hunger under slavery, we see that the idea of meal taking represents only a small part of a much larger tableau of black male hunger and self-consumption. In the dialogue from the chain gang, the white man says: "Breakfast? Want some breakfast, nigger?" To which one of the black men responds: "Yes, sir." Again, the white man: "Hungry, nigger?" To which the black man again responds: "Yes, sir." Even more incendiary than the allusions to morning meal taking and the staple nourishment that breakfast provides is the black man's admission to hunger, his being made to hunger. Confronting a long-held historical silence, Morrison gives us finally through the voice of a kneeling, helpless black man admission to the reality of black men made to undergo institutionalized hunger during slavery. Only in brief, oblique moments have black men, such as Frederick Douglass, admitted to the reality of slavery "causing us to eat our own flesh,"[23] to slavery as a gnawing, systemic hunger. But what Morrison does, mainly through the public staging of black male hunger, is hint at the range of interpretive implications of black male hunger, with hunger serving as metonymy for needing, wanting, being made to taste, lack, and the taboo desire to be filled.[24]

## Theorizing the Black Male Orifice

We can better apprehend the erotic implications of black male hunger if we begin by considering some of the history and genealogy of the mouth in black experience. The mouth represents a sacrosanct structure of black cultural production that black people have, for the most part, conceived of as outside of the domain of sexual violation under slavery. For the black male spokesperson, orator, autobiographer, and speech giver in the late nineteenth and early twentieth centuries, the mouth has symbolized, more than anything, the entrance and exit port of freedom and self-definition.[25] Slave narratives, itinerant speeches, pamphlets, abolitionist treatises, letters, reportage, poetry, and historical fiction published in the nineteenth century all serve as examples of how the foundations of black antebellum experience were laid in speech and literacy. In light of this historical trend, it is understandable that a resistance to thinking about the black male's mouth as sexual receptacle would exist in scholarship on the black slave experience.

In *Turning South Again: Re-Thinking Modernism/Re-Reading Booker T.*, Houston A. Baker Jr. provides a useful model for beginning to think about black male orifices as emblems for and receptacles of black cultural production. Working through the metaphor of "tight spots" or "tight places," Baker defines these as zones of black male experience that have both geographic and erogenous connotations. Jim Trueblood from Ralph Ellison's *Invisible Man* and Booker T. Washington serve as illustrative examples of these "tight places," which are sexually/erotically charged spaces, spaces that antebellum and Reconstruction black men had to negotiate as they moved out of home communities and into the world. For Trueblood, the father of a sharecropping family in a southern town, the vagina of his daughter is the "tight spot" that he finds himself in one night as he lies beside her in bed. The tight spot represents a number of economic and historic factors that make life for Trueblood, a poor southern man, difficult in the postbellum era. Trueblood experiences himself as limited and tightly contained as a result of having to labor for a white land owner whose family once owned his ancestors as slaves. Also constraining are impossible seasonal crop deadlines, an inherited impoverished social status, and the fact that he has no capital and therefore limited social agency. All of these factors come into play on a night in which Trueblood "accidentally" rapes his daughter, whose vagina represents, in the context of his social constriction, the impossible task of having to "move without moving."[26]

A number of black feminist scholars have taken issue with this idea of the tight space, critiquing both black men and women for using this structure to glorify and reify the phallus and to label black women's sexuality as a sign of so many unspeakable, vacuous zones within African American experience. Ann duCille brings a helpful gendered interpretation to bear upon Ellison's *Invisible Man* and Baker's glorification of the black male phallus in the novel. Speaking in terms of "male and female texts, masculinist and feminist readings," duCille offers: "It may be that at the heart of this controversy lie not only different notions of truth, art, and history, but very different readings of the phallus and the penis."[27] Counterbalancing Baker's reading of the tight place with depictions of father/daughter sex in Morrison's *The Bluest Eye*, duCille continues:

> What for Baker is an aristocratic procreativity turned inward is in Morrison's novel "a bolt of desire [that] ran down [Cholly Breedlove's] genitals, giving it length." What Baker calls "outgoing phallic energy," Morrison names inbreeding lust, a lust bordered by politeness that makes a father want to fuck his daughter—tenderly.[28]

DuCille's analysis exposes the phallus as the natural corollary to the female tight place. The phallus and the vacuous vagina are the symbolic representations of a long-standing history of black male and female sexual violence. Both Ellison and Morrison rework an antebellum and Reconstruction dynamic of the castrated black man and the raped black woman. Baker adorns and dresses up this history by imbuing the phallus with cosmic potency and positing the phallus as the organizing, ruling principle of "the entire clan or tribe, of Afro-America."[29] Morrison and other black women before her, such as Zora Neale Hurston, Jesse Fauset, and Nella Larsen, critique this perspective of the phallus in their writings.[30] But one thing that none of these women does, including duCille, is reconfigure the symbolic framework—of phallus in relationship to vagina—in a way that accounts for the male body also having erogenous orifices, tight interior regions that have a life and symbolic significance apart from the male/female dyad of sexual violation.[31]

Drawing on an example from Booker T. Washington's life, Baker extends his thinking on the tight male place into the realm of oral performance and erotic oral fixations in black men. For Washington, the erotic and historical implications of the tight place coalesce around the prospect of giving a speech. This is not just any speech; it is his famous 1895 address to the Cotton States and International Exposition in Atlanta. Washington makes history with this speech; he is the first black man in the South to publicly address an influential crowd of southern and northern property owners, heads of state, and businesspersons. Washington experiences terror and anxiety because he knows that the northern and southern whites present are looking to him to represent the Negro race and to assuage their own anxieties and fears about the Negro's emancipated place in larger society. It is a white farmer who observes and expresses to Washington: "Washington, you have spoken before the Northern white people, the Negroes in the South; but in Atlanta, tomorrow, you will have before you the Northern white, the Southern whites, and the Negroes all together. I am afraid you have got into a *tight place.*"[32]

This example from Washington's life provides an example of speaking—vocal execution combined with enlightened reason—characterizing black masculinity in this postemancipation era. We can say also that for Washington, as a former slave, this instance of speaking is further articulation of his emancipated status and that of all the impoverished black southerners whom he represents through his speech. Should he say things politically offensive to southern conservatives or offend his northern, more liberal constituency, he could very easily experience social castration (in the form of being cut off economically from donors, evicted from the land on which Tuskegee Institute sits, and literally lynched and castrated by the same types of whites who ran Ida B. Wells out of town for reporting on the horrors of lynching). Summing up the implications of "tight places," Baker describes them as

> constituted by the necessity to articulate from a position that combines specters of abjection (slavery), multiple subjects and signifiers (Trueblood's narrative is produced for a rich, northern, white philanthropist), representational obligations of race in America (to speak "Negro"), and patent sex and gender implications (the role of the Law as the Phallus).[33]

Baker describes Washington and Trueblood as struggling to come into their own phallic agency in the context of institutional and white male phallic power. He establishes a clear relationship among phalluses but does not go far enough in locating in the male body itself the tight erogenous regions that he theorizes. Trueblood's sexual penetration of his daughter is an externalization of his own tight, highly sexualized predicament. In addition, it is an externalization of the ways he feels violated and is made to reproduce plantation and postbellum share-cropping economics. Trueblood experiences a type of economic and social penetration at the hands of a number of white men: the plantation owner, the owner of the sharecropping fields, and the northern white philanthropist who takes a titillating interest in Trueblood's rape of his daughter. Trueblood's violation is unspeakable in the gendered economy of slavery and Reconstruction that Baker works with and so, within this limited context, Baker gestures toward a recurring scenario of male sexual violation but offers no incisive analysis of black male orifices as spatial, transhistoric, and, especially, sexual sites of identity formation.

Cautiously gesturing toward the sexual in his discussion of Washington, Baker does note that "there existed a deeply homoerotic bond between Washington and *all* white men—but in particular and most expressly between the Wizard of Tuskegee and General Armstrong."[34] He says little more on this topic. His comments, though, lead me to wonder how Washington's homoeroticization of militarized authority overlaps with the implied erotics of his speech. Thinking along the lines of the tight place, I wonder about Washington's mouth (his vocal acumen) as the instrument through which he orally handles and grapples with the violent, coercive, erotic interests of phallic law. So much of African American scholarship is premised on ideas such as "the talking book" and the recurring tropes of acquired literacy and oral competency in the making of black masculine identity.[35] In the context of the Atlantic slave trade, Equiano experiences reading the Bible and developing a relationship with Christian deity as implicitly erotic endeavors that serve to reinforce phallic law. We need to begin to account more fully for books and literacy as a means of reinforcing sexual silence at the same time that they enable speech. We also need to account for the particular ways that whites have eroticized the black male mouth (even in the context of acquiring the habits of civilization).[36] Homoeroticism and sexual knowing, for example, strongly inform the male slave voice and body in the slave narrative genre. The narratives of Frederick

Douglass, Solomon Northup, Austin Steward, and Moses Roper, among others, are rife with examples of gender variance, sexualized violence, incestuous master/slave dynamics, and exposed genitals, buttocks, and backs. In the context of these men's lives, speaking, the mouth, and textual presentation take on an overlapping erotic significance that has been little noted by scholars of slavery and the slave narrative genre.

Baker's idea of the tight place is important and potentially very useful, as it names a concept and mode of thinking about black male sex that black men and women have employed for the past 150 years. In 1970, Vincent Harding wrote a landmark historical essay in which he referred to black history as "emptiness," "the void, and "the chasm." He too used Ellison's Trueblood scene to characterize the chaos of black history as female and sexually castrating.[37] In other writings, though, Harding makes clear that projections onto black female anatomy and sex disguise a deeper, more problematic figure, and that is the black man who hungers, who has the capacity to ingest and interiorize. Harding alludes to himself and to blacks more broadly, fearing that they will be "devoured by inverted sexuality."[38] Harding's expressed fears illuminate the importance of theorizing and positively embodying notions of black male hunger and erotic appetite. Already we have developed a corpus of beliefs, cosmology, spatial mapping, and racial self-fashioning based in the intangible yet active presence of the hungering black male. Already the "hungering nigger" serves as an index of homoerotic and racialized experience, suggesting that our theorizing of race, black male inner life, and homoeroticism need to occur within a closer, more syncretized framework.

To counter this spatial logic of the tight place as emptiness, void, chasm, and vacuum, we might begin to think, in a more concrete manner, about the correlation between actual geospatial places and the interior space of the eroticized male mouth and anus. We already have precedence for this way of thinking. With the example of Washington, we have the erogenous oral region coinciding with Reconstruction era claims to tilled and harvested land, to postbellum sites of slavery, and to a sense of southern homeland sought after by emancipated slaves. In the 1960s and 70s, we have the eroticized black male anus made to signify black urban and inner city dislocation, the landscape of plantations and black men sexually violated under slavery, and the homespace of community defiled by the presence and desires of black homosexual men. In the late twentieth century, the black male orifice still signifies, to many, absence and a culturally threatening vacuity. What I am suggesting, though, in opposition to this logic, is that we begin to think about male erogenous regions as constitutive of place, belonging, and presence. I am suggesting that we find in the anus and the oral cavity productive and reproductive relationships to land, landscape, place, home, and homeland, among other sites. Such a shift in perspective would take us a long way toward realizing the positive implications of the tight place as inhabited, inhabitable, and a culturally productive space.

## The Black Male Sodomite

As we move to rethink and historically reinhabit structures such as the male anus, I think it crucial that we shift our thinking to a relational model. Rather than thinking about "the anus" of a particular black man, I think it much more helpful to think about anal copulation between two black men, to think about the anus as a relational structure. Within this relational dynamic, we can better conceive of the anus and anal copulation as an index of gender identity and social role, as a site of black male erotic and emotional hungers, as a regenerative space of black cultural formation.

Importantly, this relational model that I describe can help us reclaim from colonial American history those black men who were demonized and misrecognized as a result of their committing punishable acts of sodomy. Such reclamation is a crucial first step in constructing a new genealogy of the black male orifice, one rooted in slave history and African cultural legacies largely obscured through European empire building. Manuel Congo and Jan Creoli, whom we have already discussed, were convicted sodomites. They were also important markers of seventeenth- and eighteenth-century debates concerning the meaning of anal copulation between black men. The public record evinces very few documented cases of sodomy among black men. The 1646 case of Jan Creoli and Manuel Congo is one of the first of its type to be recovered by Jonathan Ned Katz in *The Gay/Lesbian Almanac: A New Documentary*. Court officials logged the Creoli and Congo case following proceedings in 1646 on Manhattan Island, New Netherland Colony. According to the record, this was Creoli's second sodomy offense. The court had found him guilty of sodomizing a ten-year-old by the name of Manuel Congo. For reasons that are unclear, Congo was also punished and executed along with Creoli: "Manuel Congo, a lad ten years old, on whom the above abominable crime was committed, to be carried to the place where Creoli is to be executed, tied to a stake, and faggots piled around him, for justice sake, and to be flogged; sentence executed."[39] It might have been the case that Creoli and Congo were close in age, causing the white colonialists to perceive Congo as somehow instigative of the sodomy act. The punishment of both Creoli and Congo suggests a correlation, to the white way of thinking, between black bodies and an innate sense of sexual taint. The sentencing of Congo and Creoli occurred approximately fifty years before the black sodomy act of the Quakers was passed. That Quakers felt the need to craft separate sodomy laws for blacks says that there were probably occurrences of sodomy among blacks prior to 1706.

*Webster's Encyclopedic Unabridged Dictionary* defines a sodomite as "1. an inhabitant of Sodom. 2. one who practices sodomy." Sodomy is defined as "1. unnatural, esp. anal copulation with a human or an animal. And 2. [as] copulation of a human with an animal; bestiality." This broad definition of sodomy was commonly accepted in the seventeenth century. When Rev. John Cotton was asked to draw up a group of sodomy laws for the Massachusetts colony, he defined sodomy as an "unnatural filthiness, to be punished with death, whether sodomy, which is carnal fellowship of man with man, or woman with woman, or buggery, which is carnal fellowship of man or woman with beasts or fowls."[40] Both Cotton's and the dictionary definition of sodomy are rife with historical and cultural presumptions. There is the obvious reference to the biblical cities of Sodom and Gomorrah. There is an embedded hierarchy of species, wherein humans predominate over animals. There are also, in these definitions, embedded assumptions about natural biological functions: Anything connected to excrement is filthy and the anus is understood as always and only an eliminative organ. Whether or not Creoli and Congo came directly from Africa (an issue that I will shortly take up), their case marks a moment when whites, among themselves, contested the meaning of the African body, some interpolating it into Puritan Christian reality and legal and theological discourses. Blacks were denied humanity, but in the context of sodomy laws and persecutions, were clearly held to a marginal, peripheral status of humanity and sexual identity. Importantly, the white American interpretation of the black sodomite served a political end that involved furthering the goals of empire building and chaining the African body to a framework of spiritual and corporeal taint.

In spite of the power and life-shaping influence of the state, we should not forget, though, that there were other meanings and implications of anal copulation, meanings that stemmed back to African homosexual practices and plantation culture and the politics of resistance. Reinserting the black sodomite into the narrative of black cultural formation challenges the antebellum and nineteenth-century myths, ideologies, values and social practices generated by black people. Also, the black sodomite helps us to get at and unpack the implications of blackness— of Anglo-Africanness and Negroness—that functioned as a homoerotic sexual category long before twentieth-century sexual politics or the labor of nineteenth-century black persons to cast the race in the mold of the virile black male and the fecund maternal black female. There is also a race, womb, and myth of cultural origins embedded in Congo's anus and Creoli's penis, or Creoli's penis in Congo's anus. The broader implications of Congo's and Creoli's sex act spanned the Atlantic and had roots in indigenous African patterns of homosexuality and gender fluidity.

Through Manuel Congo's name, we can ascertain something of his roots, his African cultural lineage. Congo's surname is a reminder of the lush, humid Bakongo region of Central Africa. Even today, "Central Africa has the continent's densest forests and a climate of high temperatures and heavy rainfall."[41] Africans brought to the Americas often retained (in name) some hint of their geographic origins. A slave often retained a first name or surname, such as Congo, Qua, Sisa, or Zambo, to signify their literal or ancestral connections to a specific part of Africa.[42] Either the slave himself or, in many cases, the master, chose to keep this name of identification. Most likely, Manuel Congo or an ancestor of his came from the Kongo (the Bakongo region of Central Africa). The Bantu Bakongo people of this region maintained complex patterns of gender variance and homosexuality that influenced patterns of religious worship, social roles, kinship ties, and a range of other relational patterns. For example, the Bantu who lived along the Congo River in the early eighteenth century maintained flexible gender frameworks. According to the French Jesuit Jean Baptiste Labat, who served among the Bantu, certain males wore female clothing and were referred to as "Grandmother" in certain sacred and ceremonial contexts. Labat, true to his Christian training, describes a man who lives as a Ganga-Ya-Chibanda as an infernal servant of licentiousness and an expert in demonology:

> A shameless, impudent, lewd man. . . . He dresses ordinarily as a woman and makes an honor of being called the Grandmother. Whatever bad action that he might commit, there is no point of law that might condemn him to death; also he is one of the very loyal Ministers of the Demon of impurity. The privileges of his character go so far, that one is not able to say the outrages that he does to married persons, may be with their women, may be with their concubines.[43]

The Ganga-Ya-Chibanda, according to the missionary, copulates with married men, their wives, and their concubines. His/her sexual appetites know no bounds. From the missionary's stereotypic demonizing and sexualizing of the Ganga-Ya-Chibanda, we get the sense that this figure had a dual gender role and social function. It is hard to surmise from this account whether this person was possessed by a female spirit or inherited his or her responsibilities through the female bloodline, but clearly a person enacting this social function reflected spiritual/ancestral affiliations. In many western and central African cultures, the Grandmother (as the embodiment of the institution of motherhood) was a respected and feared person. This woman could elevate or erode the moral and material foundations of a community. The grandmother—at the level of womb and social regeneration—mediated between the human community and the ancestral maternal legacies of the clan or group.[44]

The Jesuit priest translates gender variance into a sexually licentious act. The priest links the Ganga-Ya-Chibanda's role of keeping the ancestral shrines and presiding over ancestral practices with demon servitude, impurity, and, by extension, the impurity of same-sexual and heterosexual acts. The Jesuit priest's sexualization of the Ganga-Ya-Chibanda coincided with French interests in land, minerals, and slaves during this time period. His comments exemplify how a colonial discourse of black homosexuality existed long before Africans arrived in the Americas. This discourse did not use the language of sex and sexual practice. Rather, it embedded homosexual deviance within a larger conceptualization of the deviant nature of Africans. Other priests and missionaries made more overt connections among homosexuality, gender variance, and the transgression of Christian tenets and values. Jesuit priest Joao do Santos, who was in the Congo region in the seventeenth century, observed a type of man referred to as Chibadi. He writes: "certayne *Chibadi*, which are Men attyred like Women, and behave themselves womanly, ashamed to be called men; are also married to men, and esteeme that unnatural damnation an honor."[45] The priests Gaspar Azeveredue and Antonius Sequerius during the same time period also encountered *chibados* "who dressed, sat, and spoke like women, and who married men 'to unite in wrongful male lust with them'"[46]

In Western and Eastern Africa, other groups, such as the Bakongo, linked homosexuality with social function. In Kenya, the Meru people have maintained the role of the *mugawe* for centuries, if not millennia. The *mugawe* is a powerful religious leader who is "considered a complement to . . . male political leaders."[47] The *mugawe* wears women's clothing and women's hairstyles. In another example, the Kwanyame people of southern Angola acknowledge the *kimbanda* as an important gender-variant person. The *kimbanda*, according to ethnologist Carlos Estermann, is "essentially a man who has been possessed since childhood by a spirit of a female sex." The *kimbanda* or *omasenge kimbanda* dress like women, do women's work, and "contract marriage" with other men.[48]

The Ganga-Ya-Chibanda and the *omasenge kimbanda* were maternal types. Their respective societies acknowledged their maternal capacity by having them dress in the clothing of the female sex. With each of these figures, clothing functioned as a powerful indicator of social class, gender role, and even spiritual orientation. Even more revealing is how social institutions, religion, cosmology, and gender norms acknowledged the maternal impulse in the male. These individuals (and their creative dual-gendered capacities) did not exist in isolation. Rather, they existed in social contexts in which sexual orientation and gender configuration were thought to originate in spirit, in the pre-material. The Ganga-Ya-Chibanda had obvious connections to the dead and perhaps also to a maternal bloodline or a maternal ancestor, hence the designation of The Grandmother.

These Central and Eastern African linkings of maternity and homoeroticism provide one means of interpreting the absence of information on homoeroticism in colonial America. This issue of information reflects not only the status of the historical archive but also our theoretical and social frameworks that make sense and meaning of homoerotic behaviors that occurred among black persons in colonial America. With Creoli and Congo, the black men that originated this discussion, we see how Western systems of law and Christian fundamentalism dictate the meaning of the homosexual act and disconnect Creoli and Congo's bodies and desires from a larger diasporic interpretive framework. It is of vital importance to know if either Congo or Creoli understood themselves as fulfilling a female or maternal role and if that role took meaning from African cultural forms. Within the sexualizing logic of sodomy law, we get nothing of the intimate and spiritual ties that might have bonded Congo to Creoli and dictated the nature and significance of their bond: Did they live together? Did they share economic resources and acquired capital? Did other members of their slave community acknowledge and sanction a bond between them? Along with Creoli and Congo, other black men were also convicted of sodomy offenses. These men could easily fit into the diasporic framework suggested through Congo. Someone, such as Mingo alias Cocke Negro, had a suggestive African first name and was executed for "forcible Buggery" in 1712. With Cocke Negro, we have even less information about his affectional or social ties to other men, and black men in particular; this should inspire us to look more deeply into the implications of his being crafted, through legal discourse, into a figuration of sodomy.[49]

At a more basic level of libidinal drive and need, I wonder about Creoli, Congo, and Cocke Negro as emblems of black male hunger for self and other. In particular, I am thinking of the emotional and erotic hungers that drive these young black men to risk death in the pursuit of erotic pleasure. They all, in their own ways, surely hungered for deep connection, for familiarity and intimacy, for warmth, and communal ties. Hunger, unlike need and even desire, taps into those libidinal and spiritual urges that sustain and drive the organic being. To think of Creoli, Congo, and Cocke as hungering in the way I am suggesting also opens us up to the theoretical and erotic implications of their satiation, their momentary fulfillment, their pleasure as an index of survival praxis and cultural renewal.

Coming back to my earlier point concerning the relational, hunger, as I am thinking of it, is fundamentally a relational construct. It is significant that Creoli and Congo are both young black men rather than a young black man and a white man. As young black men, as two persons sharing the bonded condition, both young men had access potentially to a common field of cultural and ancestral experience. In such a context, the act of anal copulation might have served to unify, reconstitute, and regenerate self and society in ways that were particular to the circumstances of bondage. As symbols of sameness and erotic reciprocity, Creoli and Congo provide an opportunity to think about the anus as a generative place.

As a place, the anus serves as a site of ancestral memory, of African customs and gender practices that perhaps informed the relation between Congo and Creoli. Africa, as symbolic and geographic region, brings into greater focus the positive aspects of black male hunger, of black men made to hunger in the context of slavery. In addition, intersecting the geography of Africa with black male interior life makes available to us a rich and largely unacknowledged terrain of black cultural formation. Through Creoli, Congo, and their act of anal copulation we get an expanded sense of gender and relational dynamics on the plantation, erotic modes of resistance and self-generation, and the black male orifice as a space constituted through mutual need and desire.

## The Anus in Diasporic Context

Through the tight and seemingly confining space of the anus, we find ourselves navigating the Atlantic and quite seamlessly engaging with issues of cultural origins and racial meaning at the heart of black experience. This journeying, through the anal cavity, conveys the inherent potential of the black male orifice to complicate and advance our inquiries into the black Atlantic itself and black diasporic experience. Black Atlantic or black diasporic studies have greatly furthered our understandings of the ways African cultural practices have remained viable in the context of the new African world. In *The Black Atlantic: Modernity and Double Consciousness*, Paul Gilroy uses the emblem of the ship to symbolize migrational shifting, the moving "between . . . two great cultural assemblages" that marks the nature of black Atlantic culture.[50] He focuses mainly on routes of cultural sharing and transmission that move along the ancient arc of the slave triangle. Throughout the slave trade, but especially during the first two-thirds, slavery commerce was a black Atlantic phenomenon, a cultural sharing. Slaves would come from Africa to the Caribbean; slave traders would then transfer them to ports in Georgia, the Carolinas, and Louisiana, among other places. Sometimes whites would take slaves from American ports to trade in the Caribbean or off the coast of South America. African-based same-sex practices also migrated within this framework.

Gilroy uses the ship, the commodities ship, the coastal ship, and the slave schooner to symbolize the legacy of the black Atlantic. The image of two black men in an intimate embrace, an anal embrace, calls our attention to those first bodies held together in the ship. There is perhaps no more intimate and formative moment for black people than that moment, women chained to women and men chained to men. If the ship captures a legacy of movement, of in-between consciousness, then joined black male bodies—either through chains, terror, mutual dislocation, or anal intercourse—registers the effects of this movement on the body, the emotions, the psyche, and desire. In the seventeenth and eighteenth centuries, the black homoerotic body was a symbol of permanent rupture, a rupture in the very meaning and ontological foundations of the African body. For no longer did variance and fluidity lend this body multiple roles, sexual preferences, and social significances. Instead, in the context of slavery and colonial expansion, this intimate erotic space between two black men became a symbol of loss, of disconnection from Africa, and of deviance within black communities.

In *Biography of a Runaway Slave*, the Cuban slave Estaban Montejo depicts an alternative genealogy of black same-sex behavior. Montejo's biography records how same-sex-identified black men were tolerated and to a great extent integrated into various aspects of eighteenth-century Cuban plantation culture. Montejo, like Harriet Jacobs, uses black homoeroticism strategically. He uses it to prove slavery a dehumanizing, culturally debilitating institution. Referring to homo-sexuality, he admonished: "In my opinion it didn't come from Africa. Old men didn't like it at all. Old men wanted to have nothing to do with them."[51] "Them" means the effeminate men who partner with more masculine men on the plantation. Montejo links "effeminacy" and acts of sodomy among black men to a much larger context of forced inti-macy. These violences—rape, seasoning pens, physical beatings, and language disruption—are to blame rather than the pristine paternal legacy of Africa.

In Montejo's cosmology, the "effeminate" black male slave is a sym-bol of rupture and disconnection. This male becomes one repository for the collective treatment of black men under Cuban plantation culture: black men ruptured from land and language; black men held together with chains, vomit, and feces; black men broken in seasoning pens and made to share the mutual secret of their degradation, of constant, per-manent subjugation. Ironically, the "effeminate" black male becomes the means of forgetting and simultaneously remembering Africa. For the old men from Africa who "wanted to have nothing to do with them [the effeminate men]," such men clarified what Africa was in their imagina-tions—an idyllic place of male/female conjugal unions, a place where men did not make house together. According to Montejo, elder African men recognized nothing of their native Yoruba, Bantu, or Kikongo lands in such persons or the domestic relationships they formed. These elder men associated the effeminate male, insofar as he is associated with the pain and mangling circumstances of slavery, with forgetting Africa, not being true to the noble legacy represented by the "old men." Through the ancestral authority that he invests in the old men, Montejo establishes that "the word effeminate [within black Cuban communities] came about after slavery."[52] In this early eighteenth-century example, we see homoeroticism (the black penis inside the anus) figured into the cos-mology and memory of Africa. Making black men have unwilling and willing sex with white men did not encourage such thinking. Such acts were usually blamed upon plantation culture and the malformed appe-tites of white slavers. However, African men making love to and being loving with one another brought African legacy into view more centrally.

What Montejo thinks of as a culturally dead space (the anal, emo-tional, erotic tie between two black men) I would like to, for a moment, think about as a reproductive space. In particular, I would like to think about the effeminate men that Montejo describes as possessing symbolic wombs—regenerative spaces of their hearts, bodies, and minds. For even in Montejo's mind, such an erotic connection between two black men is charged with memory, with lineage, and African cultural legacy. As with the Ganga-Ya-Chibanda and *omasenge kimbanda* figures, the effeminate man plays a womanly and even maternal domestic role—tending and perpetuating the psychic and economic well-being of the domestic space. Montejo argues that male wives and their husbands signify a break with all things African, but I want to shift the dialogue to think in terms of continuity and recalibration.

The intimate sexual space shared between the black men that Montejo describes translated into domestic spaces and economic partnerships. Speaking of life on the plantation, Montejo recalls:

> To make a long story short, life was lonely anyway because women were pretty scarce. And to have a woman you had to be twenty-five years old and lay her in a field. . . . Many men didn't suffer because they were accustomed to that life. Others had sex with each other and didn't want to have anything to do with women. Sodomy, that was their life. Those men washed clothes, and if they had a husband, they also cooked for him. They were good workers and were busy tending their conucos. They gave produce to their husbands to sell to the guajiros. And the word effeminate came about after slavery because that situation continued on.[53]

More significant than the question of whether such behaviors originated in Africa is the way such black male intimate spaces held the potential for redefinition, self-ownership, and a fluid model of plantation masculinity. In the mercantile economics of slavery, black men "making house" and sharing resources signaled a radical break from the numerous structures designed to diminish and devitalize black male productive energy. Montejo's description of the effeminate men and their "husbands" suggests a hierarchy and range of masculinities. There is the effeminate black man, there is the male who is "more masculine" and partners with men for life, there is the male who is "more masculine" but chooses to partner with an effeminate man only out of circumstance. From Montejo's narrative, we cannot know the full

range of combinations, the ways, perhaps, that effeminate men part-
nered with one another or a so-called masculine man chose to partner
with both a womanly man and a biological woman. Furthermore, we
do not get from Montejo's perspective a sense of how effeminate men
worked alongside and in relationship to women. There were not a lot of
women in these situations, but there were some. And certainly following the abolition of slavery in Cuba, more women were readily available
to men who were not kept from women by the Spanish men who had
previously owned them. Montejo makes no mention of the effeminate
male's dress or affect, but it might be important to know how such men
dressed, what flourishes of coiffure, jewelry, or clothing they wore to
signify their wifely status.

Montejo's narrative offers ample evidence of continuities between
Central and Western African cultures and the plantation values and
cultural practices he describes. Throughout his narrative, he refers to
religious practices, work habits and skills, and folklore as coming from
different parts of Africa. He notes that most of the slaves in Cuba came
from either Yorubaland or Central Africa, the Bakongo region. His
own grandfather, Gin Congo, comes from the Congo region of Central
Africa. He says that his father was "Lucumi from Oyo," the Oyo region
of Yorubaland and the location of the once-prominent Oyo Empire.[54] J.
Lorand Matory has written extensively about what he calls "transvestite
types" among the Yoruba in the era of the Oyo Yoruba kingdom and
empire. The Yoruba maintained a fluid and complex gender system in
which male Shango priests wore the clothing and hairstyles of women
and were understood to be the brides of the king and the thunder deity,
Shango.[55] Yoruba cosmology and lore are rife with examples of men
changing into women, women into men, women with penises, and
males with reproductive genitalia. In addition, a significant number of
the enslaved population in Cuba came from Central Africa. As I have
noted earlier, if we look to Africa, there is a definite cultural precedent
for men on American and Cuban plantations acting as domesticated
wives to husbands who traversed the public domain.

Throughout the African diaspora, pockets of culture emerged that
we catch only a hint of through examples related in Montejo's narrative. From plantations in Bahia, Brazil, there also emerged documented
examples of cross-dressing, effeminacy, and same-sex eroticism directly

linked to African cultural practices. Francisco Manicongo's behaviors were so pronounced that they came to the attention of agents of the Portuguese inquisition stationed in Brazil. Portuguese inquisition officials document Manicongo's exploits in *First Visit of the Holy Office to the Regions of Brazil—Denunciations of Bahia, 1591–1593*:

> Francisco Manicongo, a cobbler's apprentice known among the slaves as a sodomite for "performing the duty of the female" and for "refusing to wear the men's clothes which the master gave him." Francisco's accuser added that "in Angola and the Congo in which he had wandered much and of which he had much experience, it is customary among the pagan negros to wear a loincloth with the ends in front which leaves an opening in the rear . . . this custom being adopted by those sodomitic negros who serve as passive women in the abominable sin. These passives are called *jimbandaa* in the language of Angola and the Congo, which means passive sodomite. The accuser claimed to have seen Francisco Manicongo "wearing a loincloth such as passive sodomites wear in his land of the Congo and immediately rebuked him."[56]

Along with familiar practices of demonization, we have in Manicongo another example of a gender- and sexually deviant black man interpolated into a European framework of sexual deviance. Manicongo's treatment in the context of the Portuguese inquisition parallels that of Manuel Congo and Jan Creoli a century later in colonial America. This patterned European response to differing African codes of gender and sexuality conveys how crucial the management of African bodies and erotic desires was to the consolidation of European imperial power in the Americas. More to the point, we see that Europeans developed implicit strategies aimed at containing the erotic significance of the male anus and the socially transgressive implications of anal sex. In Manicongo, anal copulation coincides with his gender-variant dress, his choosing to do the labor of the female sex, and his maintaining cultural practices that originate, in part, from Central Africa.

Throughout this chapter, I foreground the gender-variant or passive figure only because this person has received so little attention in our scholarship on slavery in the Americas and other parts of the African diaspora. However, despite my focus on this type of black man I do not wish to preclude broader considerations of black masculinity and of black men performing a range of interlocking roles and erotic functions in the context of plantation life. Montejo, a military man and soldier in the Cuban war of independence, would have had his views of masculinity shaped by notions of valor, images of soldiers as saving women and children and ultimately returning home to propagate and rebuild the nation. As for black men who fought in the U.S. Civil War, participation in the Cuban war of independence promised greater social belonging and civil acknowledgement.

Nevertheless, Montejo's notions of nation, family, and paternity strongly mimic those of the Spanish imperialists who were overthrown in the Cuban War and, for that matter, those of the English, French, and Portuguese. Because of his prejudices we cannot know how effeminate men contributed to child rearing or how they perhaps enabled physical and cultural resistance. From Montejo's recollection, we can safely deduce that multiple models of the domestic sphere existed. Family was a creative entity that was defined in a number of different ways. Gender was flexible and homosexuality was complex, breaking down into effeminate and masculine men, into men who chose to partner with female-men, biological women, or, in some cases, both. Montejo speaks from a male identity that arises from the colonial paradigm, so that while he has helped create a social reality that survives and thrives beyond Spanish occupation, he still occupies and employs the gender and mythic reality of the Spanish colonizer. His mythology of masculinity is one whose creativity and reproductive potential stems from the phallus and the phallic-based institutions of the military and the church, among others.

Yet gender-variant figures, such as the male wives depicted in Montejo's narrative, suggest that the phallus and phallic ideology were not the only nodes around which culture and resistance cohered. The dimorphic worldview Montejo occupied existed alongside the more flexible reality of the male-female man, this man who could substitute for a biological woman and existed somewhere between or beyond the idea of two biological sexes. In a number of the plantation contexts I describe, the anus and anal copulation symbolize cultural continuity, alternative and creative relational bonds, and sites of resistance to the dehumanizing and emotionally numbing circumstances of slavery. Beginning from the assumptive framework that the eroticized anus and oral orifice are sites of agency and black cultural formation requires us to rethink so much of what we have accepted as norms of desire, biology, race continuity, and cultural origins. Even with the expanding and prolific body of work on black slave experience, we should still know that we have only just begun to fully delve into the more complex and difficult-to-articulate regions of black experience under slavery.

The same groups that went to Cuba and Brazil from the Bakongo region, Yorubaland, Sierra Leone, and the Gambia also came to the United States. And so we should think about Manicongo and the effeminate men that Montejo describes as related to the diasporic genealogies and cultural significances embodied in men such as Congo and Creoli. What I have tried to show by placing U.S. figures such as Congo, Creoli, and Cocke Negro in a transatlantic context is that we can and should think about the black male erogenous zone during slavery as a diasporic site, a site of cultural formation informed by the geography of the slave triangle: Africa, the Caribbean, and the United States. In fact, in the antebellum period in the United States, Blacks maintained a diasporic politics that involved traveling to and connecting culturally with places such as Cuba, Haiti, Jamaica, and Brazil. Frederick Douglass served as U.S. ambassador to Haiti. In *Blake; Or, the Huts of America* (1861–1862), Martin R. Delany wrote of the political ties between U.S. blacks and the people of Cuba. Enslaved persons in the United States frequently escaped to Mexico. David Walker, the black abolitionist, spent the last portion of his political career traveling between the United States and West Africa. There is already precedent for thinking about black men during slavery as occupying and emotionally inhabiting the diaspora.

What I am encouraging, though, is a deeper exploration of habitation: of the loss and longing that dislocation encouraged; of the profound hungers to belong, to have a homeland. I am imagining a tableau of black experience that includes the experiences of Manicongo, Cocke Negro, and Congo alongside those of Montejo, Walker, and Delany. All of these black men, under varying circumstances of U.S. slavery, wrestled with the regimes of Christianity, contended with the erotic and homoerotic interests of the state, and were made to hunger for self and a larger sense of communal belonging. What figures such as Congo and others bring into focus, though, is how we have largely overlooked the interior and erotic dimensions of these black men's struggles. At varying points throughout this book—through the examples of Douglass and Sandy, Turner and Willis, Baldwin and the black men from *Ten Black Writers Respond*—I have alluded to the relational and erotic ties that have bound black men to one another throughout history. We should not limit our understandings of anal and oral copulation to the specifics of the sex act. Rather, it is my hope that we will begin, more broadly, to marshal the relational implications of these sex acts and use these energies to reconfigure and remap black masculinity, black male interior life, and even the implications of the black Atlantic and black Atlantic experience. Our new and first priority should be the mapping and excavating of the interior. Where we have feared to expose our deepest hungers and libidinal drives, we should now see these energies and domains of experience as guideposts and indicators of a new and vital terrain of black experience.

# NOTES

NOTES TO THE FOREWORD

1. Philip Brian Harper, "The Evidence of Felt Tuition: Minority Experience, Every-day Life, and Critical Speculative Knowledge," in *Black Queer Studies: A Critical Anthology*, edited by E. Patrick Johnson and Mae G. Henderson (Durham, NC: Duke University Press, 2005), 106–123.

NOTES TO THE INTRODUCTION

1. The title of this chapter is from Orlando Patterson, *Slavery and Social Death: A Comparative Study* (Cambridge, MA: Harvard University, 1982), 338.
2. James Oliver Horton and Lois E. Horton, eds., *Slavery and Public History: The Tough Stuff of American Memory* (New York: The New Press, 2006), x.
3. See James Oliver Horton, "Slavery in American History: An Uncomfortable National Dialogue," in *Slavery and Public History: The Tough Stuff of American Memory*, edited by James Oliver Horton and Lois E. Horton (New York: The New Press, 2006), 46–47. Horton rehearses a number of contemporary sce-narios in which slavery serves as a catalyst for highly contentious contemporary debates. For example, he cites the Daughters of the Confederacy, who took issue with a PBS documentary that they felt presented too much history of slavery. He also notes the controversy that continues to swirl around Confederate holi-days and flags.
4. See Joanne Melish, "Recovering from Slavery: Four Struggles to Tell the Truth," in *Slavery and Public History: The Tough Stuff of American Memory*, edited by James Oliver Horton and Lois E. Horton (New York: The New Press, 2006), 119–125.
5. Dorothy Spruill Redford, *Somerset Homecoming: Recovering a Lost Heritage* (Chapel Hill: University of North Carolina Press, 1988), 113. Regarding Josiah III's bloodline and sense of social esteem, Redford notes: "He esteemed *his* blood the bluest, *his* opinions the wisest, *his* tastes the truest, and everything identified with *him* the most perfect the world contained" (113; Redford's emphasis). In keeping with his sense of social stature, Josiah III set out to build, through Somerset Place, a world that reflected these lofty and highbrow ideas.

6. I define these terms formally at a later point in the introduction. I raise them here only as a way of alluding to hunger as an index for much larger processes of starvation and social consumption occurring on the plantation.

7. In *In the Heart of the Sea: The Tragedy of the Whaleship* Essex (New York: Viking, 2000), Nathaniel Philbrick describes how members of the Nantucket community will not talk to him about this event even in the twentieth century. For example, the daughter of Benjamin Lawrence, a white man who sailed aboard the *Essex*, told him when asked about events aboard the ship: "We do not mention this in Nantucket" (217). Philbrick also quotes from William Comstock, *A Voyage to the South Atlantic and Round Cape Horn into the Pacific Ocean* (1798; repr., New York: Da Capo, 1968), which records how Nantucket ship captains and white crew members typically thought of and treated blacks as subhuman persons, in a manner reminiscent of slave treatment. They typically referred to the ship that brought hands from New York as the "slaver" and ship captains as "Negro drivers" (27).

8. Scot French, *The Rebellious Slave: Nat Turner in American Memory* (New York: Houghton Mifflin, 2004), 279.

9. I am thinking here of Scot French and before him William Sidney Drewry, *The Southampton Insurrection* (Washington, DC: Neale Company, 1900). In *Nat Turner: A Slave Rebellion in History and Memory* (New York: Oxford University Press, 2003) Kenneth S. Greenberg offers a more evenhanded interpretation but still does not speculate about the obvious implications of Turner's literal consumption.

10. Patterson, *Slavery and Social Death*, 337. Patterson describes a continuum of human parasitism on the plantation that ranged from "true mutualism" (a more balanced, incremental consumption) to "total parasitism" (a type of consumption that results in the slave's death) (336). Parasitism is one way of conceptualizing the dynamic of human consumption on the plantation. Throughout this study, I use the terms "consumption" and "cannibalism" to more directly convey the reality of flesh hunger and appetite that the enslaved person frequently described in written document and oral narrative.

11. John S. Jacobs, "A True Tale of Slavery," in *Incidents in the Life of a Slave Girl: Written by Herself*, edited by Jean Fagan Yellin (1987; repr., Cambridge, MA: Harvard University Press, 2000), 207, 209.

12. In *Twelve Years a Slave: Narrative of Solomon Northup, a Citizen of New-York, Kidnapped in Washington City in 1841 and Rescued in 1853, from a Cotton Plantation Near the Red River in Louisiana* (Auburn, NY: Derby and Miller, 1853), Solomon Northup describes the master's feasting and gluttonous behavior as directly tied to the starvation and brutalization of the slave (215).

13. I treat this dynamic at length in Chapter 4, which focuses on Harriet Jacobs's slave narrative, *Incidents in the Life of a Slave Girl; Written by Herself*, edited by Jean Fagan Yellin (1987; repr., Cambridge, MA: Harvard University Press, 2000).

14. Quote originally appears in Samuel A. Cartwright, "Report on the Diseases and Physical Peculiarities of the Negro Race" (May 1851), but I quote from Paul Finkelman, ed., *Defending Slavery: Proslavery Thought in the Old South, A Brief History with Documents* (Boston: St. Martin's Press, 2003), 160.

15. Ibid., 159.

16. This rewriting of the master Eurocentric narrative of cannibalism is further emphasized by the other part of the *Le Rire* cartoon, which is a split frame. The first frame has a naked white man turning on a skewer; the second, amended frame focuses on the Congo Man. I rely upon a reprint of the cartoon publish in Jan Nederveen Pieterse, *White on Black: Images of Africa and Blacks in Western Popular Culture* (New Haven, CT: Yale University Press, 1992), 121.

17. Philip D. Curtin, ed., *Africa Remembered: Narratives by West Africans from the Era of the Slave Trade* (Madison: University of Wisconsin Press, 1967), records numerous examples of this belief among the Egba, Yoruba, and Bornu peoples of Nigeria; see 215, 313, 331. See also W. D. Piersen, *Black Legacy: America's Hidden Heritage* (Amherst: University of Massachusetts Press, 1993), 1–34; Michael Mullin, *Africa in America: Slave Acculturation and Resistance in the American South and the British Caribbean 1736–1831* (Urbana: University of Illinois Press, 1995), 35; Philip Verner Bradford and Harvey Bloom, *Ota: The Pygmy in the Zoo* (New York: St. Martin's Press, 1992), 31, 33, 123 for a fairly complex understanding of Congo beliefs about cannibalism applied to Europeans.

18. Curtin, *Africa Remembered*, 215.

19. Ibid.

20. Toni Morrison, *Playing in the Dark: Whiteness and the American Literary Imagination* (Cambridge: Harvard University Press, 1992), 25.

21. Jacobs, *Incidents in the Life of a Slave Girl*, 71–81.

22. Herman Melville, *Moby-Dick; or, The Whale* (1851; repr., Boston: Houghton Mifflin, 1956), 52.

23. Frederick Douglass, *Narrative of the Life of Frederick Douglass, an American Slave, Written by Himself* (1845), edited by Robert B. Stepto (Cambridge, MA: Belknap Press, 2009), 87.

24. Ibid., 19.

25. Jerry Saltz, "Kara Walker: Ill-Will and Desire," *Flash Art* 29, no. 191 (1996): 86.

26. *Webster's Encyclopedic Unabridged Dictionary of the English Language* defines homoeroticism as "a tendency to be aroused by a member of the same sex," making a distinction between arousal and the sex act.

27. In *The Golden Age of Black Nationalism, 1850–1925* (New York: Oxford University Press, 1978) Wilson Jeremiah Moses describes how "blacks as a race were [thought of] as sensual, emotional, and 'feminine,' as opposed to the hardy, aggressive and 'masculine' Anglo-Saxons" (25). The idea of the black or African race as the lady of the two races arose from this dual logic.

28. Eve Kosofsky Sedgwick, *Between Men: English Literature and Male Homosocial Desire* (New York: Columbia University Press, 1985), 1.

29. See David M. Halperin, *How to Do the History of Homosexuality* (Chicago: University of Chicago Press, 2002), 120. Specifically, Halperin refers to contemporary scholars looking for evidence of homosexuality in Renaissance literature and culture and draws attention to the misapplication of words and terms such as "homoeroticism" and "latent homosexuality."

30. Hugh Thomas, *The Slave Trade: The History of the Atlantic Slave Trade, 1440–1870* (New York: Simon and Schuster Inc., 1997), 90.

31. Ibid.

32. Pieterse explains the ideology behind this belief in *White on Black*. He writes: "When new lands were found and strange peoples encountered, whether in America, the Pacific or the African interior, the accusation of cannibalism served to affirm and secure the central place of Christian civilization" (116). Pieterse links this Christian ideology to other aspects of European Enlightenment belief and philosophy.

33. Henry Ward Beecher, "Politics and the Pulpit," *The North Star*, June 13, 1850.

34. Shirley Lindenbaum, "Thinking about Cannibalism," *Annual Review of Anthropology* 33 (2004): 475.

35. See, for example, Rosalind Shaw, *Memories of the Slave Trade: Ritual and the Historical Imagination in Sierra Leone* (Chicago: University of Chicago Press, 2002), 228–229; E. E. Evans-Pritchard, *Witchcraft, Oracles and Magic among the Azande* (New York: Oxford University Press, 1958).

36. W. Arens, *The Man-Eating Myth: Anthropology and Anthropophagy* (New York: Oxford University Press, 1979), 55–80.

37. See, as examples, Daniel Cottom, *Cannibals and Philosophers: Bodies of Enlightenment* (Baltimore, MD: Johns Hopkins University Press, 2001); Lindenbaum, "Thinking about Cannibalism"; Arens, *The Man-Eating Myth*; Petrinovich, *The Cannibal Within*; and Maggie Kilgour, *From Communion to Cannibalism: An Anatomy of Metaphors of Incorporation* (Princeton, NJ: Princeton University Press, 1990). The conceptual framework and terminology pertaining to cannibalism grows increasingly sophisticated and particularized. There is "exocannibalism," an aggressive act of consuming a person outside of a cultural group, in the context of say, warfare. "Endocannibalism" is consuming someone within one's group. There is medical cannibalism, auto-cannibalism, innocent cannibalism, and sacrificial cannibalism, among other terms. Lindenbaum's "Thinking about Cannibalism" gives a succinct inventory of the terms and conceptual frameworks newly created on the topic of cannibalism, 478–82. In addition, Lindenbaum's article ("Thinking about Cannibalism") is a good beginning interdisciplinary survey of the more cutting-edge literature on cannibalism.

38. Matthew J. Christensen documents this occurrence in "Cannibals in the Postcolony: Sierra Leone's Intersecting Hegemonies in Charlie Haffner's Slave Revolt Drama *Amistad Kata*," *Research in African Literatures* 36, no. 1 (2005): 1–19. He writes: "According to slave revolt leader Sengbe Pieh, he and forty-eight other captives aboard the *Amistad* schooner rebelled after a slave belonging to

the ship's captain gestured that their Spanish-Cuban captors intended to kill, dismember, and eat them. With this misinformation, the recently enslaved Africans unshackled themselves with a nail pried loose from the ship's woodwork, took up the cane knives stored alongside them, and stormed the deck killing the captain and his slave" (1).

39. Ibid., 2.

40. Ibid., 3.

41. When Daniel Cottom writes in *Cannibals and Philosophers* that the Enlightenment was "defined from the beginning through an obsession with guts and disgust as much as through the mind and reason," he calls to mind a world in which consumption and even cannibalism are linked to Eurocentric affluence, global dominion, and the networks of trade and discovery that allowed Europeans to traverse the globe in search of satiation (xii). See also his chapter titled "Cannibalism, Trade, Whatnot," which deals more directly with European consumptive economies and ideologies of cannibalism in a global context.

42. Houston A. Baker Jr., *Turning South Again: Re-Thinking Modernism/Re-Reading Booker T.* (Durham, NC: Duke University Press, 2001), 85.

43. Ibid.

44. Ibid.

45. Charles I. Nero, "Toward a Black Gay Aesthetic: Signifying in Contemporary Black Gay Literature," in *Brother to Brother: New Writings by Black Gay Men*, edited by Essex Hemphill (Boston: Alyson Publications, 1991), 234.

46. Ibid.

47. Joseph Beam, "Brother to Brother: Words from the Heart," in *In the Life: A Black Gay Anthology,* edited by Joseph Beam, 231–242. (Boston: Alyson Publications, 1986).

48. See Philip Brian Harper's excellent study on black masculine anxiety, *Are We Not Men?: Masculine Anxiety and the Problem of African American Identity* (New York: Oxford University Press, 1996).

49. In *Soul on Ice* (New York: Dell, 1968), Eldridge Cleaver infamously popularized the term "Negro homosexual" (102).

50. Robert Reid-Pharr, *Black Gay Man: Essays.* (New York: New York University Press, 2001), 124.

51. Ibid.

52. Ibid., 125.

53. Ibid.

54. Nero, "Toward a Black Gay Aesthetic," 232.

55. Deborah E. McDowell, "In the First Place: Making Frederick Douglass and the Afro-American Narrative Tradition," in *African American Autobiography: A Critical Collection of Essays*, edited by William L. Andrews (Englewood Cliffs, NJ: Prentice Hall, 1993), 36–58.

56. E. Frances White, *Dark Continent of Our Bodies: Black Feminism and the Politics of Respectability* (Philadelphia: Temple University Press, 2001), 160.

57. Baker, *Turning South Again*, 73.

58. See Maurice Wallace, *Constructing the Black Masculine: Identity and Ideality in African American Men's Literature and Culture, 1775–1995* (Durham, NC: Duke University Press, 2002), 85.

NOTES TO CHAPTER 1

1. William D. Piersen, *Black Legacy: America's Hidden Heritage* (Amherst: University of Massachusetts Press, 1993), 7.

2. See Patricia A. Turner, *I Heard It through the Grapevine: Rumor in African-American Culture* (Los Angeles: University of California Press, 1993), 15.

3. I take this definition of "season" from *Webster's Encyclopedic Unabridged Dictionary of the English Language* (New York: Gramercy Books, 1989).

4. See Ottobah Cugoano, *Thoughts and Sentiments on the Evil and Wicked Traffic of the Slavery and Commerce of the Human Species, Humbly Submitted to the Inhabitants of Great Britain by Ottobah Cugoano, a Native of Africa* in *Pioneers of the Black Atlantic: Five Slave Narratives from the Enlightenment, 1772–1815*, edited by Henry Louis Gates Jr. and William L. Andrews (Washington, DC: Civitas/Counterpoint, 1998), 94.

5. Joseph Wright, "The Narrative of Joseph Wright," in *Africa Remembered: Narratives by West Africans for the Era of the Slave Trade*, edited by Philip D. Curtin (Madison: University of Wisconsin Press, 1967), 331.

6. Ibid.

7. See Phillips Verner Bradford and Harvey Blume, *Ota: The Pygmy in the Zoo* (New York: St. Martin's Press, 1992). Bradford and Blume's accurate and potentially insightful description of Pygmy and Apache cannibal beliefs are undermined by their description of such beliefs serving as a form of play, verbal chicanery, and jest between Geronimo and Ota: "Geronimo, like other native Americans, was glad for the entertainment provided by the pranks of his pygmy neighbors, but he could turn the tables. Through an interpreter, the serious old Apache warned the pygmies that they would do well to keep close watch on the crowds of White Eyes. When the pygmies asked why, he replied in a whisper that in addition to being rude, some White Eyes appeared to be hungry" (16). The authors reduce the connotations of institutional consumption, occupation and cultural genocide, imperial sorcery and cannibal science that Geronimo and the pygmies, who both had a "disdain for witchcraft," observed and shared to a stereotypical exchange of happy, performing savages and heathens.

8. See Mia Bay, *The White Image in the Black Mind: African-American Ideas about White People, 1830–1925* (New York: Oxford University Press, 2000), 4.

9. Ibid.

10. William D. Piersen, "White Cannibals, Black Martyrs: Fear, Depression, and Religious Faith as Causes of Suicide among New Slaves," *Journal of Negro History* 62, no. 2 (1977): 148.

11. This quote originally appears in Carl O. Williams, *Thraldom in Ancient Iceland* (1937), but I quote it as it appears in Orlando Patterson, *Slavery and Social Death: A Comparative Study* (Cambridge, MA: Harvard University Press, 1982), 81.

12. Patterson, *Slavery and Social Death*, 81.

13. Lydia Maria Child, *An Appeal in Favor of That Class of Americans Called Africans* (1833), edited by William Loren Katz (New York: Arno Press and the New York Times, 1968), 27.

14. Patterson, *Slavery and Social Death*, 81.

15. Olaudah Equiano, *The Interesting Narrative of the Life of Olaudah Equiano, or, Gustavus Vassa, the African, Written by Himself* (1789), edited by Shelley Eversley, introduction by Robert Reid-Pharr (New York: Modern Library, 2004), xxx.

16. Frank Kelleter describes this prefatory letter as defining and dictating Equiano's political aims. See "Ethnic Self-Dramatization and Technologies of Travel in *The Interesting Narrative of the Life of Olaudah Equiano, or Gustavus Vassa, the African, Written by Himself* (1789)," *Early American Literature* 19, no. 1 (2004). Kelleter says that "Equiano's text, whatever else it may be, is first and foremost a public speech act: a strategic intervention in a public debate" (71). In terms of the topic of human consumption, Equiano's introduction prompts us, as readers, to read between the lines. Given his intention of addressing the British Parliament and the larger English audience, Equiano could not come right out and make accusations of cannibalism against Europeans. Instead, he would have to adopt an embedded and implied manner of speaking about human consumption. His text, at the level of stylistics and execution, masterfully models a dual-tongued rhetoric that acknowledges European feelings of cultural superiority at the same time that it finds within these cultural practices the most heinous and consumptive appetites for the bonded African.

17. See Akiyo Ito, "Olaudah Equiano and the New York Artisans: The First American Edition of *The Interesting Narrative of the Life of Olaudah Equiano, or Gustavus Vassa, the African*," *Early American Literature* 32, no. 1 (1997): 82.

18. This citation originally appears in Gates's introduction to Douglass's *Narrative of the Life of Frederick Douglass*, but I quote it from Akiyo, "Olaudah Equiano and the New York Artisans," 82.

19. Equiano, *The Interesting Narrative of the Life of Olaudah Equiano*, 35.

20. Ibid., 34.

21. Ibid., 46.

22. Ibid., 47.

23. Ibid., 62.

24. Ibid.

25. In "'Who's Eating Whom?': The Discourse of Cannibalism in the Literature of the Black Atlantic from Equiano's *Travels* to Toni Morrison's *Beloved*," *Research in African Literatures* 29, no. 4 (1998): 107–121, Alan Rice does more than most to complicate the issue of cannibalism in Equiano's narrative. At the same time

that he treats the subject of cannibalism stereotypically as "rumor," a "fear of cannibalism," and "a trope of cannibalism," he also alludes to the cannibalistic implications of the slave trade and suggests that depictions of whites as cannibals did speak to a "realistic level" of slave perceptions and experience. For references to others who treat the subject of cannibalism in Equiano's narrative as metaphor and linguistic device, see Rosalind Shaw, *Memories of the Slave Trade: Ritual and Historical Imagination in Sierra Leone* (Chicago: University of Chicago Press, 2002), 230; Piersen, "White Cannibals, Black Martyrs," 149; Bay, *The White Image in the Black Mind*, 3–4; and Piersen, *Black Legacy*, 6–7. In "Mobility in Chains: Freedom of Movement in the Early Black Atlantic," *South Atlantic Quarterly* 100, no.1 (Winter 2001), Gretchen Holbrook Gerzina describes Equiano's depictions of European cannibals as "playing on the stereotypes of Africans as linguistically deficient cannibals" (47). Gerzina, like most, completely overlooks the template of African beliefs about cannibalism and makes cannibalism an issue of semantics instead of a real and culturally valid domain of experience.

26. Equiano, *The Interesting Narrative of the Life of Olaudah Equiano*, 95.
27. Patterson, *Slavery and Social Death*, 81, 337. Patterson devotes an entire chapter of his text to the subject of "Slavery as Human Parasitism." This section of his text, which is one of the least discussed aspects of this widely cited book, is one of the few written documents that attempts to account for the biological and emotional reality of the consumption of slaves.
28. In *The Black Image in the White Mind: The Debate on Afro-American Character and Destiny, 1817–1914* (New York: Harper and Row, 1971), George M. Frederickson describes how Americans and Europeans characterized the Negro race as an effeminate race: "There was, in fact, a general acknowledgement among romantic racialists that women and Negroes were alike in the gifts they brought to the world. Kinmont himself had maintained that the black race was "more feminine and tenderminded" than the white (114).
29. Equiano, *The Interesting Narrative of the Life of Olaudah Equiano*, 47.
30. Ibid.
31. Snow's interview appears in *The American Slave: A Composite Autobiography*, vol. 7, *Oklahoma and Mississippi Narratives*, edited by George P. Rawick (Westport, CT: Greenwood Press, 1973), 135–142, 140.
32. See Henry Louis Gates Jr., *The Signifying Monkey: A Theory of African-American Literary Criticism* (New York: Oxford University Press, 1988), 154–158, for a description of the talking book trope within early African slave narratives and in particular in Equiano's narrative.
33. Equiano, *The Interesting Narrative of the Life of Olaudah Equiano*, 47.
34. Joseph Lavallée, *Le nègre comme il ya peu de blancs* (1789), anonymous translation from the French as *The Negro Equaled by Few Europeans* (London: J. J. G. and J. Robinson, 1790).

35. Joseph Lavallée, *Le nègre comme il ya peu de blancs* (1789), translated from the French by J. Trapp as *The Negro as There Are Few White Men* (London: Printed for the author, 1790).

36. Lavallée, *Le nègre comme il ya a peu de blancs*, anonymous translation as *The Negro Equaled by Few Europeans*.

37. Equiano, *The Interesting Narrative of the Life of Olaudah Equiano*, 38.

38. Ibid., 47.

39. Peter Farb and George Armelagos, *Consuming Passions: The Anthropology of Eating* (Boston: Houghton Mifflin Company, 1980), 166.

40. Ibid., 165–176. Working with a transcultural methodology, Farb and Armelagos examine—in cultures ranging from Indian to African to Middle Eastern—the range of economic, geographic, religious, and climactic factors that contribute to how a culture cultivates taste and acquires an appetite for a culinary object.

41. Jean Anthelme Brillat-Savarin, *The Physiology of Taste: Or, Meditations on Transcendental Gastronomy*, translated by M. F. K. Fisher (1949; repr., Washington DC: Counterpoint, 1999), 38.

42. See Eve Kosofsky Sedgwick, *Between Men: English Literature and Male Homosocial Desire* (New York: Columbia University Press, 1985), 21. Complicating the work of Sigmund Freud and Rene Girard in this area, Sedgwick called more direct attention to the deployment of gender in terms of the patriarchal power structures and psychoanalytic structures of phallic reinforcement imbricated within the traditional male homosocial relation.

43. Ibid.

44. I discuss this phenomenon at length in Chapter 2, which deals with the notion of "Christian cannibalism" in the context of the nineteenth-century U.S. debate about cannibalism.

45. Equiano, *The Interesting Narrative of the Life of Olaudah Equiano*, 62.

46. Ibid., 79.

47. Ibid., 80.

48. Ibid.

49. Ibid., 79.

50. Ibid., 80–81.

51. Ibid., 81.

52. Ibid., 95.

53. Ibid., 94–95.

54. Ibid., 95.

55. John Wesley, *Thoughts upon Slavery* (London: R. Hawes, 1774), 26, emphasis added.

56. Originally appears in John Atkins, *A Voyage to Guinea, Brasil, and the West Indies* (1735), but I quote it from Kai Wright, ed., *The African-American Archive: The History of the Black Experience in Documents* (New York: Black Dog and Leventhal Publishers, 2001), 24–25.

57. Shaw, *Memories of the Slave Trade*, 229. Shaw extrapolates from the cannibalism practices among the Mane warriors of Guinea. She then links these practices to the larger Atlantic slave trade and the Portuguese, with whom the Mane conducted much human trade.

58. Equiano, *The Interesting Narrative of the Life of Olaudah Equiano*, 91.

59. Ibid., 92.

60. Ibid., 98.

61. Ibid.

62. Toni Morrison, *Playing in the Dark: Whiteness and the American Literary Imagination* (Cambridge, MA: Harvard University Press, 1992), 25.

63. Orlando Patterson, *Rituals of Blood: Consequences of Slavery in Two American Centuries* (Washington, DC: Civitas Counterpoint, 1998), 210.

64. Shaw, *Memories of the Slave Trade*, 230.

65. Ibid., 228.

66. Ibid., 231.

67. Ibid., 232.

68. Quote originally appears in *Biography of Mahommah G. Baquaqua, a Native of Zoogoo, in the Interior of Africa . . . Written and Revised from His Own Words*, edited by Samuel Moore (1854), but I quote if from Robert Edgar Conrad, ed., *Children of God's Fire: A Documentary History of Black Slavery in Brazil* (University Park: Penn State University Press, 1994), 26.

69. Equiano, *The Interesting Narrative of the Life of Olaudah Equiano*, 95.

70. Ibid., 95.

71. Ibid., 90.

72. Ibid., 62.

73. Ibid., 214.

74. Ibid., 213.

75. Ibid., 214.

76. Ibid.

77. Ibid.

78. Ibid.

79. Ibid., 215.

80. Ibid.

81. This comes from Wyatt MacGaffey, *Modern Kongo Prophets: Religion in a Plural Society* (Bloomington, IN: Indiana University Press, 1983), 134.

82. Wyatt MacGaffey, *Religion and Society in Central Africa: The Bakongo of Lower Zaire* (Chicago: University of Chicago Press, 1986), 161.

83. Charles Dickens, "The Noble Savage," *Household Words*, June 11, 1853, 337.

84. John M. Janzen and Wyatt MacGaffey, *An Anthropology of Kongo Religion: Primary Texts from Lower Zaire* (Lawrence, KS: University of Kansas Press, 1974). The Bakongo offered the following succinct definition: "Those we call witches are malicious, greedy and jealous people who are in effect murderers because they all have the same motive: killing others or preventing them from enjoying

human happiness. Such people are witches and man-eaters. As for actual cannibalism, there was never any of that in this country; possibly among other tribes,
but not among the Bakongo. Foreigners have the idea that there was cannibalism because they did not understand what was being discussed" (45).

85. Shaw, *Memories of the Slave Trade*, 232.

86. Ibid., 238.

87. Walter Rodney, *A History of the Upper Guinea Coast, 1545 to 1800* (London: Oxford University Press, 1970), 102.

NOTES TO CHAPTER 2

1. See Lydia Maria Child, *An Appeal in Favor of That Class of Americans Called Afri-cans* (1833), edited by William Loren Katz (New York: Arno Press and the New York Times, 1968), 26.

2. Ibid.

3. Ibid.

4. Ibid., 26–27.

5. Ibid., 27.

6. A good example of this is Child's editing of Harriet Jacobs's slave narrative, *Incidents in the Life of a Slave Girl*. Child recommended that Jacobs compile all of the incidents of human consumption into one chapter that the white north-ern female reader could conveniently skip. Topics such as human consump-tion had the potential of "unsexing" women in the public domain, attracting to their bodies and persons accusations of sexual licentiousness and a socially prohibited sexual knowledge. I deal with this topic at length in chapter 4, which focuses on Jacobs's slave narrative.

7. In *An Appeal in Favor of That Class of Americans Called Africans*, Child goes so far as to implicate northern Massachusetts laws and economic wealth in the promulgation of plantation slavery (197). For this and other transgressions, Child experienced social ostracization from Boston elite society. She suffered through all of this, but still dared not speak publicly and forthrightly on the topic of the consumption of humans under slavery.

8. Child, *An Appeal in Favor of That Class of Americans Called Africans*, 27.

9. One can find evidence of this culture of human consumption in most slave nar-ratives and throughout compiled volumes of interviews of ex-slaves. From well-known scribes of the slave narrative to lesser-known persons, such as Moses Roper, Charles Ball, and James W. C. Pennington, the subject of consumption is taken up in metaphoric and more literalized instances. Given the politicized nature of the genre of the slave narrative and of speaking about slavery after emancipation, commentary on consumption always had political import that overlapped with issues of race and nation formation.

10. Orlando Patterson, *Slavery and Social Death: A Comparative Study* (Cambridge, MA: Harvard University Press, 1982), 95.

11. Ibid., 337.

12. John Hope Franklin, *The Militant South, 1800–1861* (Boston: Beacon Press, 1964), 35.
13. Theodore Dwight Weld, *American Slavery As It Is: Testimony of a Thousand Witnesses* (1839), edited by William Loren Katz (New York: Arno Press and The New York Times, 1968), 86.
14. Here I am thinking of persons such as Frederick Douglass, David Walker, John S. Jacobs, Solomon Northup, Harriet Jacobs, and Moses Roper, among others. Most of these individuals I treat in later chapters. Typically, somewhere in the body of their slave narratives or some other such writing, these African Americans made reference to a culture of human consumption that shaped and informed slave life. Their oftentimes very personal and intimate observations on this topic had the effect of implicating plantation owners or broader U.S. culture in cultural practices of consumption.
15. Horace Mann, "Slavery and the Slave Trade in the District of Columbia." This speech was serialized in two numbers of *The National Era*, April 19, 1849, 63; and April 26, 1849. All quotes are from the latter number.
16. Ibid.
17. Ibid.
18. Ibid.
19. J. G. W., "Fugitive Slaves—Letter of Daniel Webster," *The National Era*, June 6, 1850, emphasis added.
20. J. R. Giddings, "Speech of Honorable J. R. Giddings," *The North Star*, June 16, 1848. Congressman Joshua Reed Giddings represented the 20th District of Ohio in 1848.
21. George Fitzhugh, *Cannibals All!: Or, Slaves without Masters*, edited by C. Vann Woodward (Cambridge: Belknap Press of Harvard University Press, 1960), 25.
22. Ibid., 23
23. Ibid., 201.
24. W. Arens, *The Man-Eating Myth: Anthropology and Anthropophagy* (New York: Oxford University Press, 1979), 14.
25. For information about this archaic practice, see Shirley Lindenbaum, "Thinking about Cannibalism," *Annual Review of Anthropology* 33 (2004): 478.
26. Arens, *The Man-Eating Myth*, 18–19.
27. Ibid., 19.
28. Geoffrey Sanborn, "The Missed Encounter: Cannibalism and the Literary Critic," in *Eating Their Words: Cannibalism and the Boundaries of Cultural Identity*, edited by Kristen Guest (Albany: State University of New York Press, 2001), 193.
29. Henry Bolingbroke, *A Voyage to the Demerary* (London: R. Phillips, 1807), 149.
30. See Sanborn, "The Missed Encounter," 98. Sanborn cites Bolingbroke's argument and brilliantly argues that Western modernity and the objectification of traditional African and Native American cannibalistic others are interrelated. Yet even Sanborn does not take the argument to the next logical step, which

is to theorize the idea of a modern, Western cannibal type independent of the traditional Eurocentric construct of cannibalism.

31. This first appears in Owen Chase, *Narrative of the Most Extraordinary and Distressing Shipwreck of the Whaleship Essex, of Nantucket* (New York: W. B. Gilley, 1821), but I quote it from Thomas Ferral Heffernan, *Stove by a Whale: Owen Chase and the* Essex (Middleton, CT: Wesleyan University Press, 1981), 17.

32. Ibid., 18.

33. Ibid., 19.

34. Nathaniel Philbrick, *In the Heart of the Sea: The Tragedy of the Whaleship* Essex (New York: Viking, 2000), 217.

35. This originally appears in E. C. B. Lee and Kenneth Lee, *Safety and Survival at Sea* (London: Cassell, 1971), but I quote it from Lewis Petrinovich, *The Cannibal Within* (New York: Aldine De Gruyter, 2000), 54–55.

36. Philbrick, *In the Heart of the Sea*, 217–218.

37. Petrinovich, *The Cannibal Within*, 55.

38. Ibid., 166.

39. Ibid., 172–73.

40. This originally appeared in William Comstock, *A Voyage to the Pacific: Descriptive Customs, Usages, and Sufferings on Board of Nantucket Whale-Ships* (Boston: Perkins, 1838), but I quote it from Philbrick, *In the Heart of the Sea*, 26.

41. Philbrick, *In the Heart of the Sea*, 26.

42. Ibid., 27.

43. Petrinovich, *The Cannibal Within*, 51.

44. Ibid.

45. Ibid.

46. John S. Jacobs, "A True Tale of Slavery," in *Incidents in the Life of a Slave Girl: Written by Herself*, edited by Jean Fagan Yellin (1987; repr., Cambridge, MA: Harvard University Press, 2000), 207.

47. Ibid., 209, 224.

48. Ibid., 225.

49. B. E. Rogers in *The American Slave: A Composite Autobiography*, Supplement, Series 1, vol. 11, *North Carolina and South Carolina Narratives*, edited by George P. Rawick (Westport, CT: Greenwood Press, 1977), 54.

50. Lerone Bennett Jr., *Before the Mayflower: A History of Black America* (1962), 6th rev. ed. (New York: Penguin Books, 1993), 44.

51. Ibid., 150.

52. Ibid., 134.

53. Ibid., 134.

54. James L. Smith, *Autobiography of James L. Smith* (Florida: Mnemosyne Publishing Company, 1969), 9.

55. Ibid., 17.

56. Ibid.

57. Ibid.

58. Ibid., 18.

59. Ibid., 17–18.

60. Deborah Gray White, *Ar'n't I a Woman?: Female Slaves in the Plantation South* (New York: W. W. Norton, 1985), 33.

61. These descriptions of black women laboring on the plantation originally appeared in Frederick Law Olmsted, *The Cotton Kingdom* (1861), but I quote it from White, *Ar'n't I a Woman?*, 33. The women are simply laboring on the plantation. Within the rice fields, they hike up their skirts to keep their garments from getting soaked. Olmsted extrapolates from their bodies and the conditions of their labor erotic allure, a bestial corporeality, and sexual transgression.

62. White, *Ar'n't I a Woman*, 33.

63. Ibid., 78

64. Smith, *Autobiography of James L. Smith*, 19.

65. Jean Anthelme Brillat-Savarin, *The Physiology of Taste: Or, Meditations on Transcendental Gastronomy*, translated by M. F. K. Fisher (1949; repr., Washington, DC: Counterpoint, 1999), 43.

66. Citation originally appears in Montesquieu, *The Spirit of the Law* (1752), but I quote from Dwight A. McBride, *Impossible Witnesses: Truth, Abolitionism, and Slave Testimony* (New York: New York University Press, 2001), 2.

67. Smith, *Autobiography of James L. Smith*, 19.

68. Ibid.

69. Ibid., 20.

70. Equiano, *The Interesting Narrative*, 98.

71. Patterson, *Social Death*, 337.

72. See G. W. F. Hegel, *The Phenomenology of Spirit*, translated by J. B. Baillie (New York: Harper Torchbooks, 1967), 111.

73. Edward A. Pollard, "Black Diamonds," in *Slavery Defended: The Views of the Old South*, ed. Erik L. McKitrick (New Jersey: Prentice-Hall Incorporated, 1963), 164.

74. Pollard, "Black Diamonds," 162.

75. Ibid., 164.

76. Ibid.

77. See Basil Lanneau Gildersleeve, *The Creed of the Old South 1865–1915* (Baltimore: Johns Hopkins University Press, 1915), 52. Gildersleeve was a scholar of classical literature, a soldier in the Confederate army, and a slave owner. In his scholarship and personal correspondence, he frequently found justification for southern slavery in the history and literature of ancient Greek society.

78. Pollard, "Black Diamonds," 164.

79. Booker T. Washington, *Up from Slavery: An Autobiography* (New York: Doubleday, Page and Company, 1904), 71.

80. Trudier Harris, *Exorcising Blackness: Historical and Literary Lynching and Burning Rituals* (Bloomington: Indiana University Press, 1984), 43.

81. Jim Allen in *The American Slave: A Composite Autobiography*, vol. 7, *Oklahoma and Mississippi Narratives*, edited by George P. Rawick (Westport, CT: Greenwood Press, 1972), 2, emphasis added.

82. Pet Franks in ibid., 56, 58.

83. This description is taken from a photograph that I took of the house while visiting Southampton, Virginia.

84. Harriet Beecher Stowe, *Dred: A Tale of the Great Dismal Swamp* (Boston: Houghton, Mifflin, 1896), 98, emphasis added.

85. Henry Irving Tragle, *The Southampton Slave Revolt of 1831: A Compilation of Source Material* (Amherst: The University of Massachusetts Press, 1971), 253.

86. Robert R. Howison, *A History of Virginia, from Its Discovery and Settlement by Europeans to the Present Time* (Philadelphia: Carey and Hart, 1846), 2:440.

87. This comment originally appeared in a "Letter to the Editor" of *The American Commercial Beacon and Norfolk & Portsmouth Daily Advertiser* on October 31, 1831, but I quote it from *The Carolina Observer* (Fayetteville, NC), November 9, 1831.

88. Originally appeared in *The Petersburg Index*, October 1, 1869, but I quote it from Tragle, *The Southampton Slave Revolt*, 153.

89. Quotation originally appears in William Sidney Drewry, *The Southampton Insurrection* (1900), but I quote it from Scot French, *The Rebellious Slave: Nat Turner in American Memory* (New York: Houghton Mifflin Company, 2004), 279

90. Ibid.

91. Ibid.

92. Tragle, *The Southampton Revolt*, 337.

93. Ibid., 339.

94. Originally appeared in *The Tidewater News*, May 8, 1931, but I quote from Tragle, *The Southampton Revolt*, 156.

95. Ibid.

96. Lindenbaum, "Thinking about Cannibalism," 478.

97. See Karen Gordon-Grube, "Anthropophagy in Post-Renaissance Europe: The Tradition of Medical Cannibalism," *American Anthropologist*, n.s. 90, no. 2 (1988): 405–409.

98. Tragle, *The Southampton Revolt*, 254.

99. Ibid., 338.

NOTES TO CHAPTER 3

1. Frederick Douglass, *Narrative of the Life of Frederick Douglass, an American Slave, Written by Himself* (1845), introduction by Robert B. Stepto (Cambridge: Belknap Press, 2009), 87.

2. Ibid., 17.

3. David Van Leer, "The Anxiety of Ethnicity in Douglass's Narrative," in *Frederick Douglas: New Literary and Historical Essays*, edited by Eric J. Sundquist (New York: Cambridge University Press, 1990), 124.

4. Douglass, *Narrative of the Life*, 88.

5. Frederick Douglass, *Life and Times of Frederick Douglass: His Early Life as a Slave, His Escape from Bondage, and His Complete History: An Autobiography* (Hartford, CT: Park Publishing Company, 1883), 154.

6. I quote more extensively from the same passage in Williams's text in chapter 1. See Carl O. Williams, *Thraldom in Ancient Iceland* (Chicago: University of Chicago Press, 1937), 38–39.

7. Orlando Patterson, *Slavery and Social Death: A Comparative Study* (Cambridge, MA: Harvard University Press, 1982), 81.

8. Quoted in Jerry Saltz, "Kara Walker: Ill-Will and Desire," *Flash Art* 29, no. 191 (1996): 84.

9. This quotation originally appeared in John Blassingame, ed., *The Frederick Douglass Papers, Series 1, Speeches, Debates, and Interviews*, vol. 2, *1847–54* (New Haven, CT: Yale University Press, 1979). However, I quote it from Jenny Franchot, "The Punishment of Esther: Frederick Douglass and the Construction of the Feminine," in *Frederick Douglass: New Literary and Historical Essays*, edited by Eric J. Sundquist (New York: Cambridge University Press, 1990), 145.

10. Ibid.

11. Ibid.

12. I am aware of Nell Irvin Painter's point regarding this statement. She argues in *Sojourner Truth: A Life, a Symbol* (New York: W. W. Norton, 1996) that Truth may not have made this statement. She correlates Gage's depiction of Truth's speech with that of Marius Robinson, a friend of Truth's who was an eyewitness to the event. Robinson does not mention the "ar'n't I a woman" statement in his notes on the speech. I use the statement here because, first, it is not absolutely established whether Gage or Robinson was the more accurate witness and, second, I think this statement does speak to the subtext of Truth's talk, which was the question of her black womanhood and on what authoritative grounds she could articulate that position. See 126–127 and 164–169 for Painter's synopsis of both versions of Truth's speech.

13. Ibid., 139.

14. Franchot, "The Punishment of Esther," 145.

15. Ibid.

16. Douglass, *My Bondage and My Freedom* (1855), edited by John Stauffer (New York: The Modern Library, 2003), 214, emphasis added.

17. Ibid., 215.

18. Ibid., 216, emphasis added.

19. Wilson Jeremiah Moses links the nineteenth-century belief that "blacks as a race were sensual, emotional, and 'feminine'" to a general ideology of racial chauvinism that Europeans from Hegel to Guizot to Gobineau to Jefferson advocated. Educated blacks were well aware of this belief and some, such as Alexander Crummel and Sutton Griggs, agreed with whites and applied this vision of effeminacy to the black masses. See Moses, *The Golden Age of Black Nationalism, 1850–1925* (New York: Oxford University Press, 1978), 25.

20. Quoted in William Andrews, "*My Bondage and My Freedom* and the American Literary Renaissance of the 1850s," in *Critical Essays on Frederick Douglass*, edited by William Andrews (Boston: G. K. Hall, 1991), 143.

21. In *Sojourner Truth*, Painter argues that Sally Dumont, the slave mistress, was the person Truth had in mind when she obliquely referred to experiences of sexual abuse. Painter notes that then and still today it is easier to speak of black female abuse by white men than to speak of such abuse at the hands of white women (16). In the first novel (also an allegorical slave narrative) published by a black woman in America, Harriet Wilson's *Our Nig*, rev. ed. (1859; repr., New York: Vintage Books, 1983), all of the sexualized abuse perpetrated against the main character, Alfredo, is done by the white mistress, Mrs. Bellmont. The narrator frequently described Mrs. Bellmont as "excited" and consumed by a "dangerous passion" as she performs punishments that mimic, in textbook fashion, the raping of black women in slave narratives. A point that comes through in Wilson's tale is how difficult it was within the conventions of true womanhood and the sexual mores of the time to articulate the intensely erotic dynamics that could exist between a black woman and a white woman. Of course, in historical texts about black women in slavery, rape at the hand of the white male master is the only conceivable reality. See Deborah Gray White, *Ar'n't I a Woman?: Female Slaves in the Plantation South* (New York: W. W. Norton, 1985); Gerda Lerner, ed., *Black Women in White America: A Documentary History* (New York: Vintage Books, 1972); and Jacqueline Jones, *Labor of Love, Labor of Sorrow: Black Women, Work and the Family from Slavery to the Present* (New York: Vintage Books, 1995) for evidence of this viewpoint.

22. See Deborah E. McDowell, "In the First Place: Making Frederick Douglass and the Afro-American Narrative Tradition," in *African American Autobiography: A Critical Collection of Essays*, edited by William L. Andrews (Englewood Cliffs, NJ: Prentice Hall, 1993), 50.

23. Van Leer, "The Anxiety of Ethnicity in Douglass's Narrative," 131.

24. Van Leer's exact words are: "What he does not understand is that this particular horror is not and never will be his. . . . The mature narrator knows the youth to be wrong"; ibid. My point, though, is just the opposite.

25. Douglass, *Narrative of the Life*, 20.

26. For example, in *Narrative of My Escape from Slavery* (1838; repr., Mineola: Dover Publications, 2003), Moses Roper refers to acts of female rape as "too disgusting to appear in this narrative" (10). Similarly, in *Running a Thousand Miles for Freedom; or, The Escape of William and Ellen Craft from Slavery in Great Slave Narratives*, edited by Arna Bontemps (Boston: Beacon Press, 1969), William Craft says that slave women were frequently compelled to "submit to the greatest indignity" (8). This was the general language and manner in which rape was spoken about during the time period.

27. Douglass, *Narrative of the Life*, 20.

28. This is a vital point that I consider later in this chapter when discussing a letter Douglass wrote to the master/paternal figure, Thomas Auld, wherein he adopts the persona of a white daughter of a plantation owner.

29. Originally quoted in *Narrative of the Life in the Adventures of Henry Bibb*, but I quote it from White, *Ar'n't I a Woman?*, 33.

30. I am thinking of those abolitionists who used Douglass's body as their text—referring to him as a "diploma," and a "brand new fact"—mostly ignorant of the deeper layers of meaning encoded in his body's numerous scars. See Douglass, *My Bondage and My Freedom*, 214–215.

31. See Paul Giles, "Narrative Reversals and Power Exchanges: Frederick Douglass and British Culture," *American Literature* 73, no. 4 (2001): 784.

32. McDowell, "In the First Place," 45–47.

33. Ibid., 47.

34. Francis Foster, "In Respect to Females . . .": Differences in the Portrayals of Women by Male and Female Narrators," *Black Literature Forum* 15, no. 2 (Summer 1981): 66.

35. Foster samples a number of staple slave narratives that would later be compiled in representative anthologies, such as those of William and Ellen Craft, Henry Bibb, and Moses Roper, among others; ibid., 66–67.

36. While I have chosen to focus on Douglass in this chapter, it is important to note that the idea of a female genealogy undergirding his experience is relevant for a number of his contemporaries. Take, for example, Solomon Northup, forced to participate in the beating/raping of Patsey, Master Epps's favorite concubine. Northup describes Patsey as the "enslaved victim of lust and hate"; see Solomon Northup, *Twelve Years a Slave: Narrative of Solomon Northup, a Citizen of New-York, Kidnapped in Washington City in 1841 and Rescued in 1853, from a Cotton Plantation Near the Red River in Louisiana* (Auburn, NY: Derby and Miller, 1853), 189. Northup devotes a significant portion of his narrative to describing Patsey's tragic journey from "a joyous creature, a laughing, light-hearted girl" to a woman missing teeth, constantly abused, and severely depressed (188–189). Before he tells Patsey's story, Northup profiles Eliza, another woman made into a concubine and severely abused. These women serve a partially utilitarian purpose in relationship to Northup's assaulted masculinity. But a final scenario in the narrative inverts this male master/female concubine dynamic, urging us to consider how Northup himself might have fulfilled the role of concubine to his master. In this climactic scene, Northup is made by his master to administer the lash to Patsey. When he does not flail hard and fast enough, Epps tells him: "Strike harder, or *your* turn will come next, you scoundrel" (256, Northup's emphasis). Similarly, after watching his Aunt Hester's torture from the kitchen closet, Douglass thinks to himself: "I expected it would be my turn next" (*Narrative of the Life*, 20). The parallel between Douglass's and Northup's turn-taking is unmistakable. Clearly, what lies beneath these fixations upon female abuse is

an erotic anxiety that Douglass and Northup each conveys through triangulation (the male slave, the master, and the female slave).

37. McDowell, "In the First Place," 45.

38. Douglass, *The Life and Times*, 94.

39. Ibid., 97.

40. Douglass, *My Bondage and My Freedom*, 18, emphasis in Douglass.

41. William S. McFeely, *Frederick Douglass* (New York: W. W. Norton), 158.

42. Douglass, "To My Former Master," *The North Star*, September 8, 1848, column B.

43. McFeely, *Frederick Douglass*, 159.

44. I partially credit my thinking along these lines to Charles Clifton, "Rereading Voices from the Past: Images of Homo-eroticism in the Slave Narrative," in *The Greatest Taboo: Homosexuality in Black Communities*, edited by Delroy Constantine-Simms (New York: Alyson Books, 2001). Clifton feels that Douglass "positions the black male body (himself) in the role of female narrator who exposes the white rapist. The 'I' who enters, 'some dark night, in company with a band of hardened villains,' is still white men. However, it is not black females (Amanda or Esthers) who become 'a degraded victim to the brutal lust of fiendish overseers,' but rather young black men" (352). Clifton's essay, which does more speculating than working through of inquiries, does not apply this observation more broadly to Douglass's life and writing.

45. This statement from *The Life and Times of Frederick Douglass* (1882; repr., Ware: Wadsworth Editions, 1996) referred to a shared kinship between Douglass and Lincoln. I will come back to the relationship between Douglass and Lincoln shortly, as it has bearing on this dynamic of incest and institutionalized concubinage that I am establishing first through Auld.

46. Douglass, *Narrative of the Life*, 67–68.

47. Douglass, *My Bondage and My Freedom*, 129.

48. Ibid. emphasis added.

49. Ibid., 125.

50. Ibid.

51. Joseph Lavallée, *Le nègre comme il ya peu de blancs* (1789), translated from the French by J. Trapp as *The Negro as There Are Few White Men* (London: Printed for the author, 1790), 23.

52. Ibid., 24.

53. Ibid., 34, emphasis added.

54. John Saillant, "The Black Body Erotic and the Republican Body Politic, 1790–1820," in *Sentimental Men: Masculinity and the Politics of Affect in American Culture*, edited by Mary Chapman and Glenn Hendler (Berkeley: University of California Press, 1999), 89.

55. See ibid., 96–97 for a discussion of other stories, such as "Quashie; or, the Desperate Negro," which followed Lavelle's format and was also serialized in periodicals in the 1790s.

56. This quote originally appears in Thomas Nelson Page, *Red Rock: A Chronicle of Reconstruction* (New York: Charles Scribner's Sons, 1898), but I quote it from Sabine Sieke, *Reading Rape: The Rhetoric of Sexual Violence in American Literature and Culture, 1790–1990* (Princeton, NJ: Princeton University Press, 2002), 37.

57. Hazel V. Carby, *Reconstructing Womanhood: The Emergence of the Afro-American Woman Novelist* (New York: Oxford University Press, 1987), 18.

58. George Fitzhugh, *Cannibals All!: Or, Slaves without Masters* (1857), edited by C. Vann Woodward (Cambridge: Belknap Press of Harvard University Press, 1960), 33.

59. David Walker, *Walker's Appeal to the Coloured Citizens of the World*, edited by Peter P. Hinks (University Park: Penn State University Press, 2000), 65.

60. Ibid., 64.

61. Ibid., emphasis added.

62. Ibid., 65.

63. Ibid., 64.

64. As quoted by Dickson J. Preston in *Young Frederick Douglass: The Maryland Years* (Baltimore, MD: Johns Hopkins University Press, 1980), 214.

65. Ibid.

66. Ibid.

67. Douglass, *Narrative of the Life*, 48.

68. Ibid.

69. Ibid., 48–49.

70. Ibid., 49.

71. Ibid., 96.

72. Ibid., 99.

73. Ibid.

74. Douglass, *My Bondage and My Freedom*, 65.

75. Douglass, *The Life and Times*, 35.

76. Ibid., 36.

77. See ibid., 154.

78. John W. Blassingame, ed., *Slave Testimony: Two Centuries of Letters, Speeches, Interviews, and Autobiographies* (Baton Rouge: Louisiana State University, 1977), 343.

79. Douglass, *Narrative of the Life*, 151.

80. Douglass, *My Bondage and My Freedom*, 237.

81. This is from a testimonial letter originally written for Tubman at her request. It is compiled in the "Documents" section of Jean M. Humez, *Harriet Tubman: The Life and the Life Stories* (Madison: University of Wisconsin Press, 2003), 306–307.

82. Douglass, *My Bondage and My Freedom*, 18.

83. For example, see the somewhat gushing description of Lincoln's beauty in Douglass, *The Life and Times*, 444.

84. Ibid.
85. Ibid.
86. Ibid., 443.
87. Ibid., 444.
88. Ibid.
89. Ibid., 450–451.
90. Ibid., 451.
91. Ibid., 450–451.
92. Douglass, *My Bondage and My Freedom*, 64.
93. Douglass, *The Life and Times*, 553.
94. Ibid.
95. Ibid., 553–554.
96. Ibid., 554.
97. Frederick Douglass, "Oration in Memory of Abraham Lincoln," in *Frederick Douglass: Selected Speeches and Writings*, edited by Philip S. Foner (Chicago: Lawrence Hill Books, 1999), 618.
98. Ibid.
99. Douglass, *The Life and Times*, 184.
100. Ibid., 130.
101. See Jesse Weik, *The Real Lincoln* (Boston: Macmillan, 1923), 85–86.
102. For the Freedman's Savings Bank, see Kevin Gaines, *Uplifting the Race: Black Leadership, Politics, and Culture in the Twentieth Century* (Chapel Hill: The University of North Carolina Press, 1996). Gaines notes how hundreds of thousands of dollars that represented the life savings of ex-enslaved persons were "squandered in a saturnalia of overspeculation and incompetence by the bank's white directors" (22). In *The Life and Times*, 493, Douglass writes of being appointed, at the last minute, as the head of and fall guy for the bank who was blamed by members of the federal government for the squandered and lost funds.
103. Quoted in Lisa Brawley, "Frederick Douglass's *My Bondage and My Freedom* and the Fugitive Tourist Industry," *Novel: A Forum on Fiction* 30, no. 1 (1996): 102.
104. Ibid. Brawley discusses a number of the political occurrences (such as the extension of slavery into Mexico and the annexation of Cuba) that shaped Douglass's revised opinion of the Constitution.
105. Douglass, *My Bondage and My Freedom*, 22. If anything, Lincoln's ratification of the Fugitive Slave Act (1850) reinforced for Douglass how precarious was his freed status.
106. This heroic figure identifies with the values of the Revolution of 1776. He is stoic, solitary, noble, and highly moral. In "Trappings of Nationalism in Frederick Douglass's *The Heroic Slave*," *African American Review* 34, no. 2 (2000), Krista Walter notes that southern slave masters "were often particularly interested in refusing slaves access to the history of the American Revolution"

because of "fear of insurrection" (234). Douglass seizes upon these values in this
story to incite slave revolt and more importantly to "purify the tainted discourse
of nationalism" (235).

107. Frederick Douglass, *The Heroic Slave*, in *Three Great African American Novels*
(New York: Dover Publications, 2008), 3–4.

108. Ibid., 4.

109. Ibid., 6.

110. Ibid.

111. Ibid.

112. Ibid., 7.

113. Ibid., 8.

114. P. Gabrielle Foreman, "Sentimental Abolition in Douglass's Decade: Revision,
Erotic Conversion, and the Politics of Witnessing in *The Heroic Slave* and *My
Bondage and My Freedom*," in *Sentimental Men: Masculinity and the Politics
of Affect in American Culture*, edited by Mary Chapman and Glenn Hendler
(Berkeley: University of California Press, 1999), 151.

115. Patrick Henry quoted in William Wirt, *Sketches in the Life and Character of
Patrick Henry* (Philadelphia: Thomas, Cowperthwait & Company, 1841), 94.

116. Douglass, *The Life and Times*, 397.

117. I am not overlooking the fact that Douglass romanticizes the might and military
prowess of the state and presents the black male body, in a way that is partially
aligned with the white colonial imagination, as the most appropriate vessel of
a national rebirth. Washington is stereotypically hulking, Nubian in caste, and
sexually virile. In the opening part of this serialized story, Madison is described
thus:

> Madison was of manly form. Tall, symmetrical, round and strong. In his
> movements he seemed to combine, with the strength of the lion, the lion's
> elasticity.—His torn sleeves, [sic] disclosed arms like polished iron. His face
> was "black, but comely."—his eye, lit with emotion, kept guard under a brow
> as dark and as glossy as the raven's wing. His whole appearance betokened
> Herculean strength; yet there was nothing savage or forbidding in his aspect.
> A child might play, in his arms, or dance on his shoulders. A giant's strength,
> but not a giant's heart was in him. His broad mouth and nose spoke only
> of good nature and kindness. But his voice, that unfailing index of the soul,
> though full and melodious, had that in it which could terrify as well as
> charm.—He was just the man who would choose when hardships were to
> be endured, or danger to be encountered,—intelligent and brave. He had
> the head to conceive, and the hand to execute. In a word, he was one to be
> sought as a friend, but to be dreaded as an enemy.

The character of Washington is also described in this first part as stereotypically prayerful and religiously fervent, all of which reinforce the stereotypical
effeminacy of the Negro male and the race. But there is also a process of resistance and an important process of self-generation at work in this dynamic, with

Douglass using the stereotypes of male effeminacy to carve out a non-existent space of agency. "The Heroic Slave," *Frederick Douglass' Paper* 6, no. 11 (March 4, 1853), 1–2.

118. Douglass, *My Bondage and My Freedom*, 15.

119. For example, in "Picturing the Mother, Claiming Egypt: *My Bondage and My Freedom* as Auto (Bio)ethnography," *African American Review* 35, no. 3 (2001): 391–408, Michael Chaney explains this gender disparity as Douglass's attempt to revise ideas of African lineage and diasporic experience. In *Moral Choices: Memory, Desire, and Imagination in Nineteenth-Century American Abolition* (Baton Rouge, LA; Louisiana State University Press, 1978), Peter F. Walker approaches this question from the perspective of color and ethnicity, trying to understand why Douglass would find likeness to his mother "in the form of a princely man who, as far as the picture shoed, may have been white" (254).

120. James Cowles Prichard, *The Natural History of Man; Comprising Inquiries into the Modifying Influence of Physical and Moral Agencies on the Different Tribes of the Human Family* (London: H. Bailliere, 1855), 133–135.

121. Here I borrow from Randy Prus's observations in "Citizen Douglass and Gendered Nationalism," *a/b Auto/Biography Studies* 16, no.1 (2001): 76. Prus refers to Douglass's alliance with suffragist politics, an alliance complicated by Douglass's feeling that the black man should achieve the vote before the white woman.

122. David Leverenz, *Manhood and the American Renaissance* (Ithaca, NJ: Cornell University Press, 1989), 108.

123. Henry Louis Gates Jr., "From Wheatley to Douglass: The Politics of Displacement," in *Frederick Douglass: New Literary and Historical Essays*, edited by Eric J. Sundquist (New York: Cambridge University Press, 1990), 48.

NOTES TO CHAPTER 4

1. David Walker, *Walker's Appeal in Four Articles Together with a Preamble to the Colored Citizens of the World, But in Particular, and Very Expressly to Those of the United States of America* (1829), 3rd ed. (Boston: D. Walker, 1830), 77.

2. Ibid., 69, emphasis in original.

3. Douglass, *Narrative of the Life of Frederick Douglass, an American Slave, Written by Himself* (1845), introduction by Robert B. Stepto (Cambridge: Belknap Press, 2009), 88.

4. John S. Jacobs, "A True Tale of Slavery," in *Incidents in the Life a Slave Girl, Written by Herself* edited by Jean Fagan Yellin (1987; repr., Cambridge, MA: Harvard University Press, 2000), 209, 224.

5. Ibid., 207.

6. See Lydia Maria Child, *An Appeal in Favor of That Class of Americans Called Africans* (1833), edited by William Loren Katz (New York: Arno Press and the New York Times, 1968), 18, 26–27.

7. Originally appears in George M. Weston, *The Progress of Slavery in the United States* (Washington, DC: Printed for the author, 1857), but I quote it from

George M. Frederickson, *The Black Image in the White Mind: The Debate on Afro-American Character and Destiny, 1817–1914* (New York: Harper and Row, 1971), 154.

8. Ibid., 156.

9. William Wells Brown, "Narrative of the Life and Escape of William Wells Brown," in *Clotel; or the President's Daughter* (1853; repr., New York: Carol Publishing Group Edition, 1995), 4.

10. Solomon Northup, *Twelve Years a Slave: Narrative of Solomon Northup, a Citizen of New-York, Kidnapped in Washington City in 1841 and Rescued in 1853, from a Cotton Plantation Near the Red River in Louisiana* (Auburn, NY: Derby and Miller, 1853), 214.

11. Walker, *Walker's Appeal in Four Articles*, 63.

12. Harriet Jacobs, *Incidents in the Life of a Slave Girl; Written by Herself*, edited by Jean Fagan Yellin (1987; repr., Cambridge, MA: Harvard University Press, 2000), 156.

13. Ibid., 73–74.

14. Walker, *Walker's Appeal in Four Articles*, 19, 35.

15. Ibid., 70.

16. Ibid., 25.

17. James Oliver Horton and Lois E. Horton, "Violence, Protest, and Identity: Black Manhood in Antebellum America," in *A Question of Manhood: A Reader in U.S. Black Men's History and Masculinity*, edited by Darlene Clark Hine and Ernestine Jenkins (Bloomington: Indiana University Press, 1999), 384.

18. Ibid. For examples of the consumption of slaves, see Theodore Dwight Weld's famous abolitionist tract, *American Slavery As It Is: Testimony of a Thousand Witnesses* (1839), edited by William Loren Katz (New York: Arno Press and The New York Times, 1968). Weld records numerous examples of flesh taking, slaves who have "their ears cropped and the sides of their cheeks gushed out" (20). One mistress cooks the flesh of her slave with heated tongs, leading to the black woman's death: "So taking the tongs, she heated them red hot, and put them upon the bottoms of her feet; then upon her legs and body; and, finally, in a rage, took hold of her throat. This had the desired effect" (88).

19. Maria Stewart, "The Negro's Complaint," in *Maria Stewart: America's First Black Political Writer: Essays and Speeches*, edited by Marilyn Richardson (Bloomington: Indiana University Press, 1987), 57.

20. In *An Appeal in Favor*, the noble manhood and innate moral character of the Negro figure prominently in Lydia Maria Child's abolitionist argument for fair and humane treatment of black persons (Child, *An Appeal in Favor of That Class of Americans Called Africans*, 177–193). I am not disputing her methodology. However, this rhetorical strategy maintains the moral and intellectual inferiority of the slave as a somehow "lesser" person deserving special consideration. Similarly, in Northup's slave narrative, *Twelve Years a Slave*, we are led to believe that his return home to his family and children cancels out all of the horrors

and emasculations that he underwent when captured and secretly sold into slavery. However, I would argue that both before and after his return to the status of free, northern, black man, the reality of slavery impact his life and determine the agency and contours of his manhood. In both cases we see how the institution of slavery determines the lives and treatment of blacks regardless of their putative status as possessions or free persons.

21. Thomas Jefferson, *Notes on the State of Virginia* (1781), edited by Frank Shuffleton (New York: Penguin Books, 1999), 139.

22. Douglass, *Narrative of the Life*, 51.

23. Jacobs, *Incidents in the Life of a Slave Girl*, 1.

24. P. Gabrielle Foreman, "Manifest in Signs: The Politics of Sex and Representation in Incidents in the Life of a Slave Girl," in *Harriet Jacobs and Incidents in the Life of a Slave Girl*, edited by Deborah M. Garfield and Rafia Zafar (New York: Cambridge University Press, 1996), 78–79.

25. Anne Bradford Warner, "Carnival Laughter: Resistance in *Incidents*," in *Harriet Jacobs and Incidents in the Life of a Slave Girl: New Critical Essays*, edited by Deborah M. Garfield and Rafia Zafar (New York: Cambridge University Press, 1996), 220.

26. Jean Fagan Yellin, *Harriet Jacobs: A Life* (New York: Basic Civitas Books, 2004).

27. Jacobs, *Incidents in the Life of a Slave Girl*, 192.

28. Maurice O. Wallace, *Constructing the Black Masculine: Identity and Ideality in African American Men's Literature and Culture, 1775–1995* (Chapel Hill, NC: Duke University Press, 2002), 89–90.

29. Jonathan Ned Katz, *Gay/Lesbian Almanac: A New Documentary* (New York: Harper and Row, 1983), 90.

30. Ibid., 61.

31. On the most basic level, I am referring to descriptions of Luke as an example of "homosexuality" under slavery. For example, in *Dark Continent of Our Bodies: Black Feminism and the Politics of Respectability* (Philadelphia: Temple University Press, 2001), E. Frances White proffers an insightful and thought-provoking discussion of male rape under slavery. In her comments, she consistently conflates the topic of male rape under slavery with the idea of homosexuality. Referring to Morrison's depiction of a male made to perform oral sex, she writes: "Here Morrison uses homosexuality as a literary trope, just as many white writers have used Africanisms. The ritual of homosexual oral sex between master and slave clearly marks the black male captive as enslaved and subjugated." Her conflation of past and present is even more explicit in the following statement: "I must admit that I, too, feel ambivalent about lifting the veil from the possibility of homosexual rape. After all, homosexuality has already had such bad press—why add to that by pointing to instances in which it would be seen as sordid and despicable?" (159–160).

   We do not understand "homosexuality" under slavery, nor do we understand "male rape" in historical and sociopolitical context. White men's motives

for raping black women during the Jim Crow era differed from those of plantation owners and overseers in earlier periods. In *Reconstructing Womanhood: The
Emergence of the Afro-American Woman Novelist* (New York: Oxford University
Press, 1987), Hazel Carby reminds us that "rape itself should not be regarded
as a transhistorical mechanism of women's oppression but as one that acquires
specific political or economic meanings at different moments in history" (18).
Carby's comments apply as well to the topic of male rape across a historical
spectrum and within the antebellum period itself. For example, the rape of
black men within the domestic sphere of the plantation meant something different from the meanings inhering in black men who were raped by anonymous
white men in fields, in slave-breaking pens, and in hidden enclosures. Different
scenarios of rape played upon different presumptions of gender and sexuality—masters chose some black men because of their feminine characteristics,
others for their more masculine and therefore threatening sexual personas. Jan
Creoli, a seventeenth-century black man, was convicted and sentenced to death
for committing sodomy. According to the court docket, Creoli raped Manuel
Congo, a younger slave. In keeping with stereotypes of African taint and
licentiousness, the court sentenced both slaves to death. See Jonathan Ned Katz,
*Gay American History: Lesbians and Gay Men in the U.S.A.* (New York: Thomas
Y. Crowell Company, 1976), 22–23. Neither consensual sex nor rape between
black men contributed to the economy of slave society. Where white "rapists"
or pederasts from the time could undergo Christian reform and integrate back
into society, the black "rapist" or pederast reinforced white ideas of black innate
inhumanity and broader philosophical and theological denials of a black soul
and social belonging.

32. Jacobs, *Incidents in the Life of a Slave Girl*, 43.
33. Ibid., 43–44.
34. Ibid., 43.
35. Ibid.
36. Ibid., 44.
37. Ibid., 192.
38. Ibid., 156.
39. Ibid., 20.
40. Horton and Horton, "Violence, Protest, and Identity," 384.
41. See Trudier Harris, *Exorcising Blackness: Historical and Literary Lynching and
    Burning Rituals* (Bloomington: Indiana University Press, 1984), 188–189.
42. In the previous chapter on Douglass, I pointed out how the Curse of Ham
    brought together homoerotism with biblical justifications for black skin and
    the enslavement of persons with black skin. White males learned in infancy to
    romanticize and exoticize black male nursemaids, uncles, wait servants, and
    playmates. White women had similar opportunities to romanticize and eroticize
    black girls and women. Yet as Nell Irvin Painter points out in *Sojourner Truth: A
    Life, a Symbol* (New York: W. W. Norton, 1996), black women did not talk about

their sexual abuse by white women because such events would have affected their credibility. Black female rape by white women has gone down in history as "so unaccountable, so unreasonable, and what is usually called so unnatural" that black women, in the act of claiming themselves as true women, denied and virtually erased this sexual aspect of their slave experience (16). Here again, we see the category of womanhood diametrically opposed to the being and sexual reality of the slave. Without a fuller embracing of and grappling with the discursive significance of the slave, we cannot hope to excavate or make sense of the unspoken sexual realities of enslaved or emancipated persons.

43. In his "Foreword" to Lydia Maria Child, *An Appeal in Favor of That Class of Americans Called Africans* (1833), edited by William Loren Katz (New York: Arno Press and the New York Times, 1968), James M. McPherson refers to Child as "the best known woman writer in America" (para. 1). He lists a number of her publications and accomplishments: "Lydia Maria Child's first two novels, *Hobomok* (1823) and *The Rebels* (1825), had won entrance for her into the best literary and social circles of Boston. Her books on household management, cooking, and the raising of children sold many thousands of copies and were translated into several languages" (Ibid.).

44. McPherson, "Foreword," para. 2.

45. Jacobs, *Incidents in the Life of a Slave Girl*, 48.

46. Ibid., 49.

47. Ibid., 49.

48. I quote from the version of Mary Prince's narrative in Henry Louis Gates Jr., *Six Women's Slave Narratives* (New York: Oxford University Press, 1988), 4, emphasis added.

49. Ibid., 10.

50. William L. Andrews, "Introduction," in *Six Women's Slave Narratives*, ed. Henry Louis Gates, Jr. (New York: Oxford University Press, 1988), xxxiv.

51. In her otherwise sensitive biography of Jacobs's life, Yellin diminishes the idea that slavery is as evil and hellish as Jacobs describes. Yellin demonstrates the limitations of her moral imagination when she describes as "exaggerated" Jacobs's depictions of the "living hell" of slavery and of a master who is "a consummate devil" (Yellin, *Harriet Jacobs: A Life*, 23). Such perspectives diminish the documented perceptions of enslaved persons and demonstrate an inability to grapple with topics such as the moral implications of human consumption.

52. Jacobs, *Incidents in the Life of a Slave Girl*, 46.

53. Ibid.

54. Doris Witt records that the traditional preparation of collard greens involves placing a ham hock in the pot; *Black Hunger: Soul Food and America* (Minnesota: University of Minnesota Press, 1999), 12.

55. Eugene D. Genovese, *Roll, Jordan, Roll: The World the Slaves Made* (1972; repr., New York: Vintage Books, 1976), 599.

56. Jacobs, *Incidents in the Life of a Slave Girl*, 46.

57. Orlando Patterson, *Slavery and Social Death: A Comparative Study* (Cambridge, MA: Harvard University, 1982), 81.
58. Jacobs, *Incidents in the Life of a Slave Girl*, 18.
59. Ibid.
60. Ibid., 12.
61. Ibid., 12.
62. Ibid.
63. Ibid., 12–13.
64. Witt, *Black Hunger*, 22, Witt's emphasis. Witt refers in particular to the marketing and consumption of the image of Aunt Jemima, which she roots in the old slavery stereotype of the mammy figure.
65. Jacobs, *Incidents in the Life of a Slave Girl*, 13.
66. Deborah Gray White, *Ar'n't I a Woman?: Female Slaves in the Plantation South* (New York: W. W. Norton, 1985), 47.
67. Jacobs, *Incidents in the Life of a Slave Girl*, 65.
68. This originally appears in Eric Lott, *Love and Theft: Blackface Minstrelsy and the American Working Class* (New York: Oxford University Press, 1993), but I quote it from Witt, *Black Hunger*, 31.
69. Jacobs, *Incidents in the Life of a Slave Girl*, 192.
70. Ibid., emphasis added.
71. Ibid.
72. Ibid.
73. George P. Rawick, ed., *The American Slave: A Composite Autobiography*, Supplement, Series 1, vol. 12, *Oklahoma Narratives* (Westport, CT: Greenwood Press, 1977), 5.
74. George P. Rawick, ed., *The American Slave: A Composite Autobiography*, Supplement, Series 1, vol. 9, *Mississippi Narratives*, pt. 4 (Westport, CT: Greenwood Press, 1977), 1380.
75. Jacobs, *Incidents in the Life of a Slave Girl*, 192.
76. Ibid.
77. White, for example, in *Ar'n't I a Woman?*, writes of white men who raped black women and the extent to which this phenomenon was socially maintained. However, White does not include in her conception of "rape" all the ways that young boys and girls learn to eroticize slaves and, long before instances of violent abuse, think of the slave as a sexually expendable and a usable object (152). In *Incidents*, Jacobs even includes female daughters in a genealogy of sexual violence learned from the plantation father. However, in this model, which emphasizes the sexual act, she overlooks the myriad and, I would argue, more determining instances of nurturing, play, and caretaking that habituate the child to the slave's body and sexuality (50–51).
78. Mary Reynolds, in *The American Slave: A Composite Biography*, vol. 5, *Texas Narratives*, pt. 2, edited by George P. Rawick (Westport, CT: Greenwood Press, 1972), 237.

79. Jacobs, *Incidents in the Life of a Slave Girl*, 192.
80. Samuel A. Cartwright, "Report on the Diseases of and Physical Peculiarities of the Negro Race" (1851), in *Defending Slavery: Proslavery Thought in the Old South, A Brief History with Documents*, edited by Paul Finkelman (Boston: Bedford St. Martin's Press, 2003), 157–173.
81. "Aethiopis" is a term that references the country of Ethiopia and the larger idea that enslaved Africans as a race of people originated in biblical and mythical terms from Ethiopia. See Cartwright's explication of this phenomenon in ibid., 167.
82. Ibid., 160.
83. Ibid., 160–161.
84. Walker, *Walker's Appeal in Four Articles*, 70.
85. Harris, *Exorcising Blackness*, 43.
86. For example, in "Mama's Baby, Papa's Maybe: An American Grammar Book," in *Black, White, and in Color: Essays on American Literature and Culture* (Chicago: University of Chicago Press, 2003), Hortense J. Spillers advocates this appeal to gender completion. Commenting on the historical dynamic of black people stripped of gender roles, Spillers advocates that restoring these roles "would restore, as figurative possibility, not only power to the female (for maternity), but also power to the male (for paternity). We would gain, in short, the *potential* for gender differentiation as it might express itself along a range of stress points, including human biology in its intersection with the project of culture" (204; Spillers's emphasis). In the concluding section of this chapter, I treat more thoroughly a range of other African Americanist scholars who make similar appeals for the reification of a decidedly fixed model of gender normalcy.
87. Jacobs, *Incidents in the Life of a Slave Girl*, 52.
88. Ibid.
89. Painter, *Sojourner Truth*, 16.
90. Ibid.
91. I refer to editorials like the following that appeared in the *Boston Morning Post* concerning the abolitionist efforts of the Grimké sisters: "The Misses Grimké have made speeches . . . but have not found husbands yet. We suspect that they would prefer white children to black under certain circumstances, after all." Quote originally appears in the *Boston Morning Post*, August 25, 1837, but I quote it from Deborah M. Garfield, "Earwitness: Female Abolitionism, Sexuality, and *Incidents in the Life of a Slave Girl*," in *Harriet Jacobs and Incidents in the Life of a Slave Girl*, edited by Deborah M. Garfield and Rafia Zafar (New York: Cambridge University Press, 1996), 102.
92. Jefferson, *Notes on the State of Virginia*, 145–146.
93. Jacobs, *Incidents in the Life of a Slave Girl*, 33.
94. Toni Morrison, *Playing in the Dark: Whiteness and the American Literary Imagination* (Cambridge, MA: Harvard University Press, 1992), 25.
95. Jacobs, *Incidents in the Life of a Slave Girl*, 34.

96. Ibid., 34.
97. Garfield, "Earwitness," 115.
98. Ibid.
99. Ibid., 114.
100. Painter, *Sojourner Truth*, 16.
101. Morrison, *Playing in the Dark*, 25
102. Ibid.
103. Jacobs, *Incidents in the Life of a Slave Girl*, 38.
104. Ibid., 12.
105. Ibid.
106. Ibid., 34.
107. Ibid.
108. Moses Roper, *Narrative of My Escape from Slavery* (1838; repr., Mineola: Dover Publications Inc., 2003), 1.
109. Douglass, *Narrative of the Life*, especially chapter 1.
110. White, *Ar'n't I a Woman?*, 47.
111. Jacobs, *Incidents in the Life of a Slave Girl*, 65.
112. Elizabeth Fox-Genovese, *Within the Plantation Household: Black and White Women of the Old South* (Chapel Hill: University of North Carolina Press, 1988), 292.
113. Jacobs, *Incidents in the Life of a Slave Girl*, 85.
114. Ibid., 89.
115. Ibid., 11–12.
116. Ibid.
117. Another "good" white woman, Mrs. Flint's aunt, Miss Fanny, takes tea at Aunt Marthy's home, delights in the elderly black woman's sense of refinement, and partakes freely of the pastries and sweetmeats she prepares for their teary-eyed reunions. Miss Fanny, as I mentioned earlier, purchases Aunt Marthy from the auction block and frees her. She abhors the treatment of Jacobs by Mrs. Flint and her husband and feels a genuine love and admiration for Aunt Martha. Yet even Miss Fanny, in all of her demonstrative goodness, occasionally slips up and slips back into the logic of slave expendability. Summing up a conversation between herself and the elderly white woman, Jacobs recalls: "She condoled with me in her own peculiar way; saying she wished that I and all my grandmother's family were at rest in our graves, for not until then should she feel any peace about us" (Jacobs, *Incidents in the Life of a Slave Girl*, 89). Leading up to this conversation, Miss Fanny has attempted to negotiate with her niece and nephew for Jacobs's freedom. Reporting back to Jacobs and her grandmother, she probably feels a mixture of defeat, responsibility, and shame. Yet instead of wishing death upon her own kin, the elderly woman resorts to thinking of the enslaved as an expendable commodity. What is probably most painful to Miss Fanny is how goodness fails. Neither her good intentions nor those of Jacobs's grandmother have the power to extricate either woman from the legacy of the past. In fact, what Miss Fanny's misspeaking

most clearly reveals is how goodness enables and sustains both white fantasies and affections for the Negro and a prescription of social death.

118. Jacobs, *Incidents in the Life of a Slave Girl*, 11, emphasis added.

119. Ibid.

120. Mary Prince, *The History of Mary Prince, a West Indian Slave* (1831; repr., New York: Pandora Press, 1987), 4.

121. Child, *An Appeal in Favor of That Class of Americans Called Africans*, 27.

122. Jacobs, *Incidents in the Life of a Slave Girl*, 18.

123. Ibid.

124. Ibid., 48.

125. Ibid., 172.

126. Ibid.

127. Ibid., 51, emphasis added.

128. See Spillers, "Mama's Baby, Papa's Maybe," 204.

129. Harris, *Exorcising Blackness*, 43.

130. See Spillers, "Mama's Baby, Papa's Maybe," 206, Spillers's emphasis.

131. Ibid.

132. bell hooks, *Ain't I a Woman: Black Women and Feminism* (Boston: South End Press, 1981), 22.

133. Ibid.

134. Angela Y. Davis, *Women, Race, & Class* (New York: Vintage Books, 1983), 6. In particular, Davis refers to hard field work as one labor practice, among many, that masters use to equalize the gender dynamic on the plantation. She does not consider how gender operated for black women as a fluid, foundational structure in the domestic realms of the plantation. This is part of my point regarding the recovery of rigid and normative gender categories. The complexity and variance gets flattened out, leaving us with a wholly incomplete picture of black subjectivity and interior life on the plantation.

135. Michelle Wallace, *Black Macho and the Myth of the Superwoman* (1978), rev. ed. (New York: Verso, 1990), 68.

136. hooks, *Ain't I a Woman*, 22.

137. The historical reference for Wallace's discussion is the "Negro homosexual" that Eldridge Cleaver imagines in *Soul on Ice* (New York: Dell, 1968), 102. Describing Cleaver's 1970s sexual politics, Wallace writes: "Cleaver did a lot to politicize sexuality in the Black Movement. One of his most dubious contributions was the idea that black homosexuality was synonymous with reactionary Uncle Tomism"; *Black Macho and the Myth of the Superwoman*, 67.

138. Spillers, "Mama's Baby, Papa's Maybe," 204.

NOTES TO CHAPTER 5

1. This originally appeared in the *Norfolk Herald* on November 14, 1831, but I quote it from Scot French, *The Rebellious Slave: Nat Turner in American Memory* (New York: Houghton Mifflin, 2004), 278.

2. Ibid.

3. James R. McGovern, *Anatomy of a Lynching: The Killing of Claude Neal* (Baton Rouge: Louisiana State University Press, 1982), 80.

4. For example, before his death, Turner predicted that it would rain on the day of his death. When Turner's necked snapped, "the cloud and rain came as promised, and then the fearful people had to wait out a long dry spell"; Roy F. Johnson, *The Nat Turner Slave Insurrection* (Murfreesboro, NC: Johnson Publishing, 1966), 180. Following this occurrence Johnson says that "many people, both whites and blacks, were greatly alarmed" (180).

5. The citation originally appears in William Sidney Drewry, *The Southampton Insurrection* (Washington, DC: Neale Company, 1900), but I quote it from French, *The Rebellious Slave*, 279.

6. William Styron, *The Confessions of Nat Turner* (1966), rev. ed. (New York: A Signet Book, 1968). Styron makes a point of distinguishing his text from "a historical novel," which is technically a more direct engagement with historical facts. This is a confusing statement, since he says earlier in the "Author's Note": "I have rarely departed from the *known* facts about Nat Turner and the revolt of which he was a leader (vii; Styron's emphasis). In numerous interviews, Styron has had to clarify his use of and relationship to the history, "the facts" of Turner's life, in the novel. Styron comments on this issue of history as he perceived it and how his critics reacted to his usage of it in the novel in Kenneth S. Greenberg, "Interview with William Styron," in *Nat Turner: A Slave Rebellion in History and Memory*, edited by Kenneth S. Greenberg (New York: Oxford University Press, 2003), 222.

7. These statistics are taken from Donna Haisty Winchell, "Cries of Outrage: Three Novelists' Use of History," *Mississippi Quarterly* 49, no. 4 (1996): 728.

8. The list is long, but I think readily of Harriet Beecher Stowe, *Dred: A Tale of the Great Dismal Swamp* (1856), G. P. R. James, *The Old Dominion* (1858), and Arna Bontemps, *Black Thunder* (1935). Bontemps's text is based primarily on Gabriel Prosser's rebellion, but the subtext for this rebellion was Turner's Southampton revolt. The same year that Styron's novel was published, Daniel Panger published *Ol' Prophet Nat* (1967). Sherley Anne Williams's *Dessa Rose* (1986) was a response to Styron's novel, but it focused on a female revolutionary at the heart of a slave rebellion.

9. This is excerpted from John Oliver Killens, "The Confessions of Willie Styron," in *William Styron's Nat Turner: Ten Black Writers Respond*, ed. John Henrik Clarke (Boston: Beacon Press, 1968), 44.

10. One of the earliest and most frequently cited reviews is Philip Rahv, "Through the Midst of Jerusalem," *The New York Review of Books*, October 26, 1967, 6–10. Speaking to the historical authority and insight of the novel, Rahv writes that "only a white Southern writer could have brought it off." Neither a northern white nor a "Negro writer," filled as they are with a "very complex anxiety," could have successfully accomplished what Styron does, Rahv contends (7).

11. See Gertrude Wilson, "Fortas Should Be Impeached," *New York Amsterdam News*, June 8, 1968. In this article Wilson documents how Columbia University purchased a gymnasium in Harlem and allowed white students to enter in the front but required black Harlemites to enter from the back. Wilson doesn't explicitly mention race, only that Columbia students can enter the main doors and Harlem residents must enter the rear door. Supreme Court justice Abe Fortas added to the controversy by making public statements about the situation and the legal case, based on this and other racialized incidents, to be presented before the court. Wilson had venomous things to say about Styron's novel and his reception of the Pulitzer Prize in another *New York Amsterdam News* article titled "I Spit on the Pulitzer Prize!," *New York Amsterdam News*, May 18, 1968.

12. See Lerone Bennett Jr., *Before the Mayflower: A History of Black America* (New York: Penguin Books, 1988), 418.

13. Originally appears in a letter written to Styron, but I quote it from Kenneth S. Greenberg, *Nat Turner: A Slave Rebellion in History and Memory* (New York: Oxford University Press, 2003), 22.

14. Ernest Kaiser, "The Failure of William Styron," in *William Styron's Nat Turner: Ten Black Writers Respond*, edited by John Henrik Clarke (Boston: Beacon Press, 1968), 54.

15. Sarah Bradford, *Harriet Tubman: The Moses of Her People* (New York: Carol Publishing Group, 1961), 135. The full text of the letter from Douglass to Tubman is printed in the "Appendix" to Bradford's text.

16. Booker T. Washington, *Frederick Douglass* (Philadelphia: George W. Jacobs & Co., 1906), 15.

17. Ibid., 15–16.

18. John Henrik Clarke, "Introduction," in *William Styron's Nat Turner: Ten Black Writers Respond*, edited by John Henrik Clarke (Boston: Beacon Press, 1968), viii.

19. Kaiser, "The Failure of William Styron," 54.

20. Greenberg, *Nat Turner*, 219.

21. Kaiser, "The Failure of William Styron," 54.

22. See Melville J. Herskovitz, *The Myth of the Negro Past* (New York: Harper and Brothers Publishers, 1941), 1–2. In this landmark text that advocated for cultural continuity and the cultural literacy of African American linguistic and cultural practices, Herskovitz sought to debunk a number of myths pertaining to Africans and African Americans, among them that blacks were of a naturally childlike character, were of the poorer stock of Africans, were from diverse savage cultures, and so forth.

23. Kaiser, "The Failure of William Styron," 62.

24. Vincent Harding, "You've Taken My Nat and Gone," in *William Styron's Nat Turner: Ten Black Writers Respond*, edited by John Henrik Clarke (Boston: Beacon Press, 1968), 2

25. Ibid.

26. Ibid., 27.

27. Ibid.

28. Loyle Hairston, "William Styron's Nat Turner—Rouge Nigger," in *William Styron's Nat Turner: Ten Black Writers Respond*, edited by John Henrik Clarke (Boston: Beacon Press, 1968), 71.

29. Lerone Bennett Jr., "Nat's Last White Man," in *William Styron's Nat Turner: Ten Black Writers Respond*, edited by John Henrik Clarke (Boston: Beacon Press, 1968), 11.

30. Alvin F. Poussaint, "The Confessions of Nat Turner and Styron's Dilemma," in *William Styron's Nat Turner: Ten Black Writers Respond*, edited by John Henrik Clarke (Boston: Beacon Press, 1968), 21.

31. Marlon Ross makes an excellent point in "White Fantasies of Desire: Baldwin and the Racial Identities of Sexuality," in *James Baldwin Now*, edited by Dwight A. McBride (New York: New York University Press, 1999), which is that for many young revolutionaries of the 1960s, homosexuality was understood as allied "to notions of national decadence, unproductivity, waywardness, and, especially during the cold war, betrayal" (30). These black nationalists—which included Baraka, Cleaver, and others—did not want to amend this idea of homosexuality as connected to a corrupt U.S. nation-state and so refused to see Baldwin as anything more than a derivative of this political/sexual phenomenon. So even though such blacks had some awareness of the historical limitations of their assertions, their strategic deployment of homosexuality prevented them from publicly announcing such an understanding or employing a more complicated, transhistorical model of homoeroticism/homosexuality.

32. Michael P. Bibler, "'As if set free into another land': Homosexuality, Rebellion, and Community in William Styron's *The Confessions of Nat Turner*," in *Perversion and the Social Relation*, edited by Molly Anne Rothenberg, Dennis Foster, and Slavoj Zizek (Durham, NC: Duke University Press, 2003), 161.

33. Ron Eyerman, *Cultural Trauma: Slavery and the Formation of African American Identity* (Cambridge: Cambridge University Press, 2001), 12.

34. Alice Walker, Contribution to "The Revolving Bookstand," *American Scholar* 37 (1968): 551.

35. June Meyer, "Spokesman for the Blacks," *The Nation*, December 4, 1967, 597.

36. Bennett, "Nat's Last White Man," 5.

37. Quoted in Sokolov, "In the Mind of Nat Turner," *Newsweek*, October 16, 1967, 67.

38. Ibid.

39. Baldwin was writing *Another Country* (New York: The Dial Press, 1962) at the same time that Styron was writing *The Confessions of Nat Turner*. Baldwin lived for a time in a guest house behind Styron's Virginia home, which brought the two authors into very close proximity with one another. In the interview with Greenberg in *Nat Turner*, Styron says that Baldwin was writing a novel that "involved getting into the minds of white people as a black man." Conversely, Styron says, Baldwin encouraged him "to try to become a black

man" (Greenberg, "Interview with William Styron," 219). In interviews, Styron frequently mentioned the racial dynamics of Baldwin's influence upon him. It is noteworthy, though, that the central black character of Baldwin's *Another Country*, Rufus, like Turner in Styron's novel, has a homosexual connection with a white man (a French man, to be exact).

40. Harding, "You've Taken My Nat and Gone," 31–32.
41. Ibid., 32.
42. I am referring here to scholars from *Ten Black Writers*. Lerone Bennett Jr. refers to Turner's "homosexual encounter" as emasculating ("Nat's Last White Man," 11); Harding sees homosexuality as tainting the real Turner's radical Christian theology and sees homosexuals in the novel as basically "pariah-like" personalities ("You've Taken My Nat and Gone," 27); Killens wrestles with the "half-man and half-faggot" spectacle that Styron makes of Turner's life ("The Confessions of Willie Styron," 35); and Kaiser simply emphasizes how Styron's "despotic and emasculating" depictions of Turner reinforced how the culture of slavery had made black men the same ("The Failure of William Styron," 54).
43. Styron, *The Confessions of Nat Turner*, 198.
44. Ibid., 199.
45. Ibid.
46. Frederick Douglass, *Narrative of the Life of Frederick Douglass, an American Slave, Written by Himself* (1845), introduction by Robert B. Stepto (Cambridge: Belknap Press, 2009), 51.
47. Styron, *The Confessions of Nat Turner*, 200.
48. Ibid., 201.
49. Olaudah Equiano, a West African, was one of the first to write about, returning to West Africa as a missionary under the authority of the English crown; see Equiano, *The Interesting Narrative of the Life of Olaudah Equiano, or, Gustavus Vassa, the African, Written by Himself* (1789), edited by Shelley Eversley, introduction by Robert Reid-Pharr (New York: Modern Library, 2004). Amanda Berry Smith, Henry Highland Garnet, and Booker T. Washington, among other black Americans, either traveled to Africa or supported organizations for the missionary colonization of Africa.
50. Styron, *The Confessions of Nat Turner*, 200.
51. Ibid., 200.
52. Ibid., 201.
53. Poussaint, "The Confessions of Nat Turner and Styron's Dilemma," 21.
54. Douglass, *Narrative of the Life*, 111.
55. W. E. B. Du Bois, *The Souls of Black Folk* (1903; repr., New York: New American Library, 1982), 218.
56. In particular, I am thinking of Du Bois's descriptions in *The Souls of Black Folk* of black religious practices. He at first refers to "the African savage" and to the "African character" as derived from Africans who inhabit a world of overwhelming sensuality and fetishism: "The transplanted African lived in a

world animate with gods and devils, elves and witches. . . . He called up all the resources of heathenism to aid,—exorcism and witch-craft, the mysterious Obi worship with its barbarious rites, spells, and blood-sacrifices even, now and then, of human victims" (218). These more ancient African behaviors and mores find expression in the masses of "black folk" and in the "black and massive form of the preacher" (211). The preacher and his congregation embody a sensuality reminiscent of "pythian madness," "demoniac possession," and "human passion" that shocks and fascinates Du Bois (211).

57. Du Bois's review in *The Crisis* refers to the novel as "filth" and as catering to "a decadent section of the white world" who hungered for images of black "utter licentiousness"; W. E. B. Du Bois, "The Browsing Reader," *The Crisis* 35 (June 1928): 202. McKay depicts homosexuality and premarital sex in the novel. When he wrote of decadent white persons, Du Bois was referring to persons such as Carl Van Vechten, a noted white patron and homophile who desired black men. Van Vechten gave financial support to Hughes, McKay, Hurston, and numerous others.

58. James Baldwin, *No Name in the Street* (New York: Dell Books, 1972), 61.

59. Ibid., 62.

60. Ibid., 65.

61. See Michelle Wallace, *Black Macho and the Myth of the Superwoman* (1978), rev. ed. (New York: Verso, 1990). Wallace, dissecting Cleaver's notion of the Negro homosexual, uncovers a hierarchy of sexual politics that posits the sexual pen- etration of a white man as the ultimate expression of sexual power: "If whom you fuck indicates your power, then obviously the greatest power would be gained by fucking a white man first, a black man second, a white woman third and a black woman not at all. The most important rule is that *nobody* fucks you" (68).

62. Baldwin, *No Name in the Street*, 63–64.

63. This is a reference to Bryan R. Washington's comments in "Wrestling with 'The Love that Dare Not Speak Its Name': John, Elisha, and the 'Master,'" in *New Essays on Go Tell It on the Mountain* (New York: Cambridge University Press, 1996). He refers to the subtext of homosexuality in *Baldwin's Go Tell It on the Mountain* as buried and disguised (78). His observations apply also to the larger body of Baldwin's writing, which scholars have similarly found resistant to a queer analysis. I am thinking of Claude J. Summer, *Gay Fictions, Wilde to Stonewall: Studies in a Male Homosexual Literary Tradition* (New York: Con- tinuum, 1990), which has an essay on homosexuality in *Giovanni's Room*; David Bergman, *Gaity Transfigured: Gay Self-Representation in American Literature* (Madison: University of Wisconsin Press, 1991); and Lee Edelman, "The Part for the (W)hole: Baldwin, Homophobia, and the Fantasmatics of 'Race,'" in his *Homographies: Essays in Gay Literature and Cultural Theory* (New York: Rout- ledge, 1994).

64. Washington, "Wrestling with 'The Love That Dare Not Speak Its Name,'" 78.

65. James Baldwin, "Down at the Cross: Letter from a Region in My Mind," in *The Fire Next Time* (1962), rev. ed. (New York: Vintage International, 1993), 105.

66. Killens, "The Confessions of Willie Styron," 34.

67. This quote is originally from R. von Kraft-Ebbing, *Psychopathia Sexualis* (Stuttgart: Enke 1886), but I quote it from Marianne Noble, *The Masochistic Pleasures of Sentimental Literature* (Princeton, NJ: Princeton University Press, 2000), 127. Noble also refers to similar testimony documented in Sigmund Freud, *Sexuality and the Psychology of Love* (New York: Simon and Schuster, 1963).

68. Originally quoted in Marcia Marcus, *A Taste for Pain: On Masochism and the Female Sexuality* (New York: St. Martin's Press, 1981), but I quote it from Noble, *The Masochistic Pleasures of Sentimental Literature*, 126–127.

69. Noble, *The Masochistic Pleasures of Sentimental Literature*, 140. Noble extrapolates from reviews of Stowe's novel published in the *New Orleans Picayune* and from the written commentary of George Frederick Holms and William Gilmore Simms, the distinguished president of the University of Mississippi and South Carolinian author, respectively.

70. James Baldwin, *Notes of a Native Son* (Boston: The Beacon Press, 1955), 14.

71. Ibid., 22.

72. Quoted in Sokolov, "In the Mind of Nat Turner," 67.

73. Hollywood did eventually approach Styron about turning his novel into a movie. Black actors united and protested. And Baldwin, oddly enough, found himself in the role of middleman, mediating a Los Angeles debate between the black actor and activist Ossie Davis and Styron. See L. W. West III, *William Styron: A Life* (New York: Random House, 1998), 383. Baldwin's sense of discomfiture was reflected in way he publicly introduced himself before the debate as a friend of both Styron and Davis.

74. In "Learning from the Sixties," in *Sister Outsider* (Freedom, CA: The Crossing Press, 1984), Audre Lorde writes that within black political circles "as soon as any young Black woman begins to recognize that she is oppressed as a woman as well as a Black, she is called a lesbian no matter how she identifies herself sexually" (144–145). The implicit idea is that the lesbian black woman is not black, insofar as blackness is equated with a secondary position to black men. In the same essay, she recalls how "a young civil rights activist who had been beaten and imprisoned in Mississippi" was "trashed and silenced" at a national meeting of black women because she had a white husband (138). Michelle Wallace's *Black Macho and the Myth of the Superwoman* was an attempt to get at some of the ways the "black woman is haunted by the mythology that surrounds the black man" (15). This mythology, as Wallace understood it, stemmed back to slavery and the sexual treatment of black women and men at the hands of white men. See also Cheryl Clark, "The Failure to Transform: Homophobia in the Black Community," in *Home Girls: A Black Feminist Anthology*, edited by Barbara Smith, 2nd ed. (1983; repr., New Brunswick: Rutgers University Press, 2000). *Home Girls*, as a whole, foregrounds black female complexity and erotic life in a way that transcends prevailing stereotypes of the virgin/whore dichotomy.

75. Eldridge Cleaver, *Soul on Ice* (New York: Dell, 1968), 102.
76. I have already quoted Ross on this topic. In addition to him, Charles I. Nero comments upon the pathological implications of Cleaver's model in "Toward a Black Gay Aesthetic: Signifying in Contemporary Black Gay Literature," in *Brother to Brother: New Writings by Black Gay Men*, edited by Essex Hemphill (Boston: Alyson Press, 1991), 231. In *Black Gay Man: Essays* (New York: New York University Press, 2001), Robert Reid-Pharr sets Cleaver's virulent comments within the broader contexts of his ideas on gender, masculinity, and sexual violence in *Soul on Ice*. Darieck Scott deals with the psychological and historical presumptions informing Cleaver's understanding of the homosexual as a symbol of racial demise in "More Man Than You'll Ever Be: Antonio Vargas, Eldridge Cleaver, and Toni Morrison's Beloved," in *Dangerous Liaisons: Blacks, Gays, and the Struggle for Equality*, edited by Eric Brandt (New York: The New Press, 1999), 217–242; and E. Patrick Johnson deals with Cleaver's accusations of Baldwin as a performance of the former's masculinity, revolutionary politics, incarcerated status, and, most importantly, sexuality in *Appropriating Blackness: Performance and the Politics of Authenticity* (Durham, NC: Duke University Press, 2003), 51–54.
77. Baldwin, "Down at the Cross," 76–77, Baldwin's emphasis.
78. In *Why I Hate Abercrombie and Fitch: Essays on Race and Sexuality* (New York: New York University Press, 2005), Dwight A. McBride offers a compelling analysis of the complex factors that shaped Baldwin's operation as a race man who had to downplay or outright suppress his homosexual lifestyle. McBride finds that in Baldwin's fiction he more successfully speaks from a platform of homosexual consciousness coupled with racial, nationalist critique (44–53). See also Hazel Carby, *Race Men* (Cambridge, MA: Harvard University Press, 1998) for an analysis of Baldwin's double racial and sexual bind.
79. Ibid., 45.
80. I should like to add that the necessity for this politics has only increased over time and is evident in the work of late twentieth-century, self-identified black gay artists and intellectuals, who consistently found themselves entrapped and silenced by the same forces that silenced and marginalized Baldwin. For example, Samuel Delany refers to the vexing intermixing of race and homosexuality in "Some Queer Notions About Race," in *Queer Cultures*, edited by Deborah Carlin and Jennifer DiGrazie (Upper Saddle River, NJ: Pearson/Prentice Hall, 2004). In a telling reference to slavery, Delany states: "Breeding is, after all, what white slaveowners in the early years of slavery *wanted* their slaves to do. Presumably, having same- sex relationships is what they *didn't* want them to do" (208, Delany's emphasis). While this correlation between homosexuality and slave masters is more complicated, Delany's larger point is well taken, which is that procreation as the fundamental unity of black family and community is a notion fatefully tied to the legacy of slavery and that black humanity is equated with procreation. In *Why I Hate Abercrombie and Fitch*, McBride

refers to the search of black queer studies for "a usable past to define and clarify the significance of its arrival onto the scene in its current incarnation" (39). Overtly, McBride is referring to the presence of homoeroticism in slavery and the Reconstruction era. Less overtly he is alluding to issues of "archive," of the uses of and political ideologies undergirding certain predominant narratives of black and slave history. McBride's *Impossible Witnesses: Truth, Abolitionism, and Slave Testimony* (New York: New York University Press, 2001) prefigures the concerns with the slave past briefly alluded to in *Why I Hate Abercrombie and Fitch*. *Impossible Witnesses* deals with the compacted and layered discourses that shape the representative voice of the African American emerging out of slavery. See also Nero, "Toward a Black Gay Aesthetic"; and Ron Simmons, "Some Thoughts on the Challenges Facing Black Gay Intellectuals," in *Brother to Brother: New Writings by Black Gay Men*, edited by Essex Hemphill (Boston: Alyson Publications, 1991), 211–228. Both essays deal with the legacy of slavery and the problems of black male heroism and chivalrous masculinity that limit and restrict a range of expressions of black masculinity and sexuality. Both men also implicate black women, such as Julia Hare, Toni Morrison, and Frances Cress Welsing, in this dynamic. Essex Hemphill links class, racial representation, and the memory of slavery in *Ceremonies* (San Francisco: Cleis Press, 1992), castigating "the middle class aspirations of a people trying hard to forget the shame and cruelty of slavery and ghettos" (64). Hemphill states that a number of black gay men's writing on this topic can be traced back to the publication of Joseph Beam, ed., *In the Life: A Black Gay Anthology* (Boston: Alyson Publications, 1986). Speaking directly to Black Power politics and political ideologies, Beam proclaimed that "black men loving black men is the revolutionary act of the eighties, not only because sixties' revolutionaries like Bobby Seale, Huey Newton, and Eldridge Cleaver dare speak our name, but because as black men we were never meant to be together" (241–242). Beam is of course referring to slave history and other histories that were based in the denial of black male homoerotic desire and emotional well-being.

81. In *The Evidence of Things Not Said: James Baldwin and the Promise of American Democracy* (Ithaca, NY: Cornell University Press, 2001), 13–15, Lawrie Balfour describes how important witnessing is to both Baldwin's art and his political ethos.

82. Baldwin, "Down at the Cross," 60.

83. Ibid.

84. Ibid., 69.

85. Ibid., 76.

86. James Baldwin, *Nobody Knows My Name* (1961; repr., New York: Vintage International, 1993), 100–101.

87. I quote from John S. Jacobs's slave narrative, "A True Tale of Slavery," in *Incidents in the Life of a Slave Girl, Written by Herself*, edited by Jean Fagan Yellin (1987; repr., Cambridge, MA: Harvard University Press, 2000), 207. In chapter

4, I deal more extensively with this issue of paternal legacy alongside issues of motherlessness in Jacobs's narrative; in the narratives of Austin Steward, Solomon Northup, Douglass; and in the lives of ex-slaves compiled in the WPA series.

88. Baldwin, "Down at the Cross," 78.
89. Baldwin writes in *The Fire Next Time* of joining a church as a way of wrestling with the angel of his father. Contemplating the prospects of a preaching career, he recalls: "My youth quickly made me a much bigger drawing card than my father. I pushed this advantage ruthlessly, for it was the most effective means I had found of breaking his hold over me. That was the most frightening time of my life" (32).
90. Baldwin, *Go Tell It on the Mountain*, 197.
91. Ibid., Baldwin's emphasis.
92. Harding, "You've Taken My Nat and Gone," 27.
93. Styron, *The Confessions of Nat Turner*, 300.
94. Harding, "You've Taken My Nat and Gone," 25–26.
95. Mae G. Henderson, "'Where, By the Way, Is This Train Going?': A Case for (Re) Framing Black Cultural Studies," *The Journal of the Midwest Modern Language Association* 27, no. 1 (1994): 43.
96. Vincent Harding, *Beyond Chaos: Black History and the Search for the New Land* (Atlanta, GA: Institute of the Black World, 1970), 25.
97. Ibid., 26.
98. Ibid.
99. Ibid., 2.
100. Originally appears in George Washington Williams, *History of the Negro Race in America, 1619–1880* (1882), but I quote it from Harding, *Beyond Chaos*, 6.
101. Harding, *Beyond Chaos*, 31.
102. Vincent Harding, *There Is a River: The Black Struggle for Freedom in America* (New York: Harcourt Brace Jovanovich, 1981), xiv.
103. Quoted in Huey P. Newton, "Eldridge Cleaver: He Is No James Baldwin," in *The Huey P. Newton Reader*, edited by David Hilliard and Donald Weise (New York: Seven Stories Press, 2002), 287.
104. Douglass, *Narrative of the Life*, 123.
105. Ibid.
106. Ibid., 107.

NOTES TO CHAPTER 6
1. Essex Hemphill, *Ceremonies* (San Francisco: Cleis Press, 1992), 63.
2. "The typical conversion experience was preceded by a period of anxiety over one's salvation which lasted for days or even weeks," writes Albert J. Raboteau in *Slave Religion: The "Invisible Institution" in the Antebellum South* (New York: Oxford University Press, 1978), 266. Raboteau refers to beliefs about conversion and salvation that typically held sway on the plantation. During slavery, this

concern over one's salvation often coincided, following the period of worrying and fretting, with greater devotion to Christian practices and strengthening one's internal means of surviving the emotional and psychological hardships of slavery (266–270).

3. See Painter's analysis of the infamous breast-baring incident in *Sojourner Truth: A Life, a Symbol* (New York: W. W. Norton, 1996). Painter describes Truth as deftly negotiating dynamics of "infancy and adulthood" informing the dynamic between herself and the white men present (139). In this context and others where Truth made reference to children borne of her womb, children suckling at her breasts, and her laboring capacity, Truth drew upon the legacy of biblical women such as Esther and Mary Magdalene, among others (135–141).

4. Thomas R. Gray, "The Confessions of Nat Turner," in Scot French, *The Rebellious Slave: Nat Turner in American Memory* (New York: Houghton Mifflin, 2004), 292.

5. Ibid.

6. See Ron Simmons, "Some Thoughts on the Challenges Facing Black Gay Intellectuals," in *Brother to Brother: New Writings by Black Gay Men*, edited by Essex Hemphill (Boston: Alyson Publications, 1991), 218.

7. Ibid., 219.

8. Ibid., 221. Each of these black men that Simmons references has ties to larger social organizations that embody their homophobic nationalist ideas. Louis Farrakhan works through the Nation of Islam, Haki Madhubuti started and still today operates the influential Third World Press, Molefe Asante is one of the people who began the first Black Studies Program at Temple University in Philadelphia, Pennsylvania, and Baraka, of course, was connected to the Black Arts movement and with the U.S. organization. These organizational ties rendered the views held by these black men all the more trenchant and problematic.

9. Gary Fisher, *Gary in Your Pocket: Stories and Notebooks of Gary Fisher*, edited by Eve Kosofsky Sedgwick (Durham, NC: Duke University Press, 1996). Fisher's forays into sadomasochistic culture and sexual experiences with white men are overshadowed by the legacy of slavery. At one point in his recorded journal entries, he lies in bed reading *Slavery Defended: The Views of the Old South*, edited by Eric L. McKitrick (Englewood Cliffs, NJ: Prentice-Hall, 1963) an anthology of the views of white male slavery defenders. Reading this text inspires the black Fisher to write to his white lover: "Dear Master Park, Here's the letter you wanted. I'm laying here sideways in the bed with *Slavery Defended* opened to about midway, sampling the arguments and thinking about how good it felt to serve" (230). In *Slavery Defended*, whites write of blacks as infants, as more animal-like than human, as deformed, morally tainted, and lacking a soul. Fisher's disturbing correlation between "serving his master" and white male defenders of slavery speaks to the thorough, and still today largely unaccounted for, eroticization of the enslaved person in slave culture. Within Fisher's lexicon of sexual practices, he prefers to orally eroticize this embodied legacy

of slavery: "So I'm on my knees again, before God," he thinks to himself in an anonymous sex encounter: "Tall, white, wary of me, trying to work him into a froth of masterliness. . . . I should swallow his manseed, feeling that in him, the desire to feed me, nurse me even as he feeds himself on my nursing him, feeds his ego, has manness, his very strength" (208).

10. Robert F. Reid-Pharr's comments come from *Black Gay Man: Essays* (New York: New York University Press, 2001), 148. Reid-Pharr offers an extremely useful discussion of black male oral eroticism as dually lodged in legacies of black nig-gerization and black gay identity formation at the end of the twentieth century. See also Charles I. Nero, "Toward a Black Gay Aesthetic: Signifying in Contem-porary Black Gay Literature," in *Brother to Brother: New Writings by Black Gay Men*, edited by Essex Hemphill (Boston: Alyson Publications, 1991), 234.

11. In the third version of his autobiography, *The Autobiography of W. E. B. Du Bois: A Soliloquy on Viewing My Life from the Last Decade of Its First Century.* (New York: International Publishers, 1968), Du Bois made a rather veiled, if somewhat remorseful, commentary upon the incident:

> In the midst of my career there burst on me a new and undreamed of aspect of sex. A young man, long my disciple and student, then my co-helper and successor to part of my work, was suddenly arrested for molesting men in public places. I had before that time no conception of homosexuality. I had never understood the tragedy of an Oscar Wilde. I dismissed my co-worker forthwith, and spent heavy days regretting my act. (282)

12. Marsha Darling, "In the Realm of Responsibility: A Conversation with Toni Morrison," in *Conversations with Toni Morrison*, edited by Peggy Whitman Pren-shaw (Jackson: University of Mississippi Press, 1994), 247.

13. I am referring to works such as Toni Morrison, "Racism and Fascism," in *In Defense of Mumia*, edited by S. E. Anderson and Tony Medina (New York: Writ-ers and Readers Publishing, Inc., 1996). For Morrison's critique of the idea of the male as head of household and the nuclear family as the only appropriate model of family, see Bonnie Angelo, "On the Pain of Being Black: An Interview With Toni Morrison," in *Conversations with Toni Morrison*, edited by Peggy Whitman Prenshaw (Jackson: University of Mississippi Press, 1994), 259–260. Then there is Morrison's magisterial *Playing in the Dark: Whiteness and the Literary Imagination* (Cambridge, MA: Harvard University Press, 1992), which explores the theme of Africans used as figures and objects of white imagination, colonization, and American empire building.

14. Ron Eyerman, *Cultural Trauma: Slavery and the Formation of African American Identity* (Cambridge: Cambridge University Press, 2001), 18.

15. Ibid.

16. Toni Morrison, *Beloved* (1987; repr., New York: Plume, 1998), 107–108.

17. E. Frances White, *Dark Continent of Our Bodies: Black Feminism and the Politics of Respectability* (Philadelphia: Temple University Press), 160.

18. Hazel V. Carby, *Reconstructing Womanhood: The Emergence of the Afro-American Woman Novelist* (New York: Oxford University Press, 1987), 18.
19. Nero, "Toward a Black Gay Aesthetic," 232. Curiously, Nero does not actually mention the chain-gang oral sex scenario. It might have been that he overlooked it, as many people do when they first encounter it in the narrative. Drawing upon her other fiction (*The Bluest Eye, Tar Baby*) and her general depiction of the Sweet Home male slaves in *Beloved*, Nero comes to his conclusions of homophobia. His points are still valued and provide a lens for thinking about the topic of black male sexual violation under slavery and historical specificity when it comes to the topic of rape.
20. Ibid., 234.
21. See Darieck Scott, "More Man than You'll Ever Be: Antonio Fargas, Eldridge Cleaver, and Toni Morrison's Beloved," in *Dangerous Liaisons: Blacks, Gays, and the Struggle for Equality*, edited by Eric Brandt (New York: The New Press, 1999), 229.
22. Ibid. To further clarify Scott's point, what he means is that history has prepared us to respond to instances of "murder and mutilation and atrocity," but we have received no historical or social prepping for the erotic implications of the breakfast scenario. In the broadest sense, Scott implies that we have come to rely upon violence and mutilation as a means of evading the truth of other unwieldy scenarios, such as the erotic/oral breakfast scene (233).
23. Frederick Douglass, *Narrative of the Life of Frederick Douglass, an American Slave, Written by Himself* (1845), edited by Robert B. Stepto (Cambridge, MA: Belknap Press, 2009), 88.
24. This is not to say that Morrison does not fall short in her imaginative capacities, that she does not ultimately, as Nero asserts, eclipse an exploration of black male hunger through her foregrounding of traditional female domesticity; saving, heroic black masculinity; and appeals to the sanctity of nuclear family. Morrison, along with numerous other black women artists and intellectuals of her generation, did fall short in this regard. However, my point is that in the act of laboring and attempting to understand black male hunger, Morrison has provided us with an example that is still useful and usable.
25. Deborah M. Garfield provides excellent commentary on this issue in her essay "Earwitness: Female Abolitionism, Sexuality, and *Incidents in the Life of a Slave Girl*," in *Harriet Jacobs and Incidents in the Life of a Slave Girl*, edited by Deborah M. Garfield and Rafia Zafar (New York: Cambridge University Press, 1996), 100–130. She notes that for a larger American readership the writing careers of "Douglass, Henry Bibb, William Wells Brown, Henry 'Box' Brown, the Clarkes, Josiah Henson, and Moses Grandy . . . were proof of the centripetal tug of oratory, for they resumed lecturing after the narratives were published. Speech enabled narrative; narrative then facilitated a return to the 'living, speaking' Logos parenting it" (101).

26. Quoted in Houston A. Baker Jr., *Turning South Again: Re-Thinking Modernism/ Re-Reading Booker T.* (Durham, NC: Duke University Press, 2001), 46.

27. Ann duCille, "Phallus(ies) of Interpretation: Toward Engendering the Black Critical 'I,'" originally appeared in *Callaloo*, but I quote it from *African American Literary Theory: A Reader*, edited by Winston Napier (New York: New York University Press, 2000), 448.

28. Ibid.

29. Ibid., 449.

30. DuCille discusses Larsen's, Hurston's, and Fauset's writing from this perspective in ibid.

31. See also Evelynn Hammonds, "Black (W)holes and the Geometry of Black Female Sexuality," in *African American Literary Theory: A Reader*, edited by Winston Napier (New York: New York University Press, 2000), 482–497. Hammonds directly challenges black feminists, whom she sees as having "almost universally described black women's sexuality, when viewed from the vantage of the dominant discourses, as an absence" (486). As an example, Hammonds cites the literary critic Hortense Spillers as one of the first to describe black women as "the beached whales of the sexual universe, unvoiced, misseen, not doing, awaiting their verb" (487). Spiller's comments refer to a trajectory of silence and absence spanning from Sojourner Truth in the antebellum period to the black nationalist and feminist movements of the 1980s. Hammonds also cites Morrison's descriptions of black women's sexuality as "one of the 'unspeakable things unspoken'" of the African American experience. Hammonds finds black women habitually grounding black female sexuality "in metaphors of speechlessness, space, or vision, as 'void' or empty space that is simultaneously ever visible (exposed) and invisible" (487). For Hammonds, the troubling result of this dynamic is that we have little information about black women's pleasure, their interior erotic lives, and the manner in which black women have created dynamic, creative spaces around their sexuality, which is my point also concerning black male sexuality in the antebellum period. In the antebellum period, black men suffered a double dislocation because their sexual selves were based mostly in these objects of black female sexuality rather than on the real, complicated realities of black women.

32. Washington, *Up from Slavery: An Autobiography* (New York: Doubleday, Page and Company, 1904), 213, emphasis added.

33. Baker, *Turning South Again*, 15.

34. Ibid., 73.

35. I think of Henry Louis Gates Jr.'s seminal *Figures in Black: Words, Signs and the "Racial" Self* (New York: Oxford University Press, 1987). So much of his text is invested in the history of "autobiographical forms in English and in French [that] assumed narrative priority toward the end of the eighteenth century [that] shaped themselves principally around military exploits, court intrigues, and spiritual quests" (80). Gates's analysis of the literary strategies of Wheatley,

Douglass, Toomer, and Walker, among others, conform, to a great extent, to this master narrative of the African American autobiographical tradition. His *The Signifying Monkey: A Theory of African-American Literary Criticism* (New York: Oxford University Press, 1988) follows in this vein and works more aggressively with the concepts of signifying, "the Talking Book," and "the Speakerly Text"— all oral and textual templates that posit literacy as a sign of what is there, rather than an indicator of what is not, what cannot be spoken. In *Blues, Ideology, and Afro-American Literature: A Vernacular Theory* (Chicago: University of Chicago Press, 1984), Houston A. Baker Jr. uses the "blues matrix" to convey instances of black "expressive dignity," which precludes a sojourn into the less dignified, even shameful legacies of black male experience, such as rape and erotic ties to white men in the context of slavery, (13–14).

36. I attempted to get at some of these issues in chapter 1 when I analyzed the homoerotic relations among Equiano, white men, and Native Americans. As I state in that chapter, literacy is a means of reproducing white male desire and hunger in Equiano's narrative. In the final interchange between Equiano and the Indian prince, the book (the Bible), the bedside prayer, and literacy all facilitate homoerotic ties to an unseen, beloved white father, whom the Misquito youth sees as directly tied to the interests and appetites of the white slave transporters and the ship hands who work the ship that transports them to England.

37. Vincent Harding, *Beyond Chaos: Black History and the Search for the New Land* (Atlanta, GA: Institute of the Black World, 1970), 25. As with Baker, Black feminists responded in kind to Harding's analysis of black historical methodology and, by extension, experience. In "'Where, By the Way, Is This Train Going?': A Case for (Re)Framing Black (Cultural) Studies," *Callaloo* 19, no. 1 (1996): 60–67, Mae G. Henderson takes Harding's "masculinist narrative" of history to task, seeking to replace it with a black cultural studies model that "interrogates not only the categories of race, class, and nationality, but also that of gender in the construction of socio-cultural experience," 62.

38. Vincent Harding, "You've Taken My Nat and Gone," in *William Styron's Nat Turner: Ten Black Writers Respond*, edited by John Henrik Clarke (Boston: Beacon Press, 1968), 31.

39. See Jonathan Katz, *Gay American History: Lesbians and Gay Men in the U.S.A* (New York: Thomas Y. Crowell Company, 1976), 23.

40. Ibid., 20.

41. See Stephen O. Murray and Will Roscoe, "Overview," in Murray and Roscoe, *Boy-Wives and Female Husbands: Studies of African Homosexualities* (New York: St. Martin's Press, 1998), 141.

42. Robert L. Hall documents this naming practice in "African Religious Retentions in Florida," in *Africanisms in American Culture*, edited by Joseph E. Holloway (Bloomington: Indiana University Press, 1990). Hall uses Florida naming practices as a representative example of what was common throughout the slave-owning provinces. He writes: "Evidence of the persistence of African naming

practices during the second Spanish period is contained in a 1792 inventory
of the estate of Dona Maria Evans, an Anglo-American who had migrated to
Florida from South Carolina in 1763. The inventory listed a total of twenty
blacks. . . . Some had African-sounding names: Zambo, Pender, Sisa, Fibi,
Ebron, Congo" (102).

43. Giovanni Antonio Cavazzi, *Ganga-Ya-Chibanda* (1687), translated by Will
Roscoe, in *Boy-Wives and Female Husbands: Studies of African Homosexualities,*
edited by Stephen O. Murray and Will Roscoe (New York: St. Martin's Press,
1998), 163.

44. Within writings on Western and Central African gender practices, the role of
grandmother is not emphasized as much as the role of the mother. The role of
mother and then, of course, the role of grandmother each bring powers and
responsibilities that accrue with age and in keeping with other social factors,
such as class, vocation, familial lineage, marriage status, and so forth. See
Oyèrónké Oyěwùmí, *The Invention of Women: Making an African Sense of Western Gender Discourses* (Minneapolis: University of Minnesota Press, 1997); and
Wyatt MacGaffey, *Religion and Society in Central Africa: The Bakongo of Lower
Zaire* (Chicago: University of Chicago Press, 1986), 85–89.

45. Murray and Roscoe, *Boy-Wives and Female Husbands,* 147.

46. Ibid.

47. Original citation is from David F. Greenbergs, *The Construction of Homosexuality* (Chicago: University of Chicago Press, 1988). However, I use the quote from
Randy P. Conner, *Blossom of Bone: Reclaiming the Connections between Homoeroticism and the Sacred* (New York: HarperSanFrancisco, 1993), 41.

48. The original quote is from Carlos Estermann, *The Ethnography of Southwestern
Angola,* but I use the quote from Conner, *Blossom of Bone,* 41.

49. See Jonathan Ned Katz, *Gay/Lesbian Almanac: A New Documentary* (New York:
Harper and Row, 1983), 61. Cocke Negro is classified as a "buggerist," which
was another contemporary term that meant the same thing as "sodomite." It is
telling, though, that in this instance a similar strategy of erasing the particular
significance of black male anal sex is employed. Was it more dangerous for
someone like Cocke Negro to be classified as a sodomite or to embody alternative gender and lifestyle examples that contradicted the colonizing efforts of the
state?

50. Paul Gilroy, *The Black Atlantic: Modernity and Double Consciousness* (Cambridge,
MA: Harvard University Press, 1993), 1.

51. Esteban Montejo, *Biography of a Runaway Slave,* edited by Miguel Barnet, translated by W. Nick Hill (Connecticut: Curbstone Press, 1994), 40.

52. Ibid.

53. Ibid.

54. A footnote to Montejo's narrative explains the geographic origins of his grandfather's name: "It was common in the Spanish Colony for Negro slaves to use the

name of their country of origin as a surname after their given name"; Montejo, *Biography of a Runaway Slave*, 209.

55. See J. Lorand Matory, *Sex and the Empire that Is No More: Gender and the Politics of Metaphor in Oyo Yoruba Religion* (Minneapolis: University of Minnesota Press, 1994). In *The Invention of Women*, Oyěwùmí takes issue with Matory's finding evidence of transvestism and transgenderism in Oyo-Yoruba culture. She describes such thinking as "alien to the Yorùbá conception" of gender and social hierarchy (117). Oyěwùmí's comments, I believe, derive in large part from a general resistance among African scholars to Western modes of thinking about same-sex identities and roles. In my opinion, Matory's comments finesse the cultural divide and sensitively attend to gender variance within Yoruba culture.

56. This originally appears in the document produced by the Portuguese Inquisition, *First Visit of the Holy Office to the Regions of Brazil—Denunciations of Bahia, 1591–1593* (São Paolo, 1925), but I quote from Murray and Roscoe, *Boy-Wives and Female Husbands*, 146.

Andrews, William L. "Introduction." In *Six Women's Slave Narratives*, edited by Henry Louis Gates Jr., xxix–xli. New York: Oxford University Press, 1988.

———. "*My Bondage and My Freedom* and the American Literary Renaissance of the 1850s." In *Critical Essays on Frederick Douglass*, edited by William Andrews, 133–147. Boston: G. K. Hall & Co., 1991.

Angelo, Bonnie. "On the Pain of Being Black: An Interview With Toni Morrison." In *Conversations with Toni Morrison*, edited by Danille Taylor-Guthrie, 255–261. Jackson: University of Mississippi Press, 1994.

Arens, W. *The Man-Eating Myth: Anthropology and Anthropophagy*. New York: Oxford University Press, 1979.

Baker, Houston A., Jr. *Blues, Ideology, and Afro-American Literature: A Vernacular Theory*. Chicago: University of Chicago Press, 1984.

———. *Turning South Again: Re-Thinking Modernism/Re-Reading Booker T*. Durham, NC: Duke University Press, 2001.

Baldwin, James. *Another Country*. New York: Dial Press, 1962.

———. "Down at the Cross: Letter from a Region in My Mind." In *The Fire Next Time*, 23–141. 1962. Reprint, New York: Vintage International, 1993.

———. *Go Tell It on the Mountain*. 1952. Reprint, New York, Dell Publishing, 1985.

———. *No Name in the Street*. New York: Dell Books, 1972.

———. *Nobody Knows My Name*. 1961. Reprint, New York: Vintage International, 1993.

———. *Notes of a Native Son*. Boston: Beacon Press, 1955.

Balfour, Lawrie. *The Evidence of Things Not Said: James Baldwin and the Promise of American Democracy*. Ithaca, NY: Cornell University Press, 2000.

Bay, Mia. *The White Image in the Black Mind: African-American Ideas about White People, 1830–1925*. New York: Oxford University Press, 2000.

Beam, Joseph, ed. *In the Life: A Black Gay Anthology*. Boston: Alyson Publications, 1986.

Beecher, Henry Ward. "Politics and the Pulpit." *The North Star*, June 13, 1850, 1.

Bennett, Lerone, Jr. *Before the Mayflower: A History of Black America*. [1962.] 6th rev. ed. New York: Penguin Books, 1993.

———. "Nat's Last White Man." In *William Styron's Nat Turner: Ten Black Writers Respond*, edited by John Henrik Clarke, 3–16. Boston: Beacon Press, 1968.

Bergman, David. *Gaity Transfigured: Gay Self-Representation in American Literature.* Madison: University of Wisconsin Press, 1991.

Bibler, Michael P. "'As if set free into another land': Homosexuality, Rebellion, and Community in William Styron's *The Confessions of Nat Turner*." In *Perversion and the Social Relation*, ed. Molly Anne Rothenberg, Dennis Foster, and Slavoj Zizek, 159–186. Durham: Duke University Press, 2003.

Blassingame, John W, ed. *Slave Testimony: Two Centuries of Letters, Speeches, Interviews, and Autobiographies.* Baton Rouge: Louisiana State University, 1977.

Bolingbroke, Henry. *A Voyage to the Demerary Containing a Statistical Account of the Settlements There.* London: R. Phillips, 1807.

Bontemps, Arna. *Black Thunder.* New York: The Macmillan Company, 1936.

Bradford, Philip Verner, and Harvey Blume. *Ota: The Pygmy in the Zoo.* New York: St. Martin's Press, 1992.

Bradford, Sarah. *Harriet Tubman: The Moses of Her People.* New York: Carol Publishing Group, 1961.

Brawley, Lisa. "Frederick Douglass's *My Bondage and My Freedom* and the Fugitive Tourist Industry." *Novel: A Forum on Fiction* 30, no. 1 (September 1, 1996): 98–128.

Brillat-Savarin, Jean Anthelme. *The Physiology of Taste: Or, Meditations on Transcendental Gastronomy.* Translated by M. F. K. Fisher. 1949. Reprint, Washington, DC: Counterpoint, 1999.

Brown, William Wells. "Narrative of the Life and Escape of William Wells Brown." In *Clotel; or the President's Daughter.* 1853. Reprint, New York: Carol Publishing Group Edition, 1995.

Carby, Hazel V. *Race Men.* Cambridge, MA: Harvard University Press, 1998.

———. *Reconstructing Womanhood: The Emergence of the Afro-American Woman Novelist.* New York: Oxford University Press, 1987.

Cartwright, Samuel A. "Report on the Diseases of and Physical Peculiarities of the Negro Race." [1851.] In *Defending Slavery: Proslavery Thought in the Old South, A Brief History with Documents*, edited by Paul Finkelman, 157–172. Boston: Bedford/St. Martin's Press, 2003.

Cavazzi, Giovanni Antonio. *Ganga-Ya-Chibanda.* [1687.] Translated by Will Roscoe. In *Boy-Wives and Female Husbands: Studies of African Homosexualities*, edited by Stephen O. Murray and Will Roscoe, 163-165. New York: St. Martin's Press, 1998.

Chaney, Michael. "Picturing the Mother, Claiming Egypt: *My Bondage and My Freedom* as Auto (Bio)ethnography." *African American Review* 35, no. 3 (September 1, 2001): 391–408.

Child, Lydia Maria. *An Appeal in Favor of That Class of Americans Called Africans.* [1833.] Edited by William Loren Katz. New York: Arno Press and the New York Times, 1968.

———. *Hobomok, a Tale of Early Times.* [1823.] In *Hobomok and Other Writings on Indians*, edited by Carolyn L. Karcher. New Brunswick, NJ: Rutgers University Press, 1986.

———. *The Freedmen's Book*. 1865. Available online at http://www.gutenberg.org/ files/38479/38479-h/38479-h.htm#Page_206.

———. *The Rebels, or Boston before the Revolution*. 1825. Reprint, Boston: Phillips, Sampson, 1850.

Christensen, Matthew J. "Cannibals in the Postcolony: Sierra Leon's Intersecting Hegemonies in Charlie Haffner's Slave Revolt Drama *Amistad Kata Kata*." *Research in African Literatures* 36, no.1 (2005): 1–19.

Clark, Cheryl. "The Failure to Transform: Homophobia in the Black Community." In *Home Girls: A Black Feminist Anthology*, edited by Barbara Smith, 190–201. 1983. Reprint, New Brunswick, NJ: Rutgers University Press, 2000.

Clarke, John Henrik. "Introduction." In *William Styron's Nat Turner: Ten Black Writers Respond*, edited by John Henrik Clarke, vii–x. Boston: Beacon Press, 1968.

———, ed. *William Styron's Nat Turner: Ten Black Writers Respond*. Boston: Beacon Press, 1968.

Cleaver, Eldridge. *Soul on Ice*. New York: Dell, 1968.

Clifton, Charles. "Rereading Voices from the Past: Images of Homo-Eroticism in the Slave Narrative." In *The Greatest Taboo: Homosexuality in Black Communities*, edited by Delroy Constantine-Simms, 342–361. New York: Alyson Books, 2001.

Comstock, William. *A Voyage to the Pacific, Descriptive of the Customs, Usages, and Sufferings on Board of Nantucket Whale-Ships*. Boston: Perkins, 1838.

Conner, Randy P. *Blossom of Bone: Reclaiming the Connections between Homoeroticism and the Sacred*. San Francisco: Harper San Francisco, 1993.

Conrad, Robert Edgar, ed. *Children of God's Fire: A Documentary History of Black Slavery in Brazil*. University Park: Penn State University Press, 1994.

Cottom, Daniel. *Cannibals and Philosophers: Bodies of Enlightenment*. Baltimore, MD: Johns Hopkins University Press, 2001.

Craft, William. *Running a Thousand Miles for Freedom; or, The Escape of William and Ellen Craft from Slavery*. In *Great Slave Narratives*, edited by Arna Bontemps. Boston: Beacon Press, 1969.

Cugoano, Ottobah. *Thoughts and Sentiments on the Evil and Wicked Traffic of the Slavery and Commerce of the Human Species, Humbly Submitted to the Inhabitants of Great Britain by Ottobah Cugoano, a Native of Africa* in *Pioneers of the Black Atlantic: Five Slave Narratives from the Enlightenment, 1772–1815*. Edited by Henry Louis Gates Jr. and William L. Andrews. Washington D.C.: Civitas/Counterpoint, 1998.

Curtin, Philip D., ed. *Africa Remembered: Narratives by West Africans from the Era of the Slave Trade*. Madison: University of Wisconsin Press, 1967.

Darling, Marsha. "In the Realm of Responsibility: A Conversation with Toni Morrison." In *Conversations with Toni Morrison*, edited by Danille Taylor-Guthrie, 246–254. Jackson: University of Mississippi Press, 1994.

Davis, Angela Y. *Women, Race, & Class*. New York: Vintage Books, 1983.

Delany, Samuel R. "Some Queer Notions about Race." In *Queer Cultures*, edited by Deborah Carlin and Jennifer DiGrazie, 199–223. Upper Saddle River, NJ: Pearson/ Prentice Hall, 2004.

Dickens, Charles. "The Noble Savage." *Household Words*, June 11, 1853, 337.

Douglass, Frederick. *The Heroic Slave*. [1852.] In *Three Great African-American Novels*. New York: Dover, 2008.

———. *Life and Times of Frederick Douglass: His Early Life as a Slave, His Escape from Bondage, and His Complete History: An Autobiography*. Hartford, CT: Park Publishing Company, 1883.

———. *My Bondage and My Freedom*. [1855.] Edited by John Stauffer. New York: The Modern Library, 2003.

———. *Narrative of the Life of Frederick Douglass, an American Slave, Written by Himself*. [1845.] Introduction by Robert B. Stepto. Cambridge: Belknap Press, 2009.

———. "Oration in Memory of Abraham Lincoln." In *Frederick Douglass: Selected Speeches and Writings*, edited by Philip S. Foner, 615–624. Chicago: Lawrence Hill Books, 1999.

———. "To My Former Master." *The North Star*, September 8, 1848.

Drewry, William Sidney. *The Southampton Insurrection*. Washington, DC: Neale Company, 1900.

Du Bois, W. E. B. *The Autobiography of W. E. B. Du Bois: A Soliloquy on Viewing My Life from the Last Decade of Its First Century*. New York: International Publishers, 1968.

———. "The Browsing Reader." *The Crisis*, June 1928, 202.

———. *The Souls of Black Folk*. 1903. Reprint, New York: New American Library, 1982.

DuCille, Ann. "Phallus(ies) of Interpretation: Toward Engendering the Black Critical 'I.'" In *African American Literary Theory: A Reader*, edited by Winston Napier, 443–459. New York: New York University Press, 2000.

Edelman, Lee. "The Part for the (W)hole: Baldwin, Homophobia, and the Fantasmatics of 'Race.'" In *Homographies: Essay in Gay Literature and Cultural Theory*, edited by Lee Edelman, 42–78. New York: Routledge, 1994.

Equiano, Olaudah. *The Interesting Narrative of the Life of Olaudah Equiano, or, Gustavus Vassa, the African, Written by Himself*. [1789.] Edited and with notes by Shelley Eversley. Introduction by Robert Reid-Pharr. New York: Modern Library, 2004.

Evans-Pritchard, E. E. *Witchcraft, Oracles and Magic among the Azande*. New York: Oxford University Press, 1958.

Eyerman, Ron. *Cultural Trauma: Slavery and the Formation of African American Identity*. Cambridge: Cambridge University Press, 2001.

Farb, Peter, and George Armelagos. *Consuming Passions: The Anthropology of Eating*. Boston: Houghton Mifflin, 1980.

Finkelman, Paul. *Defending Slavery: Proslavery Thought in the Old South, a Brief History with Documents*. Boston: St. Martin's Press, 2003.

Fisher, Gary. *Gary in Your Pocket: Stories and Notebooks of Gary Fisher*. Edited by Eve Kosofsky Sedgwick. Durham, NC: Duke University Press, 1996.

Fitzhugh, George. *Cannibals All!: Or, Slaves without Masters*. [1857.] Edited by C. Vann Woodward. Cambridge: Belknap Press of Harvard University Press, 1960.

Foner, Philip S., ed. *Frederick Douglass: Selected Speeches and Writings*. Chicago: Lawrence Hill Books, 1999.

Foreman, P. Gabrielle. "Manifest in Signs: The Politics of Sex and Representation in *Incidents in the Life of a Slave Girl.*" In *Harriet Jacobs and Incidents in the Life of a Slave Girl*, edited by Deborah M. Garfield and Rafia Zafar, 76–99. New York: Cambridge University Press, 1996.

——. "Sentimental Abolition in Douglass's Decade: Revision, Erotic Conversion, and the Politics of Witnessing in *The Heroic Slave* and *My Bondage and My Freedom.*" In *Sentimental Men: Masculinity and the Politics of Affect in American Culture*, edited by Mary Chapman and Glenn Hendler, 149–162. Berkeley: University of California Press, 1999.

Foster, Francis. "In Respect to Females . . .": Differences in the Portrayals of Women by Male and Female Narrators." *Black American Literature Forum* 15, no. 2 (1981): 66–70.

Fox-Genovese, Elizabeth. *Within the Plantation Household: Black and White Women of the Old South*. Chapel Hill: University of North Carolina Press, 1988.

Franchot, Jenny. "The Punishment of Esther: Frederick Douglass and the Construction of the Feminine." In *Frederick Douglass: New Literary and Historical Essays*, edited by Eric J. Sundquist, 141–165. New York: Cambridge University Press, 1990.

Franklin, John Hope. *The Militant South, 1800–1861*. Boston: Beacon Press, 1964.

Frederickson, George M. *The Black Image in the White Mind: The Debate on Afro-American Character and Destiny, 1817–1914*. New York: Harper and Row, 1971.

French, Scot. *The Rebellious Slave: Nat Turner in American Memory*. New York: Houghton Mifflin Company, 2004.

Freud, Sigmund. *Sexuality and the Psychology of Love*. New York: Simon and Schuster, 1963.

Gaines, Kevin. *Uplifting the Race: Black Leadership, Politics, and Culture in the Twentieth Century*. Chapel Hill: University of North Carolina Press, 1996.

Garfield, Deborah M. "Earwitness: Female Abolitionism, Sexuality, and *Incidents in the Life of a Slave Girl.*" In *Harriet Jacobs and Incidents in the Life of a Slave Girl*, edited by Deborah M. Garfield and Rafia Zafar, 100–130. New York: Cambridge University Press, 1996.

Gates, Henry Louis, Jr. *Figures in Black: Words, Signs and the "Racial" Self*. New York: Oxford University Press, 1987.

——. "From Wheatley to Douglass: The Politics of Displacement." In *Frederick Douglass: New Literary and Historical Essays*, edited by Eric J. Sundquist, 47–65. New York: Cambridge University Press, 1990.

——. *The Signifying Monkey: A Theory of African-American Literary Criticism*. New York: Oxford University Press, 1988.

——, ed. *Six Women's Slave Narratives*. New York: Oxford University Press, 1988.

Genovese, Eugene D. *Roll, Jordan, Roll: The World the Slaves Made*. 1972. Reprint, New York: Vintage Books, 1976.

Genovese, Elizabeth Fox. *Within the Plantation Household: Black and White Women of the Old South.* Chapel Hill: University of North Carolina Press, 1988.

Gerzina, Gretchen Holbrook. "Mobility in Chains: Freedom of Movement in the Early Black Atlantic." *South Atlantic Quarterly* 100, no. 1 (2001): 41–59.

Giddings, J. R. "Speech of Honorable J. R. Giddings." *The North Star*, June 16, 1848.

Gildersleeve, Basil Lanneau. *The Creed of the Old South, 1865–1915.* Baltimore: Johns Hopkins University Press, 1915.

Giles, Paul. "Narrative Reversals and Power Exchanges: Frederick Douglass and British Culture." *American Literature* 73, no. 4 (2001): 779–810.

Gilroy, Paul. *The Black Atlantic: Modernity and Double Consciousness.* Cambridge, MA: Harvard University Press, 1993.

Gordon-Grube, Karen. "Anthropophagy in Post-Renaissance Europe: The Tradition of Medical Cannibalism." *American Anthropologist*, n.s. 90, no. 2 (1988): 405–409.

Gray, Thomas R. "The Confessions of Nat Turner, as Told to Thomas R. Gray." [1831.] In Scot French, *The Rebellious Slave: Nat Turner in American Memory*, 283–303. New York: Houghton Mifflin Company, 2004.

Greenberg, Kenneth S. "Interview with William Styron." In *Nat Turner: A Slave Rebellion in History and Memory*, ed. Kenneth S. Greenberg, 214–228. New York: Oxford University Press, 2003.

———. *Nat Turner: A Slave Rebellion in History and Memory.* New York: Oxford University Press, 2003.

Hairston, Loyle. "William Styron's Nat Turner—Rouge Nigger." *William Styron's Nat Turner: Ten Black Writers Respond*, edited by John Henrik Clarke, 66–72. Boston: Beacon Press, 1968.

Hall, Robert L. "African Religious Retentions in Florida." In *Africanisms in American Culture*, edited by Joseph E. Holloway, 224–248. 2nd ed. Bloomington: Indiana University Press, 1990.

Halperin, David M. *How to Do the History of Homosexuality.* Chicago: University of Chicago Press, 2002.

Hammonds, Evelynn. "Black (W)holes and the Geometry of Black Female Sexuality." In *African American Literary Theory: A Reader*, edited by Winston Napier, 482–497. New York: New York University Press, 2000.

Harding, Vincent. *Beyond Chaos: Black History and the Search for the New Land.* Atlanta, GA: Institute of the Black World, 1970.

———. *There Is a River: The Black Struggle for Freedom in America.* New York and London: Harcourt Brace Jovanovich, 1981.

———. "You've Taken My Nat and Gone." In *William Styron's Nat Turner: Ten Black Writers Respond*, edited by John Henrik Clarke, 22–33. Boston: Beacon Press, 1968.

Harper, Philip Brian. *Are We Not Men?: Masculine Anxiety and the Problem of African American Identity.* New York: Oxford University Press, 1996.

———. "The Evidence of Felt Tuition: Minority Experience, Everyday Life, and Critical Speculative Knowledge." In *Black Queer Studies: A Critical Anthology*, edited by E.

Patrick Johnson and Mae G. Henderson, 106–123. Durham, NC: Duke University Press, 2005.

Harris, Trudier. *Exorcising Blackness: Historical and Literary Lynching and Burning Rituals*. Bloomington: Indiana University Press, 1984.

Heffernan, Thomas Ferral. *Stove by a Whale: Owen Chase and the* Essex. Middleton, CT: Wesleyan University Press, 1981.

Hegel, George Wilhelm Friedrich. *The Phenomenology of Spirit*. Translated by J. B. Baillie. New York: Harper Torchbooks, 1967.

Hemphill, Essex. *Ceremonies*. San Francisco: Cleis Press, 1992.

Henderson, Mae G. "'Where, By the Way, Is This Train Going?': A Case for (Re)Framing Black (Cultural) Studies." *Callaloo* 19, no. 1 (1996): 60–67.

Herskovitz, Melville J. *The Myth of the Negro Past*. New York: Harper and Brothers, 1941.

hooks, bell. *Ain't I a Woman: Black Women and Feminism*. Boston: South End Press, 1981.

Horton, James Oliver. "Slavery in American History: An Uncomfortable National Dialogue." In *Slavery and Public History: The Tough Stuff of American Memory*, edited by James Oliver Horton and Lois E. Horton, 35–56. New York: The New Press, 2006.

Horton, James Oliver, and Lois E. Horton. "Violence, Protest and Identity: Black Manhood in Antebellum America." In *A Question of Manhood: A Reader in U.S. Black Men's History and Masculinity*, edited by Darlene Clark Hine and Ernestine Jenkins, 382–398. Bloomington: Indiana University Press, 1999.

———, eds. *Slavery and Public History: The Tough Stuff of American Memory*. New York: The New Press, 2006.

Howison, Robert R. *A History of Virginia, from Its Discovery and Settlement by Europeans to the Present Time*. Vol. 2. Philadelphia: Carey and Hart, 1846.

Humez, Jean M. *Harriet Tubman: The Life and the Life Stories*. Madison: University of Wisconsin Press, 2003.

Ito, Akiyo. "Olaudah Equiano and the New York Artisans: The First American Edition of *The Interesting Narrative of the Life of Olaudah Equiano, or Gustavas Vassa, the African*." *Early American Literature*. 32, no. 1 (1997): 82–102.

J. G. W. "Fugitive Slaves—The Letter of Daniel Webster." *The National Era*, June 6, 1850, 2.

Jacobs, Harriet. *Incidents in the Life of a Slave Girl: Written by Herself*. Edited by Jean Fagan Yellin. 1987. Reprint, Cambridge, MA: Harvard University Press, 2000.

Jacobs, John S. "A True Tale of Slavery." In *Incidents in the Life of a Slave Girl: Written by Herself*, edited by Jean Fagan Yellin, 207–228. 1987. Reprint, Cambridge, MA: Harvard University Press, 2000.

James, George Payne Rainsford. *The Old Dominion*. 1858. Reprint. London, George Routledge, 1903.

Janzen, John M., and Wyatt MacGaffey. *An Anthropology of Kongo Religion: Primary Texts from Lower Zaire*. Lawrence, KS: University of Kansas Press, 1974.

Jefferson, Thomas. *Notes on the State of Virginia*. [1781.] Edited by Frank Shuffleton. New York: Penguin Books, 1999.

Johnson, E. Patrick. *Appropriating Blackness: Performance and the Politics of Authenticity*. Durham, NC: Duke University Press, 2003.

Johnson. Roy F. *The Nat Turner Slave Insurrection*. Murfreesboro, N.C.: Johnson Publishing, 1966.

Jones, Jacqueline. *Labor of Love, Labor of Sorrow: Black Women, Work and the Family from Slavery to the Present*. New York: Vintage Books, 1995.

Kaiser, Ernest. "The Failure of William Styron." In *William Styron's Nat Turner: Ten Black Writers Respond*, edited by John Henrik Clarke, 50–65. Boston: Beacon Press, 1968.

Katz, Jonathan Ned. *Gay American History: Lesbians and Gay Men in the U.S.A.* New York: Thomas Y. Crowell Company, 1976.

———. *Gay/Lesbian Almanac: A New Documentary*. New York: Harper and Row, 1983.

Kelleter, Frank. "Ethnic Self-Dramatization and Technologies of Travel in *The Interesting Narrative of the Life of Olaudah Equiano, or Gustavus Vassa, the African, Written by Himself* (1789)." *Early American Literature* 39, no. 1 (2004): 67–84.

Kilgour, Maggie. *From Communion to Cannibalism: An Anatomy of Metaphors of Incorporation* Princeton, NJ: Princeton University Press, 1990.

Killens, John Oliver. "The Confessions of Willie Styron." In *William Styron's Nat Turner: Ten Black Writers Respond*, edited by John Henrik Clarke, 34–44. Boston: Beacon Press, 1968.

Lavallée, Joseph. *Le nègre comme il ya peu de blancs*. [1789.] Translated from the French by J. Trapp as *The Negro as There Are Few White Men*. London: Printed for the author, 1790.

———. *Le nègre comme il ya peu de blancs*. [1789.] Anonymous translation from the French as *The Negro Equaled by Few Europeans*. London: G. G. J. and J. Robinson, 1790.

Lerner, Gerda, ed. *Black Women in White America: A Documentary History*. New York: Vintage Books, 1972.

Leverenz, David. *Manhood and the American Renaissance*. Ithaca, NY: Cornell University Press, 1989.

Lindenbaum, Shirley. "Thinking about Cannibalism." *Annual Review of Anthropology* 33 (2004): 475–498.

Lorde, Audre. "Learning from the Sixties." In Lorde, *Sister Outsider: Essays and Speeches*. Trumansburg, NY: Crossing Press, 1984.

Lott, Eric. *Love and Theft: Blackface Minstrelsy and the American Working Class*. New York: Oxford University Press, 1993.

MacGaffey, Wyatt. *Modern Kongo Prophets: Religion in a Plural Society*. Bloomington, IN: Indiana University Press, 1983.

———. *Religion and Society in Central Africa: The Bakongo of Lower Zaire*. Chicago: University of Chicago Press, 1986.

Mann, Horace. "Slavery and the Slave Trade in the District of Columbia." *The National Era*, April 19, 1849, 63; and April 26, 1849, 65. Also published in *The Liberator*, April 27, 1849, 63; May 4, 1849, 69; and May 11, 1849, 73–74.

Matory, J. Lorand. *Sex and the Empire That Is No More: Gender and the Politics of Metaphor in Oyo Yoruba Religion*. Minneapolis, MN: University of Minnesota Press, 1994.

McBride, Dwight A. *Impossible Witnesses: Truth, Abolitionism, and Slave Testimony*. New York: New York University Press, 2001.

——. *Why I Hate Abercrombie and Fitch: Essays on Race and Sexuality*. New York: New York University Press, 2005.

McDowell, Deborah E. "In the First Place: Making Frederick Douglass and the Afro-American Narrative Tradition." In *African American Autobiography: A Critical Collection of Essays*, edited by William L. Andrews, 36–58. Englewood Cliffs, NJ: Prentice Hall, 1993.

McFeely, William S. *Frederick Douglass*. New York: W. W. Norton and Company, 1991.

McGovern, James R. *Anatomy of a Lynching: The Killing of Claude Neal*. Baton Rouge: Louisiana State University Press, 1982.

McKay, Claude. *Home to Harlem*. New York: Harper & Bros., 1928.

McKitrick, Eric L, ed. *Slavery Defended: The Views of the Old South*. New Jersey: Prentice-Hall, 1963.

McPherson, James M. "Foreword." In *An Appeal in Favor of That Class of Americans Called Africans*. [1833.] Edited by William Loren Katz. New York: Arno Press and the New York Times, 1968.

Melish, Joanne. "Recovering from Slavery: Four Struggles to Tell the Truth." In *Slavery and Public History: The Tough Stuff of American Memory*, edited by James Oliver Horton and Lois E. Horton, 199–125. New York: The New Press, 2006.

Melville, Herman. *Moby-Dick; or, The Whale*. 1851. Reprint, Boston: Houghton Mifflin, 1956.

Meyer, June. "Spokesman for the Blacks." *The Nation*, December 4, 1967, 597–599.

Montejo, Esteban. *Biography of a Runaway Slave*. Edited by Miguel Barnet. Translated by W. Nick Hill. Connecticut: Curbstone Press, 1994.

Morrison, Toni. *Beloved*. 1987. Reprint, New York: Plume, 1998.

——. *Playing in the Dark: Whiteness and the American Literary Imagination*. Cambridge, MA: Harvard University Press, 1992.

——. "Racism and Fascism." In *In Defense of Mumia*, edited by S. E. Anderson and Tony Medina, 51–52. New York: Writers and Readers Publishing, 1996.

Moses, Wilson Jeremiah. *The Golden Age of Black Nationalism, 1850–1925*. New York: Oxford University Press, 1978.

Mullin, Michael. *Africa in America: Slave Acculturation and Resistance in the American South and the British Caribbean, 1736–1831*. Urbana: University of Illinois Press, 1995.

Murray, Stephen O., and Will Roscoe, eds. *Boy-Wives and Female Husbands: Studies of African Homosexualities*. New York: St. Martin's Press, 1998.

Nero, Charles I. "Toward a Black Gay Aesthetic: Signifying in Contemporary Black Gay Literature." In *Brother to Brother: New Writings by Black Gay Men*, edited by Essex Hemphill, 229–252. Boston: Alyson Publications, 1991.

Newton, Huey P. "Eldridge Cleaver: He Is No James Baldwin." In *The Huey P. Newton Reader*, edited by David Hilliard and Donald Weise, 285–293. New York, Seven Stories Press, 2002.

Noble, Marianne. *The Masochistic Pleasures of Sentimental Literature*. Princeton, NJ: Princeton University Press, 2000.

Northup, Solomon. *Twelve Years a Slave: Narrative of Solomon Northup, a Citizen of New-York, Kidnapped in Washington City in 1841 and Rescued in 1853, from a Cotton Plantation Near the Red River in Louisiana*. Auburn, NY: Derby and Miller, 1853. http://docsouth.unc.edu/fpn/northup/northup.html.

Oyěwùmí, Oyèrónkẹ́. *The Invention of Women: Making an African Sense of Western Gender Discourses*. Minneapolis: University of Minnesota Press, 1997.

Painter, Nell Irvin. *Sojourner Truth: A Life, a Symbol*. New York: W. W. Norton, 1996.

Panger, Daniel. *Ol' Prophet Nat*. Winston-Salem, NC: J. F. Blair, 1967.

Patterson, Orlando. *Rituals of Blood: Consequences of Slavery in Two American Centuries*. Washington, DC Civitas Counterpoint, 1998.

———. *Slavery and Social Death: A Comparative Study*. Cambridge, MA: Harvard University Press, 1982.

Petrinovich, Lewis. *The Cannibal Within*. New York: Aldine de Gruyter, 2000.

Philbrick, Nathaniel. *In the Heart of the Sea: The Tragedy of the Whaleship* Essex. New York: Viking, 2000.

Piersen, W. D. *Black Legacy: America's Hidden Heritage*. Amherst: University of Massachusetts Press, 1993.

———. "White Cannibals, Black Martyrs: Fear, Depression, and Religious Faith as Causes of Suicide among New Slaves." *Journal of Negro History* 62, no. 2 (1977): 147–159.

Pieterse, Jan Nederveen. *White on Black: Images of Africa and Blacks in Western Popular Culture*. New Haven, CT: Yale University Press, 1992.

Pollard, Edward A. "Black Diamonds." In *Slavery Defended: The Views of the Old South*, edited by Erik L. McKitrick, 162–168. New Jersey: Prentice-Hall, 1963.

Poussaint, Alvin F. "The Confessions of Nat Turner and Styron's Dilemma." In *William Styron's Nat Turner: Ten Black Writers Respond*, edited by John Henrik Clarke, 17–22. Boston: Beacon Press, 1968.

Preston, Dickson J. *Young Frederick Douglass: The Maryland Years*. Baltimore, MD: Johns Hopkins University Press, 1980.

Prichard, James Cowles. *The Natural History of Man; Comprising Inquiries into the Modifying Influence of Physical and Moral Agencies on the Different Tribes of the Human Family*. London: H. Bailliere, 1855.

Prince, Mary. *History of Mary Prince, a West Indian Slave*. 1831. Reprint, New York: Pandora Press, 1987.

Prus, Randy. "Citizen Douglass and Gendered Nationalism." *a/b Auto/Biography Studies* 16, no. 1 (2001): 71–89.

Raboteau, Albert J. *Slave Religion: The "Invisible Institution" in the Antebellum South.* New York: Oxford University Press, 1978.

Rahv, Philip. "Through the Midst of Jerusalem." *The New York Review of Books*, October 26, 1967, 6–10.

Rawick, George P., ed. *The American Slave: A Composite Autobiography.* Supplement, Series 1, vol. 9, *Mississippi Narratives.* Westport, CT: Greenwood Press, 1977.

———. *The American Slave: A Composite Autobiography.* Supplement, Series 1, vol. 11, *North Carolina and South Carolina Narratives.* Westport, CT: Greenwood Press, 1977.

———. *The American Slave: A Composite Autobiography.* Supplement, Series 1, vol. 12, *Oklahoma Narratives.* Westport, CT: Greenwood Press, 1977.

———. *The American Slave: A Composite Autobiography.* Vol. 7, *Oklahoma and Mississippi Narratives.* Westport, CT: Greenwood Press, 1972.

———. *The American Slave: A Composite Biography.* Vol. 5, *Texas Narratives*, edited by George P. Rawick. Westport, CT: Greenwood Press, 1972.

Redford, Dorothy Spruill. *Somerset Homecoming: Recovering a Lost Heritage.* Chapel Hill, NC: University of North Carolina Press, 1988.

Reid-Pharr, Robert. *Black Gay Man: Essays.* New York: New York University Press, 2001.

Richardson, Marilyn. *Maria Stewart, America's First Black Political Writer.* Bloomington: Indiana University Press, 1987.

Rice, Alan. "'Who's Eating Whom?': The Discourse of Cannibalism in the Literature of the Black Atlantic from Equiano's *Travels* to Toni Morrison's *Beloved*." *Research in African Literatures* 29, no. 4 (1998): 107–121.

Rodney, Walter. *A History of the Upper Guinea Coast, 1545 to 1800.* London: Oxford University Press, 1970.

Roper, Moses. *Narrative of My Escape from Slavery.* 1838. Reprint, Mineola, NY: Dover Publications, 2003.

Ross, Marlon B. "White Fantasies of Desire: Baldwin and the Racial Identities of Sexuality." In *James Baldwin Now*, edited by Dwight A. McBride, 13–55. New York: New York University Press, 1999.

Saillant, John. "The Black Body Erotic and the Republican Body Politic, 1790–1820." In *Sentimental Men: Masculinity and the Politics of Affect in American Culture*, edited by Mary Chapman and Glenn Hendler, 89–111. Berkeley: University of California Press, 1999.

Saltz, Jerry. "Kara Walker: Ill-Will and Desire." *Flash Art* 29, no. 191 (1996): 82–86.

Sanborn, Geoffrey. "The Missed Encounter: Cannibalism and the Literary Critic." In *Eating Their Words: Cannibalism and the Boundaries of Cultural Identity*, edited by Kristen Guest, 107–204. Albany: State University of New York Press, 2001.

Scott, Darieck. "More Man than You'll Ever Be: Antonio Vargas, Eldridge Cleaver, and Toni Morrison's *Beloved*." In *Dangerous Liaisons: Blacks, Gays, and the*

*Struggle for Equality*, edited by Eric Brandt, 217–242. New York: The New Press, 1999.

Sedgwick, Eve Kosofsky. *Between Men: English Literature and Male Homosocial Desire.* New York: Columbia University Press, 1985.

Shaw, Rosalind. *Memories of the Slave Trade: Ritual and the Historical Imagination in Sierra Leone.* Chicago: University of Chicago Press, 2002.

Sieke, Sabine. *Reading Rape: The Rhetoric of Sexual Violence in American Literature and Culture, 1790–1990.* Princeton, NJ: Princeton University Press, 2002.

Simmons, Ron. "Some Thoughts on the Challenges Facing Black Gay Intellectuals." In *Brother to Brother: New Writings by Black Gay Men*, edited by Essex Hemphill, 211–228. Boston: Alyson Publications, 1991.

Smith, Barbara. *Home Girls: A Black Feminist Anthology.* 1983. Reprint, New Brunswick, NJ: Rutgers University Press, 2000.

Smith, James L. *Autobiography of James L. Smith.* 1881. Reprint, Florida: Mnemosyne Publishing Company, 1969.

Sokolov, Raymond A. "In the Mind of Nat Turner." *Newsweek,* October 16, 1967, 65–69.

Spillers, Hortense J. *Black, White, and in Color: Essays on American Literature and Culture.* Chicago: The University of Chicago Press, 2003.

———. "Mama's Baby, Papa's Maybe: An American Grammar Book." In *Black, White, and in Color: Essays on American Literature and Culture*, edited by Hortense J. Spillers, 203–229. Chicago: University of Chicago Press, 2003.

Stewart, Maria. "The Negro's Complaint." In *Maria Stewart: America's First Black Political Writer: Essays and Speeches.* Edited by Marilyn Richardson. Bloomington: Indiana University Press, 1987.

Stowe, Harriet Beecher. *Dred: A Tale of the Great Dismal Swamp.* Boston: Phillips, Sampson and Co., 1856.

Styron, William. *The Confessions of Nat Turner.* [1966.] Rev. ed. New York: New American Library, 1968.

Summer, Claude J. *Gay Fictions, Wilde to Stonewall: Studies in a Male Homosexual Literary Tradition.* New York: Continuum, 1990.

Thomas, Hugh. *The Slave Trade: The History of the Atlantic Slave Trade, 1440–1870.* New York: Simon and Schuster, 1997.

Tragle, Henry Irving. *The Southampton Slave Revolt of 1831: A Compilation of Source Material.* Amherst: University of Massachusetts Press, 1971.

Turner, Patricia A. *I Heard It through the Grapevine: Rumor in African-American Culture.* Los Angeles: University of California Press, 1993.

Van Leer, David. "The Anxiety of Ethnicity in Douglass's Narrative." In *Frederick Douglas: New Literary and Historical Essays*, edited by Eric J. Sundquist, 118–140. New York: Cambridge University Press, 1990.

Walker, Alice. Contribution to "The Revolving Bookstand." *American Scholar* 38 (1968): 549–551.

Walker, David. *Walker's Appeal, in Four Articles; Together with a Preamble, to the Coloured Citizens of the World, But in Particular, and Very Expressly to Those of the*

*United States of America*. [1829.]. 3rd ed. Boston: D. Walker, 1830. Available online at http://docsouth.unc.edu/nc/walker/walker.html.

———. *Walker's Appeal to the Coloured Citizens of the World*. [1829.] Edited by Peter P. Hinks. University Park: Penn State University Press, 2000.

Walker, David, and Henry Highland Garnet. *Walker's Appeal and Garnet's Address: To the Slaves of the United States of America*. 1848. Reprint, Nashville: James C. Winston, 1994.

Walker, Peter F. *Moral Choices: Memory, Desire, and Imagination in Nineteenth-Century American Abolition*. Baton Rouge, LA; Louisiana State University Press, 1978.

Wallace, Maurice. *Constructing the Black Masculine: Identity and Ideality in African American Men's Literature and Culture, 1775–1995*. Durham, NC: Duke University Press, 2002.

Wallace, Michelle. *Black Macho and the Myth of the Superwoman*. [1978.] Rev. ed. New York: Verso, 1990.

Walter, Krista. "Trappings of Nationalism in Frederick Douglass's *The Heroic Slave*." *African American Review* 34, no. 2 (2000): 233–247.

Warner, Anne Bradford. "Carnival Laughter: Resistance in *Incidents*." In *Harriet Jacobs and Incidents in the Life of a Slave Girl: New Critical Essays*, edited by Deborah M. Garfield and Rafia Zafar, 216–232. New York: Cambridge University Press, 1996.

Washington, Booker T. *Frederick Douglass*. Philadelphia: George W. Jacobs and Company, 1906.

———. *Up from Slavery: An Autobiography*. New York: Doubleday, Page and Company, 1904.

Washington, Bryan R. "Wrestling with 'The Love That Dare Not Speak Its Name': John, Elisha, and the 'Master.'" In *New Essays on Go Tell It on the Mountain*, edited by Trudier Harris, 77–96. New York: Cambridge University Press, 1996.

Weik, Jesse. *The Real Lincoln*. Boston: Macmillan, 1923.

Weld, Theodore Dwight. *American Slavery As It Is: Testimony of a Thousand Witnesses*. [1839.] Edited by William Loren Katz. New York: Arno Press and The New York Times, 1968.

Wesley, John. *Thoughts upon Slavery*. London: R. Hawes, 1774.

West, James L. W., III. *William Styron: A Life*. New York: Random House, 1998.

White, Deborah Gray. *Ar'n't I a Woman?: Female Slaves in the Plantation South*. New York: W. W. Norton, 1985.

White, E. Frances. *Dark Continent of Our Bodies: Black Feminism and the Politics of Respectability*. Philadelphia: Temple University Press, 2001.

Williams, Carl O. *Thraldom in Ancient Iceland*. Chicago: University of Chicago Press, 1937.

Williams, Sherley Anne. *Dessa Rose*. New York: W. Morrow, 1986.

Wilson, Gertrude. "Fortas Should Be Impeached." *New York Amsterdam News*, June 8, 1968, 15.

———. "I Spit on the Pulitzer Prize!" *New York Amsterdam News,* May 18, 1968, 17.

Wilson, Harriet. *Our Nig*. 1859. Reprint, New York: Vintage Books, 1983.

Winchell, Donna Haisty. "Cries of Outrage: Three Novelists' Use of History." *Mississippi Quarterly* 49, no. 4 (1996): 727–742.

Wirt, William. *Sketches in the Life and Character of Patrick Henry*. Philadelphia: Thomas, Cowperthwait & Company, 1841.

Witt, Doris. *Black Hunger: Soul Food and America*. Minneapolis: University of Minnesota Press, 1999.

Wright, Joseph. "The Narrative of Joseph Wright." In *Africa Remembered: Narratives by West Africans from the Era of the Slave Trade*, edited by Philip Curtin, 322–333. Madison: University of Wisconsin Press, 1967.

Wright, Kai, ed. *The African-American Archive: The History of the Black Experience in Documents*. New York: Black Dog and Leventhal Publishers, 2001.

Yellin, Jean Fagan. *Harriet Jacobs: A Life*. New York: Basic Civitas Books, 2004.

Africans, ix, 12, 17, 19, 30, 32, 48–49, 56–57, 140, 273n22, 282n13; Anglo-Africans, 36; as cannibals, 69, 248n25; central, 29; coastal, 9, 33, 200; dislocation of, 201; enslaved, 1, 269n81; as heathens, 41, 55, 67–68; imported, 53; naming of, 228; and religion, 275n56; sexuality of, 230; as subhuman, 83; West, 25
*Amistad* (ship), 17, 30, 214, 244n38. *See also* consumption: at sea
anal sex, 21–22, 134, 147, 149, 210–211, 226–227, 231, 234, 237, 266n31, 286n49
Anderson, Sam, 146
Angelo, Bonnie, 282n13
anus, 27, 139, 150, 203, 209–213, 225–228, 232, 234, 237–238
Aptheker, Herbert, 184
Arens, W., 68–69, 244n37
Armelogo, George, 40
Atkins, John, 46
autobiographies, xi, 8, 12, 22, 35, 100, 107, 121, 124, 282n11, 284n35
Azeveredue, Gaspar, 230

Bailey, Thomas A., 184
Baker, Houston, Jr., 19–20, 23–24, 27, 37–38, 52, 213, 221–225, 285n35
Baldwin, James, 174, 182, 198–199, 203, 240, 279n81, 280n89; and E. Cleaver, 196, 205, 278n76; and sexual identity, 197, 274n31, 276n63, 278n78, 278n80; and W. Styron, 186–187, 274n39, 277n73; on race and sexuality, 191–195, 199–200
Balfour, Lawrie, 279n81
Barrett, Lindon, 22
Bay, Mia, 32
Beam, Joseph, 21, 279n80
Beecher, Rev. Henry Ward, 16
Bennett, Darius, 1

Bennett, Lerone Jr., 77, 179, 182, 185, 275n42
black male interiority, 111–112, 122, 203, 212
Blume, Harvey, 246n7
bodies, 17, 39, 49, 100, 113, 147, 150, 231, 235; African, 36, 237; on auction block, 7; black, 91, 93, 99, 151, 168, 170, 210; black female, 23, 81, 156; black gay, 211; black male, 16, 98, 233; captured, 16; consumption of, 127, 141; dismemberment of, 45, 50, 60, 90, 114, 171, 223; mummification, 68; and sexuality, 9, 227, 251n6, 254n61
Bolingbroke, Henry, 70, 252n30
Bontemps, Arna, 257n26, 272n8
Bradford, Philip Verner, 243n17, 246n7
Bradford, Sarah, 273n15
Brady, Wes, 78
Brawley, Lisa, 261n104
Brown, William Wells, 103, 129, 283n25
Butler, Octavia, 214

cannibalism, xi, 6, 13, 18–19, 25, 51, 56, 68–69, 95, 97, 141, 178–181, 185, 242n10, 247n25; African accusations of, 31–32, 247n16; Africans as, 29, 244n32, 250n57, 253n30; auto-, 46, 171, 173; Christian, 19, 30, 42, 53–54, 67, 158, 249n44; culture of, 34; Europeans as, 10, 29, 36, 243n16, 245n41; linked to homoeroticism, xii-xiii, 14–15, 27; at sea, 13, 64, 70–72, 75–76, 79, 214; scholarship on, 16–17, 244n37; U.S. as cannibal nation, viii-ix, 57, 62, 66; white, 33, 35, 37, 91. *See also* consumption
Carby, Hazel, 109, 217, 219, 266n31, 278n78
Cartwright, Samuel A., 8–9, 148, 150
Chaney, Michael, 263n119
Charles, Michael Ray, 214
Chase, Owen, 71–72
Child, Lydia Marie, 59, 61, 140–141, 157, 160, 251nn6, 7, 264n20, 267n43

Christensen, Matthew J., 244n38
Christianity, 31, 35, 38, 44, 48–50, 68–69, 128, 182, 239, 244n32; African missionaries, 16; and cannibalism, 19, 30, 42, 53–54, 67, 158, 249n44; and conversion; 52, 188–189, 281n2; morality and values, 4, 40, 83; radical black, 210, 275n42; and romantic love, 43, 55; and sexuality, 134, 196, 209, 224, 228–231, 266n31; Southern, 201
Clark, Cheryl, 277n74
Clarke, John Henrik, 179, 203
Cleaver, Eldridge, 22–23, 196–197, 205, 245n49, 271n137, 274n31, 276n61, 278n76, 279n80
Clifton, Charles, 22, 125, 259n44
Coleman, Eli, 77
Collins, John A., 99
Comstock, William, 73–74, 242n7
consumption, 5–9, 12, 18, 61–64, 88–89, 127–130, 140–145, 177–178, 206, 220, 245n41; auto-cannibalism, 46, 147; of black persons, ix, xi, 13, 148, 155; and capitalism, 68; and Christianity, 48–50; culture of, 27, 95, 132, 156; in F. Douglass's works, 95–99, 109–111, 114, 125; as erotic ritual, 101, 104, 158; and homoeroticism, xiii, 14–15, 180–82, 202, 205; of humans, 26, 30, 37, 57, 69, 85, 90, 213, 247n16, 251nn6–9, 252n14; as rhetorical device, 17–19, 151–152, 174, 242n10, 268n64; at sea, 25, 70–76 (see also *Amistad*; *Essex*); social, 31, 34, 46–47, 65–66, 159, 161–165, 170, 184–185, 242n6; during slavery, 33–34, 42, 45, 51, 149–50, 248n27, 264n18, 267n51; of Nat Turner, 89, 91–94, 171, 173, 207, 242n9. *See also* cannibalism
Cottom, Daniel, 244n37, 245n41
Cotton, Rev. John, 227
Cox, Renee, 214
Craft, William, 257n26
Crummel, Alexander, 190, 256n19
Cuguano, Ottobah, 32

Davis, Angela Y., 168–69, 271n134
Delany, Martin R., 239
Delany, Samuel R., ii, 278n80
Demme, Jonathan, 214
Dickens, Charles, 55
Douglass, Frederick, 25–26, 35, 95–125, 154, 160, 178–179, 225, 239, 258n28, 258n30, 258n36; critical reception, 23, 259n44,

263n119, 263n121, 283n25, 285n35; influence, 188–190, 202, 206; on A. Lincoln, 259n45, 261n105; and sexuality, 14, 262n117, 266n42; on slavery, 13, 127–128, 133, 220, 252n14, 261n106. *See also* hunger: mother; rape
Drewry, William Sidney, 91, 172
Du Bois, W. E. B., xi, 21, 174, 190, 212, 275n56, 276n57, 282n11
duCille, Ann, 222, 284n27, 284n30

Edelman, Lee, 276n63
Eisami, Ali, 10, 12
Elkins, Stanley M., 179, 184
Ellison, Ralph, 151, 203, 221–222, 225
Eppes, General, 91
Equiano, Olaudah, 25, 31, 34, 35–48, 50–55, 84, 224, 247n25, 248n32, 275n49, 285n36
*Essex* (ship), 5, 25, 64, 71, 72, 73, 74, 242n7. *See also* consumption: at sea
Estermann, Carlos, 230
Europeans, 9–10, 52, 86, 99, 200, 226, 244n32, 248n28, 256n19; as cannibals, 12–19, 29–36, 48–51, 54, 56–57, 68–69, 92, 243n17, 245n41, 247n16, 248n25; as colonizers, 72, 74, 83; O. Equiano on, 25, 37, 41, 43, 53; and sexuality, 108, 167, 194, 237; on souls, 55
Evans-Pritchard, E. E., 123
Eyerman, Ron, 183, 215–216

Farb, Peter, 40, 249n40
Fauset, Jesse, 222, 284n30
Fisher, Gary, 211, 281n9
Fisher, M. F. K., 83
Fitzhugh, George, 67–68, 109
Floyd, John, 90, 93
Foreman, P. Gabrielle, 133
Foster, Francis, 103
Fox-Genovese, Elizabeth, 154
Franklin, John Hope, 62
Franks, Pet, 88
Frederickson, George M., 248n28
French, Scot, 91, 242n9
Freud, Sigmund, 194, 249n42, 277n67

Gage, Dana, 98, 256n12
Gaines, Kevin, 261n102
Garfield, Deborah M., 156–57, 269n91, 283n25
Gates, Henry Louis, Jr., 35, 246, 248, 263, 267, 284

gender, 9, 14–15, 129, 152, 199, 201, 222, 224, 226, 249n42, 263n119, 286n44; ambiguity, 102, 111, 115, 123, 125, 130, 155, 167–168, 220, 228; formation, 19, 23, 139, 165, 173, 232; norms, 150–151, 153, 164, 166, 185, 205, 223, 266n31, 269n86, 271n134, 278n76, 285n37; politics, 98, 124, 133, 138, 213; variance, 26, 63, 100, 131, 154, 169–170, 181, 219, 225, 229–230, 236–238, 287n55
Gerzina, Gretchen Holbrook, 248n25
Giddings, J. R., 67, 252n20
Gildersleeve, Basil Lanneau, 86, 88, 254n77
Gilroy, Paul, 16, 19, 233
Gray, Thomas R., 210
Greenberg, Kenneth S., 242n9, 272n6, 274n39

Hairston, Loyle, 182
Hall, Robert L., 285n42
Halperin, David, 15, 244n29
Hamilton, Charles V., 179
Hammonds, Evelynn, 284n31
Harding, Vincent, 179, 181, 186–187, 202, 204–206, 225, 275n42, 285n37
Harper, Philip Brian, ii
Harris, Trudier, 87, 138, 139, 151, 167, 169, 214
Hegel, G. W. F., 212, 256n19
Hemphill, Essex, 209–212, 278n76, 279n80
Henderson, Mae G., 203, 285n37
Henry, Patrick, 121, 123
Herskovitz, Melville J., 180, 273n22
homoeroticism, 63, 157, 203, 215–216, 218, 225, 228, 233–234, 239, 243n26, 244n29, 274n31; and appetite, 7, 18, 34–35; and J. Baldwin, 195, 200–201; and black culture, 174, 191–193, 197, 205, 212; and cannibalism, 13–15, 19, 62, 181, 185–186; ; in colonial America, 231; and F. Douglass, 26, 122; and O. Equiano, 31; interracial, 9–10, 12, 41, 44, 108, 213, 224, 285n36; and H. Jacobs, 130–131, 134, 152; during slavery, 8, 20–21, 24–25, 135, 140, 145, 150–51, 173, 178, 184, 198, 202; and N. Turner, 171–172, 187, 189
hooks, bell, 168, 169
Horton, Louis E., 3, 138, 241n3
Horton, Oliver, 3, 138, 241n3
Howison, Robert R., 90
hunger, 46, 81–82, 97, 143, 149, 158–159, 189, 205, 212, 240, 242n6, 276n57; for black flesh, 10, 14, 31, 39, 65, 75, 77, 91, 93, 140; of black males, 27, 122, 225–226, 231–232, 283n24; cannibalistic, 13, 18, 30; and F. Douglass,

95, 113–114, 118, 121, 124–125; emotional, 19; institutionalized, 4–5, 26, 79, 213, 220; and H. Jacobs, 130, 144–148, 151–152, 155, 157, 164–165, 170; and T. Morrison, 220; mother, 9, 23, 96, 112, 115, 117, 120, 166 (see also Douglass, Frederick); for self, 239; for soul, 49; white, 7–8, 17, 69, 85–86, 88–89, 94, 102, 127, 172–73, 196, 204, 285n36. See also starvation
Hurston, Zora Neale, 222, 276n57, 284n30

J. G. W., 67, 252n19
Jacobs, Harriet, 7, 25, 233, 242n13, 251n6, 252n14, 267n51, 269n91, 283n25; and consumption, 13, 26, 129 141–144, 165 170; and masculinity, 137–139; and rape, 153–154, 182, 219, 268n77. See also rape
Jacobs, John S., 7, 77, 128, 252n14, 279n87
James, G. P. R., 272n8
Jefferson, Thomas, 132, 155, 204, 256n19
Johnson, Charles, 214
Johnson, Patrick E., v, viii, xi, 278n76
Johnson, Roy F., 272n4
Jones, Gayle, 214
Jones, Jacqueline, 257n21

Kaiser, Ernest, 178–181, 197, 275n42
Katz, Jonathan Ned, 226, 266n31, 286n49
Kelleter, Frank, 247n16
Kenan, Randall, 214
Kilgour, Maggie, 244n37
Killens, John Oliver, 176, 193–197, 275n42

Labat, Jean Baptiste, 229
Lavallée, Joseph, 38–39, 108
Lerner, Gerda, 257n21
Lincoln, Abraham, 116–120, 204, 259n45, 260n83, 261n105
Lindenbaum, Shirley, 92, 244n37
Lorde, Audre, 277n74
Lott, Eric, 145

MacGaffey, Wyatt, 54, 250n84, 286n44
Mann, Horace, 65, 252n15
Marcus, Marcia, 194
masculinity, 22, 128, 137, 168, 180, 195, 197, 202, 204, 235, 258, 278; and J. Baldwin, 200; black, 129, 139, 181, 184–85, 196, 198, 206, 223, 238, 240, 279, 283; nineteenth century, 23–24, 103, 110, 121; and F. Douglass, 14, 26, 99–101, 111, 117, 121, 125; and H. Jacobs, 130–31, 138, 151, 154, 164–65; white, 42, 63, 74–76, 85, 91

Matory, J. Lorand, 287n55

McBride, Dwight A., ii, viii, xiii, 22, 24, 197, 274n31, 278n78, 278n80, 279n80

McDowell, Deborah E., 23, 100, 103–104, 125

McFeely, William S., 105, 106

McGovern, James R., 171

McIver, Beverly, 214

McKay, Claude, 190, 276n57

McKitrick, Eric L., 281n9

McPherson, James M., 267n43

Melville, Herman, 13

Meyer, June, 184

Montejo, Esteban, 233–236, 238–239, 286n54

Montesquieu, 83

Morrison, Toni, 12–13, 156, 158, 214–215, 220, 282n13; critical recption, 23, 27, 218–19, 222, 265n31, 279n80, 283n24, 284n31; major works, 213, 216

Moses, Wilson Jeremiah, 243n27, 256n19

Mullin, Michael, 243n17

Musgrave, J. S., 91–92

Nero, Charles I., 20, 211, 278n76, 279n80, 282n10

Newton, Huey P., 279n80

Noble, Marianne, 277n67, 277n69

Northup, Solomon, 7, 129, 225, 242n12, 252n14, 258n36, 264n20, 280n87

Olmstead, Frederick Law, 81, 254n61

Oyěwùmí, Oyèrónkeⲭ, 286n44, 287n55

Page, Thomas Nelson, 109

Painter, Nell Irvin, 154–155, 157–158, 256n12, 257n21, 266n42, 281n3

Panger, Daniel, 272n8

Patterson, Orlando, 6–7, 33–34, 37, 48, 62–63, 97, 143, 242n10, 248n27

Petrinovich, Lewis, 73, 75, 244n37,

Pieterse, Jan Nederveen, 243n16, 244n32

plantation, 60, 63–64, 81, 84–85, 88, 145–146, 149, 158, 168–170, 238, 254n61, 271n134; cannibalism on, 6, 8, 12–15, 18–19, 25, 70, 77, 252n14; and L. M. Child, 141; Cuban, 233–36; and F. Douglass, 95–96, 114, 117, 119–21; and O. Equiano, 51; historical tours, 1–3; homoeroticism on, 15, 21, 27, 37–38, 134, 202, 211, 218–19, 228, 232; as incestuous, 100, 102, 140; and H. Jacobs, 137–38, 142–43, 153, 165; rape

on, 109, 147, 154, 205, 214, 217, 266n31; religion on, 47–48, 280n2; and J. L. Smith, 79; starvation on, 4–5, 59, 113, 162, 242n6; and N. Turner, 175; and D. Walker, 127

Pollard, Edward A., 71, 85–88

Poussaint, Alvin F., 182, 184, 189

Prince, Mary, 142, 163

Prus, Randy, 263n121

Raboteau, Albert J., 280n2

Rahv, Philip, 272n10

rape, 7, 80, 82, 93, 99, 109, 125, 153–154, 212, 254; female, 22, 110, 112, 121, 159, 185, 195, 197, 206, 221–222, 224, 267n42; homosexual, 9, 23, 111, 133–135, 138–139, 151, 169, 181, 205, 219, 265n31, 285n35; during slavery, 26, 96, 101–102, 105–108, 147, 213, 216–218, 257n21, 268n77, 283n19. See also Douglass, Frederick; Jacobs, Harriet

Redford, Dorothy Spruill, 241n5

Reid-Pharr, Robert, ii, 22, 24, 211, 275n49, 278n76, 282n10

Reynolds, Mary, 148

Rice, Alan, 247n25

Roper, Moses, 159, 225, 251n9, 252n14, 257n26, 258n35

Ross, Marlon, ii, 22, 274n31

Rustin, Bayard, 21, 206

Saillant, John, 108

Sanborn, Geoffrey, 69, 252n30

Santos, Joao do, 230

Scott, Darieck, ii, 22, 219, 278n76

seasoning, 31, 46, 64, 77, 79, 142, 234; of flesh, 6, 31, 78, 106

Sedgwick, Eve Kosofsky, 15, 41, 249n42, 281n9

Shaw, Rosalind, 46, 48, 248n25, 250n57

Simmons, Ron, 22, 210, 211, 279n80, 281n8

slavery, 168–170, 179, 182, 185, 187, 189, 192, 198, 209–210, 212, 215, 219, 223–224, 233–239, 261n104, 282n9; and L. M. Child, 140, 251; and clothing, 146; and consumption, 5, 7, 9, 13, 30–31, 33, 57, 61–67, 73, 128–130, 141, 149, 173, 177–178; defense of, 68, 74, 85–88, 109, 254n77; and F. Douglass, 26, 95, 97, 103, 105, 111–112, 115, 119–120, 123, 127; economics, 41; and freedom, 161, 265n20; historical understanding of, 3–4, 20; and homoeroticism, 8, 12, 21–25, 27, 150–51, 157, 172, 174, 183–84, 191, 194–95, 197, 206, 216; and hunger, 220,

232; and H. Jacobs, 136, 165, 267n51; and mammy figure, 268n64; and masculinity, 132, 138–39; as parasitic institution, 6, 248n27; popular representations of, 108, 214, 241n3, 275n42; and religion, 200–201, 281n2; and seasoning, 78–79; and sexual identity, 131; and sexual violation, 155, 205, 217–218, 221, 257n21, 277n74, 283n19, 285n35; slave master, 33–34, 36–37, 40, 52, 57, 61–62, 88, 102, 105, 163, 261n106, 278n80; and soul food, 142–143; in Southampton, 91; and D. Walker, 110; and womanhood, 135;
Smith, Barbara, 277n74
Smith, James L., 25, 79, 88, 182, 213
Snow, Susan, 38
sodomy, 21, 134, 147, 149, 226–28, 231, 234, 237, 266n31, 286n49
Spillers, Hortense, 167–169, 269n86, 284n31
starvation, 3, 26, 46, 72, 95, 97, 113–114, 136, 143–144, 161, 166, 206, 242n12. *See also* hunger
Steward, Austin, 225, 280n87
Stewart, Maria W., 132
Stowe, Harriet Beecher, 89, 147, 194, 272n8, 277n69
Styron, William, 20, 172, 189, 191, 196, 201–202, 272n6; and J. Baldwin, 174, 186–187, 193, 195, 274n39, 277n73; critical reception, 27, 173, 175–185, 196, 273n11, 275n42; and F. Douglass, 188
Summer, Claude J., 276n63

taste, 13, 18, 41, 65, 68, 80–81, 86, 93, 162, 220, 249n40; for Negro flesh, 9, 40, 43, 62, 82, 88–89, 145, 164, 172
Taylor, Rev. Edward, 92
tight place, 27, 213, 221–225
torture, 7, 34, 77, 101–103, 113, 130, 141, 158, 178, 258n36
Truth, Sojourner, 98, 154, 157, 210, 220, 256n12, 257n21, 266n42, 281n3, 284n31
Tubman, Harriet, 115, 117, 178, 260n81
Turner, Nat, 90, 173–176, 179, 181, 186, 190, 195, 240, 272n4, 272n6; consumption of, 6–7, 27, 89, 94, 207, 242n9; and religion, 188, 201–202, 210; representation of, 26; ritualized death, 65, 91–93, 171–172, 177–178; and sexuality, 182–185, 187, 189, 191, 193, 275n39
Turner, Patricia A., 30

Van Leer, David, 96, 101, 257n24

Walker, Alice, 184, 214, 219
Walker, David, 110, 127, 129, 131, 150, 239, 252n14
Walker, Kara, 13, 214
Wallace, Maurice O., 24, 134
Wallace, Michelle, 168, 214, 271n137, 276n61, 277n74
Walter, Krista, 261n106
Warner, Anne Bradford, 134
Washington, Booker T., 20, 23–24, 86, 151, 179, 204, 221–222, 275n49
Washington, Bryan R., 192, 276n63
Washington, George, 13, 121, 123
Weiner, Marli F., 154
Weld, Theodore Dwight, 264n18
Wells, Ida B., 223
Wesley, John, 46
West, James L. W., III, 277n73
White, Deborah Gray, 81, 145, 154, 254n61, 257n21, 268n77
White, E. Frances, 23, 217
Williams, Carl O., 33, 97, 247, 256n6
Williams, George Washington, 203–204
Williams, Sherly Anne, 214
Wilson, Gertrude, 180, 273n11
Wilson, Harriet, 257n21
Witt, Doris, 267n54, 268n64
WPA Interviewees: Jim Allen, 87, 88; Sam Anderson, 146; Pet Franks, 88
Wright, Joseph, 32

Yellin, Jean-Fagan, 134, 242n13, 267n51, 279n87

ABOUT THE AUTHOR

Vincent Woodard (1971–2008) was Assistant Professor of English at the University of Colorado–Boulder. He received his PhD in American Studies and English from the University of Texas, Austin.